Queen Victoria

Queen Victoria

Daughter, Wife, Mother, Widow

LUCY WORSLEY

HODDER &
STOUGHTON

First published in Great Britain in 2018 by Hodder & Stoughton
An Hachette UK company

I

Copyright © Lucy Worsley 2018

The right of Lucy Worsley to be identified as the
Author of the Work has been asserted by her in accordance
with the Copyright, Designs and Patents Act 1988.

A CIP catalogue record for this title is available from the British Library

Hardback ISBN 9781473651388
Trade Paperback ISBN 9781473651395
eBook ISBN 9781473651401

Typeset in Bembo MT Pro by Palimpsest Book Production Ltd, Falkirk, Stirlingshire

Printed and bound CPI Group (UK) Ltd, Croydon CR0 4YY

Hodder & Stoughton policy is to use papers that are natural, renewable
and recyclable products and made from wood grown in sustainable forests.
The logging and manufacturing processes are expected to conform to
the environmental regulations of the country of origin.

Hodder & Stoughton Ltd
Carmelite House
50 Victoria Embankment
London EC4Y 0DZ

www.hodder.co.uk

To Ned and Mark

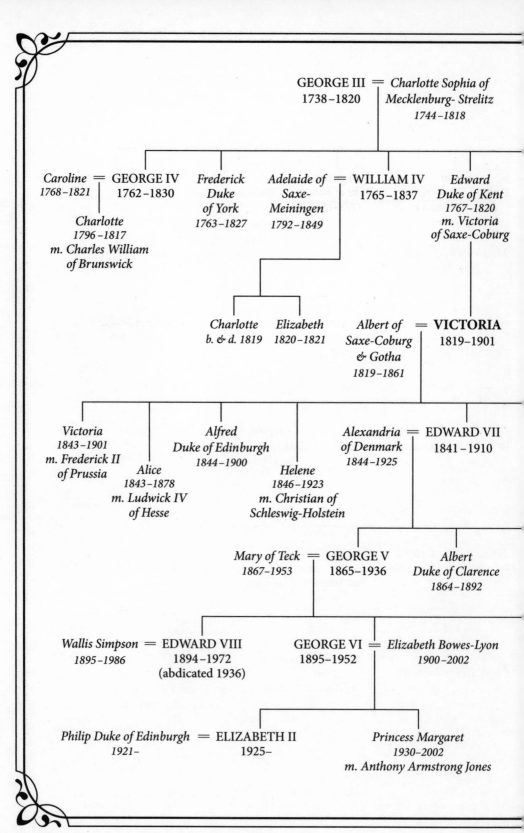

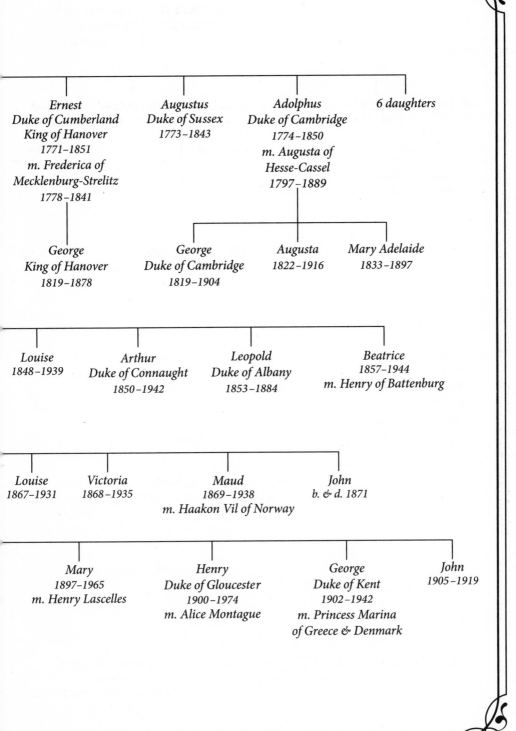

Ernest
Duke of Cumberland
King of Hanover
1771–1851
m. Frederica of
Mecklenburg-Strelitz
1778–1841

Augustus
Duke of Sussex
1773–1843

Adolphus
Duke of Cambridge
1774–1850
m. Augusta of
Hesse-Cassel
1797–1889

6 daughters

George
King of Hanover
1819–1878

George
Duke of Cambridge
1819–1904

Augusta
1822–1916

Mary Adelaide
1833–1897

Louise
1848–1939

Arthur
Duke of Connaught
1850–1942

Leopold
Duke of Albany
1853–1884

Beatrice
1857–1944
m. Henry of Battenburg

Louise
1867–1931

Victoria
1868–1935

Maud
1869–1938
m. Haakon Vil of Norway

John
b. & d. 1871

Mary
1897–1965
m. Henry Lascelles

Henry
Duke of Gloucester
1900–1974
m. Alice Montague

George
Duke of Kent
1902–1942
m. Princess Marina
of Greece & Denmark

John
1905–1919

Contents

PART THREE: THE WIDOW OF WINDSOR

Introduction

An early piano composition of mine, entitled 'Purple Velvet for Queen Victoria', was a sombre and rather menacing funeral march. Like many kids, I grew up believing that the queen was, for some unknown reason, in mourning her whole life long. The most powerful, memorable images of Victoria show her as a little old lady, potato-like in appearance, dressed in everlasting black.

In recent years, there have been many attempts in popular culture – for example, the cinema film *Young Victoria*, or the television series *Victoria* – to overturn this funereal image. The big and small screens have both shown us a less decorous, more passionate young princess who loved dancing. We seem to have ended up with two Victorias, bearing no clear relationship to each other. How did she go from dancing princess to potato?

That's a tale worth telling, but in this book I also want to present a third Victoria. The little old lady, sullen in expression, gloomy in dress, proved to be a remarkably successful queen, one who invented a new role for the monarchy. She found a way of being a respected sovereign in an age when people were deeply uncomfortable with having a woman on the throne.

Perhaps the Victorians were even less comfortable with women in power than, say, the Tudors, with Elizabeth I, or the Stuarts, with Queen Anne. I believe that Victoria got around this by working out rather a clever way of ruling that we might characterise as stereotypically feminine. She operated by instinct rather than logic, emotion rather than intellect. This turned out to be perfect for an institution like the monarchy. It had lost its cold hard *power*, but it might – through gesture and spectacle – be able to retain its *influence*. The accident of her gender turned out to be just what the monarchy needed.

But what did this cost Victoria as a human being? An awful lot, I think. As well as a queen, she was also a daughter, a wife and a widow, and at each of these steps along life's journey, she had to perform all sorts of troubling mental contortions to conform to what society demanded of a woman. On the face of it, she was deeply socially conservative. The idea of votes for women, for example, disgusted her. But if you look at her actions rather than her words, she was in fact tearing up the rulebook for how to be female.

And I'm particularly interested in Victoria's years as a widow. Her early life was so traumatic and dramatic that biographers in the past have tended to concentrate upon it, and there's a plethora of books about the young queen.[1] But historians have more recently begun to swing the other way, and I stand with them in believing that she became her best self in old age.[2] Only in maturity did she come out of the shadow of her husband's domineering personality, to emerge imperious, eccentric and really rather magnificent.

People in the process of writing a biography are often asked, do you *like* your subject? In the case of Victoria, the answer is complex. She could be a monster. Her children could have told you of terrible flaws in her parenting. She could be inconsistent, dictatorial and selfish. But her own horrid upbringing, redeemed only by occasional bright shafts of love and light, means that it would be a stony heart that felt no pity for the human being she was.

And there's much to admire too. She was never vain. She was, in her peculiar way, hard-working, and deeply committed to her unchosen task. Her job made impossible demands upon her, and yet there's a sense of buoyancy about her, and idiosyncrasy, and an energy that sweeps you onto her side. I think that her life was, all things considered, a hard one. Not materially hard, but hard in the sense that enormous wealth and celebrity can put pressure on a human being. She required massive mental resilience. So, do I like her? The answer is yes, initially hesitant, but ultimately resounding.

And I have also loved telling her story by peering through twenty-four different windows into her life. The idea came to me in 2012 when my colleague Alexandra Kim – we worked together as curators at Queen Victoria's birthplace, Kensington Palace in London – completed a loan request for a parasol from the Museum of London. Made of black lace, it was the very one carried by Victoria as she drove through London on 22 June 1897 to show herself to the crowds who'd gathered to celebrate her Diamond Jubilee. The parasol was a gift from the 'Father of the House' of Commons, Charles Pelham Villiers, Member for Wolverhampton. Aged ninety-five at the time of the jubilee, he'd entered Parliament when Victoria was sixteen, two years short of becoming queen in 1837. He was one of the few people living who could remember what it was like before the long, colourful Victorian age began.

This parasol was just one item in an exhibition where we attempted to recreate that one particular day when she, and her empire, were perhaps at their zenith. We pulled together intimate items like the parasol with objects on a grander scale, like a huge model of the late-Victorian London she glimpsed from her carriage. Our exhibition also featured what the millions of her subjects on the streets that day saw, how they celebrated and, indeed, what they criticised. The sight of her colonial troops marching through the streets of London, so many of them, so utterly subordinated, caused some viewers to begin to question the British right to use so much violence in pursuit of so much empire.

Our exhibition also made me think about how Victoria's reign gave the monarchy a living legacy; it was opened by Her Majesty the Queen and, watching the flickering film footage of the Diamond Jubilee procession, she commented how remarkable it was that her great-great-grandmother's carriage had eight horses, a real feat of equestrianism that is hard to match today. Of course, she'd gained the insight from driving in similar processions herself. It was a reminder that many of the traditions and rituals of today's monarchy were 'invented' by Victoria.

Another reason I decided to follow this principle of recreating individual days in detail was because with Victoria – uniquely – I *could*. She was a prolific diarist, spilling out millions of words over her lifetime, three or four thousand some evenings. And now they are more accessible than ever because of a wonderful feat of digitisation by the Bodleian Libraries, the Royal Archives and ProQuest, including every single surviving word of the queen's voluminous journals.

But the journals can only take us so far. I have also selected important days from her parents' lives, the date of her own birth and days when her children came into her life and she was too busy to pick up a pen. And it's also worth remembering even the journals (or especially the journals?) can be false friends. Every Victorian woman who wrote a diary did so with circumspection: secrets revealed could lead to loss and shame. Even as Victoria wrote, she suspected that her words would one day be read. A queen has no privacy. 'You will be,' Victoria's mother told her when she was sixteen, 'more severely observed than any one else in [the world]. You know that very well yourself.'[3]

So Victoria's journals lay traps for us, leaving us a blandly smiling account of a day containing a desperate quarrel. Or else her past editors have tripped us up by leaving out details that they in their own times thought unimportant. Most notoriously, Victoria's youngest daughter Beatrice, for example, made transcriptions of her mother's diaries before burning most of the originals, deleting certain names and incidents as she went. This means we must also probe areas where the journals haven't got much to say. As historian Paula Bartley points out, Victoria's eldest son, Bertie, destroyed 'all the correspondence in the Flora Hastings affair, all the letters to Disraeli if they concerned the family and all the correspondence between the Munshi and his mother'.[4] Flora Hastings, Benjamin

Disraeli and her Indian bodyservant Abdul Karim, 'The Munshi', as he was known, are all therefore characters who will make an extended appearance.

Later in her life, Victoria published extracts from her journals, using her simple, unpretentious prose very powerfully to describe her love and her grief. Her words were important, but her subjects knew her even better in the form of her unmistakable image, firstly through the work of artists and then, as the century wore on, in the form of those ubiquitous, instantly recognisable photographs. This book tries to conjure up her physical body in words, not from prurience but because so much of the success of her reign lay less in doing than simply in *being*. The pictures still hold the eye today because there is something so countercultural about them. Why does she not smile? Why does she look so unamused? It's almost shocking to us today to see a female world leader looking so lugubrious. We forget that 200 years ago, it was surprising to see a female at all.

I've also selected the days when she met people like Florence Nightingale, or the Maharaja Duleep Singh, because of their significance to the age to which Victoria gives her name. No other monarch's reign has so shaped the world in which we still live. At the end of her life, she was ruling over nearly a quarter of the population of the globe. We're all still Victoria's subjects, in the sense that we have a constitutional monarchy, and many of us still follow its births, deaths and marriages with interest. We're still dealing with the legacy of having seized and lost an empire. We follow the Victorian game of football, travel from London to Birmingham by train, as the Victorians could, and we still (just about) stick the Victorian invention of stamps on letters before placing them in 'VR' postboxes.[5] The Victorians gave us public lavatories, the underground railway, the nursing profession, the cigarette, the annual seaside holiday. We still enjoy their treats, from curry (one of Victoria's favourites) to chocolate Easter eggs, Oxo, Rose's Lime Juice Cordial, Bird's Custard, Cadbury's Cocoa and Lyle's Golden Syrup.[6]

What about Albert? Previous historians have very often favoured him at Victoria's expense, partly, I think, because he had the qualities that historians themselves tend to possess and therefore admire. He was orderly, dispassionate, logical, a thinker rather than a feeler. Of course, he had an impressive intellect. But if you value emotional intelligence as a component of leadership, then you realise that in many ways Victoria outshone him, and you get a new narrative of her reign. Stanley Weintraub, in one of the gold-standard biographies of the queen, concludes that what lingers longest in the memory of her reign is the sad 'long afternoon of her post-Albert seclusion'.[7] But no, what interests me – and indeed many others today, now women's contributions to history are better recognised – is her eventual return to fiery form. 'While the Prince Consort lived,' she told a visitor in the early 1860s, 'he thought for me, now I have to think for myself.'[8]

I hope that seeing her up close, examining her face-to-face, as she lived hour-to-hour through twenty-four days of her life, might help you to imagine meeting her yourself, so that you can form your own opinion on the contradictions at the heart of British history's most recognisable woman.

PART ONE

A Naughty Daughter

I

Double Wedding: Kew Palace, 11 July 1818

Kew Palace, a little brick building peeping out from among the trees in west London's Kew Gardens, is an unlikely-looking royal palace. You might mistake it for a giant doll's house. But it has in fact been notorious since the late-Georgian period as both the asylum and prison of George III, who retreated here during his episodes of critical illness. If he were alive today, it's likely that George III would be treated for bipolar disorder. In his own lifetime, though, people thought him 'mad'. The king's 'madness' would cast a long shadow over the life of his best-known granddaughter, Queen Victoria.

In his healthier, happier youth, George III, Victoria's grandmother Queen Charlotte and their fifteen children had loved visiting their pocket-sized palace in the gardens. 'Dear little Kew', Charlotte called it.[1] Their home was a seventeenth-century merchant's dwelling with curved gables, repurposed as a royal hideaway. It was ideally situated for enjoying the botanical wonderland of Kew, which extended from right outside the building's front door.

On Saturday 11 July 1818, however, the mood inside Kew Palace was sombre. A curious double wedding was to take place there that afternoon. Two of George III and Queen Charlotte's sons were simultaneously to marry two German princesses, but in an atmosphere of duty rather than joy.

Charlotte, the mother of the grooms, was now seventy-four years old. Her fifteen offspring had once played contentedly in the gardens at Kew, but the family once known as 'the joyous band' had since been atomised by misfortune. Charlotte's three final children had died horribly young. Her formerly loving husband became estranged, and was sometimes even crude and cruel towards her as he lost control of his speech and descended into his own incoherent hell. Today he was absent from his sons' weddings, living as he was under medical supervision at Windsor Castle. There he was said to be 'perfectly happy, conversing with the Dead'.[2]

As well as twelve surviving children, Charlotte also had a significant number of grandchildren, totalling at least fourteen.[3] Yet the wedding party now gathering did so in response to a crisis in the royal line of succession. The problem with George III and Charlotte's living grandchildren, and the reason for the doubt about their number, was that in 1818 every single one of them was illegitimate, born outside the sanctity of wedlock.

This extraordinary situation had arisen because George III, a strict father, had been anxious to prevent his children from making inappropriate matches. His Royal Marriages Act of 1772 made it illegal for his progeny to marry without his personal permission. But the unintended consequence had been to discourage his sons – the Royal Dukes – from getting married at all. By the end of the eighteenth century, only three of the seven had taken the plunge. The union of the eldest, the Prince of Wales, had produced just a single daughter – a second Charlotte – before ending in separation. Another brother's marriage had been undertaken in secret, without royal permission, and was therefore not recognised by law.

Two of the remaining unmarried Royal Dukes, William, Duke of Clarence, and Edward, Duke of Kent, were now making their way to their mother's house at Kew in order, at 4 p.m., to attend their own weddings. This double ducal marriage ceremony had been triggered by the recent death, in childbirth, of their niece Princess Charlotte. As the one legitimate royal grandchild, the late princess had been her generation's only possible monarch.

For the sake of the succession, then, Princess Charlotte's death forced her uncles to do their patriotic duty. They were now expected to stop tottering comfortably towards middle age with their mistresses, find themselves proper brides and perpetuate the royal line.

As Queen Charlotte watched for the arrival of her sons from the sash windows of her first-floor drawing room, her view embraced a bizarre landscape. The dinky toy palace in which she sat was positioned within a royal compound that included several other mansions, since destroyed, where princes had once dwelt. Nearby on the riverbank stood the unfinished turrets of the Castellated Palace, a bonkers construction begun but not completed by George III. It was aptly described as a building in which princesses might be 'detained by giants or enchanters – an image of distempered reason'.[4] The leafy landscape, bordered by the Thames, was studded with the temples, follies and palaces of a royal family that liked to retreat to its fantastical garden world for refreshment and rehabilitation.

Anyone watching from below as Charlotte peered through the panes would have noticed her striking hair, teased high and powdered white. Contemporaries often commented on her 'true Mulatto' or mixed-race appearance, and the cast of her features in her portraits does seem to hint at the African heritage she possessed via her Portuguese ancestors.[5] Her cheeks, though, were also deathly pale, and her health today was in a perilous state. She had paused here at Kew merely as a staging post on a journey to Windsor and her husband, before being taken too ill to continue. Today's events were unfolding after a postponement during which she had desperately tried to regain her strength.

One of the causes of Charlotte's malady was her heart, now beating 'most unequally & irregularly'.[6] It had taken many 'exertions of the doctors' to make her ready for the 'rather lugubrious' ceremony, and to administer painkillers strong enough to get her out of bed and into her wheelchair.[7] Her condition was physical, but also partly mental. 'My Mind & feelings,' she wrote, thinking of her husband's illness and her unsatisfactory children, 'have been very much harassed . . . my Strength and Spirits are not equal to Trials.'[8] She was served now by just a few long-standing, intimate members of her formerly vast staff, including her wardrobe maid and her 'Necessary Woman to the Private Apartments'. This last character was Charlotte's fellow German Mrs Papendick, whose job it was to empty the queen's 'necessary', or commode.[9]

Charlotte's chair upon 'rollers' had been a gift from her eldest son, who now watched and waited by her side. The Prince of Wales, a 'very stout' man of fifty-five, had often been at odds with his parents in his youth.[10] In more recent years, though, he had become a thoughtful, regretful son, frequently visiting his mother, and making contrivances for her comfort. He was now designated as the Prince Regent, his sick and absent father's official stand-in.

Despite having her plump, punctilious son to hand, Charlotte was lonely, and heartsick for her husband. 'I wish I was with the king,' she would say. Charlotte had married her George at seventeen, the very same night of her arrival in London from her native Mecklenburg in Germany. It was an arranged match, but nevertheless became notable for its fidelity and felicity. Charlotte understood that she was now dying. She'd wanted to get to 'dear, dear Windsor' not only to say goodbye to her husband, but also to destroy certain private papers.[11] Instead, though, she was stuck here at Kew.

On the floor above the queen's suite, her daughters Princesses Augusta and Sophia were also preparing for the wedding. Like their brothers the grooms, they were also unmarried, middle-aged and disgruntled. At events like this, they were expected to dress in striped gowns of matching design to demonstrate their membership of the joyous band. Charlotte insisted that everyone at court still act according to the habits of earlier, luckier times.

In reality, Augusta and Sophia would rather have been almost anywhere else than Kew. Charlotte believed that it was improper for her daughters to take part in society while their father was ill. It would be the *highest mark of indecency*', she claimed, for them to appear in public.[12] But the king's illness had by now lasted for years, placing the princesses in a terrible limbo. If they ever emerged from their seclusion, it would be taken as an admission that the king's family had lost hope that he would ever recover. And this Charlotte would not tolerate.

Trapped at Kew, Augusta and Sophia had grown to hate its quiet, and called it 'the nunnery'. This was a dangerous joke for princesses to make, as a 'nunnery' was also a contemporary word for a brothel. And indeed, Sophia had provided one of her mother's many illegitimate grandchildren, giving birth to a child out of wedlock. The father was one of the king's valets, a gentleman described as 'a hideous old Devil, old enough to be her father, and with a great claret mark on his face'.[13] And so the princesses lived their lonely lives, 'secluded from the world, mixing with few people, their passions boiling over'.[14] When warned that her life was nearing its end, Charlotte had wept, and said to Augusta: 'I had hoped to see you all happy, and now I fear I shall not arrive at that wish of my Heart'.[15]

For Augusta and Sophia, their brothers' weddings were at least a diversion from the usual dull routine. There was an unfamiliar bustle within the building as the first-floor drawing room was furnished with an altar for the ceremony, and four red velvet cushions were brought in to receive eight royal knees. The 'ancient silver plate' from the Chapels Royal had been conveyed specially to Kew.[16] The cramped drawing room of an invalid was a somewhat makeshift venue for a royal wedding, but the conventions would be observed as far as possible.

Just before four, the family began to assemble, the Prince Regent leading his mother to her seat near the altar. The smallish room, with its walls of pale panelling, wobbly floor and ancient fireplace, soon grew crowded. The guests were a select group including the Prime Minister and the Lord Chancellor, while the Archbishop of Canterbury was to officiate. The Prince Regent was ready to give away the brides, and the stage was set for the grooms.

༄

The two couples were William, Duke of Clarence, who was to marry Princess Adelaide of Saxe-Meiningen, and his younger brother Edward, Duke of Kent, whose spouse-to-be was Princess Victoire of Saxe-Coburg.

The names, the titles, sparkle like diamonds on a necklace, but behind them lay very different characters and hopes. William, the future King William IV, stepped up to the altar first. Aged fifty-two, he was widely known as 'Coconut Head' for his pointed skull. He was the unfortunate victim of the spurious 'science' of phrenology, which decreed that the shape of one's head determined one's character. His cranium was thought to indicate mental instability. 'What can you expect,' commented someone who knew him, 'from a man with a head like a pineapple?'[17] Little, in fact, had been expected of William. By 1818, he had two careers behind him: one in the Royal Navy, the other as the lover of the actress Mrs Dorothy Jordan. As profligate as the rest of his Royal Duke brothers, William had lived off Mrs Jordan's earnings until reaching the conclusion that a wealthy heiress might suit him better. At that point he unceremoniously abandoned her.

William's bride-to-be was twenty-five, less than half his age. Princess Adelaide of Saxe-Meiningen must have fully understood that she'd been chosen in desperation. Even after marriage had been 'pressed upon' William 'as an act of public duty' in the light of the succession crisis, he'd struggled to find a bride who'd accept him.[18] Adelaide was, in fact, the eleventh young lady he'd asked.[19]

The Prince Regent now escorted Adelaide into the drawing room upon one arm, while Victoire clung to the other. Adelaide was of a perfectly average height, but because she never made a strong personal impression she has left behind her the idea that she was unusually small. 'A small, well-bred, excellent little woman', was a favourite judgement from a British courtier; 'a poor little bad-ish concern' was one that went the other way.[20] Even today she looked far from impressive, despite her dress of silver tissue and the 'superb wreath of diamonds' upon her head.[21] She'd arrived from Germany just a week earlier, and had been staying at Grillion's

Hotel in Albemarle Street. As it would turn out, there were distinct advantages to Adelaide's lack of colour. She would become a calming presence in the royal family, conciliatory, loving and beloved. Knowing no English and having no intimates in this foreign country, Adelaide and Victoire had already become allies. They were at least able to 'talk the same mother tongue together, it makes them such real friends'.[22]

At the altar, William watched Adelaide approach with serious misgivings. She was only just older than his own illegitimate daughters. His elder brother had made a terrible hash of his own marriage, and had separated from his wife. Feeling guilty about his similarly shabby treatment of his actress-mistress Mrs Jordan, William promised himself that he would now make a fresh start. '*I cannot, I will not, I must not* ill use her,' he vowed.[23] It wasn't an auspicious beginning.

The second couple, Edward Duke of Kent and Princess Victoire of Saxe-Coburg, had already been married once, in May, using the Lutheran version of the ceremony. This had taken place in the Hall of Giants at Victoire's family's castle, Ehrenburg, in her native state of Coburg, Germany. They were now making a second marriage under the rules of the Church of England. When the royal succession might well flow through a match, it was just as well to make doubly sure it was legal.

Towering over his short, pointy-headed brother, Edward, Duke of Kent, was a tall man, of 'soldierlike bearing' despite his 'great corpulency'. He'd lost most of his hair. Despite the unconvincing dye job he'd had done upon the remaining tufts, he was physically impressive, and 'might still be considered' handsome.[24]

Born in 1767, the man who would become Queen Victoria's father had been much the largest of Queen Charlotte's fifteen babies.[25] He grew up to be calmer and quieter than his brothers, speaking 'slowly and deliberately' in a manner both 'kind and courteous'.[26] Edward had spent his youth at a military academy in Hanover, before moving to Geneva. There he'd acquired debts, various actress lovers and then, more seriously, a mistress who was a musician named Adelaide Dubus.

This other Adelaide gave Edward a baby daughter, named Adelaide Victoire, an illegitimate shadowy half-sister to the future queen. But Adelaide Dubus died in childbirth, and little Adelaide Victoire did not survive much longer herself.[27] Edward couldn't cope. Bereaved, indebted and distraught, he returned to London. Unfortunately, he did so without his father's permission. George III, angry at the breach in protocol, immediately shipped Edward off to Gibraltar, presumably in the hope that there he would cause less embarrassment.

Edward's job in Gibraltar was to lead the Royal Fusiliers, who were commonly called the 'Elegant Extracts' (after the popular anthology of prose) for their recruitment practice of poaching the best-looking men from other regiments.[28] Their new colonel was well-intentioned but ineffective. He loved to interfere in everyone else's business, maintaining a correspondence so vast that 'his name was never uttered without a sigh by the functionaries of every public office'.[29]

Edward and his brothers were once described by the Duke of Wellington as 'the damndest millstone around the necks of any government that can be imagined'. When Parliament failed to vote the Royal Dukes the financial allowances they believed that they deserved, Wellington had a ready explanation. The profligate and arrogant Royal Dukes, he explained, had 'insulted – *personally* insulted – two thirds of the gentlemen of England,' so 'how can it be wondered at that they take their revenge?'[30]

Edward's wedding was in fact to be the last in a series of similarly undignified couplings between Royal Dukes and German princesses, made for the sake of the succession, but also in the hope of getting Parliament to award each duke a bigger allowance as a married man. His younger brother the Duke of Cumberland had married his Princess Frederica three years ago, and the Duke of Cambridge his Princess Augusta just six weeks before today's ceremony. 'With a noble spirit of patriotism,' wrote one strait-laced Victorian historian, the Royal Dukes 'set about their arduous duties of procuring heirs to strengthen the succession'.[31] Well, that was one way of putting it. A less unctuous contemporary satirical poet claimed instead that:

> Hot and hard each royal pair
> are at it, hunting for the heir.[32]

This semi-ridiculous rush to reproduce became known as the Baby Race. Of course, with hindsight, we know that Victoria will win it. But at the time, it was very far from certain.

Edward decided to whip the garrison of Gibraltar into shape with the ferocious severity he'd experienced himself as an army cadet in Hanover. He was no stranger to corporal punishment. One of his sisters remembered seeing the Royal Dukes in their youth being 'held by their tutors to be flogged like dogs with a long whip'.[33]

Unfortunately, when it came to discipline, Edward tried too hard. Accusations of brutality – deserved or not – would haunt him for the length of his army career. He also had great difficulty in knowing how or when to relax, and his household servants found him a trying master. They complained of his 'strictness', it was said, 'and his extraordinary love of order'.[34] This was something he would bequeath to his daughter Victoria, who would likewise prove herself to be detail-orientated, and dedicated to the task in hand.

Another of the problems Edward experienced in Gibraltar was the climate, which he thought bad for his health; a third was his loneliness. Adelaide Dubus had taught him what love looked like, and having lost both her and his child, he found himself longing for female company. He felt himself to be above merely sensual pleasure, and looked, in short, 'for a companion, not a whore'.[35]

It was time for the entrance of Thérèse-Bernardine Mongenet (1760–1830), known as Madame Julie de Saint-Laurent, Edward's long-term companion and mistress, who would stick with him for the next twenty-eight years.[36] A friend of Edward's had scouted out Julie, previously the mistress of a French aristocrat, in Marseilles in accordance with Edward's detailed brief. He'd said that he wanted 'une Jeune Demoiselle' who was also a talented singer.[37] Julie's arrival was a great relief to Edward's staff in Gibraltar, who believed that the appointment of an official mistress would save him – and them – from other liaisons that might prove 'dangerous as well as disgraceful'.[38]

Despite Edward's reputation for cruelty, there is something cruelly sad about his life. His father forced him to live in exile from Britain for many decades. His financial problems depressed him. They were the inevitable consequence of an upbringing that gave all the Royal Dukes a strong notion of their status and the style in which they ought to live, alongside a weak notion of the value of money.

Edward did not last long in Gibraltar, and was next posted to Canada. 'I am left to vegetate,' he wrote, 'in this most dreary and gloomy spot on the face of the earth.' Years went by. He was now nearly thirty, Edward complained, 'and the only one of the Brothers, kept abroad'.[39] He was missing all the excitement of the Napoleonic Wars, and the chance to prove himself in action. After much pleading, he was allowed to return to London, but then caused scandal by going about with Julie. 'This may be done abroad,' cautioned one of his younger brothers, 'but you may depend upon it, that it cannot be done at home.'[40] Edward was becoming a misfit, unwelcome even among his own family. Perhaps because he'd come to feel like an outcast, Edward was among the more liberal of the extremely conservative Royal Dukes, and spoke at various times in favour of education, the ending of slavery and Catholic emancipation. He even became interested, unlikely though it sounds, in 'socialistic theories'.[41]

Victoria's father, then, was a tortured man, unsure of his life's purpose. Duty had taken him to Germany, Switzerland, Spain and Canada, but he really longed for home, security and romantic happiness. He tried to make himself feel better with absurdly spendthrift behaviour, particularly in the matter of houses and interior decoration. He ran up such huge debts that in 1816 a committee was formed to run his finances for him. The committee awarded him just £11,000 out of £27,000 a year for his annual living expenses, reserving £16,000 a year for his creditors. Dealing with the consequences of her father's debts would later help shape his daughter's much more stringent attitude towards money.

Having eventually left the army, Edward took Julie to live in Brussels because of its low cost of living.[42] Yet, like his brothers, he could see one way out of the financial wilderness: marriage. 'I shall marry,' he claimed in one grandiose statement, 'for the succession.' But then he revealed another motive: 'I shall expect the Duke of York's marriage to be considered the precedent. That was a marriage for the succession, and £25,000 was settled . . . I shall be contented with the same.'[43]

And so, Edward began quietly to look around for a suitable spouse. His hunting ground was Germany, then still a patchwork of small principalities rather than a single united country. In these small courts, bloodline was highly prized, and the German states had a thriving export business in thoroughbred Protestant princesses. Edward was cowardly enough to neglect to mention his new mission to Julie. It is not pleasant to read of how, from the day of his decision, he found himself 'in the practice of daily dissimulation' with her. Eventually poor Julie read in the *Morning Chronicle* that Edward had been looking for a wife. Finishing the article, she made such an 'extraordinary noise' and such a 'strong convulsive movement' that people thought she was ill. The press had told her what her live-in lover had not: that their relationship was over.[44]

Edward's chosen bride – Queen Victoria's mother – was Marie Luise Victoire, then generally known as Victoire, Dowager Princess of Leiningen (1786–1861). She was tall and well-built, 'rather large, but with a good figure', and she had 'a very white skin, black eyes and black hair'.[45] According to one fashion journalist, her high colouring was 'compounded of ravens' plumes, blood and snow'. People thought Victoire lucky not to have inherited her Coburg birth family's distinctive hooked nose.[46] Victoire was not only a fine physical specimen but also a showy dresser. Her wardrobe included her white silk with a low neck, 'trimmed with a deep turnover of lace and tartan ribbon', and her 'mauve flowered-satin'.[47] She was capable of spending more than £100 on a single, spectacular hat.[48]

As she now entered the drawing room on the Prince Regent's other arm, Victoire by far outshone Adelaide. Pale Adelaide wore silver, but Victoire's naturally dramatic colouring was complemented by a dress of 'rich gold trimmings' and Brussels lace, 'tastefully ornamented with gold tassels'.[49] Queen Charlotte herself had ordered this wedding gown, which cost £97, the equivalent of four years' salary for a well-paid governess.[50] It was a dress of dreams, and would be described in detail in *The Times*. Victoire liked, and looked good in, the new, super-tight muslin gowns that made the wearer look like a classical Grecian column. The body-hugging fit of these gowns required the wearing of a novel form of underwear – ankle-length drawers – so that modesty was preserved under the flimsy white fabric. A pair of Victoire's own drawers still survives at the Victoria and Albert Museum.

Golden-tasselled Victoire was now thirty-one. Like Adelaide, she was marrying a man much older than herself, but she was relaxed about this. Her Coburg relatives were an ambitious, upwardly mobile bunch, and through marriage they had infiltrated many of the first families of Europe. Victoire's brother Leopold was the widower of the deceased British princess Charlotte, whose death had been the root cause of the ceremony today. With Charlotte's death Leopold had lost the chance of becoming consort to the Queen of England. But where one Coburg fell down, another sprang up.

Victoire's first husband had always paid rather less attention to his wife than to his hobby of hunting. But the Prince of Leiningen, long since deceased, had at least left her comfortably off. She and her two children, Feodore and Charles, lived in their own palace at Amorbach in Germany. This made her reluctant, at first, to accept Edward's offer. If she married this second aging suitor, Victoire would be sacrificing a quiet and pleasant life.

Her friends, though, thought she would be foolish to turn down such a catch as a British prince. She did confess that Edward's fine figure had made a deep impression when he came wooing. 'How,' one of Victoire's circle asked her, 'could you reject such an honourable proposal?'[51]

But it was still with some misgivings that she eventually accepted him. 'I am leaving an agreeable, independent position,' Victoire wrote to Edward, 'in the hope that your affection will be my reward.'[52] Victoire knew all about Julie, and knew that Edward still cared for her. She could only pray that she would find more happiness in her second marriage than her first.[53] Her craggy-faced brother Leopold shared her nervousness. His sister was marrying into a messed-up family, 'whose members hate one another with an inconceivable bitterness'. And then Britain itself had a more commercial, critical, open society than the Coburgs were used to in their deferential German home. 'Poor Vicky,' Leopold confessed, 'is very afraid that she will be somewhat ridiculed' in England.[54]

At face value, today's ceremony at Kew Palace would be a strangely unlovely wedding, with doubts on all sides and none of the participants marrying for affection. But Edward and Victoire were living at a time when the new art-form of the romantic novel was sneaking its way into libraries. In this still-fresh nineteenth century, people were beginning to think that couples ought to be brought together by the lightning bolt of love, as well as by family duty and economic necessity. This concept was particularly slow to permeate the royal families of Europe, whose position forced them to be utilitarian in their relationships. Yet Edward and Victoire could glimpse the potential for their marriage to be something more than that. Like Jane Austen's heroine Anne in *Persuasion*, a book that was also published in 1818, Victoire would come to believe in the possibility of having a second chance of love.

As she stood before the altar, Victoire had to hand a piece of paper with the words of the Anglican service written out for her upon it in German. When the Archbishop asked Victoire, 'Wilt thou have this man to thy wedded husband?' her crib sheet prompted her to respond: 'Ich will.'[55] She did so not in resignation but in hope.

The Prince Regent now signed the marriage register twice, firstly for the absent king and then for himself.[56] Queen Charlotte signed too, then quickly left the room. She had just about managed to avoid being sick, but certainly wasn't up to the 'most sumptuous dinner' to be served up at five. The other wedding guests descended the narrow staircase to the dining room below, there to toast each other's health. The Prince Regent particularly enjoyed his food, as the 55-inch waist of a pair of his surviving breeches indicates. During a royal dinner the table was spread, twice, with a buffet of dishes from which the diners grazed according to their desire. The first course included a choice of soups, fish and the mixed dishes known as 'removes' and entrées, while the second course was roast meat and fancy vegetables. If the pickiest guest even then couldn't see anything to fancy, there was always cold meat on the sideboard.

It was quite a business getting your fellow diners to serve you if the dish you wanted was placed on the other side of the table. Communication and conversation did not flow freely, not least because of the language barrier. Victoire had carefully rehearsed a speech, writing out the phonetical sounds of the English that she could not speak:

> 'Ei hoeve to regrétt, biing <u>aes yiett</u> so littl cônversent in thie Inglisch lênguetsch, uitsch obleitschës – miy, tu seh, in a <u>veri fiú words</u>, theat ei em <u>môhst grêtful</u> for yur congratuleschens end gud uishes.'[57]

After the stilted meal, Edward and his new Duchess of Kent drove away by carriage, while William and his new Duchess of Clarence joined the Prince Regent for tea-drinking in a cottage out in the gardens.

Queen Charlotte was too ill to join the tea-party, and in fact she would never again leave Kew Palace. Four months after her sons' weddings, and just two rooms away from the scene of the ceremony, she died. The queen's agonising end left Kew tainted not only by illness but by death, and the funny little palace would now fall from the royal family's favour. In due course Queen Victoria would use her parents' wedding venue as a country holiday home for her children, and would eventually give it to the nation and open it up to visitors on her seventy-ninth birthday in 1898. Among the items on display was the very chair in which her grandmother passed away.

As for Edward and Victoire, two months after their marriage they were off back to Germany, to live cheaply on her estates. As they passed through the Low Countries, they were spotted at a ball for the Allied Army, which was still in occupation after 1815's Battle of Waterloo. Edward was observed tenderly touching the cheek of his waltzing wife, 'to feel if she was not too hot'. He was anxious because they suspected that she was already pregnant.[58]

This compassionate touch of the cheek, though, was an important sign that something else had begun too. This inauspicious, pragmatic union, with money and succession at its heart, would catch fire, grow passionate and produce a daughter capable of great passion herself.

2

Birth: Kensington Palace, 24 May 1819

In the early hours of 24 May, a light rain was falling. It sprinkled the lime tree avenues and the dull mirror of the Round Pond outside Kensington Palace's long, low east-facing facade. From where she lay in bed, Victoire could see the coming dawn reflected in the pond. She was wide awake. Although this was the third time she had given birth, she was as edgy as if it were the first: 'everything is new for me . . . it is eleven years since I had a child.'[1]

Kensington Palace has a sylvan quality, protected by its green gardens against the hubbub of central London. This rambling, red-brick palace was the centre of court life in Georgian times. By 1819, though, it had become a rather run-down retirement home for minor members of the royal family, and was entirely rural in character. To the south lay market gardens. To the north were gravel pits, and the pleasant swell of Campden Hill. Placed practically in the countryside, the palace had originally been built for the asthmatic King William III, who'd struggled to breathe in the smog of riverside Westminster.

Victoire's bed was positioned, rather eccentrically, in the first-floor dining room of her husband Edward's apartment. The space had been converted to a makeshift hospital suite.[2] Its walls were papered in blue, it had a 'handsome' mirror of silvered glass and there was direct access via a back staircase to the kitchens below. These stairs were usually used for bringing food, but they would now be equally handy for fetching hot water.[3]

The dining room had also been chosen for the birth because it was adjacent to a saloon, where members of the Privy Council including the Duke of Wellington, the Home Secretary and the Archbishop of Canterbury could wait and watch in comfort. These luminaries would, by long tradition, gather to observe any royal birth. It was their job to ensure that the child was born alive and well, and to check that no imposter baby could be slipped into the mother's bed to replace a stillborn child.

Their presence was demanded by the legacy of the events of 1688, when a replacement baby, concealed inside a warming pan, was said to have been smuggled into Queen Mary of Modena's bed as a substitute for a stillbirth. It was 'fake news', but the ensuing scandal contributed to a successful coup against Mary's husband, the unpopular Catholic King James II. Scrutiny of the process was supposed to make sure that nothing like this could ever happen again.

When the wife of Edward's younger brother the Duke of Cambridge had given birth to a baby in March, just a couple of months earlier, the Duke of Clarence had rushed into the room to 'determine its sex by actual inspection' before sending off messengers to announce that the Cambridges had just taken the lead in the Baby Race.[4] Victoire's lying-in was being followed with a similar level of interest. Boys gathered in the courtyard behind the palace, ready to run to the newspaper offices. The line of carriages bringing well-wishers to call reached all the way from Kensington Palace to Hyde Park Corner.[5] London was agog to find out if a more senior Kent baby would arrive safely to trump the little Cambridge.

Present at Victoire's side in the dining room was her husband, who was turning out to be a surprisingly modern father. Throughout the night just past, Edward had been struck by the 'patience and sweetness' with which his wife bore her sharpest pains. 'I did not leave her from the beginning to the end,' he would proudly claim afterwards.[6]

And these two unlikely candidates for love had discovered in each other, perhaps to their surprise, something each had long sought. There was no more talk of brutality. Confronted with Victoire's initial doubts, Edward had doubted himself. 'I want you to know,' he wrote, 'my very dear Princess, that I am nothing more than an old soldier of 50 years and after 32 years of service not very fitted to captivate the heart of a young and charming Princess, who is 19 years younger.'[7] This kind of self-deprecation, so unexpected in the corpulent prince, was irresistible. He also displayed a touching level of self-knowledge: 'I would have wished to be able to say all this to you in pretty verses but you know that I am an old soldier who has not this talent.'[8] His laboured pleasantries have a note of authenticity. The year of his marriage, Edward told Victoire, 'saw the birth of my happiness by giving you to me as my guardian angel'. If Heaven preserved his wife's health, and gave him a child, Edward swore that he would be consoled for all his 'misfortunes and disappointments'.[9]

For her own part, Victoire was naïve, certainly, but the best part of her character was her trusting optimism. Her nature, wrote someone who knew her well, was 'confiding to a degree that no good heart could withstand or betray'.[10] This emotional vulnerability had made her unlovely husband love Victoire, and it was something she would bequeath to her daughter.

During the early months of the pregnancy, which they'd spent in Germany, Edward enjoyed commissioning extensive (and unaffordable) improvements to Victoire's first husband's schloss, the thousand-year-old abbey of Amorbach. The Kents arrived back in England only just in time for their baby to be born. The difficulty he'd faced in borrowing sufficient money for the journey had forced Edward to leave it a little late, in turn compelling his heavily pregnant wife to endure a madcap carriage race across the Continent to reach Kensington Palace before she came to term. One of the postilions who assisted with the driving was killed in an accident along the way, and Edward had to pay a pension to his widow. He was also still paying for Julie's carriage, china and living expenses.[11] Edward was by now so greatly in arrears to Coutts bank that he'd been compelled to place 'the very last shilling' he possessed into their hands, forcing him ever deeper into debt.[12]

The debts and the scramble were worth it, though, for Edward and Victoire to be able to claim that their child, a possible future monarch, was born on British soil. Edward thought it was essential that his child should be born in 'the old palace of our ancestors'.[13] 'Say as oft as possible that you are born in England,' Victoire's brother Leopold would in due course counsel his young niece. 'George the III gloried in this, and as none of your cousins are born in England it is your interest.'[14]

The medical team in the Kensington Palace dining room included a novelty at a royal lying-in. Plump, matronly, herself childless, Charlotte Heidenreich von Siebold was a German obstetrician. Most unusually for a woman, she was a qualified physician, with a specialism 'in all Ladies complaints'.[15]

Charlotte had begun her career assisting her midwife mother, who, hidden behind a curtain during lectures so as not to distract the male students, had been the very first German woman to win a doctorate in obstetrics. Charlotte followed her mother through medical training at the University of Göttingen. The Siebolds' motivation had been financial. Before they could call themselves doctors, they'd had difficulty in getting their high-society clients to pay their bills.[16] Frau Siebold came warmly recommended as well as highly qualified, and it must have been a relief for Victoire to have a doctor who spoke her native tongue.

The eminent Welsh doctor David Daniel Davis was also present. He was author of a textbook on obstetrics that advised readers how to use the horrible-sounding instruments he now laid out in case of need: the 'Blunt Hook', the 'long Scissors' and a variety of tools 'for the Extraction of the Head, others for that of the Body'.[17] Should Frau Siebold fail to bring out the baby naturally, force might become necessary.

Despite having these experienced staff standing by, Edward was growing ever more anxious as the labour progressed. He no longer even cared about the succession, only about the health of his wife and child. 'I have no choice between Boy and Girl,' he wrote, 'and I shall always feel grateful for whichever of the two is bestowed upon us, so long as the Mother's health is preserved.'[18]

But Victoire at thirty-two was young, still, and very strong. She had a habit of rushing around the palace so fast that one gentleman she overtook in a corridor 'almost lost [his] wig to the gale'.[19] Edward's prayers were answered. After a short, smooth labour of six hours, it was at 4.15 on the morning of 24 May 1819 that 'a pretty little princess, plump as a partridge' was born.[20] Edward's 'Mayflower', as he called her, was perfect in his eyes, 'truly a model of strength and beauty combined'.[21]

Once his daughter's safety was assured, Edward began to think about what her life might hold. Although she was at this point only fifth in line to the throne, he had a peculiar premonition about her future importance. 'Take care of her,' he said, for 'she will be Queen of England.'[22]

The throne he wished for his daughter was a prize rather less worth pursuing than it had been in previous centuries. Never had its status or sparkle been lower or duller. This was, in part, the fault of Edward himself, and his other 'damned millstone' brothers including the Prince Regent. Before his disappearance from public sight behind the walls of Windsor, George III had won widespread respect, and his subjects celebrated each time his illness seemed to abate. But with his sons it was different. George III had been a curiously inadequate father, by turns too strict and too disengaged. His sons grew up to be lazy, selfish, uninterested in the painful upheavals that their subjects were experiencing as Britain became an industrial nation. Later the same year Percy Bysshe Shelley would write his damning poem 'England in 1819' about the dangerously unpopular royal family and its bloodsucking Royal Dukes. 'Rulers who neither see, nor feel, nor know', Shelley thought them, who 'leech-like to their fainting country cling'.

Now it was time to tell the world that this ill-starred royal family's latest member had arrived. In later years, Victoire would claim that there was also someone present at her daughter's birth who hasn't been mentioned yet.[23] This was Captain, later Sir John, Conroy. Edward's aide-de-camp from his army days, Conroy was the household's administrator. Chisel-cheekboned, black-eyed and exactly the same age as Victoire, Conroy was a figure of great importance in the family's life. Perhaps it was he who now told the Privy Councillors that they could examine the child.

If Conroy really was present at the birth, no one at the time mentioned it. It's also odd that the birth certificate was now signed by 'D. D. Davis', the Welsh doctor. He is not singled out for praise or indeed mention by anyone else present, so it looks like he was booked as a fallback, to mitigate the risks of employing a female doctor, while Charlotte Siebold did the work.

But Dr Davis nevertheless took the credit. The sheer novelty of Frau Siebold's gender must have led to the numerous false reports circulated afterwards that she had run into difficulties, forcing Davis successfully to intervene.[24] However, having managed the royal birth with perfect ease, Frau Siebold was soon on her way back to Germany. Three months later, in Coburg, she would deliver a little son to Victoire's brother Ernest. This cousin to the new Kensington baby would be named Albert.

Victoire must have been filled with pride and satisfaction as she recovered over the next few days. She had not only fulfilled the royal family's demands for an heir; she had also given the man she now truly loved his heart's desire.

She had become completely the mistress of this palace of Kensington, even though she lay in the dining room of the suite formerly occupied by her predecessor Julie. (Fully aware of Edward's previous relationship of nearly three decades, Victoire gave her husband 'every reason to believe that she respects it'.[25]) Ten years earlier, George III had insisted that Edward should eject poor Julie from Kensington Palace, where censorious gossip maintained that she'd 'occupied *eighty* rooms'.[26]

Over the decade since Julie's unceremonious departure, Edward had done up his apartment at Kensington in an increasingly grumpy and bumpy process paid for by the Treasury. George III, in his lucid moments, attempted to control his extravagant son's purse. According to one source, George III ordered that the rooms merely be whitewashed. Edward, though, could not resist embarking on ever more elaborate decorating schemes. He simply did not ask or tell his father, explaining his actions by 'saying *He had once been a bad boy, and would not be so again*, or subject himself to a refusal by asking what the King might not approve'.[27]

Somehow, through persistence, and by borrowing money, Edward had provided himself and Victoire, and now their daughter, with an interior at Kensington Palace that was elegant and up to date. The baby passed her first weeks in an apartment of exuberant Regency colours: crimson, white, amber, geranium, mint-green, pink. The drawing room of buff and black had furniture including something called a 'large indulging sofa with scrolled ends'. The suite's doorcases and cornices were burnished gold.[28] Edward, then, was something of a contradiction: as well as an uptight military martinet, he was also a sybarite.

In the year 1819, true to her own character, Victoire herself managed to spend more than £100 on clothing for her baby, although this probably included a christening robe and bedding for her cot.[29] Edward did not mind at all, as there was never a prouder or more indulgent father. He found his daughter decidedly masculine, more of a 'pocket Hercules, than a pocket Venus'.[30] Contrary to custom, Victoire insisted on breastfeeding, which was unusual enough to be reported in *The Times*.[31] 'Everyone is so astonished,' she admitted, but 'I would have been desperate to see my little darling on someone else's breast.'[32] She was besotted, and told anyone who'd listen that her daughter was '*mon Bonheur, mes delices, mon existence*'.[3] This was all very unusual. Babies were usually removed from their royal mothers to be brought up by professionals. Breastfeeding would inhibit the next conception, and aristocratic women were expected to get on with providing the spare as well as the heir as soon as possible. The little family at Kensington Palace were acting more like the close-knit, affectionate families of contemporary fiction than the couples joined by convenience more commonly found in the royal palaces of Europe. The Kents also followed the latest scientific advice in having their baby inoculated against smallpox. One suspects the influence of Frau Siebold, who'd become licensed to perform this operation early on in her career.

Even if his daughter was a mere fifth in the succession, Edward could legitimately brag that he had now pulled ahead in the Baby Race. Two of his brothers also produced children in 1819, one just before, one just three days after him. But these younger Royal Dukes were Edward's juniors. Their sons lay behind Edward's daughter in the pecking order.

However, the eldest of all the brothers, the Prince Regent, did not like to think of Edward as the father of a future queen. After all, the Regent thought, he might himself make a second marriage, and might even have another child of his own. He decided, therefore, that Edward needed putting in his place.

Edward was anxious that his 'little Queen' should be named after a good role model, Queen Elizabeth I.[34] But the final decision on her name was to be the Prince Regent's. He now rejected not only Elizabeth, but also Georgina and Charlotte after the baby's grandparents. All these names seemed presumptuously royal for such a negligible child. The christening at Kensington Palace was well underway before anyone knew which name the Regent would approve.[35] At the moment in the ceremony when it was required, there was a long pause. Everyone knew that the Regent must make the final choice.

'Alexandrina,' he pronounced. The name would be a compliment to the baby's godfather, the Tsar of Russia.

But it was quietly suggested that she needed more than one name.

'Give her the mother's name also then,' he conceded, grumpily.

He then left, and failed to attend the dinner party that Edward and Victoire hosted at Kensington Palace that evening.

And so, the baby girl was given the English form of her German mother's name almost as an afterthought, and certainly with no inkling that it was a name that would come to define an age.[36]

3

Wet Feet: Sidmouth, 23 January 1820

The January of 1820, in the Devon seaside resort of Sidmouth, was colder than anyone expected. England's average temperature that month was 0.3 degrees below freezing. Ice floes were spotted in the Humber estuary, and Poole Harbour was frozen.[1] At Windsor Castle, George III, dying at long last, 'suddenly drew himself up in his bedclothes', and, quoting *King Lear*, said, 'Tom's a cold.'[2]

The cold was particularly unwelcome to the genteel visitors who'd been drawn to the seaside resort of Sidmouth, Devon, in the hope of a mild West Country winter. Here the January sun usually shines through the spray of waves crashing onto the muddy red cliffs, or else upon Sidmouth's shingle beach. You come upon this beach unexpectedly, just a few steps from the main market-place, almost as if the town did not realise that the sea was so close. In 1820, the beach was the destination of the donkey rides of a visiting family of a boy and two girls. They were the children of a literary lady, a friend of the novelist Frances Burney named Althea Allingham.

The hottest Sidmouth town gossip that winter was all about the Duke and Duchess of Kent's decision to bring the Princess Victoria down to Devon for a winter holiday. 'Little Sidmouth was elated with the honour' of hosting the princess, Althea observed. Her own little daughters were 'full of eager anxiety to see the baby Princess, who might perhaps one day be Queen of England'. [3]

Their wish was quickly fulfilled, as the royal baby soon became part of Sidmouth life. The Allingham girls would watch at the gate of Edward and Victoire's rented temporary home, Woolbrook Cottage, waiting for the eight-month-old baby's nurse to bring her out for an airing. When the infant appeared, Althea was likewise fascinated. She described the princess as a 'very fair and lovely baby' with her large blue eyes and her mouth with its 'sweet but firm expression'.

On one day of bright sunshine, the Allingham family ran into the Kent family, who were out together in search of 'interesting maritime plants' on the 'sand at ebb tide'.[4] It was a charming picture, Edward and Victoire 'linked arm-in-arm', while the baby, in her 'white swan's-down hood and pelisse', reached out for her father. Alethea, who never neglected an opportunity for sentimentality, later recalled the smile on Victoria's 'rosy face' and Edward's 'delighted out-stretched arms'. The Allinghams asked permission, which was granted, for all three of their children to give the princess a kiss. (No wonder, with all this indiscriminate smooching with strangers, that Victoria was soon discovered to have caught a cold.)

The adults talked about the weather, Edward disagreeing with the general view that Sidmouth's climate was unusually healthy. 'Yes, yes,' he had said, in response to the Allinghams' enthusiasm for Devon, 'but for all that there is a treacherous wind from inland; it is blowing to-day.' Approving of this genteel family met by chance, Edward invited them to visit Woolbrook Cottage.

A few days later, therefore, Althea Allingham and her army-colonel husband received a card suggesting a six o'clock dinner. They were in the very act of climbing into their carriage to drive to Woolbrook Cottage 'when a groom wearing the Duke's livery rode up, bearing a second card'. It said that dinner was cancelled because Edward was ill. 'Little did we, or anyone suppose,' Althea recalls, 'that this announcement [of his sickness] was the first note of warning as to what was to come.'[5]

૭

By 23 January, two weeks later, Edward was struggling for his life. Woolbrook Cottage was an incongruous setting for a combat with death. It was that Regency dream, a *cottage orné*, a decorative kind of cottage where aristocrats played at living a simple country life. Before it took on its name of Woolbrook Cottage, it was known as 'King's Cottage', not for any royal reason but because it had been a Mr King of Bath who had transformed it from an old farm into a Gothic villa with castellations in the 1770s. Grander than its name suggests, Woolbrook Cottage was really a substantial holiday home for members of the gentry.

The cottage still exists today, a white-rendered, compact mini-castle at the head of a little valley running down to the beach. Of three storeys, the building in 1820 was 'covered with climbing plants' to cast summertime shade over its whimsical curved verandah.[6] The valley's western wall sweeps up to meet the second storey of the house, meaning that you can see the sea through the first-floor windows of the drawing room, but also step out eastwards through French windows onto the verandah 'entwined with honey-suckle and roses', and thence onto the sloping lawn.[7]

This large, oval-shaped drawing room was the prettiest room in the house, with a carpet patterned with rose wreaths.[8] That January of 1820, though, the roses and honeysuckle were little in evidence, and the cottage was musty and distinctly chilly. Victoire in a candid moment described it as a 'wretched little house, so cramped in space and so impossible to keep warm'.[9] However hard her servants tried, the fireplaces simply could not heat the flimsy building. Half castle, half villa, the cottage was slightly gimcrack in construction, and even today draughts whistle violently through the pretty but impractical pointed panes of its Gothic windows.

Edward's brothers wondered how 'he could think during such a dreadful cold season of leaving his comfortable apartments at Kensington'.[10] But he didn't mind the cold. He was hearty and hale. 'My brothers are not so strong as I am,' he would declare. 'I have led a regular life, I shall outlive them all; the crown will come to me and my children.'[11]

Edward's 'regular' life was in fact something of a trial to his household. He kept the hours of a clockwork machine. The pernickety side of his personality comes over in his super-neat, slanting handwritten letters, issuing a multitude of instructions that one thing must be done 'in the strictest literal sense' and 'in the strictest conformity' with another.[12] One servant had to stay up all night, in order 'to call him in the morning, not being allowed to go to bed until he had lit a fire in the dressing-room'. Then, at six, a second servant brought Edward's cup of coffee, while a third removed the tray. One can see how his living expenses mounted up so quickly. He kept control of all these staff with a system of bells, a different chime sounding for each of the five he summoned most frequently. The system was considered so ingenious that it was adopted by the Treasury.[13]

Edward and Victoire had come to Sidmouth for the stated reason of its warm weather and its health-giving saltwater baths.[14] In the summer, Sidmouth was a thriving resort, made popular by the 'fashionable rage for bathing', as one guidebook put it. It had just short of 3,000 inhabitants, but its population swelled seasonably: you might find an extra 300 visitors of good family in August.[15] But Edward's real reason for choosing Sidmouth was debt. He'd employed an Exeter solicitor to search out a suitable property that he could rent at a low price out of season.[16]

As well as being cold, Woolbrook Cottage was also too small to accommodate all the family's servants, who had to be lodged elsewhere in the town. Sidmouth's shopkeepers were delighted. In eighteen months of marriage, Edward had showered Victoire with gifts paid for with borrowed money: a piano, jewellery, millinery, muslin, perfume and lace.[17] The local tradesmen now queued up to offer their services, and John Taylor, a Sidmouth shoemaker, was selected for the honour of making Victoria's first pair of shoes. He ended up making three pairs, each four inches long: one for the baby to wear, one to keep for himself and a third that he gave to a potter in the town to be memorialised as ceramic copies for sale. In due course Queen Victoria would become the most merchandised monarch thus far in history, and the process had already begun.

Despite the cold, Edward believed that his daughter was doing well. She'd been weaned at six months. At eight months, she was already the size of a one-year-old, and had successfully sprouted two milk-teeth 'without the slightest inconvenience'.[18] 'My little girl,' Edward wrote, is 'strong and healthy; *too healthy*, I fear, in the opinion of some members of my family, by whom she is regarded as an intruder.'[19] He was hinting here at the resentful feelings that his younger brothers, losers of the Baby Race, were thought to harbour against her. If Victoria were to die, their own sons would move up the order of succession.

But Victoire was more familiar than Edward with the ways of children. Observing the little girl more closely, she found her daughter 'restless', and suffering from a sore throat. The baby was 'beginning to show symptoms of wanting to get her own little way'.[20] Victoire was finding her 'pocket Hercules' more challenging than her first two children. 'I am over anxious,' she confessed, 'in a childish way with the little one, as if she were my first child . . . my dearest darling has torn me completely out of my normal way of life.'[21] For her, Sidmouth was 'a dreary time'.[22]

Then Victoire's daughter Feodore, now twelve, also fell ill. But having both girls sick was only a prelude for what was to come. On 7 January, Edward had gone out walking in the rain with his friend and advisor John Conroy. Six feet tall like Edward himself, Conroy had been forced to leave the army after a 'disagreement' in 1816. He became his former commander's 'chief administrator' instead.[23] He was by now so deeply embedded into the Kents' household that they could not imagine doing without him.

On returning from the wet walk, legend tells, Edward then failed to change his damp boots and stockings: 'attracted by the smiles of his daughter, he unfortunately delayed until he was dressed for dinner.'[24] Thus his love for his daughter, it's suggested, caused his subsequent illness. It's pleasing reasoning, but Edward himself had no time for the wet socks theory. He dated the decline in his health from his very arrival in the West Country. He thought that something in the water of Sidmouth had 'begun to play the very deuce [with] his bowels'.[25] No one yet understood about germs or viruses, and everyone thought that water or air were the means through which sickness travelled and entered the body. The true cause of Edward's malady was the pneumonia virus, and the result was 'acute inflammation of the lungs, which soon assumed an alarming aspect'.[26]

But Edward refused to take his 'cold' very seriously. Determined to ignore the fact that he was ill, he asked Captain Conroy to invite guests to a party.[27] He even wanted to take a sea bath in 'the terribly cold wind', but his wife would not let him.[28] He also refused the medicines of the local physician.[29] These included the purgative calomel, highly dangerous because of its mercury content, mixed with 'Dr James's Powder for Fevers', with its active ingredient of another poison, antimony.[30] After a few days, though, Edward's breathing difficulties forced him to take to his bed. On the Wednesday, 12 January, Victoire had his bed moved to a warmer room. On Saturday 15 January, the blistering began.

Now real anxiety entered the cottage, this 'badly built house which is quite unfit for anyone who is ill'. 'Oh!' Victoire wrote, 'I was in such desperate anxiety, in spite of the Doctor's renewed assurances.'[31] Feodore in later life remembered how her mother had barely coped. 'I well remember the dreadful time at Sidmouth,' she recalled. 'I recollect praying on my knees.'[32] The weather had turned truly nasty – 'the cold is almost unbearable' – and there were no trusted local doctors.

The painful process of blistering involved placing heated cups over slits cut in the patient's skin, so that as they cooled down the air inside them contracted and sucked out the blood. In reality, draining Edward's plasma made matters worse. In response to Conroy's urgent messages to London, the late Queen Charlotte's doctor, Dr William Maton, came down to Sidmouth. This was an unfortunate choice, as Maton could not speak French or German, and Victoire was still not fluent in English. She could not make him understand that she didn't want her husband blistered or bled. 'For four hours they must have tormented him,' Victoire claimed. 'It made me nearly sick.'[33]

On Wednesday 19 January, Dr Maton ordered six pints of blood to be removed from his patient, in two separate sessions. When Edward was told about the second session, he wept.

You can feel nothing but sympathy for Victoire, watching her husband being put through these barbarous treatments, while instinctively knowing that they were doing no good. She had to help him out of bed, and grew terribly frightened when he fainted and vomited. There was 'hardly a spot on his dear body', Victoire wrote on 20 January, left untouched 'by cupping, blisters or bleeding'. 'I cannot think it can be good for the patient to lose so much blood when he is already so weak,' she continued, 'he was terribly exhausted yesterday after all that had been done to him by those cruel doctors.'[34]

By Saturday 22 January, the crisis had drawn important people to Sidmouth, Victoire's brother Leopold and his advisor Baron Stockmar. Stockmar, himself a trained doctor, felt Edward's pulse and knew at once he could not survive: he 'rattles in his throat and is despaired of'.[35]

Edward did rally briefly, during which time they tried to get him to sign his will. This document would leave Victoire in an unusual, indeed, a startling position. For her husband's will left everything to her. In effect, this meant she'd get nothing, for, as one of his sisters sighed, 'Edward had nothing in the World but debts.'[36] But the will also left Victoire – a single woman – something intangible but vital: responsibility for bringing up and educating the heir to the throne. 'I do nominate, constitute, and appoint my beloved wife, Victoire, duchess of Kent,' he wrote, 'to be sole guardian of our dear child, to all intents and for all purposes whatever.'[37]

This surprising development was partly to do with the distaste and disinterest of Edward's elder brother, the Prince Regent, who was dealing with his own demons in this late stage of his life. The

Regent did indeed write and request to be made his niece's guardian in the event of Edward's death, but the letter arrived too late. And it was also due to Victoire's aggressive and pragmatic brother, whom she called '*gut, gut,* Leopold'. Present on the spot in Sidmouth, Leopold pressed the claims of his sister's birth family, the Coburgs, at the expense of those of Edward's family, the Hanoverians. Disappointed of the British throne himself, Leopold could still use his sister to exert his influence.

It was probably Baron Stockmar, as Leopold's right-hand man, who drew up the will.[38] Victoire worried that Edward wouldn't have the strength to sign it, but then, having heard it read aloud twice, he gathered all his vitality. 'With difficulty,' Stockmar recalled later, 'he wrote "Edward" below it, looked attentively at each separate letter, and asked if the signature was clear and legible. Then he sank back exhausted on the pillows.'[39]

This will would leave Victoire in a position that was stronger than she could ever have imagined. A monarch had a right, indeed a duty, to control the person and education of his heir. Just a couple of generations previously, George I had removed his grand-daughters from the care of their parents after a disagreement. Victoire now had enormous responsibilities. She would have to find untold strength to deliver them, and no one had ever encouraged her to have much confidence in herself.

When the dark morning of Sunday 23 January finally dawned, Victoria's father was very near death. An eyewitness who was standing 'by the curtain of his bed' in the last hours heard him say, 'with deep emotion, "May the Almighty protect my wife and child, and forgive all the sins I have committed."' Edward's last recorded words, addressed to Victoire, were 'Do not forget me.'[40] It was at ten o'clock 'in the dim light of the January morning' that 'the tolling bell of the old parish church told a sorrow-stricken village that the Duke was dead'.[41]

His hand was still in hers. Victoire had given him all his medicine during his illness, and not changed her clothes for five days, nor slept for five nights except on a little couch at the end of his bed. She had 'quite adored poor Edward', wrote someone who knew them both, 'they were truly blessed in each other.'[42] 'Our dear Mama,' wrote her elder daughter Feodore, 'was very deeply afflicted.'

For the sake of her baby, though, Victoire did her best not to give 'way too much to her grief'.[43] There was work to do. Edward's spirit had left the cottage, but his body remained. It now had to be embalmed, and laid in state in the rose-wreathed drawing room. Local people trooped into the house to stare, passing between two men at the door each holding a black flag. Anyone well dressed was allowed to enter to pay their respects, and so many people turned up that a one-way system had to be instituted. 'We all went,' wrote a young lady from nearby Salcombe, to see the drawing room hung with black cloth, and lit only by candles 'larger than any you ever saw and placed on very high candle-sticks'.[44] Trestles held an urn containing Edward's heart and viscera as well as his huge coffin. Seven and a half feet long to accom-modate his great height, it weighed more than a ton beneath its 'rich velvet pall'.[45]

The lying-in-state continued for longer than anyone had expected, and it was two whole weeks later, on 7 February 1820, that a magnificent procession finally formed up to transport his remains to Windsor.[46] The reason for the delay was that on 29 January, just a week after Edward, George III had finally passed away. This meant that within seven days, Victoria had taken two steps nearer to the throne. There were now just three lives – George IV, the Duke of Clarence and a late entry to the Baby Race in the form of the Duke of Clarence's two-month-old baby – between it and her.

Edward's will gave Victoire sole control over his daughter. But he also left her a more malign legacy. On his deathbed, he'd begged her not to forget him, and she certainly would not. Yet he'd also recommended she place her trust in his friend and servant, John Conroy. The black-haired, theatrical-looking ex-army captain would now find himself the devoted, trusted servant of the lonely, isolated duchess, with almost unlimited opportunities for power and self-advancement.

Conroy could be of immediate use to Victoire at this 'critical time of her life', and raised a new loan for her at Coutts bank.[47] He had wonderful 'activity and capability', she thought, while 'good Leopold is rather slow in the uptake and in making decisions'.[48] She had no cash, and wasn't even certain that the Prince Regent, who was in fact now the brand-new King George IV, would even let her return to Kensington Palace. Conroy and Leopold escorted her back to London in 'bitter cold and damp weather', looking 'very sharp after the poor little baby'.[49]

Within eighteen months, Victoire had lost her placid life in Amorbach, her husband and all prospect of security in this foreign land of England. 'My poor head is so confused, I can hardly think,' she admitted, finding comfort only in 'dear, sweet little Vickelchen'.[50]

But Edward had also bequeathed his family something more significant than debts and the service of the dubious Captain Conroy. Despite his frustrating, wasted life spent largely in exile, Julie had shown Edward what a functioning romantic relationship looked like, and he had put it into practice with Victoire. Under his lasting influence, Victoire would now fight like a lion to remain close to her daughter, even if the effort was fraught with danger. She could have retired to Amorbach, as the British establishment now wished that she would. She could have left her baby to be brought up by the grudging George IV. And yet she would stay, standing 'alone, almost friendless and unknown' in this country where she 'could not even speak the language'.[51]

Victoria, then, would grow up surrounded by people with strong passions, for her, and for her future. From them she would gain a lesson that was doubly hard for a king or queen to learn: how to create a family, and how to love. This lucky chance would ultimately save the monarchy.

4

'I will be good': Kensington Palace, 11 March 1830

Her teacher hands her a book. Folded within its pages is a chart listing Britain's kings and queens. Victoria, in her white dress and coral necklace, has pretty light brown hair and a chubby lower lip that tends to fall open unless she remembers to keep it closed. She's just short of eleven years old. The knowledge of her place in the succession has so far been kept from her. Look at the chart, she is told. Her uncle the king George IV is gravely ill. He cannot live long. Who will come next?

What follows is one of the best-known and most dramatic scenes in Victoria's life. Sitting at the rosewood table in Kensington Palace where she did her lessons, she studied the chart, thought it through and worked it out. When her oldest uncle George died, her next oldest uncle William would take over. And when he died, she must herself become queen.

'I see I am nearer the throne than I thought,' Victoria is supposed to have said. 'I will be good!'

It would become the most celebrated statement of Victoria's childhood, rousing words, with a message of responsibility and duty: one must step up to the challenge of ruling one's country, as well as learning one's French.

But did it really happen?

One detail at least is agreed by all sources: that the setting was Kensington Palace. It was the sleepiest and most sedate of the numerous royal palaces. Kensington was 'a place to drink tea', by contrast to Windsor Castle – 'a place to receive monarchs' – and Buckingham Palace, where you went 'to see fashion'. During Victoria's Kensington childhood, anyone going for a walk 'quietly along the gardens, fancies no harsher sound to have been heard from the Palace windows, than the "tuning of the tea-things"', or the playing of a piano.[1]

Behind closed doors, though, the atmosphere at Kensington was far from peaceful. Victoria would come to believe it was not so much a palace as a prison. Deep in the gardens, she was growing up in isolation. Her guardians deliberately kept her well away from both the greedy eyes of her future subjects, and the disreputable, high-society world of George IV. She was comfortable, she was well-fed, she had toys. But she was also under considerable psychological strain. She formed the centre of a small and close-knit circle whose adoration placed her under what was sometimes intolerable pressure.

In later life, Victoria admitted that as a child she'd been spoiled, and 'very much indulged by everyone'. 'Everyone' included her mother's devoted lady-in-waiting, Baroness de Späth, who'd been with Victoire since her first marriage, Victoria's nurse Mrs Brock – 'dear Boppy' – and an elderly dresser named Mrs Louis. They all of them 'worshipped the poor little fatherless child'.[2] With Baroness de Späth, it even became 'a sort of idolatory', and 'she used to go on her knees' before her charge.[3]

Looking at Victoria's little face, with its typically Hanoverian, slightly bulging blue eyes, these ladies discerned 'a very striking resemblance to her late Royal Father'.[4] It was hard to chastise someone who'd lost a parent so young. Victoria was as close as she could be to her half-sister, but Feodore was eleven years older. What she lacked was a playmate on an equal footing, someone to laugh at her. 'You must always remember,' said a person who knew her well later in life, that she never had companions her own age to 'knock any nonsense out of her'.[5] Victoria was developing a streak of selfishness that stemmed from the indulgence of Boppy and Späth.

Into this pressure-cooker of adulation came the bracing influence of Johanna Clara Louise Lehzen. She'd arrived at Kensington in 1819 as Feodore's governess. Five years later, Victoria was old enough to need a governess of her own. Prince Leopold, still giving financial help to his sister's household, decided that Lehzen should do the job. Although he did not live at Kensington, his influence was very great. Victoire had £6,000 a year, voted by Parliament at the time of her marriage. Leopold, though, had £50,000 annually, a wildly generous provision made at the time of his short-lived marriage to the late Princess Charlotte. The wider royal family considered that Leopold could easily bear some of the living costs of his sister and niece. Yet leaving Leopold to shoulder the financial responsibility like this meant that the royal family also sacrificed a good deal of their own power over Victoria. Because he paid for things, Victoria would become almost the property, indeed the puppet, of her beloved 'Uncle Leopold'.

And Leopold now chose Lehzen. This was partly because he thought she would be a counter-influence against Captain Conroy, who controlled much of what went on at Kensington, and whom Leopold distrusted. 'Lehzen', as the household called her, was an intense character, with dark-eyed, dark-haired 'Italian' looks, and a disordered digestion.[6] She'd say that she 'did not know the feeling to be hungry' – something that would later cause trouble with her pupil – and that all she ever 'fancied were potatoes'.[7] She suffered from migraines, which some people misinterpreted as a drinking problem. It was family tragedy that had forced Lehzen to find work as a governess. She was the youngest daughter of a pastor in Hanover; her mother had died when she was young, and three of her sisters had also passed away before reaching twenty. Lehzen was born the wrong side of the scenes to sit down at table with aristocrats and courtiers, and was eventually made a baroness to eliminate the difficulties in etiquette that this caused.[8]

Lehzen had the self-discipline, plus the selfless dedication, that her position demanded. But she considered the job offer that Leopold made (via Victoire) very carefully before accepting. 'After a short silence,' Lehzen recollected of the interview, 'I said that I had often thought of the great difficulties which such a person might have to encounter in educating a Princess.'[9] As a condition of her service, Lehzen asked that she might always be present when Victoria met third parties, so that her influence would be paramount. Although Victoria met few outsiders, this did not mean that she spent much time alone. Every aspect of her progress through girlhood was kept constantly under watch. 'I never had a room to myself,' Victoria claimed in later life, 'till I was nearly grown up always slept in my Mother's room.'[10] Victoria told one of her own children that she was not even allowed to walk downstairs unaccompanied in case she fell.[11] Even when she walked out in Kensington Gardens, the young princess felt, people constantly 'look at me . . . to see whether I am a good child'.[12]

As she was already living at Kensington Palace, Lehzen must have been aware that her charge would be difficult to manage. The celebrated fiery temper of the Hanoverian dynasty was already visible in the little girl: people called her '*le roi Georges* in petticoats'.[13] 'Did she not feel *unhappy* when she had done wrong?' a tutor once asked her. 'Oh no,' Victoria replied.[14] Her mother Victoire was still finding all this very difficult. Her younger daughter 'drives me at times to real desperation', she admitted.[15]

But Lehzen, thoughtful but strict, had the strength of character not to let Victoria's tricks get out of hand. 'Lehzen takes her gently from her bed,' we hear of the morning routine, 'and sits her down on the thick carpet, where she has to put on her stockings.' 'Poor Vicky!' Victoria would say, 'She is an unhappy child! She just doesn't know which is the right stocking and which is the left!'[16] She usually appeared in the white, pink or pale blue of a nice young girl. She'd been wearing figure-moulding stays – or at least the softer, unboned equivalent thought suitable for children – since the age of six.[17]

In later years, Victoria's memory convinced her that her life at Kensington was bleak and gloomy, and another of its inhabitants did once call the place a 'hospital for the decayed and poor royalties'.[18]

While Victoria's childhood was far distant from the real depriv-
ation of the many truly poor children of London, it was true that
the palace did not run smoothly. Her father's financial problems
still dogged the household, and luxuries were carefully controlled.
'I never had a sofa, nor an easy chair,' Victoria claimed, and 'there
was not a single carpet that was not threadbare.'[19] The very 'Cribb
Bedstead in which Her Majesty first reposed', purchased from Mr
Francis of Bond Street, was never paid for: its maker was still
complaining that his invoice was unpaid eighteen years after her
birth.[20] Still, Victoire's accounts do show a steady stream of small
extravagances flowing into the palace: honey from Fortnum &
Mason's; porcelain from Josiah Wedgewood; a silver muffin-
toaster.[21]

Victoria's food was an odd mixture of grand and mean. She
recalled eating 'bread and milk out of a small silver basin', with
tea 'only allowed as a great treat'.[22] 'The Princess only eats plain
roast mutton,' claimed Captain Conroy, wanting praise for running
a thrifty and wholesome household.[23] If given the opportunity,
Victoria would gorge. One of her passions was fresh fruit. When
she could get them, she would devour peaches, gooseberries, grapes,
cherries, apples, pears.[24] In fact, the close control exerted over her
diet meant that the seeds of a dysfunctional eating pattern were
being planted. In a story written by the young Victoria, the heroine,
a 'naughty girl', behaves in a way that's thoroughly 'naughty greedy
and disobedient' yet somehow manages to escape punishment. Even
better, in this tale of wish fulfilment, she gets 'rewarded' for her
bad behaviour with a profusion of sweetmeats.[25]

Victoire watched Victoria so closely and carefully because of
the legitimate fear that despite her late husband's will, George IV
might at any time try to remove her daughter from her care.
Previous kings had always made their own educational arrangements
for their heirs, and precedent was everything in the royal family.
George IV's personal dislike of Victoire meant he was constantly
'talking of taking her child from her'.[26]

The lonely Victoire, with her debts and responsibilities and grief, was scatterbrained, and prone to making poor judgements of character. But she redeems herself with her charm and warmth, and clearly loved her children. 'Her kindness and softness,' it was said of her, 'are very delightful in spite of want of brains.'[27] She was gradually learning the language of her adopted country, but still apologised to visitors 'for not speaking English well enough to talk it'.[28] This is one of the reasons she had grown so dependent upon Captain Conroy.

Victoire never wrote – nor presumably spoke – quite as a native. Did she therefore talk to her daughter in German? The unpopularity of the German Hanoverians in Britain explains Victoria's own later insistence that she did not. 'Never spoke German . . . not allowed to,' she stoutly claimed.[29] Her schoolroom timetable does reveal, however, that she had a formal German lesson twice a week.[30] And the German accents of Victoria's mother, Lehzen and Späth did certainly affect her spoken English. Her tutor Mr Davys, brought in to supplement Lehzen with more formal lessons, recollected that at first 'she confused the sound of the "v" with that of "w", and pronounced *much* as *muts*.'[31]

Despite her account of tarnished silver, threadbare carpets and uncomfortable chairs, Victoria also had plenty of toys, especially dolls. She was 'quite devoted' to her dolls, '& played with them till she was 14'. She believed that they were her friends in place of real little girls: '*she* was an *only* child,' she wrote, '& except occasional visits of other children lived always *alone*, without companions.'[32]

As well as her dolls, Victoria had a wonderful doll's house. For her eighth birthday, her presents included furnishings for it, including 'a tiny melon-shaped silver tea-pot, with a very short spout' and marked with a 'V'.[33] This is one among other pieces of evidence that, contrary to common belief, she *was* usually called 'Victoria', her second name, rather than 'Drina', the diminutive of her first, even in childhood. The dolls had an educational purpose even beyond the making of their costumes. They also provided a training in the court life that Victoria in seclusion was failing to experience. 'Upon a long board full of pegs, into which the dolls' feet fitted,' we're told, 'she rehearsed court receptions, presentations, and held mimic drawing-rooms and levees.'[34] Even so, Victoria's limited social opportunities were making her bashful. For her whole life, she could sometimes lose confidence in a conversation, and allow it to peter out in a 'shy way she had'.[35]

As well as helping to sew the dolls' costumes, Lehzen was sacrificing private life and friends for her privilege of training a probable future queen. She even refused to keep a journal, an action that would have been considered indiscreet. In return, Victoria developed 'great respect and even awe of her' but also 'the greatest affection'. Victoria later claimed that for thirteen years her governess 'never once left her'.[36] This wasn't quite true: Lehzen took a holiday in Paris in May 1831, for example. But she was rewarded for her service with the devotion of her charge.

It must have been hard for Victoire when her own daughter began to talk about 'my <u>angelic</u> dearest Mother, <u>Lehzen</u>, who I do <u>so</u> love!'[37] But a coldness was gradually creeping into Victoire's relationship with Victoria, not least because Victoria had picked up on her Uncle Leopold and Lehzen's distrust of Captain Conroy. 'I have grown up all alone,' Victoria later declared.[38] This was not technically true; it was more that she *felt* alone. In reality, she was constantly surrounded not only by servants but also, as time went on, by Conroy's family. His wife was a frequent visitor, and his daughters, Jane and another Victoire, became Victoria's approved playmates. With them, she played with rudimentary jigsaws called 'dissected prints', made cottages out of cards, dressed up as 'Nuns' or 'Turks' or rode upon a pony called Isabel.[39] It doesn't sound like a lonely life, but the loneliness that she experienced stemmed from the fact that her intimates were chosen for her.

Conroy, for his part, had insinuated himself completely into Victoire's confidence. It's clear that he was adept at exploiting her lack of self-belief. 'So often, so very often,' she confessed to him, 'what you said so often and what hurt me, but unhappily is true, I am not fit for my place, no, I am not. – I am just an old stupid goose.'[40] Victoire also worried that Conroy had appointed a rather dubious clerk to pay the palace bills. She later admitted that 'she was afraid of him – he might be dishonest'.[41] Victoire's own vagueness confused and irritated Conroy in return. 'The Duchess lives in a mist,' he said, 'and therefore she is very difficult to deal with.'[42]

But the ditzy duchess nevertheless drew emotional support from a position she developed for herself within the tightly knit Conroy family unit. The young Queen Elizabeth I, lacking a conventional family life, decided that she didn't need one. The young Queen Victoria was excluded from, but forced to watch, a happy family life being played out all round her by the hated Conroys. Their enjoyment in each other was easy to see, yet utterly out of reach. In later life, she would seek to replicate such a close family for herself.

Unlike the 'misty' Victoire, or the devious Captain Conroy, Lehzen had a crystal-clear idea of right and wrong. 'I adored her, though I also feared her,' Victoria remembered.[43] Lehzen would say that 'she could pardon *wickedness* in a Queen', but not '*weakness*'.[44] With her 'great judgement and yet greater strength of mind', it was Lehzen who coached Victoria in something in which she would always excel: in telling people when 'they were wrong'.[45]

Victoire and Lehzen went so far as to begin a regime of moral surveillance called the 'Good Behaviour Book'. Beginning in 1831, it was a journal recording Victoria's conduct, and it's a striking record of both submission and rebellion. Victoria would often admit to sins ranging from having been 'very thoughtless' or 'very impertinent' through to 'very very very very horribly naughty!!!!!' This daily task of recording her life became a habit that grew into something quite remarkable: the millions of words eventually embodied in the journals that she would keep lifelong. The project owed something to the contemporary evangelical current within the Church, which required worshippers to confess their sins. Also, Victoria was repeatedly told that she was chosen for a special destiny; that her life deserved memorialising.

Later she would take this idea of becoming the historian of her own life through into keeping significant dresses from her wardrobe, and into the compulsive taking and collecting of photographs. In due course, even certain rooms of her palaces would be maintained with their furniture unchanged as shrines to earlier times. Ultimately Kensington Palace itself, where the first words were written in the 'Good Behaviour Book', would be thrown open to visitors by Victoria. Her subjects would be allowed to see where she was born, and implicitly to judge if she'd lived life well.

The reading material that Lehzen gave Victoria included Miss Edgeworth's *Moral Tales for Young People*. These stories showed the world as good or bad, white or black, a vision of life that Victoria would retain. Edgeworth's purpose was to produce children who could solve moral dilemmas for themselves. Yet her stories also made it clear that society was hierarchical. In 'The Bad Governess', for example, the girlish heroines 'could not bear to think that a person should be treated with neglect or insolence merely because her situation and rank happened to be inferior'.[46] Victoria was brought up by Lehzen to respect servants, but also to believe that they were lesser than herself.

Miss Edgeworth's was a monochromatic, melodramatic view of the world, but it suited troubling times. While Victoria was safely distanced from it in the garden groves of Kensington, the regime of her uncle George IV was going dangerously adrift. The long-lived George III had been so personally popular that he made the institution of monarchy more palatable too. But there was no such affection for his son. Politicians were beginning to detect a growing feeling that the monarchy could not survive, and that there was a gathering list of arguments 'in favour of some undefined change in the mode of governing the country'.[47] In other words, the unpopularity of Victoria's uncles, combined with the human cost of industrialisation, might bring about revolution.

This only placed further pressure upon Victoria to 'save' the monarchy. One visitor to Kensington Palace found her 'a born

Princess', lacking in affectation, and representing a welcome fresh start. 'I look to her to save us from Democracy,' this lady concluded, 'for it is impossible she should not be popular when she is older and more seen.'[48] But the royal family itself did not think that their salvation lay in a mere girl. 'Good heavens! A woman on the throne of so great a country – how ridiculous,' scoffed one of her cousins.[49] Victoria's gender also presented a problem in that Britain and the German state of Hanover had been ruled for the last century by a single king. But the law prevailing in Germany prevented a female from inheriting Hanover's throne. Under Queen Victoria, Hanover would be divorced from Britain and the monarchy's possessions split asunder.

In 1823, when Victoria was just short of four, she began a regular course of studies under her academic tutor, a clergyman named George Davys. She was far from swottish. 'I was not fond of learning,' she remembered later, 'and baffled every attempt to teach me my letters up to 5 years old.'[50] Victoire apologised in advance to Mr Davys for any bad behaviour: 'I fear you will find my little girl very headstrong,' she told him, 'but the ladies of the household will spoil her.'[51] Victoria herself repaid Mr Davys's efforts with a considerable dislike, thinking him always 'in a bad temper'.[52] He does sound a bit of a bore. His published works included patronising homilies for village folk and an exposition on the importance of thrift. 'His ambition through life,' as his obituarist would put it, 'was rather to be good than great.'[53]

Dutiful Mr Davys nevertheless instituted a timetable of regular lessons with a roster of visiting tutors. Generally, Victoria studied for two hours in the morning and one in the afternoon. Her schoolroom routine involved an eight o'clock breakfast of bread and milk and fruit with her mother. She then rode her donkey round Kensington Gardens, followed by lessons until a very plain luncheon. After more lessons, she drove out with her mother, dined at seven on more 'bread and milk', and at nine 'went to her little French bed with its pretty Chintz hangings, placed beside that of her mother'.[54]

On Saturdays, she gave Mr Davys a recap of everything she'd learned that week. His curriculum favoured the arts, rather than the ancient languages that would have been studied by a boy. The majority of the time was spent on music, drawing (where she excelled), dancing, history, poetry, religion, French and German. It was the standard education for a genteel young lady being prepared for a society debut and marriage. Her tutors reported her as 'indifferent' in spelling, but 'good' at most other subjects, with a 'very good' reserved for French.[55] It was a lightweight curriculum for a future sovereign, but the household was not intellectually curious. As one of Victoria's Prime Ministers would later observe, 'old Davys instilled some Latin into her during his tutorship' but 'the rest of her education she owes to her own natural shrewdness and quickness'.[56]

This meant that there was a basic contradiction in Victoria's position. She was, as historian Stanley Weintraub notes, clearly born into power, and those about her fought hard for her prerogatives. And yet, at the same time, she was educated 'by pious spinsters and cautious clergymen', exhorted to behave demurely, and to live simply.[57] 'It had been very early instilled into her,' wrote someone who knew the adult queen well, 'that it was man's province to be clever, and that it was best for woman not to intrude into it.'[58] She was special, and yet she had to pretend to be ordinary. This strange contradiction – I believe – would in due course become the key to her surprisingly successful reign.

By early 1830, when Victoria was ten, it was clear that George IV – blind, obese, addicted to laudanum and hiding away at Windsor – was dying. Lehzen has left a description of her pupil in early adolescence. 'My Princess,' as Lehzen calls her, 'is not tall, but very pretty, has dark blue eyes, and a mouth which, though not tiny, is very good-tempered and pleasant, very fine teeth, a small but graceful figure, and a very small foot.'[59] Victoria's minuscule feet were well displayed in the pretty, flat, ribboned pumps of contemporary fashion. At the age of fifteen, her foot would be 21.3 centimetres long, making her, in modern terms, a British size two.[60]

It was George IV's impending death that eventually made it clear that the truth of Victoria's position must be revealed to her. William, Duke of Clarence, and his wife Adelaide (from the double wedding at Kew) were next in line to reign. But the tragic early deaths of their four children meant that when William took the crown, Victoria would become his heir presumptive. This she needed to know.

There are two rival accounts, Lehzen's and Mr Davys's, of how she learned of her future fate, and 11 March 1830 is the most likely date.[61] Yet each witness has a self-serving desire to claim the honour of having announced her destiny to the little girl, and their accounts are incompatible.

Mr Davys later told his son that *he* had been the one to reveal her future to Victoria. During lessons, he says, he had 'set her to make a chart of the kings and queens. She got as far as "Uncle William", before coming to a stop.' Who, Mr Davys asked, was the next heir to the throne? 'She rather hesitated, and said, "I hardly like to put down myself."'[62]

According to Lehzen, though, it was she, not Mr Davys, who slipped a 'chronological table' of the kings and queens of England into Victoria's history book. Possibly this was a well-known teaching aid called 'Howlett's Tables'.[63] 'When Mr Davys was gone,' Lehzen reminisced, years later, 'Princess Victoria opened, as usual, the book again and seeing the additional paper said: "I never saw that before."'

'It was not thought necessary you should, Princess,' Lehzen answered.

'I see I am nearer to the Throne than I thought,' Victoria declared. Lehzen next produces a record of a speech that is quite frankly implausible for a little girl. 'Many a child would boast,' Victoria is supposed to have said, 'but they don't know the diffi-culty; there is much splendour, but there is more responsibility!'

In Lehzen's sentimental – and highly Victorian – version of the scene, Victoria then raised her right forefinger, as if making an oath. She 'gave me that little hand', Lehzen continued, saying the words that everyone remembers.

'I will be good!' the princess promised.[64]

It seems too good to be true, a parable told by a fond governess that shows both teacher and pupil in the best possible light. Yet Victoria, reading this account years later, certainly recollected that something along those lines had indeed occurred. She noted her own memory of the day in the margin of Lehzen's account: 'I cried much,' she records, on learning that she would be queen, 'and ever deplored this contingency.'[65]

However, there is a third, rival account of what happened, which yet again challenges those of Victoria's tutor and governess. Unfortunately, it comes from someone who might be considered an unreliable witness, the 'misty' Victoire. Far from its being a carefully stage-managed session with Mr Davys, her recollection is that the revelation of Victoria's destiny to her came about without planning, and she genuinely just discovered it 'by accident, in pursuing her education'.[66]

On 13 March 1830, Victoire reported to the Bishop of London that her daughter knew all, and that there had been no stage management by Lehzen or Davys and their family trees and exhortations. 'What accident has done,' Victoire wrote, 'I feel no art could have done half so well . . . we have everything to hope from this Child!'[67]

And Victoire gains credibility as a witness if you look at the dates on which the various accounts were written. Lehzen's and Davys's were set down years later, deep into Victoria's reign, when each was eager to claim a legacy in the formation of her character. I think that we have, after all, to trust the daffy duchess's account from just two days after the event, and accept that one of the most dramatic scenes in Victoria's life – 'I will be good!' – was merely dramatic licence.

The Duchess of Kent's educational arrangements also had another advantage. Victoria's curious upbringing, despite the strain it placed upon her, despite her hostility to Captain Conroy, would turn out to be an excellent strategy in terms of public relations. Her childhood seclusion meant that she could, in due course, be presented to her people as a most interesting young lady.

The most interesting young lady, in fact, that the world contained.

5

The Three Missing Weeks: Ramsgate, October 1835

In October 1835, Victoria was sixteen, quite old enough to be married. She was taking a seaside holiday in Ramsgate, at Kent's easternmost tip, to recover her health after an arduous tour. During the previous weeks, she'd been travelling all over England.

Victoria had been to Ramsgate many times before. Uncle Leopold gave his sister and niece £1,000 annually to spend on a stay by the sea, as a substitute for the country house they did not have, and the resort of Ramsgate was popular with second-rank royals. Albion House, the holiday home that the Duchess of Kent rented on this autumn visit, had been taken the previous year by one of William IV's many illegitimate sons.

Victoria and her mother usually made their way to Kent by steam yacht.[1] These steamers took seven or eight hours to get from London to Margate. There could be as many as 300 holidaymakers on board, enjoying the bars, restaurants and band.[2] The common holiday herd disembarked and stayed put at Margate, but 'people of quality' tended, like Victoire and Victoria, to continue by carriage to the slightly classier resort of Ramsgate, where 'the company is more select'.[3]

But this was hardly a low-key, relaxing holiday. As Victoria's carriage trundled down the streets of Ramsgate towards the harbour that September, the pavements were crowded with spectators, and the town decorated with greenery and bunting.[4] 'Englishmen,' wrote the journalists, 'like to see the Royal Family coming frankly among them.'[5]

Her Uncle Leopold had told Victoria that 'high personages are a little like stage actors – they must always make efforts to please their public.'[6] But appearing in public sapped her energy. Part of the problem was the conventional model of nineteenth-century feminine behaviour, which emphasised modesty and retirement. She was not *supposed* to enjoy being a princess, being observed and applauded like this. She was, however, gradually becoming more accustomed to it, through a careful strategy devised by her mother and Captain Conroy.

Over the previous ten years, the two of them had refined and perfected a semi-formal 'System' to control and protect not only Victoria's physical body, but also her public image. The 'System', as Conroy named it, with a capital 'S', was intended 'to make the Princess "The Nation's Hope".' 'The basis of the whole system,' explains one Kensington insider, was to bolster Victoire's influence so that in case of need 'the nation should have to assign her the Regency'.[7] If William IV died before Victoria reached her majority, her Regent would otherwise be one of those unpopular and disreputable Royal Dukes. The association would taint and damage her.

The wider Conroy family, fully dedicated to the 'System' their paterfamilias had conceived, convinced themselves that this danger represented by the Royal Dukes was very real. One of them even explained the 'System' as a response to a threat upon Victoria's very life from the most sinister of the Royal Dukes, her uncle, the Duke of Cumberland. The Conroys convinced themselves that Cumberland had spread harmful rumours that Victoria had 'bad health, could hardly walk, was diseased in her feet and would never grow up'. Cumberland, they believed, was 'seized with the terrible temptation, to remove the only life, that then stood between him and the throne'. Captain Conroy's side of the story ran that 'the life of the Princess was at stake'.[8]

But this was lurid scaremongering. If the Duke of Cumberland ever did become Regent, he'd certainly deny Victoire and Conroy the rewards and influence they thought they deserved. Some people discerned a significant element of self-interest in Conroy's actions. There were murmurings that he was taking his 'System' too far, belittling, even bullying Victoria. The household's doctor, for example, thought Conroy a 'foolish bad man – whose ambition was to make the D.[uchess] Regent by proclaiming her Daughter an Idiot!'[9]

The result was enormous tension within the household. On the one hand, Victoire and Conroy were intent upon winning power and regencies. Meanwhile Lehzen, agent of the absent Uncle Leopold, encouraged Victoria to resist. Because of Lehzen's lack of loyalty to the 'System', Victoire decided that the governess must go. As mother and daughter were no longer on speaking terms, Victoire had to employ a written letter to tell Victoria that Lehzen would soon be getting the sack.[10]

Yet Victoria would not accept this, nor give up her beloved governess, without the fight that now unfolded beside the English Channel.

To the outside observer, the 'System' looked like a smart strategy. Most genteel young ladies of Victoria's age would be launched upon the marriage market. Yet Victoria's debut was being made before the whole country. She had spent the summer of 1835 travelling and making a carefully stage-managed series of public appearances, intended to introduce 'the Princess to the affections of the English people'.[11] And 'the English people' liked what they saw. In September, when Victoria attended the music festival in York, for example, 'an expression of enthusiastic feeling broke forth' as she was conducted to her seat.[12]

But there was an emotional cost involved in coming to maturity in public like this. Historian Lynn Vallone noticed that Victoria's journals in these teenage years reveal complaints of malaise in the third week of each month, of tiredness and discomfort probably connected to menstruation.[13] The record suggests that Victoria began her periods at what was then the unusually early age of thirteen. It could be one reason for her lack of height, for girls generally stop growing within a couple of years of starting to menstruate.[14] Victoria found it hard to cope with both hormones and all this scrutiny of her manner and person. At Norwich, for example, she described herself as 'well-nigh dead by the heat of this long and tiresome day'.[15] She complained of headaches, and backache, and said she 'could never rest properly' while she was travelling. She was exhausted by 'the long journeys and the great crowds' she'd endured throughout the tour.[16] She told her mother that she found it all fatiguing and 'disagreeable'.[17]

On display, on duty, never left alone, being forced to fit into the distasteful 'Conroyal Family' (as it was named by its detractors) was creating a cauldron in which the young princess was being slowly boiled. She was low and irritable. One of the doctors who treated her for mental problems as an adult detected their cause in this period of her adolescence. She'd been 'reared midst fears and quarrels', he wrote, and had 'never known what was true repose'.[18] Yet Victoria's mother piled on further pressure, in the false assumption that her daughter was malingering. 'Can you be dead to the Calls your position demands?' she wrote to her. 'Impossible! . . . Turn your thoughts and views to your future station, its duties, and the claims that exist on you.'[19]

Victoria's thinking herself ill, and her mother's denial of it, explains the background to the strangely negligent, almost inhuman, treatment she'd now receive in Ramsgate.

Their home for September and October 1835 was Albion House, number 27 at the end of Albion Place, perched close to the edge of a chalk cliff. The boundless ocean, Victoria wrote, 'looked very refreshing . . . there is nothing between us and France but the sea'.[20] Ramsgate's sea views were much admired. 'Truly picturesque', the guidebooks said, they must appeal to 'every admirer of the sublime and beautiful'.[21] Visitors in this Romantic age thought the place looked exceptionally fine during a storm. Ladies would watch 'tempestuous weather' with highly enjoyable 'emotions of terror'.[22]

But in calmer seasons before their relationship had broken down,

Victoria and her mother had spent many happy holidays here. Ramsgate's new-ish pier had caused a magnificent sandy beach to gather in its lea. Down upon these sands, 'the finest in Kent', numerous bathing machines 'may be seen crossing each other's path, busily engaged, conveying their inmates to the briny ocean'.[23] During Victoria's first visit when she was four, tourists spotted her on 'the noble sands . . . she wore a plain straw bonnet . . . she was allowed to play with other children and used to have donkey rides'.[24] Victoria and her mother went shopping at Lewis's 'Temple of Fancy', borrowed books from Burgess's Library and ate potted shrimps provided by Mr Cramp.[25] Charles Fisher on the High Street, Ramsgate's chemist, also claimed them as his customers, and added a royal coat of arms to the front of his shop.[26] Ramsgate welcomed its royal visitors by naming Kent Place, Royal Kent Terrace, Kent Baths and Victoria Baths in their honour.[27] Autumn was considered a particularly good time to visit. 'Rain, as a rule, fights shy of Ramsgate,' it was said, and 'the nights, too, are lovely in October . . . it is a calm delight to sit at the window and watch the moonlight effects on the sea.'[28]

Victoria could see this sight for herself from her first-floor bedroom, where she slept in her 'own little bed which travells always with me'.[29] She described Albion House as 'small', and complained about having to do her lessons in Lehzen's cramped bedroom.[30] Both Feodore and Victoria would rather have been on the beach. 'You used to torment Lehzen and myself during my French lessons at Ramsgate,' Feodore reminisced to Victoria in later years.[31]

Most people today would not find Albion House, with its three principal floors, its garrets and basements, as 'small' as Victoria claimed. Twice as wide as the similar terraced houses all around, it was part of a new residential area rushed up after the successful conclusion of the Napoleonic Wars in 1815. Britain's victory was reflected in the names of the surrounding streets: Wellington Crescent, the 'Plains of Waterloo' and La Belle Alliance Square. Ramsgate was on the up. In 1824, an Act was passed to supply the town with gas; in 1826 it gained a licensed theatre and in 1827 a new church.[32]

This was a very modern type of holiday, but in 1835 Victoria was not enjoying it. 'Even before the journey to York,' Lehzen noticed, she had been 'markedly unwell in body and soul'.[33] While Lehzen was apparently on Victoria's side, she did in fact represent another source of subtle pressure, the influence of Uncle Leopold, who was paying for everything.

Among Victoria's complaints was an absence of hunger: 'I forced a cup of cocoa down.'[34] Like many other teenage girls feeling impotent, Victoria noticed that when she refused food it caused the adults anxiety and distress. It was the one little piece of power that she did possess. Her doctors understood that something was wrong. One of them, asked to treat Victoria's constipation, gave her rhubarb pills, and believed her condition was caused by 'irregularity of the diet'.[35]

It was a new experience for Victoire to have to try to persuade Victoria to eat, because her daughter had always had such a good appetite. She'd been considered chubby ever since she was a baby 'so fat it can scarcely waddle'.[36] 'She eats heartily,' wrote one observer, 'I think I may say she gobbles', and she copied Lehzen in having a 'great weakness for potatoes'.[37] Her Uncle Leopold reproved his niece for eating 'a little too much, and almost always a little *too fast*'.[38] Even Feodore, who was unconditionally on Victoria's 'side', tried to intervene: 'pray think of your older sister when you look at the salt cellar with the intention of mixing so much of its contents with your knife in the gravy, you have a peculiar quick and expert way of doing it.' Food historian Annie Gray notes that even if it was well meant, 'there was no escape from the criticism'.[39]

But once she was settled into her seaside home, something happened to cheer Victoria up. Uncle Leopold came to visit. Because of his responsibilities abroad, Victoria hadn't seen him for four years, and was filled with 'a state of excitement' and joy.[40] Albion House was too small to accommodate Leopold and his French wife Louise, so he stayed at the Albion Hotel, a short walk away by the harbourside. Mr Bear, its proprietor, was 'very attentive to the accommodation of the nobility and gentry'.[41]

Victoria spent as much time as possible walking and dining with her uncle. 'I look up to him as a Father,' she wrote, in a clear snub to Conroy, 'with complete confidence, love and affection. He is the best and kindest adviser I have.'[42]

An experienced politician, Leopold explained to his niece that Conroy's unpleasant 'System' had nevertheless been working well in terms of public relations. It was distancing her from the unpopular Royal Dukes. 'Your immediate successor, with the mustaches,' he claimed, meaning the Duke of Cumberland, 'is enough to frighten them into the most violent attachment for you.'[43] Victoria was beginning to emerge from the 'System' just as Conroy – to give him credit – had intended, as 'The Nation's Hope' and 'The People's Queen'.[44]

Leopold soothed Victoria's spirit. But soon he had to leave, and she waved his steamer off from Dover dock on 7 October. Once again, Victoria felt abandoned, beleaguered, alone. Her response was to fall sick. Immediately after Leopold's boat had sailed, recorded Lehzen, Victoria got into the carriage to drive back to Ramsgate, where she 'collapsed, and was apparently very ill'.[45] Returning to Albion House, she 'felt so ill and wretched' that she went up to her room and stayed there.[46] At this point, the entries in Victoria's daily journal abruptly come to an end.

Victoire decided the situation was serious enough to send for her daughter's new medical advisor, Dr James Clark. The Scottish Dr Clark was considered something of a maverick by the medical establishment.[47] But he possessed the great qualification, in Victoria's eyes, of having nothing to do with Conroy. He'd been recommended by her Uncle Leopold.[48]

Conroy, however, believed that summoning Dr Clark was unnecessary, and insisted that there was nothing wrong with Victoria apart from teenage temper. He was eventually forced to admit that

Dr Clark wasn't even close to hand in Ramsgate; Conroy had sent him back to London, believing that Clark's services were surplus to requirements. Victoire, half-persuaded that there was nothing wrong with her sulky daughter anyway, was too timid to defy him.

Meanwhile Victoria, believing herself 'very unwell', was too sick to leave her sitting room and bedroom. Nevertheless, two whole days had to pass after Leopold's departure before Conroy admitted that Victoria might truly be ill. She begged that Dr Clark be sent for, and eventually he agreed.

After Dr Clark arrived from London but before he saw his patient, he was given a briefing. Lehzen was called in to meet the doctor in Albion House's drawing room. 'I was required to give him,' she recorded, 'in the presence of the Duchess, an account of the Princess's state of health.' But just when Lehzen was 'about to describe to him the dangerous symptoms of the illness', she was brusquely 'ordered to be silent'. 'Nothing but Victoria's whims, and your making believe,' Victoire said, sharply. Clark himself was then permitted to take only a cursory look at the patient before he set off back to London, 'convinced that everything was exaggerated'.[49]

Conroy, meanwhile, was engaged upon damage control. The local press noticed that Victoria hadn't been seen for some days. When they made a 'special enquiry' to find out why, they were fobbed off with the excuse that one of the servants was ill, and that Victoria herself had only 'a slight cold'. As pressure increased, though, Conroy began to have to issue public denials. 'All the stories you will have read of the Princess's illness were not true,' he wrote, 'she was never confined to Her bed, or to Her bedroom. She was never carried up or down stairs, or shaded with screens, never having had any beatings in her limbs.'[50]

Victoria's and Lehzen's testimony shows this up as a manifest falsehood. After the quick inspection by Dr Clark on 9 October, she grew too weak to leave her bed. Her condition grew desperately serious. The fever 'rose dreadfully', recorded Lehzen, 'and delirium set in'.[51] All the evidence suggests that Victoria was suffering from typhoid fever, a horrible, twitching state of violent illness. A victim turns deathly pale, vomits blood and has vicious diarrhoea. In the severest cases, a stretch of the bowel may split open, and internal bleeding and death can follow.

But the typhoid wasn't even the worst of it. Conroy and her mother now tried to take advantage of Victoria's weakness to bully her into consolidating their position. Although she was 'very ill', Victoria wrote, they now attempted to force her to promise that she would make Conroy her Private Secretary and chief advisor.[52] He wanted to be the power behind her throne. There were 'awful scenes in the house', Conroy threatening to lock Victoria up if she didn't do what he wanted. These would become terrible memories for Victoria, which she could hardly bear to think about in later years, and which 'she hoped were buried for ever'.[53]

Yet still she 'resisted'. This was 'in spite of my illness, and their harshness', she explains, 'my beloved Lehzen supporting me alone'.[54] Years of resentment against Conroy had come to a head at this moment, and Victoria sensed that this was the ultimate test. She simply refused to submit.

It's possible that there could be an even more visceral explanation for Victoria's defiance and her hatred of Conroy. Some contemporaries believed that she detested him because she had seen him and her mother engaged in 'familiarities'.[55] Certainly Uncle Leopold thought that the influence Conroy had gained over Victoire had 'a degree of power which in times of old one would have thought to proceed from witchcraft'.[56] The evidence for a physical relationship is exceedingly flimsy. Yet Victoire's friend and fellow-bride Adelaide attempted to warn her that to outsiders, at least, it all looked very bad. Conroy was clearly trying 'to remove everything that might obstruct his influence', Adelaide told her sister-in-law, 'so that he may exercise his power alone'.[57]

As Victoria's illness continued into its second week, Lehzen perceived that Victoire was gradually changing her mind and becoming convinced that her daughter was truly in danger. 'Now I saw the Duchess's anxiety mounting,' Lehzen wrote, although she 'tried to hide it from me. A long, fearful day and a bad night passed, the signs of an inflammation were unmistakable . . . the Duchess could contain her terror no longer.'[58]

Lehzen went to confront Conroy, and even he conceded that Dr Clark must be brought back. But there was no chance that Clark could arrive in Ramsgate until late that night. Lehzen demanded that a local doctor should be summoned. At this, Conroy was 'visibly upset'. Yet he could not stop Victoire and Lehzen ordering Dr Plenderleath from across the harbour to arrive within half an hour.

Conroy fretted about how this would play in public opinion, and how badly his charge's illness would reflect upon her mother and himself as her guardians. 'He warned me,' Lehzen records, 'against how dangerous such a step could be from a political point of view.' Lehzen, though, could stand up to Conroy where Victoire could not. No, she told him. She would not 'gamble with the life of the Princess'.[59] It was a spirited confrontation, which helps to explain Victoria's deep devotion to the governess who loved her.

And so Conroy was overruled, and Dr Plenderleath arrived at Albion House and was rushed up the stairs. A single man of forty-four, and a fixture on the Ramsgate medical and charitable scene, he lived with his cook and footman in a house in Nelson Crescent.[60] Everyone in Ramsgate knew Dr Plenderleath, and now everyone would know that the princess had become his patient. Plenderleath 'was very grave' on seeing how ill she was. But after his visit, and perhaps simply as a result of having been taken seriously, Victoria's condition at last stabilised.

The next day Dr Clark returned. During his time in the navy, Clark had won the distinction of twice being shipwrecked. Despite his career as a man of action, though, his special skill as a doctor lay less in deeds than in words. He was particularly good at talking a patient into feeling better, a skill not to be underestimated in an age when many drugs were inefficacious, or indeed made things worse.

He and Dr Plenderleath began to treat Victoria with quinine, a muscle relaxant. It might have eased her fever, but it can have had no effect on the salmonella bacteria that had poisoned her digestive system. Only good hygiene and the strength of Victoria's constitution could save her, and the latter had already been undermined by stress.

And now Dr Clark's contribution as a psychologist was just as important as his quinine draughts. Lehzen couldn't thank him enough for restoring to Victoria 'the necessary peace of mind'.[61] Clark has often been slated as a useless doctor on the evidence of his habit of claiming that a dying patient was on the mend, but a doctor's optimism could sometimes be a vital means of encouraging a sick person to believe in the possibility of recovery. His calm confidence was just what Victoria needed. Lehzen herself, and her love, were also important for Victoria's return to health. 'My dearest best Lehzen has been . . . most unceasing and indefatigable in her great care of me,' Victoria wrote afterwards. 'I am still very weak and am grown very thin. I can walk but very little and very badly. I have not yet left my room.'[62] There was no more talk of Lehzen leaving. 'They had tried to keep me from Lehzen, thinking it would weaken my love for her,' Victoria wrote, 'whereas it only increased it.'[63]

Three weeks later, on 31 October, Victoria resumed her journal. She was recovering, though her hair had fallen out and she'd lost muscle and mobility. 'Lay down on my couch,' she wrote. 'Played with Mamma on the piano till 12. Took my luncheon at 12 which consisted of some potato-soup. Looked at some things, walked a little weakly.' Victoire, feeling guilty, showered her daughter with gifts of flower jars, books and Dresden china figures.[64]

During November, Victoria regained her strength with the help of soup, boiled rice, orange jelly, biscuits and draughts of quinine. Although she was on 'a strict regime in terms of diet', she was allowed 'the pleasure of eating two' cakes every day.[65] It seemed that life was returning to normal, but with all the participants somewhat chastened by the experience.

Conroy's biographer Katherine Hudson notes the connection

between the histrionic tone of events at Albion House and the melodramas so popular in contemporary theatres and novels. Victoria herself loved reading tales of vulnerable female victims in desperate danger from cruel men. The first novel she was allowed to consume, *The Bride of Lammermoor* by Sir Walter Scott, opens with the striking image of a bride gone mad, sitting in a corner wearing nothing but a shift 'dabbled in gore'.[66] Victoria adored this sort of thing. She was also particularly enamoured, for example, of the moment in a Donizetti opera when a diva 'stares wildly about her, her hand raised to her head, and giving a frantic scream falls prostrate and lifeless to the ground'.[67]

Conroy likewise enjoyed secrets, plots and intrigue. He chose to believe (quite without evidence) that his own wife was another illegitimate daughter of Victoria's father Edward, but nevertheless kept it quiet, thinking it 'indelicate'.[68] He encouraged the spies and informants who helped him to implement the 'System' always to tell him 'the blackest stuff'.[69] Conroy writes as if he, not Victoria, were the sixteen-year-old girl. Even Uncle Leopold took an unhelp-fully melodramatic view of events in Ramsgate. 'Had I not had the courage,' he claimed, 'to tear apart the whole web of intrigue . . . God knows what would have become of the Princess.'[70]

Here Victoria's own lifelong enjoyment of scenes of high emotional intensity is prefigured. She saw herself as the heroine of her own melodrama. In some ways, she enjoyed it. But in more reflective moments, she understood that histrionics were bad for her. She later compared a dangerous episode of postnatal depression to what had happened at Albion House, claiming that the earlier illness was mental, and that it had arisen 'at once suddenly on reading . . . a very foolish story about death'. Dr Clark himself believed that the stresses of the 'System' had warped Victoria's character, bringing out 'all her bad passions'.[71]

The terrible holiday in Ramsgate also had other consequences from which Victoria would never fully recover. She was confirmed in her violent distrust of Conroy, but she now also definitively turned against her mother. 'I never knew what it was to live as mother & daughter ought to,' she wrote later, for her own mother 'did nothing without Conroy's advice & whatever was told him'.[72] How could she respect a mama who 'tamely allowed Conroy to insult her'?[73] Victoire herself was deeply unhappy, and 'hardly ever sleeps' because of 'her constant anxiety to the future'.[74]

Perhaps this was Victoire's bitterest legacy to her daughter. She'd taught Victoria all about affection, and she often spoke or wrote to her daughter to express her love. Through her actions, though, Victoire presented a role model of a woman who had lost her self in the more powerful personality of a man. It was a lesson that even the self-willed Victoria would learn all too well.

6

Albert: Kensington Palace, 18 May 1836

Wednesday 18 May 1836 started out just like so many other quiet days at Kensington Palace, with no indication that it would mark a pivot point in Victoria's life.

She got up at half past eight. She walked in the gardens with Lehzen, wrote in her journal and read scripture for forty-five minutes. She played the piano and sang, as was her daily habit, practising her accomplishments like any other young lady. And then, at a quarter to two that afternoon, her journal tells us,

> we went down into the Hall, to receive my Uncle Ernest, Duke
> of Saxe-Cobourg Gotha, & my Cousins Ernest & Albert, his sons.[1]

Thus, without fanfare, the love of Victoria's life enters the scene.

After the distressing events in Ramsgate, an uneasy truce settled over the household. Back at Kensington Palace, Victoire and Conroy continued to prepare Victoria for her entrance into the world. The setting was a grander, more palatial apartment at Kensington Palace, fit for the princess whom they intended to become 'The People's Queen'.

On their return from Ramsgate, Victoria and her mother moved upstairs to the magnificent second floor of the building. A lofty new suite had been created for them out of reception rooms completed 100 years previously for George I. The Long Gallery, for example, was partitioned off to make Victoria a sitting room, and her bed was moved into the very chamber used by former kings. These improvements were carried out in defiance of William IV's instructions. He'd said his sister-in-law and niece might make use of the rooms, but also commanded that the painted Georgian interiors should be left intact in character and appearance.[2] When William IV discovered what had happened, a huge row broke out.

The changes, as the angry king eventually discovered, were numerous. In the Grand Saloon, beneath William Kent's painted ceiling, the walls were divided up by false columns and hung with enormous looking glasses, while the windows were adorned with 'rich draperies of pink'. Victoire now began to use the room for entertaining, sometimes on a gigantic scale. She invited 200 people, for example, to a concert held there for her daughter's birthday.[3] Victoire hosted a ball once a week. She was networking, making connections with important people, preparing her daughter for queenship. It was all part of the 'System.'

Victoria, for her part, found that constantly having to be polite to all these grown-up strangers bored her dreadfully. 'I am very fond of pleasant society,' she told Uncle Leopold, 'and we have been for the last 3 weeks immured within our old Palace. I longed sadly for some gaiety.'[4] Kensington Palace now thrummed with social activity, but none of it involved people Victoria's own age, nor qualified as 'gaiety' in her eyes.

At nearly seventeen, she had become a little 'taller', with a 'pretty figure'.[5] After Ramsgate, Dr Clark had instructed that she must lead a healthier life than the 'System' had previously allowed. She should swing Indian clubs to build up her muscles, and use her exercise machine with 'pullies & Weights on Chains'.[6] Most importantly, for the sake of her troubled digestion, she was to pay attention to the 'perfect and deliberate mastication' of her food.[7] Victoria's preferred forms of exercise were riding and dancing, although she regretted being forbidden from trying the newfangled and energetic 'valze' or waltz. This involved the man entwining the woman in his arms and spinning her round.[8] But Conroy insisted that a future queen should display instead a 'very dignified demeanour'.[9]

Dr Clark also stipulated that Victoria was to be outdoors as often as possible, and in '<u>healthy</u>, <u>bracing</u> air' at that. He'd made a particular study of tuberculosis, and had written a student thesis on the curative effect of cold air on the human body. His patients were sometimes surprised to find him checking their lungs with a medical novelty: the stethoscope. In reality, Clark's theories about 'good' and 'bad' air, resulting from the belief that illness was caused by a 'miasma' travelling through the ether, would soon be discredited. But because he had 'saved' Victoria at Ramsgate, he had enormous influence, and instilled in her a lifelong passion for fresh air and chilly temperatures.

Victoria's physical appearance was beginning to signal that she was ready to be married. Although she remained short, she had blossomed into 'a very charming young lady', and visitors to Kensington Palace noticed that 'her bust . . . is remarkably fine'.[10] The people around her began to draw up lists of potential princely husbands from all round Europe. William IV was in favour of a prince from the Dutch House of Orange. In the influential eyes of Uncle Leopold, though, the front-runners for his niece's hand lay, of course, among her Coburg cousins.

And so, in the run-up to Victoria's seventeenth birthday, the current head of the Coburg family, Duke Ernest, brought his sons, another Ernest, and Albert, to Kensington for a visit of inspection. The time was ripe for a match to be made.

What did Victoria look like, now, as she stood at the top of the Stone Stairs, while her Uncle Ernest and the two young men walked in from the courtyard below? Someone who described her particularly attentively was the American artist Thomas Sully, creator of one the most attractive portraits there is of the young Victoria. You can tell from it that he found her charming.

Even if Sully was smitten, he was clear-eyed enough to give us some solid information about her height and build. 'She is short,' he admitted, '5 feet 1 & ¼ of an inch.' He made, and kept, a tape measure to prove it.[11] All her life Victoria's lack of stature would be an issue thought worthy of comment. 'It is a pity she is so small,' wrote another person who'd also met her in the flesh, 'I am told she regrets it very much herself.'[12]

Although Sully's tape measure proves that she was 5 feet 1¼ inches, Victoria's height was always stated in public to be 5 feet 2. That imaginary extra three-quarters of an inch was important because height was much more affected by nurture, rather than nature, than it is in modern times. Diets for the very poorest in 1830s society had recently been declining in quality, and with this, the adult height of working people and paupers had shrunk. There was as much as a 4-inch difference, in some areas, between middle- and working-class children of thirteen.[13] If Victoria was short, argues food historian Annie Gray, it looked like she had not been properly fed. This reflected badly on Conroy and Victoire. They made both their princess and themselves look a little bit better by adding a little bit on.

Sully found his sitter's face young for her years, slightly 'infantine in the contour'. He conceded that her large, light-blue eyes were 'a little prominent', but he liked her nose, which reminded him of those he'd 'frequently seen in persons of wit and intellect'. Her mouth particularly attracted him: 'a lovely, artless mouth when at rest – and when so, it is a little open, showing her teeth'.[14]

This pursed little mouth of Victoria's divided opinion. Another observer thought it 'her worst feature . . . generally a little open, her teeth small and short, and she shows her gums when she laughs, which is rather disfiguring'. Whenever Victoria sat for her likeness, Feodore would say, 'Do, Victoria, shut your mouth!'[15]

But the most attractive thing about Victoria wasn't a physical feature. It was her laugh. 'So full of girlish glee and gladness,' people noticed; she 'laughs in real earnest, opening her mouth as wide as it can go'.[16] In the right company, she could be exuberant, cordial, eager to please. The actor Fanny Kemble was not alone in admiring the bell-like quality of Victoria's voice. 'The enunciation as perfect as the intonation was melodious,' she gushed, 'it is impossible to hear a more excellent utterance than that of the Queen's English by the English Queen.'[17]

But had she not been a future queen, her cousins now arriving at Kensington Palace would have beheld a rather ordinary, dumpy, giggly teenager – 'nothing to criticise, nothing particularly to admire' – with an unfulfilled desire for parties.[18] She looked nice, but not special, with 'a pleasing countenance . . . though nature has certainly not stamped the seal of "Majesty" upon it'.[19] Neither had she yet learned to be 'independent and unembarrassed' in manner. Still stuck in the coils of the 'System', Victoria kept her lovely laugh for Feodore alone. She described her social manner during this period as 'extremely crushed and kept under . . . hardly dared say a word'.[20]

On this particular day that Albert first set eyes upon her, there's also cause to suspect that we can identify the very gown Victoria was wearing. The reason is that she was a great hoarder of the clothes worn on significant occasions, and the Royal Collection today still contains a high-waisted, dark-coloured, tartan velvet dress. With short puffed sleeves worn just off the shoulder, its style dates it to exactly the right period.[21]

The tartan was important, for despite the fact she had never been there Victoria had fallen passionately in love with the country of Scotland. This had happened four months previously when she'd devoured Sir Walter Scott's *The Bride of Lammermoor*. In it, a fearsome Scottish lord feasts upon the human flesh of his tenants, shocking observers when he throws back 'the tartan plaid with which he had screened his grim and ferocious visage'.[22] 'Oh!' Victoria panted in her journal, 'Walter Scott is <u>my beau ideal</u> of a Poet; <u>I</u> do so admire him both in Poetry and Prose!'[23] 'Grim and ferocious' does not sound like a particularly winsome look. Yet Victoria, at odds with the authority figures in her life, wanted to demonstrate independence and maturity through her dark, tartan gown. Casting aside the white or pink muslin dresses that had previously dominated her wardrobe, she was going through a phase and adopting a look that in our own times we might call goth.

And what did Victoria herself see as the Duke of Coburg and his sons began to climb the Stone Stairs towards her? She did not know it, but one of the young men down below loved Sir Walter Scott as much as she did herself. Yet she did not notice him. Her eye was first taken by Albert's eighteen-year-old brother Ernest with his 'dark hair, & fine dark eyes & eye-brows' and his 'very good figure'.

Only after sucking in every detail of the toothsome Ernest did Victoria's eyes move on to Albert. Now she noticed that the younger brother, sixteen like herself, was 'extremely handsome', more handsome even than Ernest. Albert's hair, she observed, 'is about the same colour as mine . . . he has a beautiful nose, & a very sweet mouth with fine teeth; but the charm of his countenance is his expression . . . full of goodness & sweetness, & very clever & intelligent'.[24]

Albert did not lack the poise required to stand up to this considerable feminine scrutiny. His mother Louise, Duchess of Coburg, had abandoned him and his brother when he was five, but even before then she had managed to instil in him a strong sense of his own self-worth. Louise 'made no attempt', claimed Albert's tutor, 'to conceal that Prince Albert was her favourite child. He was handsome and bore a strong resemblance to herself.'

This same gentleman thought that Louise was 'wanting in the essential qualifications for a mother', but a closer look at the circumstances suggests that 'abandon' is not quite the right word for her action in leaving her sons behind.[25] She had come to the small, wooded, hilly state of Coburg, in modern-day Bavaria, upon her marriage to its Duke. She was sixteen; he was seventeen years older. Her new husband loved to dress up as a knight, and staged a medieval-style tournament to celebrate their wedding. It was a fairytale start, but Albert's parents' marriage soon floundered. The Duke's affairs were legion, but when Louise indulged in one of her own, it was unforgivable. Her husband forced Louise to leave Coburg, to give up her claims upon it and never to see her sons again. She died unhappily at thirty, in Paris with her lover. 'Parting from my children,' she wrote, 'was the worst thing of all.'[26] As for Albert, he 'could not bear to think about his childhood, he had been so unhappy and miserable, and had many a time wished himself out of this world'.[27]

A beautiful, dreamy boy, Albert in his childhood home of Rosenau Castle could at least find comfort in books. There were no fewer than twenty-three novels by Victoria's own favourite, Sir Walter Scott, in the castle's turreted, neo-Gothic library.[28] During the course of this visit to Kensington Palace, Victoria and Albert would be rather shy together, but they would bond over books, and something else they both loved: music. Later that first afternoon, her cousins asked Victoria to sing to them, which she did, and she was delighted to find them 'excessively fond of music, like me'.[29]

This was definitely a step towards falling in love. The piano stool, a well-known hotspot in the romantic geography of any drawing room, forces singer and accompanist, or two duet players, into physical proximity. And in many ways Victoria and Albert seemed destined for each other. When Frau Siebold delivered Albert just three months after delivering Victoria at Kensington Palace, the newborn baby had looked all around him, alert and inquisitive as 'a little squirrel'. with the 'large blue eyes' that were just like Victoria's own.[30] Victoria and Albert's common grand-mother, Duchess Augusta, matriarch of the Coburg clan, described him at once as the 'pendant' to his 'pretty cousin'.[31] Albert's older brother Ernest would have to stay in Coburg to be Duke after his father's death. But Albert, the younger son, could be sent abroad. From birth, he had the duty and destiny of extending the Coburg family's influence in Britain.

Judging from what she wrote in her journal, though, Victoria seems to be telling us that she was charmed, but far from infatu-ated. There is no doubt that she liked her cousins' company: 'they speak English very well, & I speak it with them.' In the entry for the day of their arrival, though, she also mentions that her uncle the Duke gave her a gift of a scarlet-and-blue exotic bird. It was the type of parrot called a 'lory' or 'lorikeet', and it was impressively big, even 'larger than Mamma's Grey Parrot'. The lory was wonderfully tame, so much so that 'it remains on your hand, & you may put your finger into its beak, or do any thing with it without its ever attempting to bite'. This bird makes at least as much impact in Victoria's journal as the man who turned out to be the love of her life. And that evening Albert was left behind when she went out to a grand dinner.[32]

During the course of the next few days, Albert gave the impression that he was a little too young, and a lot too naïve, to know exactly what a prince was supposed to do when he met a princess. He had a strong sense of pride, but lacked *savoir faire*. He failed to join in properly, remaining detached from and uncommitted to the programme his aunt had arranged. 'The different way of living, and the late hours, do not agree with me,' he admitted to his stepmother. He found the long evenings – one social gathering ending at 1 a.m. – particularly challenging. There was no time for reading, and he had 'many hard battles to fight against sleepiness'. As for Victoria herself, he damned her with faint praise. All he had to say was that she was 'very amiable'.[33]

Two days later, there was a lengthy reception and dinner at St James's Palace. The day after that, Albert had to meet 3,800 people for William IV's birthday. On 23 May, during what was supposed to be another crowded reception at Kensington Palace, he 'was not quite well & went soon to bed'.[34] On 24 May, Victoria's birthday, what was meant to be the centrepiece of the stay, Albert finally collapsed. He remained only 'a short while in the ball-room' and then, 'having only danced twice', he 'turned as pale as ashes' and had to go to bed.[35] It wasn't just Albert. Ernest too was left thinking 'old England' and Victoria's life of relentless royal socialising were extremely 'peculiar'.[36]

Albert's upbringing – his missing mother was replaced by a male tutor – had left him overly serious and no good at small talk. 'He will always have more success with men' was Baron Stockmar's way of putting it. At Uncle Leopold's request, Stockmar had involved himself in Albert's education, and pronounced his pupil 'too indifferent and too reserved' when it came to women.[37] Stockmar was a self-effacing man who nevertheless had a steely commitment to the ideal of constitutional monarchy. As Leopold's advisor, he involved himself behind the scenes in many European affairs. Feodore was quite clear about which brother she preferred, and it wasn't Albert. 'Although Albert is much handsomer and cleverer', Ernest was the better company, Feodore thought, as he was so 'good natured'.[38] 'Good natured' was ladylike code for saying that Ernest was a flirt. In due course, Ernest would go on to reveal that he had a dishonest and manipulative side to his character.

Victoria agreed that Albert was 'the more reflecting of the two'.[39] Yet there could also be an additional reason for Albert's reserve with her during this first meeting. Given his preternatural cleverness, he must have known that he was being inspected as a potential future member of Britain's royal family. However, he had no guarantee that he would meet the required standard, and this was damaging to his pride. He must have been all too aware that the Coburgs, including his father, his Uncle Leopold and his Aunt Victoire, wanted him to marry his cousin. But he might also have picked up on the fact that William IV had other plans for his niece. The king had not wanted the Coburg boys to come to Kensington Palace at all, and Lord Palmerston reported that he was 'vexed and annoyed' by their presence.[40] Albert admitted later that he was fully 'aware at the time of our visit in 1836 of the difficulties attending it'.[41] By this, he can only have meant the unseemly jostling between Victoria's paternal uncle William IV and her maternal uncle Leopold to be the one to choose her mate.

Victoria, then, at sixteen, was generically excited about boys, but showed no sign of falling in love. She was soon gushing in her journal that she adored Ernest and Albert 'so <u>very very</u> dearly' but equally: '<u>much more dearly</u> than any other Cousins in the world'. To her they remained a pair, 'dearest Ernst and dearest Albert', both of them equally 'grown up in their manners . . . sensible and reasonable, and so really and truly good, and kind-hearted'. The only thing that distinguished Albert from Ernest in her mind was his superior intelligence.[42] Albert, likewise, claimed that there was nothing but cousinly feeling in the visit. 'We stayed from 3 to 4 weeks at Kensington, Princess Victoria & myself . . . & were much pleased with each other, but not a word in allusion to the future passed.'[43]

And yet, underneath this delicate dance of compliments, Victoria *did* fully understand her Coburg family's intentions. Her journal was not a private place in which to admit her feelings. The 'System' obliged others – Lehzen, her mother – to read it, and other sources directly undermine its credibility as a true record. Victoria's half-brother, Charles, for example, understood that despite the king's views a Coburg marriage was practically a done deal. 'The connection,' he claimed, 'was regarded as the one aim to which all energies should be directed.'[44]

Outside the semi-public pages of her journal, Victoria acknow-ledged her place in all this. She understood deep down that she *would* do what her Uncle Leopold wanted, even if maidenly modesty required her to be coy about it. 'I must thank you my beloved Uncle,' she wrote to him in a private letter, 'for the prospect of great happiness you have contributed [sic] to give me in the person of Dear Albert. Allow me then . . . to tell you how delighted I am with him, and how much I like him in every way. He possesses every quality that could be desired to make me perfectly happy.'[45]

The compensation for not being allowed to choose her own husband was that Albert really was almost faultless, definitely clever and seemingly kind. In addition, he was much more physically attractive than she was. In fact, he had 'the most pleasing and delightful exterior and appearance you can possibly see', Victoria judged. 'I have only now to beg you, my dearest Uncle,' she wrote to Leopold, 'to take care of the health of one, now so dear to me.'[46]

History likes to think of Victoria's marriage to Albert as a great love match. It both was and yet wasn't. The example set by her parents, the romantic novels she devoured and the expectations of the wider world ensured that Victoria would noisily insist upon finding love within her marriage. But this was clearly an arranged match, and Victoria understood that even at sixteen. Two years later, in 1838, she's found writing to Uncle Leopold again, saying that it was her 'firm resolution' not to marry her cousin until she was twenty, at the 'very earliest'. She wasn't, she thought, 'yet quite grown up', or 'strong enough in health' to bear children. But she reassures her uncle that she won't be 'faithless to my promise and change my mind'. She just wants, Victoria explains, 'to enjoy two or three years more of my present young girlish life before I enter upon the duties and cares of a wife'. Besides, Albert still needed to improve his English.[47]

And it wasn't just the prospect of the 'duties and cares of a wife' that daunted her. It was also the prospect of becoming a queen.

7

Accession: Kensington Palace, 20 June 1837

At five o'clock on the fine morning of Tuesday 20 June 1837, a mere quarter-hour after sunrise, the Archbishop of Canterbury and the Lord Chamberlain 'knocked and rang and thumped' on the door of Kensington Palace.[1]

This unlikely-looking pair, 'toil-worn and dust-stained with their night ride', had travelled post-haste from Windsor Castle.[2] The two messengers had come on a mission vital to the monarchy: to let William IV's successor know that he had died at two o'clock that morning. Victoria, still sleeping upstairs, had been queen for the last four hours.

The Archbishop and the Lord Chamberlain kept thumping away, but it was a long time before they could get anyone to let them in. Then, once again, Conroy insinuates himself into the story. A footman eventually fetched him, he received the visitors, and only then sent a maid to tell the Duchess of Kent.[3]

Unaware of the tumult below, Victoria was pretty much the last person in the palace to learn what had happened. Her struggle to free herself from the 'System' was clearly not quite over yet.

Victoria was asleep in the cavernous bedchamber formerly used by Kings George I and II that her mother had commandeered for their joint use. This room was 'very large and lofty', gloomy most of the day, yet 'very nicely furnished' by Victoire for her daughter.[4] Flowered papered walls looked incongruously feminine in such a large, high space. Its windows faced east towards the sun now rising over the Round Pond in the gardens below.

Not only had Victoria (unknowingly) reached the throne, she'd also reached her majority. Just three weeks earlier, she'd celebrated her eighteenth birthday at last. 'How old!' she confided to her journal, 'and yet how far am I from being what I should be.'[5] Conroy must have been gnashing his teeth. There would now be no need for a Regency by his pawn Victoire. When Victoria became queen, she would rule in her own right.

But it had been a dangerously close-run thing. It was a mere two days after Victoria's birthday that William IV fell seriously ill. He developed pneumonia on top of an existing heart condition. 'Our King is in a very precarious state,' wrote Lord Palmerston, 'it is not likely he can last long.'[6] William IV did surprise everyone by clinging onto life for a couple of weeks, 'like an old lion', as people said.[7] He asked his doctor to 'tinker [him] up to last out' until the anniversary of the Battle of Waterloo, the great annual celebration on 18 June that he'd always particularly enjoyed. He was determined to stay alive until then, despite the lungs full of blood, distended heart and double-sized spleen that his post-mortem revealed.[8]

In these final days of her royal uncle's life, the tension ratcheted up for Victoria at Kensington Palace. Even if the position of Regent was no longer in play, there was the question of the appointments she would make as queen, and the issue of reward for those who had brought her up. Uncle Leopold dispatched Baron Stockmar as an agent to maintain his own influence. Stockmar reported back that at Kensington Conroy continued 'the system of intimidation with the genius of a mad-man, and the Duchess carries out all that she is instructed to do with admirable docility'. Victoria had so far firmly refused 'to give her Mama her promise that she will make [Conroy] her confidential advisor'. But, Stockmar admitted, 'whether she will hold out, Heaven only knows, for they plague her, every hour and every day'.[9]

This struggle had taken place behind closed doors. On 6 June,

Victoria stopped going out in public, out of respect for her dying uncle, and the following day her lessons came to an end, for ever, as it turned out.[10] On 16 June, Stockmar reported that Victoire was being 'pressed by Conroy to bring matters to extremities, & to force her daughter to do her will by unkindness & severity'.[11] Conroy, beginning to lose control over himself as well as the situation, was even heard saying that 'if Princess Victoria will not listen to reason, <u>she must be coerced</u>'.[12]

For her part, Victoire had convinced herself that if Victoria failed to appoint Conroy as advisor she would be condemned for the omission. 'Ach, she has much, much to learn,' Victoire complained. Victoria's mother thought her far too 'young and inexperienced', blithely ignorant of just how challenging it would be to sit on the throne. The self-doubting duchess simply could not comprehend her daughter's faith that she *was* going to manage. Victoria was certainly anxious, but she had confidence that she was just about 'mature enough to undertake the heavy duties'. Or at least, she felt confident enough to try.[13]

Outside the palace, it was true that many other people were worried too. 'There would be no advantage,' thought Lord Palmerston, for example, in having 'a totally inexperienced Girl of 18 just out of a strict Guardianship to govern an Empire'.[14] But even Conroy could only coax the dippy duchess to go a certain distance towards supporting him against her daughter. While he himself thought that Victoria should be 'coerced' into cooperation, he 'did not credit the Duchess of Kent with enough strength' for carrying through 'such a step'.[15]

Victoria also drew strength from the knowledge that the endgame was in sight. 'Avoid quarrels,' her Uncle Leopold advised her. 'You must keep up your usual cool spirit, whatever may be tried in the House to teaze you out of it.' He also warned her to 'be not alarmed at the prospect' of coming to the throne 'perhaps sooner than you expected'.[16]

And despite her calm manner in public, Victoria was indeed alarmed. 'The poor King was <u>so</u> ill,' she told her diary on 19 June, 'he could hardly live through the day.'[17] That night, she had stayed up until 10.15, reading Sir Walter Scott while her maids took down her hair. Some suspected, but no one knew for sure, that this was her last evening as a princess.

Victoire had been complicit in the 'System' and had placed too much trust in Conroy. Yet she now becomes a truly pitiful figure, when, at the very first dawn of Victoria's reign, she returns softly to the bedchamber where she and her daughter had slept the night side by side. Victoire looks down at the still-sleeping girl. She has given up so much for her younger daughter, but in return Victoria seems so ungrateful and unaware. 'What is to become of my beloved Child, so young?' now Victoire asks herself. 'My greatest of fears was that I loved her too much.'[18]

Eventually Victoire broke off brooding, and she tells us that she 'awoke the dear child with a kiss!'[19] But in Victoria's own journal account of the day, penned that evening, she does not mention this at all.[20] She was by then cutting every interaction with her mother out of her mind.

Rising from the little bed next to her mother's 'with much quickness', Victoria put on a white dressing gown. She passed through the maid's room adjoining the bedroom, and into her sitting room.[21] She went entirely by herself. Victoire, who had once hoped as Regent to accompany her daughter throughout the first day of her reign, did not even attempt to go with her.[22]

There in the sitting room, Victoria saw a remarkable sight. Two men, one elderly, one middle-aged, were kneeling before her on the carpet. Archbishop William Howley and Lord Chamberlain Francis Conyngham were telling her that the life of King William IV had flickered out at twelve minutes past two that morning.[23] Conyngham, the dead king's senior household officer, was the first person to call Victoria 'Your Majesty'. He handed her the certificate of her uncle's death.[24]

The man on his knees was typical of the complicated, louche aristocrats who'd circled around the Royal Dukes and thereby helped to tarnish the image of the monarchy. Conyngham's mother had been the last, and most impressively buxom, of George IV's string of bosomy mistresses. A celebrated description of Lady Conyngham claimed she had 'not an idea in her head; not a word to say for herself; nothing but a hand to accept pearls and diamonds with, and an enormous balcony to wear them on'.[25] She got her son Francis a job as a page to her lover, George IV, and then as Lord Chamberlain to William IV. Francis Conyngham is chiefly remembered today as one of the hated absentee landlords whose tenants were to suffer so badly in Ireland's Great Famine. Was this someone that Victoria should retain in post? From now on, she would have to judge the status, character and qualities of everyone with whom she came into contact, for thus she would create the moral tone of her court.

According to one Victorian historian, the new queen now burst into tears, 'turned to the Primate, and said, "I ask your Grace to pray for me."' 'And so was begun,' this sentimental account continues, 'with the tears and prayers of a pure young girl, the glorious reign of Victoria.'[26] This was certainly a tearful age, in which men as well as women felt it was a sign of good breeding to cry frequently. Until the 1850s, even judges sobbed at affecting cases.[27] Victoria *should* have cried, according to contemporary understandings of what a young lady might do. But she did not.

She later spoke of her calmness and self-possession at that moment, and her absolute lack of tears. 'The Queen was not overwhelmed,' Victoria claimed, and was 'rather full of courage, she may say. *She took things as they came, as she knew they must be.*'[28]

Even her grief for her uncle had to be kept measured. 'Poor old man,' she thought, 'I feel sorry for him, he was always personally kind to me.'[29] Yet there was no time to mourn. Victoria quickly returned to her maid's room to be dressed. She already had a black mourning gown just waiting to be put on. Still remaining at Kensington Palace to this day, this dress is a tiny garment, with an extraordinarily small waist and cuffs. With it, she wore a white collar and, as usual, 'her light hair' was 'simply parted over the forehead'.[30] Her girlish appearance explains quite a lot of the indulgence and romance with which her reign was greeted. It also meant that she would consistently be underestimated.

Victoria knew exactly what to do next. 'The moment you get official communication,' Uncle Leopold had counselled her, 'you will entrust Lord Melbourne with the office of retaining the present Administration as your Ministers.'[31] Stockmar was on hand to reinforce his master's words, and William Lamb, second Viscount Melbourne, was already making his way to the palace while Victoria ate breakfast. Leopold, Victoire, indeed Victoria's whole circle, all supported the Whigs who currently dominated Parliament, not the excluded Tories.

At half past eight, Victoria wrote to her Uncle Leopold. She also penned a kind letter to her bereaved Aunt Adelaide, telling her that she need not leave Windsor Castle just yet. And she wrote to Feodore: 'two words only to tell you, that my poor King died this morning . . . that I am well, and that I remain for your life your devoted attached sister V.R.'[32] Her first thoughts were of her uncle, her aunt and her sister: the people who had supported her from outside the 'System'.

At nine, Victoria's Prime Minister came in to see her. This would be the very first of many such meetings. An indecorous farce had been in progress for the last few days, a whispering campaign to brief Melbourne against the new queen. Conroy was anxious to pass on to the Prime Minister his belief in Victoria's possible mental subnormality. But her faithful Dr Clark wrote as soon as he could to verify the opposite.[33]

Melbourne, stooping to kiss Victoria's hand, was by then sixty-one years old. A serial monogamist who enjoyed intense romantic relationships, he had loved then lost first a mentally unstable wife followed by two successive serious mistresses. A rather late bloomer as a politician, he spent a good deal of effort maintaining an air of languid insouciance ('I generally find that nothing that is asserted is ever true, especially if it is on the very best authority').[34] He was disarmingly candid about his poor health (he drank too much) and his lost looks (he once had three hairdressers spend three hours pulling all the greys out of his opulent, formerly auburn, hair).[35] 'I like him very much,' Victoria decided, 'and feel confidence in him.' She told him that he and his government were to stay in office.[36]

Melbourne also briefed her about what would happen next: her first public appearance in her new role at a meeting called the Accession Council. Members of the Privy Council had already been summoned for the purpose to Kensington Palace. The job of the councillors, mainly seasoned statesmen, was to protect and advise the monarch. Clerics in black coats, gentlemen in gold-braided court dress and even the surviving Royal Dukes in their old-fashioned breeches all started to arrive soon after eleven.[37] Those invited to attend included Cabinet ministers, the great officers of state and officials of the old royal household. They numbered some 220, and every single one of them who'd received the message in time to make the journey to Kensington Palace turned up. 'Her extreme youth and inexperience,' recorded the Privy Council's clerk, 'and the ignorance of the world concerning her' had piqued their curiosity as well as their sense of duty.[38] The councillors were uneasy, and ready to disparage this little girl who now had the power – as Walter Bagehot put it in his work *The English Constitution* – to 'declare war, make peace, negotiate treaties, disband the army, dismiss all sailors, sell off all warships, make every parish a university and pardon all offenders'.[39]

The meeting, held down below in the Red Saloon, started at 11.30, half an hour late. Victoria's own recollection, though, placed it at 2 p.m. So much had happened since she had woken up that morning that she could scarcely believe that only five hours had passed.[40] To reach the Red Saloon, she had to descend a steep and curving staircase. She'd previously always been forbidden from using it without someone holding her hand.[41] The sudden swing of this precipitous stair, once you have seen it in real life, makes such a precaution understandable for a young child. In addition, Victoria had one slightly weak knee that twinged when she climbed.[42] But today – significantly – she negotiated the difficult stair all alone.

And now she had to make her entrance. Surprising everyone waiting within, Victoria came into the Saloon entirely unaccompanied, 'a small, slight, fair-complexioned young lady, apparently fifteen years of age', her dress black, her hair simply dressed close to her head, and her whole appearance 'glossy and clean-looking'.[43] There was no sign of her mother or Conroy. Composedly, she 'took her seat on a throne'.[44]

Under Melbourne's adroit stage management, a remarkable transformation had just occurred. It was considered to be difficult for a young lady simply to appear before a room full of men without blushing or simpering or shedding tears. When the news got out of what she'd done, the *Examiner* newspaper thought it most remarkable and novel that the queen had appeared 'without any female attendants in the midst of a large assemblage of men'.[45] The Duke of Wellington believed she showed exceptional courage in coming in 'unattended by any other Lady', and then by running the meeting 'as if she had been performing the part for years'.[46] She 'read her speech in a clear, distinct and audible voice, and without an appearance of fear or embarrassment'.[47]

And once this gathering of powerful old men had seen her, they began to believe in her. 'Only those who lived in that time can understand,' wrote Alethea Allingham, from Sidmouth days, 'how the hearts of the people were moved as the heart of one man, when this fair young girl was called upon to fill the throne of this realm.'[48] This process, which would eventually sweep the whole of Britain, began here and now in the Red Saloon. 'There never was anything like the first impression she produced,' admitted even Charles Greville, the gossipy, grumpy clerk of the Privy Council known in his circle as 'The Gruncher'. He himself found it 'very extraordinary, and something far beyond what was looked for'.[49] 'She not merely filled her chair,' agreed Wellington, 'she filled the room.'[50]

Victoria made her oath to govern the kingdom according to

its laws and customs, then each of her ministers approached in turn and, kneeling, took his own oath of allegiance.[51] Each then kissed her hand. Throughout the ceremony, more and more Privy Councillors kept arriving. The kneeling and kissing took place in complete silence, which added 'to the impressive solemnity of the scene'.[52]

When called upon to sign her name, the new queen put just plain 'Victoria'.[53] This wasn't her own idea. Her mother and Conroy had some time ago agreed that the 'Alexandrina' from her christening should be dropped. People had become 'accustomed to Victoria – and do not dislike it – it being a high sounding name'.[54]

After the Privy Council, she met the Lord Mayor and a deputation from the City of London, with 'all the decision, thought, and self-possession, of a queen of older years'.[55] But then, just as soon as the audience was all over, Victoria was seen to 'run off like the girl she is', with all the 'high spirits' people expected of her youth.[56]

There was just one sour note in the day's triumphant harmony. During the Privy Council meeting, Conroy and Stockmar were walking in the garden, and Conroy was making some proposals about his future. He had a list of requirements, in return for which he would retire from court life and be no further trouble to anyone. He wanted a peerage, the Order of the Bath, membership of the Privy Council and a pension of £3,000 a year.[57]

As soon as Melbourne emerged from the Privy Council meeting, he was handed this list of demands. The Prime Minister was astonished. 'This is really too bad!' he fumed, 'have you ever heard such impudence?'[58] His hand shook so much with rage that he dropped the paper.

Stockmar was not quite so quick to condemn. He was anxious, now, that Victoria should not turn too far or too fast against her mother and Conroy. If she appeared ungrateful, or disrespectful of parental authority, she would '*never* be able *to retrieve her reputation*'.[59] Perhaps Stockmar could see, too, that in some ways Conroy had done a good job. He had safely delivered Victoria to the throne, her public image not only intact but glowing. Even the emotional trauma Conroy had administered had only toughened Victoria's will. Part of the venom that Conroy aroused may be explained by snobbery. Despite having to do business with aristocrats, Conroy was a meritocrat. His dedication to his duty wasn't at fault.

And so, two days later, it was agreed that John Conroy *should* be offered an Irish peerage. This, though, would involve a long wait. In the meantime he could, and did, become a baronet. Regrettably, this situation gave Conroy permission to continue hanging around Queen Victoria's court causing mischief.

That first evening of her reign, overwhelmed by her day, Victoria ate her dinner alone.[60] Victoire was elsewhere in the palace, having experienced the 'most distressing day of [her] whole life'.[61] Her heart was aching. 'If my beloved Victoria should ever read these leaves,' she wrote in her private diary, 'I beg her to believe, that I never did anything to hurt her.'[62] Yet Victoria would shortly announce that not even her mother could come into her room without permission. 'I was obliged to remind her who I was,' she would confide in Melbourne. 'Quite right,' he agreed.[63]

So Victoria – calm, confident and callous – simply booted her mother out, and appointed Melbourne to the paternal role that Uncle Leopold had previously filled. 'My poor Mother,' she wrote with cruel complacency, 'views Lord Melbourne with great jealousy.'[64] She had another long, 'very important and a very comfortable' talk with him that evening, until ten o'clock, after which she said a quick goodnight to Victoire. This was a formal ceremony of dismissal, for they would no longer share a bedchamber, and Victoire was expelled to the old suite on the lower floor.

Then Victoria cast her mother from her mind. Sitting alone, recording the day in her journal, she ruminated. 'I shall do my utmost to fulfil my duty towards my country,' she promised herself. 'I am very young and perhaps in many, though not in all things, inexperienced, but I am sure, that very few have more real good will and more real desire to do what is fit and right than I have.'[65]

The words are humble, and heartfelt. Victoria was all too well aware that she was not particularly blessed with either looks or brains. She really was quite astonishingly ordinary. Her touching little declamation even parroted the clichés of many a nineteenth-century heroine: duty, inadequacy and piety. They were just the kind of thoughts reproduced in fiction (by Dorothea Brooke in *Middlemarch*) and in real life (by Florence Nightingale and so many others). What Victoria had, which these other women did not, was a socially approved stage upon which to perform her intentions.[66] The blind luck of such a commonplace girl's winning the Baby Race would be one of the most significant things about her reign. She would prove that even ordinary girls could do extraordinary things.

In the coming days, Victoria placed herself even further from her mother's reach. Soon she moved out of Kensington Palace altogether, taking her household to a new home at Buckingham Palace. People were impressed by her decisiveness. 'In all trifling matters connected with her Court and her palace,' they said, 'she already enacts the part of Queen and mistress as if it had long been familiar to her.' Once freed from the glooms of Kensington, Victoria began to behave a little more like the forceful woman that she would one day become.

Their first glimpse of the new queen in the Red Saloon may have encouraged her ministers and courtiers to believe that her diminutive figure and slender years would make her malleable. But the clerk of her Council could already see otherwise. 'As she gains confidence,' he thought, 'and as her character begins to develop, she will evince a strong will of her own.'[67]

And Conroy, who knew this already, would come to learn it better than ever.

8

Coronation: Buckingham Palace, 28 June 1838

'Thursday, June 28!' she wrote, underlining the date. It was a day to live long in the memory. 'I was awoke at four o'clock,' continues Victoria's journal for her coronation, 'by the guns in the Park, and could not get much sleep afterwards on account of the noise of the people, bands, &c.'[1] She'd passed her broken night at Buckingham Palace, George IV's grand and elegant mansion of tawny stone. It was then a much more graceful building than it is today, for later in her reign Victoria would add the clumsy east-facing wing that the palace now presents towards London. All over the capital, other people were waking up early too, ready for one of the greatest shows the city had yet seen.

Victoria got out of bed at seven, and braced herself for the long day by eating two breakfasts, one before and one after getting dressed. At half past nine, she came out of her own suite to see the people who mattered most to her: her Uncle Ernest, Duke of Coburg, and her half-siblings Charles and Feodore. She does not mention her mother. Despite Victoria's lack of sleep, they thought she looked 'perfectly composed'.

For her journey to Westminster Abbey, Victoria was wearing red robes over a stiff white satin dress with gold embroidery. She had a 'circlet of splendid diamonds' on her head. Her long crimson velvet cloak, with its gold lace and ermine, flowed out so far behind her little figure that it became a 'very ponderous appendage'.[2] Harriet, the beautiful and statuesque Duchess of Sutherland, Mistress of the Robes, was responsible for Victoria's appearance. This 'ponderous' mantle must have made her anxious, and indeed it would get in the way and cause kerfuffle all day long. The stately duchess rather dwarfed the queen when they stood side by side, and Victoria was slightly jealous of Harriet's habit of flirting with Melbourne. But she did trust her surer dress sense. Onto Victoria's little feet went flat white satin slippers fastened with ribbons.[3]

At ten o'clock, Victoria was ready to go. She clambered into the golden state coach made for her grandfather George III, guarded at its four corners by gilded Tritons brandishing tridents. Britannia had ruled the waves since the naval victories of the eighteenth century, and her monarch as she travelled was therefore rightly guarded by sea creatures. Eight white horses strained to jerk the coach into motion, creating its characteristically unpleasant 'perpetually swinging movement'.[4]

It lumbered its cumbrous way out of Buckingham Palace, beneath the Marble Arch that then stood right outside the building. The most stunning and novel coronation procession in history had begun.

Victoria had sailed triumphantly through the first year of her reign, hardly putting a foot wrong. 'John Bull' – that imaginary personification of an Englishman – 'was so pleased at the idea of being governed by a girl,' claimed one newspaper, that 'he would cut off his ears if her little Majesty required them.'[5] The *Caledonian Mercury* thought the virgin queen 'the rainbow of a blessed promise'.[6]

These had been the best months of Victoria's life. 'I prorogued Parliament yesterday,' she'd written in July 1837, 'and am not at all tired to-day, but quite frisky.'[7] 'I had a very brilliant Levee again yesterday,' she boasts a little later.[8] 'I have been dancing till past four o'clock this morning; we have had a charming ball,' she wrote the day after her nineteenth birthday. It was so agreeable to be able to dance, to choose her own companions and to be free from the disapproving scrutiny of the now 'Sir' John Conroy and her mother. 'Oh, how different to last year!' she wrote. 'Everybody was so kind and so friendly to me.'[9]

When Britain was at peace, and when a new monarch was young and in good health, it wasn't unusual for a whole year to pass between accession and coronation, to allow the planning of a magnificent ceremony. In March 1838, a whole nine months into her reign, Victoria's Cabinet began to discuss the subject. Dispute at once broke out. London's traders banded together to ask for an August date, to give them more time to order merchandising. Others were horrified that the traditional, exclusive banquet in Westminster Hall for the great and the good was to be cut from the proceedings, and replaced by a crowd-pleasing public procession through the streets.[10] The Cabinet eventually decided that the coronation should be at the end of the parliamentary session in June. On 7 April, the order was given, and a huge machine moved into motion.[11]

The final plans for Victoria's coronation, as they emerged from the fog of discussion, were carefully calibrated to appeal to a broader range of people than any preceding ceremony. Budgeted at £70,000, it was to be cheap, but not cut-price like the previous coronation, which had been staged for Victoria's uncle William IV. Costing just £30,000, this one had caused disappointment, and subsequently became known as the 'Half-Crown-ation'. Yet Victoria's would nowhere near approach the £240,000 cost of the one before that, her uncle George IV's, which was considered over the top.

Victoria's coronation, poised as it was between parsimony and panache, was also a clever blend of old and new. The ceremony inside Westminster Abbey would appeal to society's elite. Members of the peerage would be invited to attend, but even non-peers could buy the expensive tickets for entry. From their seats in specially – and precariously – constructed stands, they'd be able to look down upon a small, virginal figure taking part in the ancient ritual below. Eyeing her slight figure with approval, the new queen's aristocracy would be able to reassure themselves that this little girl wasn't going to give them any trouble.

However, this coronation was to be witnessed not only by the peerage but also by some 500 members of the House of Commons.

It was the first coronation since the passing of the Great Reform Act of 1832, and the extension of the franchise to people whom we would in modern times think of as middle-class. So, Victoria now had also to sign invitations to be sent to Britain's Members of Parliament, requesting them to make their 'personal attendance' at 'the Solemnity of Our Royal Coronation'.[12] And then, to please the great mass of John Bulls who couldn't physically squeeze into the abbey, there was to be that great procession through the streets.

This was a revival of an idea that was centuries old. Coronation processions had once run from the monarchy's ancient fortress of the Tower of London to Westminster, but there hadn't been as lengthy a route as that now planned for Victoria since 1660. Victoria's procession would also recognise the fact that the monarchical HQ had moved, abandoning the stronghold of the Tower in favour of chic Buckingham Palace in the classy West End. Victoria's would be the first procession to start from Buckingham Palace, thus initiating the route so familiar from televised royal weddings and ceremonies in modern times. Finally, in the most crowd-pleasing touch of all, there was to be a huge fair in Hyde Park. It was initially planned to last two days, but popular demand ensured that it was extended to four.

'The great merit about this coronation,' thought 'The Gruncher' Greville, was 'that so much has been done for the people.'[13] He meant the people then called 'the lower orders', the manual workers who constituted 75 per cent of the population. The official estimate was that 400,000 of them had come to London specially to see the royal show.[14] In the week beforehand, these floods of incomers brought the city to a standstill. Victoria's own private carriage got stuck in Piccadilly for forty-five minutes because of the carts taking the fair goods into Hyde Park. The traffic was so solid that nobody could move.[15] There was 'not a fly or cab to be had for love or money', it was said, and the drivers of hackney carriages were charging 'double to foreigners!'[16]

All along the route of the procession, seating was constructed for the spectators. 'There was scarcely a house,' ran one report, 'or a vacant spot along the whole line from Hyde-park corner to the abbey, that was unoccupied with galleries or scaffolding.'[17]

On the morning of 28 June, as Victoria prepared to leave Buckingham Palace, these stands were already filled with humanity, and the squash at street level was so great that the crowds had to be held back by soldiers with rifles. 'I was alarmed at times,' Victoria admitted, 'for fear that the people would be crushed and squeazed on account of the tremendous rush and pressure.'[18] It was not entirely safe, or comfortable. This was still an age of mobs, and public disorder, as the Duke of Wellington had discovered only a few years previously when a London crowd had attacked his house at Hyde Park Corner for his opposition to the Great Reform Act.

At ten o'clock, Victoria's procession began with a bang. Following a ground-shaking gun salute, an enormous royal standard, 30 feet broad, was slowly hoisted up above the Marble Arch (which in 1838 stood in front of Buckingham Palace) to indicate that she was on the move. The early part of her cavalcade included foreign ambassadors, the Household Cavalry, the carriages of many members of the royal family and forty-eight members of the Queen's Watermen marching along on foot.[19] It was a gorgeous sight. The 'liveries were so fanciful and such a mass of gold', wrote one happy onlooker.[20] The carriage occupied by the Russian envoy, Alexander Stroganov, was particularly pleasing, with 'crowns all over the top', although disappointingly not 'of a proper *czarrish* shape'. Prince Esterházy's vehicle was likewise thought very fine, even though the prince himself 'wriggled about therein like an imprisoned worm'. Then there was the Mexican ambassador's carriage, sporting admirable 'nobs of leather'.[21]

Yet the vehicle everyone was waiting for was the queen's. Slowly, ponderously, the 'cumbrous state-coach' emerged from beneath the Marble Arch to the 'general and hearty cheering' of the crowd.[22] According to the composer Felix Mendelssohn, who saw it, it was a 'golden fairy-like' vehicle with windows revealing glimpses of a 'graceful girl' within, bowing to left and right to acknowledge the cheers. As soon as the coach appeared, 'the mass of people was completely hidden by their waving handkerchiefs and raised hats, while one roar of cheering almost drowned the pealing of the bells, the blare of the trumpets, and thundering of the guns'. 'One had to pinch oneself,' Mendelssohn concluded, 'to make sure it was not all a dream.'[23] Victoria herself was overwhelmed. 'Their good-humour and excessive loyalty was beyond everything,' she recorded, 'and I really cannot say how proud I feel to be the Queen of such a Nation.'[24]

It took Victoria a whole hour to cover the half-mile between Buckingham Palace and Westminster Abbey, but at last the golden coach reached the abbey's great east doors, and she descended. Mendelssohn, who'd been mixing earlier among the crowd, managed to get right up to the abbey's doors and 'peered into the solemn obscurity' before being barred from entry by the scarlet-clad Yeomen of the Guard, whose 'cheeks suggest beef and whose noses tell tales of whisky and claret'.[25]

As Victoria's little white foot touched the ground, there was the biggest roar of approval so far. And then, she was gone, disappearing inside. The noisy, public part of the coronation was over. Upon the waiting crowds there now 'fell a sudden silence, the silence of a church'.[26]

The people with tickets to the abbey had for the most part risen at four and been en route by five. They had generally arrived in the abbey cloisters at six, there to stand shivering in the wind until the doors opened at seven. One attendee, a young MP named Benjamin Disraeli, hadn't even been to bed, having only finalised the court costume he was required to wear at half past two.[27] By eleven, the congregation had already spent three or four hours inside the abbey, sitting, standing, talking or indeed snoozing. But now, as one body, they turned towards the east doors. 'I was glad,' burst out the choir and orchestra, 237 musicians in all, 'when they said unto me: We will go into the house of the Lord.'[28]

Victoria gasped at the sight that met her within. Lady Wilhelmina Stanhope, one of the young ladies carrying the queen's train, noticed that 'the colour mounted to her cheeks, brow and even neck, and her breath came quickly.'[29] 'Splendid', Victoria thought the congregation, many of them, like herself, swathed in red velvet, 'the bank of Peeresses quite beautiful, all in their robes'.[30] Among a host of impressive outfits, that of the Austrian ambassador was particularly noteworthy. Even the heels of his boots were bejewelled. One lady thought that he looked like he'd 'been caught out in a rain of diamonds, and had come in dripping!'[31]

Victoria was accompanied not only by the young ladies who were to carry her train, but also by the Duchess of Sutherland as Mistress of the Robes, who 'walked, or rather stalked up the Abbey like Juno; she was full of her situation.'[32] Throughout the whole ceremony the Bishop of Durham stood near to the queen, supposedly to guide her through the ritual. But he proved to be hopelessly unreliable. The unfortunate bishop 'never could tell me', Victoria recorded later, 'what was to take place'. At one point, he was supposed to hand her the orb, but when he noticed that she had already got it, he was left, once again, 'so confused and puzzled'.[33]

Another hindrance came in the form of the trainbearers' dresses. Their 'little trains were serious annoyances', wrote one of their number, 'for it was impossible to avoid treading upon them . . . there certainly should have been some previous rehearsing, for we carried the Queen's train very jerkily and badly, never keeping step properly'.[34] It was the Duchess of Richmond, not the stylish Sutherland, who had signed off the design of the bearers' dresses, and she found herself 'much condemned by some of the young ladies for it'. But the Duchess of Richmond had decreed that she would 'have no discussion with their Mammas' about what they were to wear. An executive decision was the only way to get the design agreed.[35]

Yet many of the spectators watching the little procession's erratic progress up the aisle were delighted by what they saw. 'The Queen came in as gay as a lark,' wrote one of them, 'and looking like a girl on her birthday.'[36] Charles Leslie of the Royal Academy was given a well-placed seat because he had a commission to paint Victoria receiving the sacrament, and needed to be able to see her doing it. He was surprised to find that 'the first sight of her in her robes' brought tears into his eyes, because she looked 'almost like a child'.[37]

But her high spirits faded away by the time she reached the middle of the abbey and the 'foot of the throne', and Victoria grew subdued.[38] The enormity and solemnity of what she was about to undergo seemed to overcome her. She was given a little stool to lean against while she prayed for strength for what was to come. The art historian Marina Warner notes that in the sketches that Victoria made afterwards of the day, she recorded nothing of the splendour of the abbey, nor indeed of the long and chaotic ceremony. She captured simply this moment of private devotion. Her drawings of herself at prayer reveal her sense of the purpose, poignancy and deep power of the occasion.[39]

When Victoria rose from her knees, the Archbishop of Canterbury swivelled her round to face, one by one, the four corners of the abbey. He boomed out the words 'Sirs, I here present unto you the undoubted Queen of this realm. Will ye all swear to do her homage?' Back from every side there came the sounding of trumpets, the waving of banners and thunderous shouts. 'God Save Queen Victoria,' they yelled, with such spirit that it 'made the poor little Queen turn first very red and then very pale'. 'Most of the ladies cried,' recorded one of their number, 'and I felt I should not forget it as long as I lived.'[40]

As the shouts subsided, it was now time for a change of dress, to mark the beginning of Victoria's transformation from girl to sovereign. Retreating to a special robing room, she took off her crimson cloak and put on 'a singular sort of little gown of linen trimmed with lace'. This white dress represented her purified, prepared state.

When she re-entered the abbey, she did so bare-headed. She was presented one by one with the items that would turn her into a monarch. First came the golden robe of a medieval bishop, to show the religious nature of the occasion. Seated upon her throne, she was handed the ancient symbols of kingly authority: spurs, a sword, the sceptre, her ring. Then at last came the very moment of 'the Crown being placed on my head – which was, I must own, a most beautiful impressive moment; all the Peers and Peeresses put on their Coronets at the same instant.'[41] The sound of this moment of the lifting of the coronets had been heard at coronations going back to the Middle Ages, and was once exquisitely described as 'a sort of feathered, silken thunder'.[42]

The ritual was timeless, but this time it was slightly remodelled to suit a girl. Usually a monarch was anointed with holy oil upon his breast. For Victoria, though, this action was thought indelicate and she was anointed just on the head and hands.[43] Usually a king wore his blue velvet Order of the Garter round his leg, but Victoria wore hers round her left biceps instead.[44] St Edward's Crown, traditionally used at the climax of the ceremony, had been made for Charles II, a man over 6 feet tall and well able to bear its 5-lb weight. But here problems had been anticipated. A new and smaller 'Crown of State' had been specially made 'according to the Model approved by the Queen' at a cost of £1,000.[45] The orb, however, was still the old one designed for a man. When it was handed to Victoria, she asked what she was supposed to do with it. On being told that she was supposed to carry it in her hand, she was incredulous. 'Am I?' she asked. 'It is very heavy.'[46]

Her new crown weighed less than half the load of St Edward's Crown, but it still gave Victoria a headache. She'd had it made to fit her head extra tightly, so that 'accident or misadventure' could not cause it to fall off.[47] The jewellers Rundell, Bridge & Rundell had made the new crown, and during the build-up towards the coronation it had become the focus of an angry controversy. Mr Bridge had displayed his firm's finished handiwork to the public in his shop on Ludgate Hill. This was much to the dismay of the touchy Mr Swifte, Keeper of the Regalia at the Tower of London. It was Mr Swifte's privilege to display the Crown Jewels kept at the Tower to anyone who wanted to see them, for one shilling each, and he'd been counting on a lucrative flood of visitors to pay for the feeding of his numerous and sickly infants. But the new crown proved a greater attraction, and hundreds of people went to Mr Bridge's shop, Mr Swifte complained, when they would otherwise have come to the Tower. Mr Bridges was not very sympathetic about stealing Mr Swifte's business. 'If we were to close our Doors,' he claimed, 'I fear they would be forced.'[48]

Victoria later confessed that her firmly fitting crown had hurt her 'a good deal', but nevertheless she had to sit on her throne in it, while the peers came up one by one to swear loyalty and kiss her hand.[49] Most of them did it awkwardly because 'the throne was very slippery'.[50] Indeed, there was a catastrophe when the aged Lord Rolle somehow 'slipped and rolled down the five or six steps from the throne, on his head, which was a dreadful sight'.[51] Victoria leapt up to help him, her spontaneous action earning her a round of applause. A transatlantic pundit, one of the sort whose successors still report upon royal occasions, gravely passed on to his countrymen his misapprehension that 'the Lords Rolle held their title on the condition of performing the feat at every coronation'.[52] When it was Melbourne's turn to pay homage, Victoria tells us, she grasped his hand 'with all my heart, at which he looked up with his eyes filled with tears'.[53]

Next came one of the subtle, popularising innovations in the service. For the first time in history, 500 members of the House of Commons, seated in their own special 'Gallery over the Altar', now gave nine cheers.[54] The members were, in the main, excited to take part. They 'hear, hear'ed' those among their number who were usually notoriously scruffy in appearance, but who'd risen to the occasion with 'splendid attire'. The loudest cheers went to a Scottish MP who turned up in 'the plaid of his clan', and to another who appeared in a 'peach-coloured velvet Court dress'.[55] But some, like the radical Joseph Hume, had refused to wear court dress, and had therefore been banned from attendance.[56]

Seated at the centre of all these excited people, Victoria herself was dignified and calm, going through the ceremony with panache, 'as if she had often been crowned before'.[57] She felt comforted by Melbourne's 'fatherly look' and by the occasional glimpse of 'dearly beloved angelic Lehzen'. Seated in a box high up towards the roof of the abbey, Lehzen was watching her former pupil so intently that when the queen's eyes finally fell upon her, they were able to exchange smiles.[58] The proud glance of a governess presents quite a contrast to the stir caused at George IV's coronation when he was observed to exchange fond looks with his mistress Lady Conyngham.

Victoria's mother was, of course, present in the abbey as well, but Victoria does not mention her once in her whole long description of the ceremony. His friends (he did have *some* friends) noticed that Sir John Conroy was absent: 'I glanced my eye yesterday from Mother to Daughter,' wrote one of them, 'then ran it along the line, in the rear, & missed you.'[59] Victoire must have missed Conroy too. She'd had him by her side for twenty years, longer than either of her husbands.

Rather than reaching a magnificent conclusion, the ceremony had overrun, and it tailed off into a certain amount of confusion and disorder. The Lord Treasurer dispersed commemorative medals to the participants, and found himself 'nearly torn to pieces' as the pages leapt up to grab them. Victoria was eventually released back into her robing room, where she 'complained of a headache'. She put down the weighty orb and sceptre, 'unclasped her mantle, took off her crown, and, having got rid of all her royalty, sat down on the sofa'.[60] She found it hard to remove the coronation ring, for the Archbishop had shoved it onto the wrong digit, and it came off only 'with great pain' and iced water.

The misfortune with the ring was just one of a number of mistakes. Disraeli thought the whole affair revealed a sad 'want of rehearsal'. He judged that Melbourne had held the sword of state ineptly, 'like a butcher', and he'd spotted Lord Ward 'drinking champagne out of a pewter pot, his coronet cocked aside'.[61] Melbourne, too, 'completely tired', had felt it necessary to refresh himself from the sandwiches and bottles of wine scattered across the altar of St Edward's Chapel behind the scenes.[62] No wonder, after such an early start. It was traditional for peers to conceal sandwiches inside their coronets, and some of those attending the 1911 coronation of Victoria's grandson George V, another June occasion, would admit to journalists their fears that the butter in their sandwiches might melt and leak.[63] And now everyone had a long wait before they could leave the abbey. One spectator, the writer Harriet Martineau, had brought her own sandwich, and book, and read the latter comfortably while 'leaning against my friendly pillar', but others, less well prepared, simply 'sat or lay down' on the dirty floor, 'in dust half a foot deep'.[64]

Despite her ordeal, Victoria was 'really <u>not</u> feeling tired' when she arrived back at Buckingham Palace a little after six.[65] One celebrated account of the day has her skipping into the palace to hear her dog 'barking with joy in the hall' and running upstairs '*to go to wash little Dash*'.[66] It seems highly unlikely, yet it was a story that gained circulation because of the way it illustrated something that was plain to see: the young queen's 'great animal spirits'. They were noticed and praised even by 'The Gruncher', who described how she entered into 'the magnificent novelties of her position with the zest and curiosity of a child'.[67]

The evening was occupied by a relatively small dinner for thirteen, then Victoria stayed to twelve 'on Ma.'s balcony looking at the fireworks in Green Park, which were quite beautiful'.[68] This reference to her mama's balcony at midnight is the only time in Victoria's record of the day when her mother appears. It is striking how much of the long entry is taken up instead with the actions and words of Melbourne. For her, he had become the centre of the world.

Witty, worldly, but fatherly, Melbourne was the real reason that Victoria had so enjoyed these early months of being queen. His charming, sophisticated conversation was exactly the opposite of the guarded gloom of the 'System'. But some of Victoria's subjects thought that she was showing an unhealthy favouritism to, indeed a dangerous dependence upon, the man she called 'Lord M.' And behind the splendour of her coronation day, there was a quiet but persistent grumbling note.

To many it seemed that it wasn't just Westminster Abbey that was covered in 'dust half a foot deep', but also the monarchy itself. Had Victoria been less young, less loveable, it might well have been an institution in danger. Underlying the comments upon the many mess-ups during the ceremony was the idea that in this modern age a coronation, medieval at its heart, had become an anachronism. This was an age of reform; was the mummery still necessary? Coronations were fit only for 'barbarous' earlier ages, announced one speaker in the House of Lords, 'for periods when crowns were won and lost by unruly violence and ferocious contests'.[69] Harriet Martineau in her high balcony, a popular and much-read journalist, had watched the peeresses with much distaste. She found the archaic outfits below most unseemly, and would have preferred 'the decent differences of dress which, according to middle-class custom, pertain to contrasting periods of life'. She particularly criticised the peers' wives, 'old hags, with their dyed or false hair', their bare arms and necks so 'wrinkled as to make one sick'. She did not like the 'mixing up of the Queen and the God, such homage to both, and adulation so like in kind and degree that, when one came to think of it, it made one's blood run cold'.[70]

But what carried over the doubtful, what marked a fresh start after the unpleasantness of the Royal Dukes was the figure of the young queen herself. Even radicals couldn't dislike a girl. In fact, as the historian John Plunkett notes, the most important part of Victoria's coronation wasn't taking place in the abbey at all. It was happening out in the Hyde Park Fair, awash with 'iced champagne, ditto soda water, and ginger beer'.[71]

It was happening on the streets of London, and indeed in other towns far away. By contrast with the creaky ancient ritual in the abbey, the celebrations outside were full of novelty. At the very moment of the crowning, 2 p.m. on coronation day, one 'Mrs Graham' ascended from the Hyde Park fairground in her hot air balloon. (Unfortunately, as she landed in Marylebone, the descent of her craft damaged a building, and falling masonry crushed a man to death.[72]) Meanwhile, in Preston, a local printer had his press drawn through the town by horses as part of the local celebratory procession, and he continuously printed off handbills outlining Victoria's life story so far for the crowd to buy. A penny a pop, they powerfully combined monarchy and the modern media.[73] Cheap, sometimes crude, but ubiquitous pictures of the new queen, plastered onto all sorts of products, enraged the more sophisticated observers who despised Regina-mania. The popular prints dwelt constantly on Victoria's (non-existent) beauty, not only of her 'face and features, but of her feet and even of her slippers'.[74]

With the forces of technology on her side against the monarchy's detractors, Victoria must have concluded that being queen was fun, and that it suited her. It seemed, on coronation day, that she could do no wrong. Yet there wasn't enough ginger beer and champagne in the world to win over all the unconvinced, and her honeymoon wasn't to last long.

9

In Lady Flora's Bedchamber: Buckingham Palace, 27 June 1839

Victoria was on the move, swishing along the dim corridors of Buckingham Palace. Finding her way about her palace challenged both her eyesight and her sense of direction. Any newcomer to its 'long passages and open courts' would quickly get lost without a guide, and Victoria was now heading to an unfamiliar zone of the enormous building.[1]

Her new home, with gardens behind but with a roaring thoroughfare in front, was much more prominent and public than Kensington Palace. When Victoria asked a footman to open the windows, she heard not birdsong, but 'a constant dull roar from afar, the noise of carriages driving around the city'.[2] Beyond the grimy glass, London's polluted air was visibly grey. One new servant was 'almost frightened' when she 'glimpsed through this mass a great round fiery ball, quite dark red in colour: that is what the sun looks like here!'[3] Despite the work of Victoria's First and Second Lamplighters, and their seven assistants, Buckingham Palace was always dark indoors.[4] A visitor arriving even at midday was surprised to discover the staircase illuminated by 'a candelabra with a Lamp burning . . . it was always lighted'.[5] 'It is cruelty,' claimed one of the staff, 'for human beings to have to live in this great prison all the time.'[6]

This sprawling building, extended and made palatial by architect John Nash for George IV, had originally been a private house. Even after Nash had finished, it was nowhere near as well built as might have been expected for a project that had cost the government half a million pounds. The vast overspend on the initial estimate of £200,000 had resulted in the Treasury 'making a hash of Nash'.[7] Despite another round of improvements carried out for William IV by the architect Edward Blore, Buckingham Palace still possessed major flaws. When the Thames tide was high, the palace sewer would overflow and flood the underground kitchens.[8] At Victoria's accession, the suite made for her elderly predecessor had to be jigged about, with new walls and doorways hastily thrown up to make it more suitable for a young woman.[9] The Inspector of Palaces, Mr Saunders, who was supposed to manage this work and keep the building in good condition, got sacked for leaking details of what was going on 'to parties connected with the public press'.[10]

The reception rooms, though, were marvellous. George IV, with his flair for interior decoration, had left his niece the magnificent state apartments that are still in use today. 'His Majesty plans all the alterations himself,' his courtiers noted, 'it is his great amusement.'[11] One of Victoria's guests found these 'rich and gorgeous apartments' in red, white and gold reminded her of 'the descriptions in the Arabian Nights'.[12]

Victoria now had a lady-in-waiting with her to guide her on her unaccustomed route through this almost subterranean world. Two separate households coexisted under the one palace roof, her own and her mother the Duchess of Kent's. The two were increasingly at odds, and it was highly unusual for Victoria to be crossing, as she now was, to the other side.

Eventually they reached an ordinary bedroom door, and Victoria gestured that her companion should wait outside. The bedchamber beyond was the sickroom of the thirty-three-year-old Lady Flora Hastings, a lady-in-waiting employed by Victoria's mother. 'I went in alone,' Victoria wrote in her journal for 27 June 1839, and 'found poor Lady Flora stretched on a couch.'[13]

Like all ladies-in-waiting, Flora Hastings served on a roster for a couple of months at a time. When she was in 'waiting' (or on duty) her duties included helping with correspondence, handing shawls, fastening bracelets, entertaining boring guests and generally providing the duchess with company. The ladies got no time off during their 'waiting' and had to be constantly on hand. Flora's bedroom was therefore near to her mistress's own rooms, which had been completed and occupied just a few months before. Situated at the eastern end of the palace's north wing, the duchess's suite was a long way from her daughter's at its western tip.[14] Propriety dictated that Victoria's mother should live with her as a chaperone, even if in practice they remained as distant from each other as possible.

Only extreme circumstances had forced Victoria to come so far out of her accustomed territory. As she now stepped forward into Flora's bedroom, someone else quickly retreated through another door. This was the sick woman's sister, Sophia, who very deliberately, and very disrespectfully, left without making a curtsey.[15] The wider Hastings family had lost their loyalty to the Crown. They believed that Victoria had done something to Flora that had put her terribly in the wrong.

Flora was a tall, thin woman, with a long body and long nose, and Victoria found her lying upon a sofa. The queen thought she could detect 'a searching look' in the eyes in Flora's haggard face; indeed the patient had 'a look rather like a person who is dying'. But as the visit unfolded Victoria convinced herself that Flora spoke in just her usual voice, managing a few moments of 'friendly' conversation in the faint Ayrshire accent she'd had since her Scottish childhood. The two women had known each other for many years. Recalling the visit in her journal that evening, Victoria quoted Flora as saying that she 'was very comfortable, and was very grateful for all I had done for her'.[16] The illness had created extra work for the palace staff, who had to send a separate dinner to Flora's room each evening.[17]

'I said to her,' Victoria's journal entry concluded, that 'I hoped to see her again when she was better, upon which she grasped my hand as if to say "I shall not see you again".'[18]

〰

Victoria's visit to the sickroom of a suffering servant sounds like a generous action. But Flora's sister Sophia had walked out because she believed the queen's apparent concern was just a cynical gesture. Victoria, Sophia felt, was paying the visit reluctantly, and only because she'd been strongly advised that the lack of sympathy she'd shown thus far was damaging her public image. When Sophia asked Flora afterwards what had passed, she replied that it had only been empty talk, 'nothing particular'.[19] And some newspapers – for this palace scandal had become of great interest to the press – reported that all Victoria had said was 'Lady Flora, I am sorry you are still ill', and remained less than five minutes.[20]

Whatever the truth, it was undeniably a short visit. And Victoria did heartily resent Flora, and her illness, thinking her a 'detestable person'. This was not least because Flora was an old family friend of John Conroy's. Victoria had only turned twenty a month previously, and could summon up no sympathy for a spinster thirteen years older than herself. Flora would never get a husband, the queen was heard to scoff, unpleasantly, for she 'has neither riches nor beauty nor any thing!'[21]

Victoria was also chagrined that this sickness had created a chilly atmosphere in the palace and put a damper on her social life. The summer of 1839 had been particularly wet, but the London Season was now reaching its June climax before high society would disperse to its country houses with the approaching end of the parliamentary term. The previous day, Victoria had been forced to cancel a ball. The night before that, though, she had gone merrily to the opera. Melbourne had been trying to talk her out of staging an upcoming 'great dinner . . . for fear that the carriages might disturb Lady Flora'.[22] 'It would be very awkward,' he'd muttered, 'if that woman was to die.'

Melbourne was quite right to be concerned that to those outside the palace Victoria's actions did not read well. The *Morning Post*, for example, had criticised the queen for 'the absence of every other thought than for the amusement and ill-timed enjoyment of the passing hour'. Its writer even thought her responsible for tarnishing 'the cause of Royalty'.[23] 'Can't you make a treaty of peace, and speak to Lady Flora?' Melbourne had begged Victoria.[24]

He saw what she could not: that the situation was becoming a stain upon the honour of Buckingham Palace. Victoria's people were beginning to think that the girl who'd so recently been their Queen of Hearts was in fact revealing herself to be entirely heartless. Just one day short of a full year after her coronation, circumstances had combined to discolour both Victoria's reputation and her happiness.

Back in Victoria's private drawing room, with its round bay window overlooking the garden and lake behind the palace, Melbourne was pacing about and awaiting her return. Although he thought that this visit was part of the solution to the bad press Victoria had been getting, he did not realise that he was himself part of the problem.

Melbourne had been one of the earliest people to meet Victoria as queen, at nine o'clock in the morning of the first day of her reign. Uncle Leopold had already told her that 'Lord M.' could be trusted. She thought him 'straightforward', but in reality he was anything but. With his black brows and commanding height, he was famously handsome, and the 'quaint, queer, epigrammatic turn of his mind' made Victoria laugh 'excessively'.[25] Although he was much sought after in fashionable Whig society, he had been cuckolded by his wife, and sought satisfaction instead in spanking his housemaids. He had a fetish for the 'large and extensive field of the *derrière*, which is so well calculated' to receive the birch.[26] Melbourne made rather a surprising Prime Minister, for he had never shown much ambition in his youth, and his friends were astonished by just how hard he worked once he got into government. He wasn't even wholeheartedly a Whig, and perhaps conservative or Tory values lay closer to his core. It's important to realise, though, that the very words 'Whig' and 'Tory' are difficult to define, and bear little resemblance to modern well-organised political parties. And although Britons followed elections with enthusiasm, still only one in seven of them – despite the Reform Act – had the vote.

When William IV's death gave Melbourne an unexpected opportunity 'to educate, instruct and form the most interesting mind and character in the world', he grasped it. Given the great responsibility – or gift, depending on which way you looked at it – of guiding this girl through the first few months of her reign, Melbourne had devoted himself to the task, often spending six hours a day with Victoria. This was not least because having lost his wayward wife, and two short-lived children, he was 'a man with capacity for loving without anything to love'.[27] He was indulging in an old man's *amitié amoureuse*.

It gradually became clear, though, that Victoria was making a strategic error in associating herself so closely with Melbourne and his friends. The convention was developing that a British monarch should remain 'above' party politics. However enjoyable his witty and worldly company might be, Victoria's favouritism towards the Whigs was earning her the hostility of the Tories.

Yet she still saw Melbourne nearly every morning in her closet 'for Political Affairs', rode out with him in the afternoon and would sit 'near him constantly after dinner'.[28] 'I love him like a Father!' she began to exclaim in her journal.[29] In return, Melbourne gave her his undivided attention. 'I have no doubt he is passionately fond of her,' observed 'The Gruncher'. He thought that she loved her Prime Minister right back again, with feelings that were '*sexual* though she does not know it'.[30] Victoire advised her daughter in vain to keep a sense of proportion. 'You do not know the world,' she wrote to Victoria, scribbling crazily and passionately in pencil. 'Take care Victoria,' she went on, 'take care that Lord Melbourne is not King.'[31]

These warnings about Melbourne angered Victoria, and she'd also fallen out with her mother over the question of money. Having resolved to pay off the ancient debts of her father, Victoria found Victoire shifty on the subject of her own finances, unable, or at least unwilling, to say exactly where she stood. Melbourne's opinion was that the duchess and Conroy had told 'incalculable falsehoods' on the subject, 'which really is infamous.'[32]

Conroy was still working for the duchess, and Uncle Leopold's spies told him that he was 'with her constantly, meditating vengeance on the Queen',[33] Conroy's own financial affairs were also becoming a matter of public interest. He'd begun a case for libel against *The Times* when the newspaper wrote about 'a certain estate' he'd purchased in Wales. Where had Conroy got the money from, the article asked? Given that the rest of the paragraph was about the Duchess of Kent's debts, the implication was clear: that he'd embezzled her money.[34]

And it was Conroy, his hunger for money and power, his persistent malign influence, that lay behind the mysterious, troubling business of Lady Flora's illness.

On her return to her own sector of the palace and to Melbourne, Victoria described to him how she'd 'found poor Lady Flora stretched on a couch looking as thin as anybody can be who is still alive; literally a skeleton'.[35] Flora's hair had fallen out, forcing her to wear 'a little bonnet cap'.[36] But Melbourne was more concerned about the look of the visit than the appearance of the patient, as the palace walls had eyes and ears. 'You remained a very short time,' he complained.[37]

Victoria and Melbourne had become so intimate that he could speak astonishingly freely to her. Victoria had noticed immediately that Flora had grown thin as a living skeleton. This was partly because she herself, by contrast, had grown decidedly plump. She'd developed a fuller figure than of which 'nice & nervous observers of health would quite approve', and this formed one of the topics that queen and Prime Minister would frequently discuss.[38] Melbourne set her a terrible example, with his love of 'consommés, truffles, pears, ices, and anchovies, which he does his best to revolutionise his stomach with every day'.[39]

'Oh', but she had 'such a horror of being fat,' Victoria told him, and he advised her to eat only when she felt truly hungry.[40] If she did that, Victoria responded, she'd be 'eating all day'.[41] After the restricted diet she'd been given under the 'System', Victoria was finding it almost impossible to exercise self-control. 'A great deal of eating,' wrote one of Flora's fellow ladies-in-waiting, 'always goes on at the Palace.'[42] In the first ten days of her reign alone, Victoria's household got through £33-worth of the fruit she loved: oranges, grapes, apples, gooseberries, currants, cherries and strawberries. This cost was the equivalent of a year's wages for a bank clerk.[43] Dr Clark was also worried about Victoria's weight, and had ordered her 'not to eat luncheon any more'.[44] This must have been a severe test of willpower, for even the simplest 'Ladies Luncheon' served in the royal household consisted of ribs of lamb, roast chickens, mutton cutlets, croquettes, ham and fowl, jelly and pastry.[45]

Despite these precautions, when Victoria was weighed at the end of her first year as queen, she found – to her 'horror' – that she weighed 8 stone 13 (56.6kg).[46] Again Melbourne, in a surprisingly personal exchange, became her confidant. 'Talked of my weight,' her journal once again recorded, 'my weighing near 9 stone, which I thought incredible for my size.'[47] He soothed her by telling her that the ideal woman had a 'full' figure. Her reported weight would give Victoria, at 1.52 metres tall, a modern body mass index of 24.4. It is healthy, but only just. She was very close to being classed, in today's terms, as obese. Her physicians also recommended more exercise, and advised her to stop sitting so often for the many artists who wanted to paint her portrait.[48]

Victoria had also started to complain of cold hands and feet, and lethargy. Combined with some loss of hair, this might suggest that she had an endocrine malfunction, a hormonal disorder that can affect the body's ability to turn food into energy.[49] But she herself believed that her loss of vitality had a psychological element. It was the 'worry and torment' of the Kensington 'System', she claimed, that had prevented her from growing as tall as she might otherwise have done.[50] Yet again, it was something that she perceived to be the fault of Conroy.

ᕋ

It was Conroy who'd introduced Lady Flora, from a grand if impoverished family of Scottish aristocrats, into the service of the Duchess of Kent. And his name inevitably came up in connection to an aspect of the situation that Victoria and Melbourne now must have talked over once more. Although Flora had looked thinner than a rake as she lay upon her couch, her stomach appeared, as it had done for some months now, '*very* much swollen like a person who is with child'.[51]

Was Flora pregnant? The topic had occupied Victoria and Melbourne for the past few weeks. Four months previously, on 16 February 1839, Flora in her room had received a visit from Dr Clark. He'd come to see her, she recorded, to ask 'if I were privately married, giving as his reason that my figure had excited the remarks of "the ladies of the palace".' When Flora denied this, Dr Clark grew 'excited' himself, urging that a 'confession' was 'the only thing' that could save her from ruin.[52]

Flora's waistline had for some time been the subject of suspicion and surveillance by the household's other ladies. Indeed, it had been Victoria herself, in tandem with Lehzen, who'd first noticed a change in Flora's shape. The queen believed that there was 'no doubt that she is — to use the plain words — with child!!'[53]

Among the other court ladies who agreed that there was something amiss with Flora's middle was Emma, Lady Portman. She was incensed by Flora's denial to Dr Clark of what was very obviously a pregnancy. Lady Portman had five children herself, and her husband was a noted breeder of cattle.[54] She knew a big belly when she saw one. Lady Portman insisted on seeing the Duchess of Kent, as Flora's direct employer, face-to-face. She told Victoire that if the suspicion of pregnancy was unfounded, 'it should be removed as soon <u>as</u> possible'. Otherwise, Flora must 'leave the Palace immediately'.[55]

Flora reluctantly accepted that a medical examination might be the only means to dispel the rumours. It was to be performed by Dr James Clark, and by a doctor of Flora's own choice, who was coincidentally and confusingly called Sir Charles Clarke. Lady

Portman and Flora's own maid were present. Those who afterwards heard what happened during this examination considered that it was highly intrusive, a 'dreadful mortification' and a most 'indelicate enquiry' into her person.[56]

Lasting forty-five minutes, reluctantly undergone, this examination was nothing less than an assault upon Flora's body. The latest writer on the subject, Kathryn Hughes, has discovered that Sir Charles, a doctor specialising in women's medicine, once lectured his students on how such an assessment should be performed. The patient – or victim – should be under the covers of a bed, 'knees drawn towards the belly'. The doctor should 'cover the two fore fingers of the right hand with pomatum or cold cream', and then 'that finger is to be introduced into the vagina'.[57]

Flora's maid found all this horrifying. She described how her mistress 'nearly fainted' when the doctors uncovered her, and she thought Sir Charles Clarke 'rough & coarse & indecent in the way he moved her clothes.'[58] Clarke may have been hoping to feel if the uterus was enlarged. If Flora really was four months pregnant, he might have been able to do so. But – as was forcefully pointed out in the following furore – he might also, through his examination, have 'taken' Flora's 'virginity' himself, breaking her hymen with his cold-creamed finger. This had terrible implications for Flora's future, as it would leave her unmarriageable. It was grave violence upon Flora's person, a sort of rape, and it happened under Victoria's roof at Buckingham Palace with Victoria's own connivance.

The two doctors agreed that they hadn't found any conclusive evidence of pregnancy. But that wasn't quite the end of the story. Sir Charles Clarke reported back to the queen that he'd definitely felt 'an enlargement in the womb like a child'. Flora *might* be pregnant despite her virginity: 'one could not tell if such things could not happen.'[59] Indeed, the *London Medical and Physical Journal* had recently reported on the curious case of a pregnant woman who had not experienced penetrative sex.[60] After all, there were other forms of sexual intimacy.

And there, unsatisfactorily, matters had to rest. 'D—it,' cursed Melbourne. He couldn't even dismiss anyone from the household for spreading false rumours. After all, the gossip had been begun by the queen herself.[61]

In March, then, Buckingham Palace was 'full of bickerings and heart-burnings'.[62] And as spring turned into summer, the scandal seeped out from the palace walls and began to appear in London tittle-tattle and in the newspapers too.

Some people thought that Conroy was behind the leaks, with the aim of damaging Victoria. Yet this is unlikely, because he had much to lose. The very darkest rumours named him as the father.

Conroy and Flora certainly shared a sturdy personal bond, strong enough to appear sexual even if it wasn't. She once wrote to him naming him as her 'dearest Friend', and thanking him for allowing her 'to enter into [his] feelings'.[63] Victoria herself was only too eager to believe that Conroy, a 'monster and demon incarnate', had committed adultery with Flora Hastings.[64] It was noted that at the end of her period of waiting the previous October, Conroy had escorted Flora by carriage to the docks to catch a steamboat to Edinburgh.[65] No one else had been present in the vehicle. Probably the baby had been conceived then.

These flames of rumour took on political significance. They were vigorously fanned by the Tories, who suggested that Melbourne was the lazy, immoral guardian of the young queen's virtue, failing in his responsibility to keep her household in order. The position of Melbourne and the Whigs, their enemies said, was 'most dicta-torial, most despotic'.[66] 'The Gruncher' thought Melbourne's government 'miserably weak, dragging on a sickly existence' supported only by the favouritism of the queen.[67]

Others, though, considered the business more damaging to Victoria, because it brought her grievance against her mother out into the public sphere. Flora was technically part of the household of the duchess. Dr James Clark had served both mother and daughter, but the duchess had dismissed him at once after the horrible examination, while Victoria had kept him on. This had been observed. Melbourne was warned that the rift was becoming 'the great topic of conversation all over London', and that Victoria was being painted as that worst of all possible things, an ungrateful daughter.[68] 'It would augur unfavourably for her character and the prospects of her reign,' ran one newspaper comment, 'were she not submissive of the guidance of her mother.'[69] If Victoria threw off such a powerful bond, surely she must be dangerously out of control?

Three months after Flora's waist first drew attention, this scandal born in a bedchamber came to have serious political consequences. In May, Melbourne's government had fallen. By tradition, the monarch's inner circle and closest servants would stand down at a change of government, to be replaced by others politically affiliated with the new regime. The incoming Tory Prime Minister, Sir Robert Peel, requested that Victoria dismiss her women-of-the-bedchamber as tradition dictated. She stubbornly refused. She argued that the custom must change for a female ruler, whose private life should remain more private than a male's, and whose intimate staff should therefore stay in post.

Intellectually, Victoria had a good point. Emotionally, though, she was also revealing that she was still in the grip of the 'System'. She had grown over-reliant on her Whig courtiers like Lady Portman because they were her allies against her mother.

But Victoria now defied the whole constitutional apparatus of the country in the way that she had once defied Conroy. When she was angry, her complexion would turn 'slightly purple . . . the contrast of the darkening countenance and the light rapid movements of her blue large eyes suggests the aspect of a stormy sky'. As the unfortunate Robert Peel now discovered when he asked her to dismiss her staff, 'there is force . . . in her face'.[70] She looked imperious. She *was* imperious. 'They wanted to deprive me of my Ladies,' she wrote, furiously, to Melbourne, in a letter that was laid before the Cabinet. 'They wished to treat me like a girl, but I will show them that I am Queen of England.'[71]

In consequence of her wrath, Peel felt he had no choice but to step down, therefore returning Melbourne to power once again. To Victoria, it seemed like victory: she still had 'Lord M.' coming to visit her each day. But she'd damaged her authority. An anonymous open letter addressed to the queen appeared in *The Times*; it was in fact written by her future Prime Minister Benjamin Disraeli. With 'the rapidity of enchantment', he warned her, she would find herself the mere puppet of a clique.[72]

The issue may seem trivial. Yet pulling back to see the bigger picture reveals that Victoria and her ministers were really in the process of thrashing out how politics was going to work following the Great Reform Act. The convention had long been that a monarch invited a Prime Minister to form a government. Only then did the Prime Minister go to the voters to ask for support. Elections had traditionally been just a final rubber stamp of approval upon the monarch's choice.

But there was now a larger, more confident electorate, harder for a monarch to ignore. And in any case a wise monarch had always chosen a Prime Minister with great care, taking the trouble to discover which candidate would be able to win the support of his colleagues in Parliament, and placing good government above personal gratification or pique. Following Victoria's tantrum of 1839, and her rejection of Peel, Melbourne did indeed continue to serve for a couple of years. In 1841, though, for the very first time, the opposition would win a general election, and Melbourne would be gone for good.[73] When she stamped her foot at Peel in the summer of 1839, Victoria was in fact blithely squandering some of the influence her predecessors had possessed.[74]

Victoria, then, was perilously overconfident in the last week of June. After her visit to Flora's sickroom, she told Melbourne that the latest doctor on the case was a worrier, and 'overrated danger'. Melbourne disagreed, but rather than argue, he went off to the Houses of Parliament to help pass a Beer Bill. Victoria rode out in the park, had twenty-two people to a dinner of turbot and 'Sir

Dinky Kew Palace where Victoria's parents were married in a double wedding ceremony. Victoria's father and uncle were both contestants in a slightly farcical 'Baby Race' to produce a legitimate heir to the throne.

Contemporaries described Victoria's German grand-mother, Queen Charlotte, as having a 'mulatto,' or mixed-race, cast to her features. She did have distant African ancestry via her Portuguese forbears.

Victoria's father Edward, Duke of Kent, unexpectedly found love in a marriage made purely for power and money. He died before his baby daughter's first birthday.

Victoire, Duchess of Kent, Victoria's warm-hearted and affectionate mother, loved fashion and feathers, and was described being 'very delightful in spite of want of brains'.

Kensington Palace, set in its large and leafy gardens. Within the palace, the so-called 'Kensington System' kept the young princess under surveillance and control.

Victoria's father left her 'nothing in the World but debts.' He moved his family to Woolbrook Cottage in the seaside resort of Sidmouth to save money, but promptly died there from pneumonia.

Victoria's widowed German mother, amiable, malleable, not fluent in English, fell under the spell of the dashing but dubious Captain John Conroy.

But Victoria's governess Lehzen gave her pupil a strong moral compass. She used to tell the young princess that 'she could pardon *wickedness*' but not '*weakness.*'

Victoria had few childhood friends, but among them was her little dog Dash. It was reported that on returning to Buckingham Palace on the evening of her coronation day she ran upstairs to give him a bath.

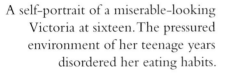

A self-portrait of a miserable-looking Victoria at sixteen. The pressured environment of her teenage years disordered her eating habits.

Yet Victoria sometimes managed to escape from the 'System' through her love of drawing, music, reading the novels of Sir Walter Scott, and above all, visiting the opera and theatre.

The American painter Thomas Sully clearly had a crush on the teenage queen, and created this delightful image of her youthful grace and charm.

The tartan velvet dress which Victoria was very likely wearing on the day she first met Albert. They shared a love of Scotland and Romantic literature.

Victoria's sketch of Lord Melbourne, her first Prime Minister, with another of Victoria's many dogs on his knee. People thought her strong feelings for older, glamorous 'Lord M.' were *sexual though she does not know it.*

Victoria's coronation involved her travelling in her golden carriage as part of a vast, people-pleasing procession through London. She arrived at Westminster Abbey 'as gay as a lark' and 'looking like a girl on her birthday'.

The solemn moment during the coronation ceremony when Victoria received the sacrament. The artist Charles Leslie was given a valuable seat near the front of the packed Abbey so he could watch closely to prepare for making this painting.

Victoria took an unfortunate and unjustified dislike to the unmarried Lady Flora Hastings. A merciless mob of courtiers claimed that Flora's swollen stomach must mean she was pregnant out of wedlock.

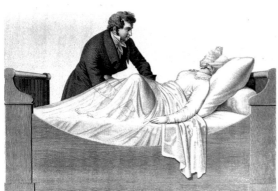

Flora was forced to undergo an intrusive medical examination like this one. But after her death, her supposed pregnancy was revealed to have been the liver disease which killed her.

Victoria's lack of sympathy for Flora became a dangerous scandal which spilled out of gloomy Buckingham Palace, and tarnished the young queen's reputation.

Victoria's family expected her to marry her German cousin Albert (right), pictured here with his rakish brother Ernest. Victoria and Albert met aged sixteen, but she insisted on waiting four years before proposing marriage.

After the scandal of Lady Flora Hastings's death, Victoria summoned Albert back to Windsor Castle. He climbed the castle's Grand Staircase (seen here) most reluctantly, having grown tired of waiting. But eventually he accepted her proposal.

Albert hated the balls and late nights that Victoria adored. But they did both love music, and played the piano and sang together nearly every day.

Victoria was determined that she was going to get married not as a queen but as a woman. She therefore wore what was considered to be a radically simple white gown.

The queen herself, a talented sketcher, designed the dresses of her bridesmaids. Her wedding was a bigger affair than she wanted, but Lord Melbourne insisted that this would please her people.

Victoria was known to regret her lack of height, but she was far from frumpy. This beautiful embroidered organza evening dress, worn in her early twenties, belies her reputation as the little old lady in black.

Loin of Roast Beef' and spent the evening ('Alas!') with 'no Lord Melbourne at all'.[75]

And unfortunately for Victoria, the pessimistic doctor was proved right. In the days that followed, Flora grew ever worse, constantly vomiting, swollen in the belly and experiencing something the *Court Circular* called 'black jaundice'.[76] She remained heroically dignified to the last. 'Is it not well,' she wrote in a poem addressed to her sisters called 'The Swan Song', 'to pass away ere life hath lost its brightness?'[77] She was also kind and wise enough to give the young queen the benefit of the doubt. 'I do not believe,' she wrote, that Victoria even '*understands* that I can have been injured by a rumour.'[78]

On Friday 5 July, at two o'clock in the morning, Flora did finally die, 'without a struggle', just raising her hands into the air, and giving one single gasp.[79] And then, at long last, the truth was revealed. A post-mortem showed that she'd been suffering from highly advanced liver disease. The 'enlargement of the person' had been caused by a swollen liver, not by pregnancy after all.[80]

Victoria was determined to show '*no* remorse' and felt '*I* had done nothing to kill her.'[81] But many of her subjects disagreed. 'The public, the women particularly, have taken up the Cause of Lady Flora,' it was said.[82] When Victoria rode out, she found 'the people in the Park cold, & not taking off their hats'. Even within doors, at her regular Buckingham Palace receptions, 'she was slightly hissed'.[83] In later life, when she'd developed more self-awareness, Victoria admitted that she'd made a costly mistake. 'Yes! I was very hot about it,' she recalled, many years later, 'but I was <u>very</u> young, only 20 & never should have acted so again.'[84] Melbourne, she came to realise, 'was too much a party man', and had made her 'a party Queen'.[85]

But the personal results of the Lady Flora affair were even more far-reaching than the political. The people who mattered in the political establishment concluded that Victoria could not go on as she was, making misjudgements like this. She picked this up, and gradually began, in turn, to lose confidence in herself. Her letters of later 1839 reveal growing anxiety, fears for her health and fatigue. Not even Uncle Leopold's good advice could help. 'I have had so much to do and so many people to see,' she told him, 'that I feel quite confused, and have written shockingly.'[86]

Victoria may have been brought up by Lehzen to admire Elizabeth I, but she wasn't capable of emulating her. She didn't have the brains, the background or the dedication to remain on the throne alone. She also had the misfortune to live in an age that was beginning to expect less of women. The family had previously been an economic unit, with all its members working and contributing. But the Industrial Revolution had begun to provide working men with large enough wages to aspire to keep their wives at home. These changing expectations applied even to the queen. 'You lead rather an unnatural life for a young person,' Melbourne told her. 'It's the life of a man.'[87]

And it was Melbourne who presented the possible solution. Victoria complained what a 'torment' it would be to have her mother living with her as a chaperone for as long as she remained unmarried. 'Well then,' Melbourne said. 'There's that way of settling it.'[88]

Oh, but she 'dreaded the thought of marrying', Victoria said at once. She was 'so accustomed' to having her own way.[89] But Melbourne did not give the customary light and jokey reply she might have expected. Instead he asked whether Prince Albert wasn't coming over to England again soon.

And so, out of Flora's stuffy sickroom, and Victoria's failure to grasp its significance, the process of taming the nation's naughty daughter finally began.

PART TWO

The Good Wife

10

The Proposal: Windsor Castle, 10–15 October 1839

Not just Melbourne, but the whole nation of Britain had come to believe that Victoria needed a man about the house.

Waking up at Windsor Castle on the morning of Thursday 10 October 1839, she was shocked to find the glass of her dressing-room window shattered and her two looking glasses broken. It was the work of a stranger throwing stones over the castle wall while an inattentive guard was on duty. The next month, a lunatic was apprehended actually inside the castle grounds. He explained that he'd climbed over the gate because 'like all other men who wanted wives', he was looking out for one, and he thought Her Majesty would do for him. The following intruder, in December, was a 'personage attired like a foreigner of distinction' with 'a boa round his neck, and furred gloves'.[1] He had dispatches that, he insisted, he must personally deliver into the hands of the queen.

Even the lunatics of Britain believed that their queen was all too single. And the German side of Victoria's family believed it most strongly of all. 'It is carried *nem. com.* by the Coburgs,' the satirical papers said, 'that she ought to be in the family way, and forthwith someone is sent over for the purpose . . . just like a parish bull.'[2]

The ship bringing the Coburgs' chosen 'parish bull' to Britain moored at the quay by the Tower of London at 4 p.m. of the very same day of the window-breaking incident, 'after a very bad and almost dangerous passage'.[3] Albert, always a poor traveller, must have been very green. Two of the queen's carriages, each drawn by four horses, were waiting on the quayside to convey him and his brother Ernest to Windsor.

The journey through London and out to the west was made through falling autumn rain. 'Never was such weather known,' the papers complained, 'and all the crops are injured.'[4] It was evening before Albert and Ernest began the steep ascent towards Windsor Castle. Its many windows glowed, for the lamps were lit throughout the whole building at four. As it hugged the skyline, the castle's 'thick walls and numerous towers' gave 'the impression of a small citadel'.[5] It was an impressive, but not a welcoming sight.

When the cavalcade finally drew to a halt before St George's Tower in the castle at 7.30 p.m., Albert was ready to give up on the suggestion that he might become the husband of this cold country's queen.

Despite the long-standing agreement between their families, Albert felt he had been kept waiting for an intolerably long time. He'd only agreed to come to England now with the intention of putting an end to all the speculation. He climbed out of the carriage 'with the quiet but firm resolution to declare' that, exhausted by delay and hesitation, he was going to withdraw 'entirely from the affair'.[6]

A proud man, Albert felt that he was becoming a laughing stock. Never mind that, as the second son, he wasn't the heir to his father Ernest, Duke of Coburg-Gotha. Never mind that Coburg – at 201 square miles – was merely half the size of the Isle of Wight. Never mind that its 40,000 inhabitants gave it a population comparable only to the town of Leicester. Albert still had a decent sense of his own worth.

The biographer A. N. Wilson points out that British historians writing about the nineteenth century ritually compare the small geographical size of German states like Coburg to English counties with the purpose of belittling them. And what Albert had to offer wasn't really his background in Coburg, even though his home state had an impressive reputation among its peers for being forward-thinking. Instead, Albert's qualifications as a queen's husband were his pure, ancient blood and his beautiful face and body. In this he was fulfilling the conventional role of a princess in a royal marriage. At 5 feet 7, he was just the right amount taller than Victoria. In modern times people might worry about the genetic consequences of first cousins mating, but in a century when people believed that they could only marry within their social class, the pool of potential spouses was smaller – for royalty, the pool was a puddle – and needs must. It would be impossible for Victoria to find a socially acceptable suitor to whom she wasn't in some way related.

And, perhaps most importantly, Albert had the innate confidence, almost the arrogance, of the Coburgs. Under the leadership of his and Victoria's common grandmother, the old Duchess Augusta, the sons and daughters of Coburg had not only survived, but thrived, upon the upheavals of the Napoleonic Wars. They'd made a string of dazzling marriages into the royal families of Europe. One of Albert's aunts had married the Russian Tsar's brother. An uncle would sire the Portuguese royal dynasty. And Albert was retracing the footsteps of his Uncle Leopold, husband to Victoria's cousin Charlotte, whose tragic early death had deprived Leopold of the chance of becoming Prince Consort of Great Britain.

Although he suffered so terribly from motion sickness, Albert had travelled far and wide since his ungracious visit to Kensington Palace for Victoria's seventeenth birthday. Now twenty years old, he'd been on the traditional educational Grand Tour, spending eighteen months at the University of Bonn, studying languages in Florence and then going on to Rome, where he'd met a serious German circle of antiquaries, archaeologists and artists who would become his taste-makers.[7] He'd been accompanied on his travels by his Uncle Leopold's sidekick Baron Stockmar, and by a young British army officer whose job (at which he had not been entirely successful) was to get Albert to speak English like a native.[8] Albert was a hard worker. 'Every morning by five o'clock,' he told his tutor, 'I sit down by my little student's lamp.'[9] He felt that his 'power of forming a right judgement' had been much increased by his travels.[10] He liked nothing better than to complete an essay on an abstract topic such as 'The Mode of Thought of the Germans', and he would stick at such projects 'despite all the distractions of our life'.[11]

It was clearly a serious young man, 'prudent, cautious and already very well informed', as Stockmar put it, who stalked stiffly towards the entrance to the castle's state apartments. There was a certain stiffness to his character, too, 'a thoughtfulness, quite unusual at so young age', which made him seem 'older than he is'.[12] But his precise, proud nature was countered by his wonderful body. 'Externally,' Stockmar explained, 'he has everything attractive to women.'[13] The many close descriptions of Victoria, treating her purely as a physical specimen, make her sound like an animal, but Albert comes in for the same treatment. Specifically, he was 'wide shouldered, rather too short in the neck – well proportioned as to the length of his limbs, though the knees are not quite cleanly knit'. His handsome face was pretty much 'impossible to resist'.[14] What a shame, then, that he'd come to Windsor to break his unspoken engagement.

Inside the castle, waiting at the top of the Grand Staircase beneath the lofty lantern roof rising far above, stood a pale young woman of twenty. Windsor tradition demanded that Victoria stand 'in the entrance at the head of her family and household' to receive important visitors, the stairs below lined with her red-clad Yeoman Warders (or 'Beef Eaters', as she called them).[15] Albert and Ernest now had to climb up this immense flight of steps, built by the architectural magician George IV, beneath the pressure of the gaze of Victoria and her court. The theatrical setting put extra weight upon this reunion of the three cousins after three years, and made it strikingly clear that one of them was now a queen.

Victoria herself was feeling uncharacteristically nervous and lethargic. She had no insight into Albert's current state of mind. They'd once exchanged cousinly letters, but after her accession the correspondence was broken off on the grounds of propriety.

And now she was very anxious that he should like her and, despite her own earlier equivocation, marry her. Once she had come around to the idea that she needed a husband, there really was no other option for her. She told Melbourne that she 'heard Albert's praises on all sides, and that he was very handsome'.[16] She'd grown impatient for his arrival, which she'd expected much earlier. She considered that Albert hadn't shown 'much *empressement* to come here, which rather shocks me'.[17] For his part, Melbourne was secretly jealous. 'I do not like the Duke of Coburg,' he grumbled in private, and 'we have Coburgs enough.' But then, he was resigned to what must happen. Victoria unmarried had become such 'a troublesome commodity'.[18]

Standing there at the head of the stairs, flanked by beefeaters, Victoria was feeling cold, and headachey, and was worried about the 'unwholesome' effects of the previous day's pork.[19] She'd been out that afternoon, touring the park in a pony carriage and visiting her castle's piggery, followed, as always, by a crowd of courtiers.[20] She was growing bored of this sort of thing, which had once amused her so much after the 'System'. Victoria believed that she was ready for a change, a more serious mode of life.

When her 'dear cousins' at last reached the top of the Grand Staircase, she found her hopes confirmed. They might very well be able to save her from herself. They were 'looking both very well, and much improved', she thought, far better than three years ago.[21] 'It was with some emotion that I beheld Albert,' she later confided to her journal, 'who is <u>beautiful</u>.'[22] Perhaps everything would be all right. She took them through to meet her mother, their aunt, who understood exactly what was in play. 'My heart felt very anxious when I looked at V & Albert,' she wrote in her diary that evening, 'they are both still so young.'[23]

The boys were spared the agony of a late and formal dinner of the kind that Albert hated, having the excuse that their formal court uniforms had not yet been unpacked. They went off to the 'three charming rooms' they'd been given, overlooking the park.[24] But Victoria insisted that they come into the drawing room and join the court after dinner in their travelling clothes.[25] This was a mistake, for the evening was deeply disappointing. Melbourne thought the two boys 'very sleepy', while he himself drank more liquor than Victoria thought good for him.[26]

And all this time, Albert seemed strangely chilly. In reality, he was simply trying to find the right moment to explain to Victoria that their match was off. He braced himself for 'telling her . . . she must understand that he could not now wait for a decision, as he had done at a former period, when this marriage was first talked about'.[27] His coldness left her in a quandary. How could she show suitable maidenly modesty, yet also signal to this beautiful man that her feelings had changed, and that she no longer saw him as just a cousin? He wasn't going to make it easy.

Victoria had to discover some means of getting a message to him. She felt it necessary to write to Uncle Leopold to tell him how the reunion was progressing. Albert's '*beauty*' is '*most striking*', she informed her uncle, but in the letter the 'cousins' were still just 'cousins' to her: a pair, companions, whose presence was 'amiable' and 'delightful' but in no way romantic. The two of them, she told Leopold, were together at the piano 'playing some Symphonies of Haydn under me at this very moment'.

You can almost imagine Victoria pausing, at that point, with her pen in the air. Haydn. Music. Silent Albert could only make stilted conversation, but he was 'passionately fond' of music.[28] This was something they still had in common. Perhaps she should employ the piano. On the second evening, she arranged dancing and stood up with him, twice, in a quadrille. As she clasped his hand, released it, seized it again as the dance required, he began to understand that something was different, and that he was wanted after all.

In the end, Albert never found the correct opening to explain that he wasn't going to marry her. Three days after her cousins' arrival at Windsor, on 13 October, Victoria felt it was going well enough to tell those around her of her intentions. She admitted to Melbourne that she had 'a good deal changed [her] opinion (as to marrying)'.[29]

Melbourne, perceptive as ever, could see exactly what was up. The courtship was 'evidently taking the course which I expected', he wrote, 'he seems a very agreeable young man, he is certainly a very good looking one.'[30] Along with writing his essays, Albert had also been polishing up his manners in the drawing rooms of Europe. He'd 'become more lively than he was, and that sits well on him'.[31] As they danced, and sat, and talked, Victoria was eyeing up every feature, assessing his 'beautiful blue eyes' and 'exquisite nose'; his 'pretty mouth with delicate mustachios' and his 'beautiful figure, broad in the shoulders and a fine waist'.[32] It really was as if she were measuring him up as the father of her children.

But Albert was still a little slow to respond to what Victoria was saying with her heartfelt playing and her speaking looks. She found the whole business 'agitating', and a cause of growing anxiety. 'It makes you ill,' said Melbourne, 'very naturally'. He could see that she was suffering, sick with suspense. A woman, he told her, 'cannot stand alone for long'. He advised her just to get on with it, and to propose.

Her mentor's approval set the final seal on the matter for Victoria. For his own part, the old premier was quietly devastated. He told her, in the same conversation, that he was 'quite a monogamist'.[33] For a long time, now, he had been monogamous with her, giving her all his time, his energy and his late-life love.

That very evening of her conversation with Melbourne, Victoria sent a more explicit message to Albert. She got Lehzen (still the person Victoria trusted the most) to tell Albert's equerry, Baron von Alvensleben, that she had almost decided to choose him as her future husband, and would 'probably make her declaration' to him in person very soon.[34] Victoria knew the message had been received. That evening, as they said goodnight in the drawing room, Albert pressed her hand with 'particular significance'.

Despite that special squeeze of the hand, Victoria was still uncharacteristically jittery on Tuesday 15 October. After all, it was possible to misinterpret a handshake. It was, as she put it, 'a nervous thing' to propose to a man. But Victoria had come to realise that even if Albert was gradually thawing, he 'would never have taken such a liberty as to propose to the Queen of England'.[35]

She steeled herself with the thought that if she had done this a year ago it would have prevented the unpleasant business of having to watch Flora die. 'Had she been engaged to the Prince a year sooner,' Victoria explained in later life, 'she would have escaped many trials.'[36] Victoria often used the third person like this to describe her own actions as queen.

That Tuesday morning Albert went out hunting. Once again, she had to wait for him, unable to settle to anything until he came back to the castle. At last she spotted him from her closet window, charging 'up the hill at an immense pace' on horseback. As was customary on important days in her life, Victoria wrote to her sister Feodore. Then she sent a message summoning Albert to her room.

In public, Victoria would be very careful to indicate that she was greatly troubled by the indelicacy of taking the initiative like this. In a book about Albert's life, which Victoria essentially wrote herself although it did not appear under her name, she described how readers could 'well understand any little hesitation and delicacy she may have felt' in proposing. Her position was painful, she suggested, as it was 'the privilege and happiness of a woman to have her hand sought in marriage'.[37]

But that was Victoria writing for public consumption. In her private journal, she did not beat around the bush. When talking the previous day to Melbourne, she'd asked him 'if I hadn't better tell Albert of my decision soon?'[38] (I love the 'tell' in that sentence.) 'My mind is quite made up,' she informed Uncle Leopold, 'and I told Albert this morning of it.'[39] The one concession she made was to prepare a speech in German, 'since she knew Albert was at a disadvantage in English.'[40] She even, contrary to expectation, gave *him* a ring.[41]

But once Victoria had taken the plunge and committed herself, and after Albert of course had said 'yes', she transformed herself into the socially acceptable, blushing maiden of romantic fiction:

we embraced each other over and over again, and he was so kind, so affectionate; oh! to <u>feel</u> I was, and am, loved by <u>such</u> an Angel as Albert, was <u>too great delight</u> to describe! he is <u>perfection</u>; perfection in every way, – in beauty – in everything! I told him I was quite unworthy of him and kissed his dear hand.[42]

It was a passage fitting for a Victorian heroine, submitting herself to the greater goodness of her man. She made herself comfortable with the unwomanliness of her actions by convincing herself that it was Albert who was making a sacrifice. Subsuming herself to him was how she justified, in her mind, the two opposing roles of queen and wife.

Over time Albert would come to believe this too; that he was the giver, not the receiver. But now, in that Windsor Castle closet, he was bewildered. It had all been so quick. The interview was over in twenty minutes. Albert was commanded to go to tell Lehzen, and his brother. And just one hour later, Victoria recorded in her journal, she was discussing the whole business in a much longer conversation with Melbourne. Her engagement wasn't even the first topic they discussed. First of all, she made sure that her Prime Minister 'was well and had slept well', and then, with wonderful British sangfroid, they 'talked of the weather'. Only then did she break it to him that she was engaged. He approved, if for characteristically worldly reasons. 'You can then (when married),' he said, 'do much more what you like.'

An hour later Victoria was lunching with her mother, who, they all agreed, was not to be told of the engagement until the public announcement. That night the queen sat next to Melbourne as usual. It is devastating to read in her journal her record of his reaction to events, although she herself was blind to his pain. He was realising that she had, in effect, at long last broken up with him, and complimented her on her engagement 'with tears in his eyes'. And then he pointed to a brooch she had given him, depicting a little golden hand. As Victoria explains:

I told him if the little gold hand I gave him broke, I would give him another; 'It won't break,' said Lord M. He always wears it.

So the heart of Lord M. was broken, and Victoria's overflowed, and, then, to cap it all, Lord Palmerston talked boringly of peasants, and 'dear Albert was obliged to go away for a moment as his nose bled'.[43] With bathos and with bleeding, thus Victoria concluded her entry in her journal for the day she made her proposal.

But how did Albert experience the same day? His own account tells how 'Victoria declared her love for me, and offered me her hand, which I seized in both mine and pressed tenderly to my lips.'[44]

Despite all this tender pressing and kissing, Albert felt out of his depth. 'I ought to be gay and carefree at this joyful event,' he told his father, 'and yet I feel sad. I don't myself know why.'[45] He understood that he was not of a 'demonstrative nature', and he now found himself 'at a loss to believe that such affection should be shown to me . . . seriously . . . I am too bewildered.'[46] But he was moved by the strength of Victoria's obvious passion and 'the joyous openness of manner' with which she told him of it. 'I was quite carried away by it,' he explained.[47] Dr Clark was asked his opinion on whether Albert was in love. His conclusion was negative. In Clark's view, everyone at Windsor Castle could see that Victoria was 'doting and attached to him, and cannot bear him out of her sight'. In return, though, Clark believed that Albert only 'liked her'.[48]

The evening of the engagement, both Coburg princes, Albert and Ernest, put on 'Windsor Uniform' for the first time. This was a suit of dark blue with red facings, worn only by those connected to the royal family, and to be invited to wear it was a particular privilege. The dinner consisted of lamb cutlets, and a wonderful dessert course of marrons glacés, jelly, blancmange, *gâteau à la Russe*, vanilla biscuits, peach cake and Macedonian flan. But even so, the meal was muted, for Albert was feeling guilty about the decision not to tell his future mother-in-law.[49] 'She cannot keep her mouth shut,' he justified himself, 'and might even make bad use of the secret.'[50] So there were no toasts to the engaged couple. Indeed, Albert probably looked askance at the wine in his intended's glass. People had already started to notice that she liked alcohol. Stockmar had taken it upon himself to warn Victoria that 'a Queen does not drink a bottle of wine at a meal'.[51] This is not quite as debauched as it sounds as the wine would have been much weaker than its modern equivalent, but Albert, with his fear of losing control, was always extremely temperate.

There were other early signs, for those who took the trouble to see them, that Victoria and Albert had very different temperaments. He knew already that she was 'fearfully obstinate', and found it disturbing.[52] He also hated the English habit of 'quizzing', or teasing. One of the maids-of-honour described Albert as having a 'complete absence of that frankness which was such a charm' in Victoria's own manner when she was relaxed, and his 'jokes were heavy and lumbering'.[53]

Historian Marina Warner correctly identifies a significant difference between their two characters. Victoria's greatest gift was transparency, honesty and communication: hence her journal. Albert, on the other hand, was a private person.[54] Keeping most of his thoughts to himself, he's hard to come to know, and harder still to like, although it's easy to admire his logical, cerebral qualities.

So what did Albert see in his future wife? He clearly felt a certain amount of physical attraction. He found her 'very much improved', and she was rounder and more shapely than she had been when he had last seen her at seventeen.[55] The young queen's bust came in for particular paeans of praise. One American observer found it to be very good, 'like most Englishwomen's', while another complimented her 'neck and bosom – plump but not fat . . . I should say decidedly that she was quite pretty.'[56] 'I am come back quite a courtier & a bit of a lover,' wrote one gentleman, after meeting Albert's future wife. 'Though not a beauty nor a very good figure she is really in person and face & especially in eyes & complexion a very nice girl – & quite such as might tempt.'[57]

Albert also thought he would be marrying into money. Uncle Leopold had been rewarded for marrying Victoria's deceased elder cousin Charlotte with a wildly generous income of £50,000 a year, and Albert probably expected something similar. When Parliament in due course only voted him £30,000 annually, his fiancée was furious. 'I cried with rage,' Victoria told her diary, 'Monsters!'[58] Yet even £30,000 a year equated to the entire income of Albert's father's duchy.

But there were still many anomalies to his situation that Albert would have to work hard to swallow. Even as a very little boy, he had shown a 'great dislike to being in the charge of women'.[59] He liked 'above all things', wrote one of his friends, 'to discuss questions of public law and metaphysics'.[60] He continued to find it easier to talk to his betrothed of music, or art, or books, than feelings. Even holding hands was something of a challenge. Her 'hands were so little', Albert thought, 'he could hardly believe they *were* hands.'[61] As one artist observed, Victoria's hands were 'very pretty, the backs dimpled, and the fingers delicately shaped'.[62] But Albert's physical strength and her physical softness seemed only right. They were well briefed about the respective roles of a lady and her knight by their jointly admired Sir Walter Scott. 'The fine delicate fragile form' of the female, as Scott put it, required 'the support of the Master's muscular strength and masculine character'.[63]

And when it came to money, Victoria would in fact be the only married woman in the whole country who'd retain control over her own income and property.[64] This was important. The reason Albert had nearly given up on the courtship was because it placed him 'in a very ridiculous position'.[65] Even now, everyone would know that he wouldn't really be master in his own household. Albert would also have to deal with the uncensored British press, which would depict him as a stud bull, good merely for the process of reproduction. And then again, there was the distressing fact that she'd been the one to speak first. 'Since the Queen did herself for a husband "propose",' ran a London ballad,

> the ladies will all do the same, I suppose;
> Their days of subserviency now will be past,
> For all will 'speak first' as they always did last![66]

In other words, it was a complete inversion of the natural order. It was a man's job to worry about wealth and worldly success, and a woman's merely to adorn him. A contemporary advice book said that 'a contented mind, an enlightened intellect, a chastened spirit, and an exemplary life' were all that a lady was required to bring to the altar.[67] The printers of London would mock Albert merrily while making as much money as they could. 'Vill you buy the *poortreat*,' was one particular print-seller's cry that assaulted the ears of Londoners, 'of the wonderful furriner vot's to have our beautiful Queen for his loving and confectionery wife?'[68]

And one final aspect of the 'wonderful furriner's' anxiety was the prospect of parting from his home, and from the person to whom he'd previously been closest: his brother. Ernest was a pallid, fretful figure at the Windsor Castle engagement dinner. While Albert was sexually inexperienced, almost prudish, Ernest, on the other hand, had in his private life followed their father's dissipated example. 'Poor Ernest has been suffering since Wednesday last with the jaundice,' Victoria wrote, 'which is very distressing.'[69] She would have been more distressed still had she known that Ernest was in truth suffering from venereal disease. There was a striking contrast between the two brothers: so close, yet so different.

Albert therefore had much on his mind. But Victoria at least was uncomplicatedly glad. Even an ordinary 'poor girl has not much free choice', she thought, when it came to choosing a husband, and for a princess it was even harder: 'a very sad, bad lookout!'[70] But now – and for ever – she was persuaded that she *had* chosen for herself. She chose to be delighted by Albert, basking in the luxury of his love and attention. 'These last few days,' she told her Uncle Leopold, 'have passed like a dream to me . . . I do feel very, very happy.'[71]

Albert would frequently find it easiest to meet his future wife's emotional expectations through presents, and he came up with a plan to give her a lover's gift of a brooch with enamel orange blossom, symbol both of chastity and of weddings.[72] But late that night of his engagement he also sat down to write her a letter expressing the words he so often found it difficult to speak out loud.

It was to be the first of many such paper expressions of love, warning, admonition and, eventually, of anger, which would travel down the corridors of Windsor Castle between their two rooms. Yet this first one, written by Albert when he was still the supplicant, not yet the master, when everything still lay ahead of them, was the most perfect. 'I hardly know how to answer you,' he admitted. 'How is it that I have deserved so much love, so much affection? . . . in body and soul ever your slave, your loyal ALBERT.'[73]

Victoria had not cried at her accession, or indeed at her coronation. But alone in her own room at Windsor Castle that night, reading her first love letter, she did at last shed tears.

II

Wedding Day: three palaces, 10 February 1840

'Oh! this was the happiest day of my life!'[1] Victoria was writing about her wedding. It was a wet February morning at Buckingham Palace, a mere four months after her engagement. Even the lace that Victoria was to wear on her cream silk dress was older than that: she'd ordered it before Albert had accepted.[2]

The announcement of the engagement had wonderfully increased the standing of the monarchy. Then – as now – the births, deaths and marriages of the royal family provided both a background beat to everyone else's lives, and a sense of renewal. The very fact that Victoria was to be married made her more attractive. There was a new 'blush on her cheek', thought the clerk to her Privy Council, 'which made her look handsomer and more interesting'.[3]

'The last time I slept alone,' Victoria wrote in her journal of the night just past.[4] Having sought solitude for so much of her childhood, she was now desperate to be alone no more. As soon as she opened her eyes, she at once wrote a note to Albert, in the German he found reassuring: 'Dearest, How are you today and have you slept well? . . . What weather!'[5] She folded it up into a tiny triangle, addressed it to 'His Royal Highness The Prince' from 'The Queen' and sent it with a servant along the palace corridors to his room. This was the last time she would need to write to Albert for a long period, as they would be much together, and the note forms the climax to several months of correspondence. Much of it regards finance and titles and politics, but the queen nevertheless wrote on a variety of incongruously girlish pads of paper, some with purple Pierrots, others with pink edging.

Albert, too, began his wedding day with his pen in his hand. But his heart was in the Germany from which he had only returned two days previously. 'In less than three hours,' he wrote to his grandmother, 'I shall be standing before the altar with my dear bride.' His nerves are apparent. 'I must end,' he concludes, as time began to run out. 'May God be my helper!'[6]

Although Albert was exactly the same age as Victoria, and although he had travelled further and seen and learned much more, he was less well prepared for public life. He'd sat out his engage-ment 'rather exasperated about various things, and pretty full of grievances'.[7] He already had quite a long list of grudges against his new country. He hadn't been allowed to appoint German staff to his household, Parliament had voted him a smaller than expected income and his credentials as a Protestant had been questioned.

Albert would have liked a smaller, more private wedding. But another of his grievances was having to share his wife-to-be with her subjects. Not even the queen was able to get her own wish for a traditional royal wedding, held in the evening behind palace doors. It was Melbourne who insisted that the ceremony should take place in daylight. Victoria would travel through the park from Buckingham Palace to St James's Palace as a bride-to-be, then back to Buckingham Palace as a married woman, then on to Windsor Castle in the evening. This meant there would be no fewer than three separate opportunities for her subjects to see her.

The date and time of the ceremony was announced in the *London Gazette* five days in advance so that people could make their plans.[8] The papers were pleased. 'She is kept by the nation as a spectacle,' claimed the *Penny Satirist*, establishing a current of thought that would flow through Victoria's whole reign, 'and it is right that she should be seen. In fact it is her duty to come out and show herself, that we may have value for our money.'[9] But while Melbourne was gleefully calculating the political gain to be had from crowds of citizens cheering their sovereign on her wedding day, Victoria was annoyed. 'Everything,' she grumbled, 'was always made so uncomfortable for Kings and Queens.'[10]

And not even Melbourne could persuade her to compile the guest list for the ceremony in the manner he thought best. Still displeased by the incident with her bedchamber ladies; still smarting from the House of Commons' failure to vote Albert the income she thought he deserved, Victoria refused to invite more than a couple of her hated Tories. This was widely considered to be politically inexpedient. 'Nothing could be more improper and foolish than to make this a mere Whig party,' wrote the critical 'Gruncher'.[11] In his opinion, Victoria's insistence on inviting only her friends to her wedding was 'wilful, obstinate and wrong-headed'.[12]

And yet on this point Victoria would not budge. 'It is MY marriage,' she said, digging in her heels, 'and I will only have those who can sympathise with me.'[13]

Victoria had her breakfast at nine o'clock, and to judge from past form it was a large one. She judged 'a good breakfast' to consist, for example, 'of a mutton chop and mashed potatoes &c'.[14] But avoiding luncheon had paid off. She had dropped down from her heaviest of 8 stone 13 pounds in 1838 to just 7 stone 2 a year later.[15] She hadn't been particularly well in the weeks before the wedding, exhibiting signs of stress, 'nervous and feverish, so much so that they fancied she was going to have the measles'.[16]

Once her mother had finally been allowed to know of Victoria's engagement, there had been something of a rapprochement between them. Conroy had eventually agreed to leave court, and Victoire was much relieved. Now she came in to Victoria's rooms to give her daughter a 'Nosegay of orange flowers'.[17] 'My beloved Child enters a new life,' Victoire thought. 'She does not know how I love her & what I feel.'[18] But while Victoria's journal entry does mention her mother's flowers, it doesn't dwell on them, and quickly sweeps on to say that immediately afterwards 'my dearest kindest Lehzen gave me a dear little ring'. The governess and her gift was obviously more warmly received.[19]

Even though she had written to him, Victoria also met Albert face-to-face. She knew that she needed to brace him up for the big day. He had only come back to Buckingham Palace from Coburg a couple of days previously. A glittering levee of courtiers had assembled to meet him, but as soon as his carriage was announced Victoria threw ceremony out of the window. 'Nobody could conceive what she was going to do,' it was reported, 'and before anyone could stop her, she had run downstairs and was in his arms.'[20] This passionate, enthusiastic Victoria was her very best self.

Once she had reassured Albert both on paper and in person, it was time to get ready. She had her hair dressed in loops upon her cheeks, and a 'wreath of orange flowers put on.' Her dress was 'a white satin gown, with a very deep flounce of Honiton lace, imitation of old'.[21]

This simple cream gown of Victoria's was a dress that launched a million subsequent white weddings. She broke with monarchical convention by rejecting royal robes in favour of a plain dress, with just a little train from the waist at the back to make it appropriate for court wear.[22] It was a signal that on this day she wasn't Her Majesty the Queen, but an ordinary woman. She wore imitation orange blossom in her hair in place of the expected circlet of diamonds. She'd had the lace for the dress created by her mother's favoured lacemakers of Honiton, in Devon, as opposed to the better-known artisans of Brussels. A royal commission like this was a welcome boost – then as now – to British industry.[23] This piece of lace would become totemic for Victoria. She would preserve it, treasure it and indeed wear it until the end of her life.

Victoria had personally designed the dresses of her bridesmaids, giving a sketch to her Mistress of the Robes, still Harriet, Duchess of Sutherland. Harriet – rich, beautiful, Whiggish – had by now become the closest thing to a female friend that Victoria allowed herself. Her courtiers noticed Albert's wish that she should place a greater distance between herself and them. They sensed his desire that she become 'pretty indifferent' as to which maid-of-honour or lady-in-waiting was on duty, being on 'more natural terms' only with her lower servants.[24] 'No familiarity,' Victoria schooled herself, 'no loud laughing . . . watch yourself, and keep yourself under restraint.'[25] She could well have felt threatened by her Mistress of the Robes, whom, it was said, 'moves like a goddess' and 'looks like a Queen'.[26] But Victoria was always conspicuously generous to people more beautiful than herself, and made Harriet an exception among her staff in treating her more like a comrade.

Since her accession, Victoria had been granted a dress allowance roughly twice as large as her predecessor William IV's, but she and Harriet thought that how they spent this public money was entirely their own affair. Harriet engaged tradespeople including dressmakers, a habitmaker, furrier, silk mercer, hosier, glover, perfumer and a specialist 'umbrella maker'. 'Her Majesty,' she wrote, loftily, when the Treasury wanted to know where the money had gone, 'does not wish to send some of the Bills (like those of the Dressmaker's etc.) to the office.' Abstracts only would be provided.[27]

But whatever Victoria's private feelings, her dress was certainly for public consumption. 'I saw the Queen's dress at the palace,' wrote one eager letter-writer, 'the lace was beautiful, as fine as a cobweb.' She wore no jewels at all, this person's account continues, 'only a bracelet with Prince Albert's picture'.[28] This was in fact completely incorrect. Albert had given her a huge sapphire brooch, which she wore along with her 'Turkish diamond necklace and earrings'.[29] It was the beginning of a lifetime trend for Victoria's clothes to be reported as simpler, plainer, less ostentatious than they really were. The reality was that they were not quite as ostentatious *as people expected for a queen*. This is really what they meant by their descriptions of her clothes as austere, and pleasingly middle-class. In other countries, members of the middle classes would join the working classes on streets and at barricades and bring monarchies tumbling down. But in Britain, part of the reason this did not happen is that Victoria, her values and her low-key style appealed with peculiar power to the respectable slice of opinion at society's upper middle.

And so, dressed but not overdressed, the unqueenly looking queen was ready for her wedding day to begin.

At 11.45, Albert left Buckingham Palace with his father and brother to travel through St James's Park in a procession of nine carriages. They were heading to the Chapel Royal of St James's Palace, originally built by Inigo Jones as a private Catholic chapel for the French queen Henrietta Maria, but long since brought into the Church of England. Anti-Catholic feeling had been behind the slanders that Albert, a Lutheran and a foreigner, therefore probably wasn't a true Protestant. Before 1828 Catholics, even powerful ones like the Duke of Norfolk, were barred from holding public office, and anti-papistry was poisoning England's troubled relationship with Ireland. As Albert was marrying the Head of the Church of England, he ostentatiously held his green-velvet-covered Protestant prayer-book in his hand.[30]

Fifteen minutes afterwards, Victoria followed in his wake, travelling with her mother and the Duchess of Sutherland in the seventh of seven more carriages. The ride took her through enormous crowds of people, even though it was 'a dreadful day – torrents of rain, and violent gusts of wind'.[31] The park was completely packed, to the extent that 'there was scarcely room to get along at a foot's pace'.[32] Despite the weather the spectators were in a mellow mood, and *The Times* reported that when some of them were catapulted into the crowd by the breaking of the branch of a tree they'd climbed, the accident was greeted only with 'roars of laughter'.[33] The gathering presented a fine opportunity for commerce. One ballad-seller offered for purchase printed lyrics for as many as twenty-three different songs about the wedding of the queen.[34]

Arriving at the rambling, red-brick St James's Palace, Victoria was taken to an upper dressing room. Here, her waiting bridesmaids were highly relieved to see her. These twelve tense young ladies had been 'immured' in the room for an hour and a half. They'd been asked to arrive early, then had nothing to do but ogle the soldiers beneath the window, 'who looked a good deal rusted by the rain'.[35]

The identities of these bridesmaids had been a matter of much moment. Albert had tried to suggest that some of those proposed were inappropriate because their mothers were not respectable. Among their number was Lady Sarah Villiers, whose mother, Lady Jersey, had been one of George IV's mistresses. Lady Eleanor Paget's parents had both been divorced. Lady Ida Hay was the illegitimate grandchild of William IV. But Melbourne quietly overruled Albert, pointing out that there simply weren't twelve young ladies with completely blameless mothers to be found in the whole of the aristocracy. It was more evidence of the degeneracy of the culture of the preceding court, to which Victoria – and even more particularly Albert – would bring a moral cleanse.

The bridesmaids wore white roses around their heads, with further blooms pinned to the tulle overskirts of their dresses. Victoria's opinion was that they 'had a beautiful effect', but others disagreed.[36] Used to seeing golden tassels, velvet robes and colourful jewels at royal ceremonies, onlookers thought that the trainbearers 'looked like village girls'.[37] The pale colour scheme was even carried through to the complexion of Victoria's face. One of the young ladies, as she shook out the bride's skirts, noticed that the queen was 'as white as a sheet'.[38]

Inside the chapel, galleries had been erected to cram the congregation into every upper corner. The chapel's furnishing scheme of dark panelling, crimson cushions and yellow fringes was pulled together by a 'rich Brussels carpet'.[39] The guests in their gowns of 'white, amber, crimson, purple, fawn' sported 'wedding favours' or bows of white satin ribbon or gold lace topped with orange blossom.[40] 'We were miserably cold,' complained one American invitee, with the bare arms and neck required by formal court dress, and nothing to keep her head warm but the regulation white plumes of feathers.[41]

The guests passed the time watching the arrival of 'embroidered heralds', 'robed prelates' and 'surpliced singing-boys', but they were getting bored as well as cold by the time a 'flourish of drums and trumpets' announced that the ceremony was beginning.[42] With relief, they saw Albert enter to the strains of 'See the Conquering Hero Comes' and welcomed him with applause and handkerchief-waving. Albert was wearing tight white breeches with his red coat; his neck was constrained by his high golden collar, and his shoulders were braced to bear the heavy chain of the Order of the Garter. He didn't much look like a conquering hero.[43] The best that one reporter could find to say was that he was no longer visibly seasick, as he had been upon his arrival in London. It was thought that the ladies, however, were pleased by his 'pale and pensive' looks.[44]

Beneath his jewelled chain he wore the uniform of a field marshal, with white satin rosettes on his shoulders.[45] Albert was wearing the clothes that 'no doubt he borrowed to be married in', sniffed Florence Nightingale, who was staying with her aunt in London.[46] She was joining in a general disparagement of Coburg's relative penury, and Albert must have been all too aware that he was not particularly popular. His departure from Coburg had been an occasion of celebration: his people could see that their boy was going up in the world. But in Britain, Coburg hardly counted at all. One member of the congregation thought it would be difficult not to laugh at the point in the ceremony when Albert was supposed to endow his wife 'with all his worldly goods'.[47] As Albert complained to Victoria, all this mockery 'makes my position here no very pleasant one'.[48]

She was just a short distance behind. As she left the dressing room, her trainbearers walking behind her in pairs, she passed crowds of servants, courtiers and guests, 'ranged on seats one higher than the other, as also in the Guard room, and by the Staircase, – all very friendly'.[49] Unlike Albert, she'd learned that she must walk with dignity, 'very slowly, giving ample time for all the spectators to gratify their curiosity, and certainly she was never before more earnestly scrutinized'. She was used to it, but even so people saw her shaking.

At the coronation her train had been too long to handle, but now there was the opposite problem. The long back part of Victoria's white satin skirt, trimmed with orange blossom, was 'rather too short for the number of young ladies who carried it' and they ended up 'kicking each other's heels and treading on each other's gowns'.[50] Even so, after a discordant fanfare of trumpets, they got Victoria up the aisle. At its head, she 'threw herself on her knees at the foot of the altar as if her whole soul was in the petition she was offering up for a blessing'.[51] It brought a wobble to many a lip. 'She looked very pale and pretty, and her hands trembled very much,' recorded one spectator.[52]

Victoria now takes up the description of what she saw before her: 'At the Altar, to my right, stood my precious Angel; Mama was on my left . . . Lord Melbourne stood close to me with the Sword of State. The Ceremony was very imposing, and fine and simple, and I think <u>ought</u> to make an everlasting impression.'[53] For her whole life she would favour a 'simple' religious ceremony and wasn't attracted by the contemporary High Church movement towards Rome. She would even, in due course, cause some official dismay by taking part in the 'low' services of the Presbyterian Church of Scotland.

The words were exactly the same as any other wedding ceremony, and the couple just called themselves 'Albert' and 'Victoria'. When the Archbishop asked Victoria if she promised to 'obey' her husband, he got a strong, loud, positive response.[54] She *wanted* to obey. And everyone present could clearly see this intention. 'She turned her sweet & innocent looks upon him,' wrote on observer, 'with an expression that brought tears into every eye . . . they left the chapel together hand in hand.'[55] Royal marriages were not expected to contain this element of giddy high romance, but Victoria's mother had taught her that this was how love should look. It just remained to be seen how sustainable this mode of marriage would be for a royal life.

At a quarter to one, the firing of guns alerted the whole of London to the very moment Albert 'placed the ring on the finger'.[56] Even the weather took notice, and 'a nice gleam of sunshine appeared'. The nervous entrance of the groom and his pent-up bride had been difficult to watch, 'for I know not which looked the most uncomfortable', but now, as they went out, 'they each had a colour; and with countenances much brightened'.

There were, however, some unhappy faces in the congregation. Victoria's mother 'looked disconsolate and distressed', people saw, with 'the traces of tears on her countenance'.[57] She had reason to cry. At each step of her daughter's progress – accession, coronation, marriage – Victoire's role had shrunk. She was being pushed further and further away from the power she had once thought might be hers. And now even Lehzen too was being superseded. Her pale face attracted 'considerable attention' in the dark corner where she sat, 'white as marble, which appeared all the whiter by contrast with her black velvet Spanish hat'.[58] Victoria's life as daughter and surrogate daughter was now over. Victoire realised this, but Lehzen did not, and would find it painful to learn.

Next came the signing of the register, then it was time to return to Buckingham Palace. The bridesmaids 'consigned the train to Prince Albert's care, who seemed a little nervous about getting into the carriage with a lady with a tail six yards long'.[59] And at last she and he were alone together, for the short journey to the wedding breakfast. Again the 'crowd was immense', Victoria recorded, and the palace 'full of people, they cheered us again and again'.[60] Victoria and Albert were 'observed to squeeze each other's hands'.[61] It was a signal that they should escape, to sit on the sofa in her dressing room for half an hour. Here they exchanged solemn words. Albert decreed that there should 'never be any secrets between us'. Much later, years later, when many things in their world had changed, Victoria added a poignant comment to her record of this moment. '& so it was,' she wrote.[62]

But Victoria had her social duty to do, and a feast was waiting below. 'I talked to all after the breakfast,' she recorded, 'and to Lord Melbourne whose fine coat I praised.' She and Albert drank a reconciliatory 'glass of wine' with Melbourne, and he 'seemed much affected by the whole'.[63] Then she went to change, putting on 'a white silk gown trimmed with swansdown', and a going-away bonnet trimmed with false orange flowers that still survives to this day at Kensington Palace. Then 'we took leave of Mama and drove off . . . I and Albert alone, which was so delightful'.[64]

They travelled to Windsor followed by just a small escort of three other coaches.[65] In one of them came Lehzen. The scale of the ceremony was tapering off, but there was still 'an immense crowd of people outside the Palace' and the roads were lined all the way to Windsor with spectators whose cheers were 'quite deafening'.[66] No fewer than thirty triumphal arches had been constructed across the road for the newly-weds to drive beneath. People also placed cut-out paper shades in their windows all along Windsor High Street so that the town glowed with 'crowns, stars and all the brilliant devices which gas and oil could supply'.[67]

Victoria's cheering 'subjects took the rain as quietly as if it had been a passing April shower'.[68] The unpopularity she'd earned over Flora had passed like a shower too. This wedding was wonderful politics. Unlike previous royal weddings, writes historian Paula Bartley, it was 'a demonstration of love and respectability'. This was a completely new way of doing things, yet done with such panache that it seemed like things had always been done this way. It was, in Eric Hobsbawm's phrase, 'the invention of tradition'.[69]

At last, by seven, Victoria and Albert were back at Windsor, and retreated to what was now their joint suite of rooms. 'After looking about our rooms for a little while, I went and changed my gown,' Victoria tells us, putting on her third outfit of the day. Any of their days together would be incomplete without music, and when she went through to Albert's new sitting room, she found him playing the piano. 'He had put on his Windsor coat,' she says, and 'he took me on his knee, and kissed me.' The gown that Victoria wore that evening was possibly the plainer, and very slender, cream silk one surviving in the Royal Collection with a traditional association with her wedding evening. If she did wear it for that first dinner together, then she could hardly have eaten a thing. It laced even tighter than her wedding dress.

But she did not eat, because reaction from all the excitement was setting in. 'We had our dinner in our sitting room,' Victoria records, but her 'sick headache' meant that she couldn't manage the cherry soufflé.[70] They talked 'of many family affairs'.[71] Her headache meant that she was obliged to lie down 'for the remainder of the evening, on the sofa'. Even so, it was delightful:

> I never, never spent such an evening!! My dearest dearest dear Albert sat on a footstool by my side, and his excessive love and affection gave me feelings of heavenly love and happiness, I never could have hoped to have felt before! He clasped me in his arms, and we kissed each other again and again!

But there would be no ritual undoing by the groom of his bride's ethereal gown. That, as always, had to be done by Victoria's dressers. 'At ½ p.10 I went and undressed and was very sick,' she says. These women, the bedrock of her life, ever present, ever watchful, must have been with her as she finished retching and went into the bedchamber, where 'we both went to bed; (of course in one bed), to lie by his side, and in his arms, and on his dear bosom'.[72] Their wedding night continued the serious, almost sombre mood of the evening. There was 'purity and religion in it all', Victoria remembered afterwards, recording that 'we did not sleep much'.[73]

The next morning, 'poor Albert was feeling very poorly,' Victoria reported, '& had to remain quiet in his room.' But later the very same day his social obligations once again began, with a dinner for ten.[74]

In fact, the honeymoon in Windsor would only last four days. Its shortness, and Victoria's public appearances during it, were seized upon as 'indelicate',[75] Albert would have liked to spend longer away, but his wife told him that they couldn't. 'I am the Sovereign,' she reminded him, and 'business can stop and wait for nothing.'[76]

Albert grumbled to a friend that he was 'only the husband, and not the master in the house.'[77] And yet, as a contemporary advice book put it, 'it is unquestionably the right of all men . . . to be treated with deference, and made much of in their own houses'.[78] According to the model of Victorian marriage, something here was amiss. Victoria had *said* one thing, she had promised to 'obey'. Yet she was *doing* another, placing her work before her husband. 'The Gruncher', hostile witness as he was, saw this clearly. Her strain and sickness in the weeks before the wedding, he thought, had been caused by doubts about Albert, by her 'dread of being thwarted, and her love of power, stronger than love'.[79] Albert swallowed the short honeymoon without making a fuss, but in fact he was merely biding his time before beginning to readjust the power balance between himself and his wife.

Even if she hardly valued it at the time, Victoria had lost something as well as gaining a husband and the prospect of the family life her childhood had lacked. Historian John Plunkett points out that this loss was symbolised in the changes now made at Madame Tussauds waxworks display. The coronation tableau was replaced in 1840 by a marriage group. Queen had been shrunk down to wife.[80]

12

'Oh Madam it is a Princess': Buckingham Palace, 21 November 1840

In the early hours of Saturday 21 November 1840, lights were lit at Buckingham Palace. Victoria's first labour had begun. But everyone's thoughts went back to another November night, almost exactly twenty-three years before. That was the night of the 'Triple Obstetrical Tragedy', deaths that had resulted in the Baby Race and Victoria's own conception.

The memory of what had gone wrong for the short-lived Princess Charlotte, the cousin Victoria never knew, placed extra pressure upon her first pregnancy. In childhood Victoria had loved visiting the English home of her Uncle Leopold at Claremont House in Surrey. There she would talk to 'dear old Louis', the former devoted dresser 'and friend' of Leopold's late wife. 'Old Louis' had been with Charlotte the night she'd died, and had much to tell Victoria about the cousin whose place she'd taken as queen.

The doctor overseeing Charlotte's fatal fifty-hour labour, Sir Richard Croft, afterwards came in for heavy criticism. He was berated for his failure to use forceps to get out Charlotte's stillborn son, and for the way he bled her heavily and denied her food. Harassed and depressed, Croft subsequently shot himself. By his corpse was found a copy of Shakespeare's plays, opened to reveal the line 'Fair Sir, God save you! Where is the Princess?'

As footmen from Buckingham Palace began to pound the knockers of homes across the capital in the darkness before dawn of 21 November 1840, Victoria's medical team must have been astonished to receive the message that labour had begun. No one was expecting the baby just yet.

Dr James Clark was woken up, as were the celebrated accoucheurs Dr Charles Locock and Dr Robert Ferguson. The latter had a sideline in mental health, and they were partners in 'the highest midwifery business in the metropolis'.[1] A messenger was also sent to Mr Richard Blagden. As a surgeon, he was socially inferior to the physicians. He had to be willing to get his hands dirty and, if necessary, cut a baby out. Mr Blagden was battle-hardened from his nights on duty at Queen Charlotte's Lying-In Hospital, the first in Britain 'to have compassion on unmarried women with their first child'.[2]

Hard upon the heels of any concern for the queen's well-being in the minds of these men must have been the fate of Sir Richard Croft, and what might happen to them if anything went wrong.

It wasn't the British way to announce a royal pregnancy, even though in the goldfish bowl of the palace Victoria's staff soon became aware of it. She conceived distressingly soon after the wedding. 'I was in for it at once,' she wrote, '& furious I was.' Perhaps it was the knowledge of Princess Charlotte's fate that had caused her anguish. She had 'the greatest horror of having children, and would rather have none'.[3] But she also knew that she had no choice, and indeed had a lifelong horror of birth control too. A queen 'never appears so queenly, so true a woman, as when surrounded by her children', wrote one Victorian educator.[4]

As early as the April following the February wedding, 'it was known & understood' by Victoria's household that she was 'in an interesting condition'.[5] Melbourne advised that she must continue to attend court events, even if she wasn't able to stand up – as etiquette required – for very long.

And it turned out that this first pregnancy of hers rather suited Victoria. She was 'wonderfully well', she claimed, 'really the Doctors say they never saw anybody so well . . . I take long Walks, some in the highest wind, every day, & am so active.'[6] Her pharmacist's

account book suggests that she suffered from the occasional headache, which was treated with 'cooling lotion' and – that universal
panacea – castor oil.[7] Contemporary medical advice recommended
that she avoid sexual intercourse and 'all masculine and fatiguing
employments'.[8] This particular author, Dr William Bull, was clearly
addressing the literate, middle-class readers who might buy his book:
working women simply had to go on working. But for those who
could afford doctors, the scandal of Charlotte's death had caused
something of an upheaval in medical practice. Charlotte had been
severely bled throughout her pregnancy and illness, but Dr Bull
now vigorously condemned the removal of blood.[9]

Friday, the day before Victoria's labour began, was in no way
remarkable. She spent it resting, writing letters, chatting to
Melbourne and playing Mozart on the piano.[10] She had dinner
with Lehzen, as usual, a meal of 'potage a la Tête de Veau' (beef
brain soup) and grouse.[11] She and Albert stayed up until nearly
eleven. It was only in the early hours of Saturday that she began
to feel 'very uncomfortable'. With some difficulty, she woke up
her husband. Dr Clark came into their bedroom at half past two,
but thought that it was a false alarm and went away again. It was
at four in the morning that Victoria again insisted, 'with great
firmness', that she needed her medical team.[12]

Dr Ferguson arrived at Buckingham Palace at six, and found his
colleagues already present in 'a little room, heated by insufferably
hot air and gas'. Because it was so early, both in the morning and
in the pregnancy, the doctors were disorganised, and had not agreed
who would do what. Victoria also allowed Lehzen to get involved
in the discussions, which quickly became unhelpful. 'We were left
to make out our respective positions during the very brunt of
attendance,' Ferguson admitted, 'a most unwise, and unsafe plan.'
He was cross because a few months previously he'd 'written to
Clark to ascertain what was expected from each of us – but with
no definite answer'.[13]

Dr Charles Locock, the head obstetrician, nevertheless managed
to soothe the patient. 'The Baby was on the way & everything

was all right,' he said. This was better. All she'd wanted was re-assurance. 'I did not feel at all nervous,' was Victoria's later claim.[14] For his part, Locock might well have felt uneasy on behalf of his short, small-boned patient, whose physique was not obviously suited to childbearing.

As well as displaying notable sangfroid, the young queen exhib-ited little of the vaunted Victorian quality of modesty. Later in life her views would change, but now, in her twenties, the queen's ease with her body rather shocked her doctors. It was customary, when a doctor arrived at a contemporary confinement, for him to request permission to 'make an examination' through a female friend of the patient. It was equally customary – 'from false modesty' – for this to be refused, until the pregnant woman's pains grew bad enough to destroy her inhibitions.[15] But concerns for Victoria's health throughout her childhood had got her thoroughly accus-tomed to doctors. This was even to the extent that Dr Locock, physician to the Westminster General Lying-In Hospital, found his royal patient's frankness rather distressing.

Locock had a reputation among his male companions as 'light hearted and genial, a pleasant, vivid talker, a lover of news, a good storyteller', and he doubtless owed some of his medical success 'to his social qualities'.[16] It's telling that he had specialised in midwifery for the better money, and unfortunately he is on record as trying to impress his high-society friends with gossip that was disrespectful and crude. His views were as frank as he claimed the queen herself to be. Every statement that he made, Locock declared, 'was invari-ably considered by Her Majesty in the least delicate sense'.[17] Garrulous, judgemental Locock does not give the impression of being on the same side as his patient. In later years, when chloroform was available to ease the pain, he thought it was wrong of Victoria to insist upon using it. It only made labour last longer, Locock thought.[18] He often found himself 'not a little digusted with the Queen's manner', and Victoria was clearly annoyed in return by her obstetrician's delicate doublespeak.[19] 'Those nasty doctors' was an item she once included in a list of the downsides of childbirth.[20]

Dr Locock was also indiscreet enough to share his views on his pregnant patient's shape, which he thought 'ugly & enormously fat'. She had left off wearing stays, becoming 'more like a barrel than anything else'.[21] Victoria herself, although she felt well, 'unhappily' had to admit that she was 'a <u>great</u> size'.[22] A fine cotton lawn petticoat from this early married period, which once had the same dimensions as her wedding dress, shows evidence of having been let out around its high empire waist, quite possibly to accommodate this pregnancy.[23] The work was done with tiny stitches as if by the needle of a fairy. There were many hands available in Victoria's wardrobe department, and indeed no shortage of clothes either. This particular petticoat survives because it was given away after becoming soiled with blood. She also had an expandable dressing gown for pregnancy, of thin white cotton, with 'gauging tapes' to widen the waist as pregnancy progressed.[24]

Once Victoria is married, we hear no more about her concerns over her weight or her appearance, just a frank acceptance that they were not perfect. 'God knows,' she would later exclaim, 'there is nothing to admire in my ugly old person.'[25] As a married woman, she had begun to feel more physically confident. This was Albert's doing. Since his unhappiness and uncertainty at the time of his whirlwind engagement, Albert had come to be delighted with his buxom little wife. Sculptor John Gibson in 1844 was commissioned to model Victoria in evening dress. He recorded how 'she came into the room accompanied by the Prince, who, like a fond young husband, had his arm round his wife's neck, and pointing to her shoulder said, "Mr. Gibson, you must give me this dimple."'[26]

Victoria's favourite portrait of herself was the so-called 'secret picture', which she commissioned from Franz Xaver Winterhalter without telling Albert in order to give it to him as a surprise gift. It shows her at twenty-four with a ripe, luscious body, plump white shoulders revealed, mouth very slightly and very sexily open. That was perhaps how Albert liked to see her, as his wife. However, in a self-portrait that Victoria would also sketch in her twenties, she shows herself looking much more stern and queenly. In this image, she has a dogged look of concentration, and seems tired, with the beginnings of a double chin. She was discovering that it was a pressing business being Albert's spouse, and hard to combine with the role of queen.[27]

Dr Locock found Albert much more congenial than his plain-speaking, plain-looking wife. When Victoria boasted of her ability to 'bear pain as well as other People', Dr Locock found that her husband held a contradictory view. Locock was slightly pleased to discover that Albert thought that when the pains began 'she would make a great *Rompos*'.[28]

But during her labour Victoria did not make a great *Rompos*; or, at least, no witnesses have recorded that she did. From 4 a.m. onwards, various people came and went from the room, a screen providing Victoria's bed with a modicum of privacy. Dr Locock also found her pragmatic about the need, according to royal trad-ition, to have witnesses to the birth. 'She would not care one single straw,' he thought, 'if the whole world was present.'[29]

The lesser doctors argued about who should and shouldn't be allowed in.[30] Albert remained present throughout, as did Mrs Lilly, a specialist nurse for newborns. Victoria's mother, who now lived elsewhere but who'd arrived at the palace before breakfast, had to wait outside, where her 'anxiety was <u>great</u> . . . How I would have liked to suffer for her.'[31]

Albert's witnessing of the births of his children was reported in the newspapers and considered laudable. This was how modern fathers were supposed to behave.[32] In due course Victoria would come to be unable to imagine giving birth without him, as he would always be present to 'direct every thing'.[33] This morning he was 'pale and obviously very anxious', with 'bloodshot eye, and haggard expression'. But Albert never lost his cool and there was nothing 'tumultuous' about his manner.[34] His talent for micro-managing was on full display, and he succeeded in easing the disagreements among the doctors. They had not yet 'quite found out how to treat me', Victoria complained afterwards. She took her own notes, in order to be able to pass them on to her medical team next time.[35]

Early on in labour, Victoria would have been given a dose of castor oil to empty her bowels, to avoid 'exceedingly disagreeable' consequences later. She would have worn her loose dressing gown over a chemise and bedgown 'folded up smoothly to the waist' and beneath that, 'a petticoat'. Stays were absent, despite the common belief among women that wearing them during labour would 'assist', by 'affording support'. The latest medical advice was that this was 'improper'.[36] The chemise that Victoria was wearing would acquire special lucky significance for her. Nine childbirths later, she'd still insist upon donning the exact same one.[37]

As the morning wore on, 'a dark, dull, windy, rainy day with smoking chimneys', the doctors began to grow worried.[38] It was taking longer than they would have liked. 'I began to believe that if not assisted,' Dr Ferguson admitted, the baby 'would be still born.'[39] He tried to go into the room in order to help, 'but Locock immediately vociferated that the Queen did not desire to have us'.[40] The 'disputes and squabbles', Victoria thought, were partly the result of her frantically anxious 'old governess who would meddle'. Lehzen was finding herself increasingly marginalised, now that Albert was on hand to manage every aspect of his wife's life.

The crowded room, the squabbling doctors, meant that it was all 'far from comfortable or convenient'.[41] The 'last pains', Victoria wrote, 'which are generally thought the worst . . . began at half past twelve and lasted till ten minutes to two'. But finally, just after two, 'a perfect little child' was born.[42] Carried along, this first time, by a cloud of pride and dopamine, Victoria proudly, if implausibly, claimed that she 'never had any pain'.[43]

For wife, husband, wife's mother, three doctors, governess and a nurse, it was a wonderful moment of success and harmony after a lengthy labour and considerable disquiet. But then Dr Locock spoke, and the words were a blow to them all.

'Oh Madam,' he said, 'it is a Princess.'[44]

∽

'I fear it will create great disappointment,' Victoria replied, imme-diately seeing the implications of the baby's gender.[45] It would have been better politics to have produced a male heir straight away, as she and Albert 'had so hoped & wished for. We were, I am afraid, sadly disappointed.'[46] And now, on close observation, it also became clear that the baby girl, having been born so early, was also 'sickly and delicate'.[47] Victoria's work was not done. She did her best to gather herself, and mouthed the phrase that disheartened royal mothers have used throughout the centuries. 'Never mind,' she said, 'the next will be a Prince.'[48]

At least Albert was on hand for consolation. 'Dearest Albert hardly left me at all,' Victoria noted, '& was the greatest support & comfort.'[49] Nothing could have exceeded his 'tender anxiety', one of the doctors agreed. 'He sat by her bedside during the whole time, cheered and sustained her – and covered her face with kisses.'[50] Now it was Albert's privilege to announce the baby's birth. He led the way through to see the Cabinet ministers gathered next door, and a nursemaid, Mrs Pegley, 'carried the baby into the room in which they were assembled'.[51]

The commencement of the labour had also been the signal for the Privy Council to be summoned to Buckingham Palace. Victoria's bedchamber lay at the end of a run of rooms linked by folding doors. During labour these were left open, so that the space where the ministers gathered at one end of the suite was visually connected with her very bed, although a screen shielded its lower end. The witnesses, present and correct in court uniform, consisted of Lords Melbourne and Palmerston, the Archbishop of Canterbury, the Bishop of London and Lord Erroll, who was Lord Steward of the Household. Through the open doors, Lord Erroll later claimed, 'he could see the Queen plainly the whole time and hear what she said'.[52]

The Bishop of London likewise reported that it was only 'one minute after the birth' that the little thing was brought in to them, wrapped in flannel, 'the nurse laying it on the table for inspection'. There the baby lay wriggling on a table for a moment, screaming 'of her discontent in being brought into this working-day world in so public a manner'.[53] The Privy Councillors now ordered that Londoners be advised of the news of the birth by the 'firing of the Tower guns,' and people recorded with satisfaction that 'the old etiquette of the court has strictly kept up'.[54] There'd definitely been no cover-up of a stillbirth, or slipping of an imposter into the succession. The baby would be another Victoria, but generally known as Vicky.

Victoria was by now getting the better of her disappointment and was beginning to feel pride and pleasure in the novel sensation that she now had a daughter. She discovered that Vicky had 'large dark blue eyes' and 'pretty little hands', and looked more 'like Albert' than herself.[55] The bedroom for 'the young lady', as her mother called her, was to be Victoria's own dressing room, 'fitted up as a temporary nursery until her little royal highness's apartments were got ready'.

As Vicky's arrival had been unexpected, very little had been prepared, with the exception of her 'marble and silver bath' and 'her gorgeous cradle made in the form of a nautilus'.[56] Gilded, lined with green silk and canopied in gaudy green and gold, it had arrived a week previously, from Mr Seddon, George IV's favourite furniture supplier.[57] The timing of the birth also meant that there was no wet nurse to hand. An old palace page was given the job of travelling as fast as he could to the Isle of Wight to bring back a midwife, one Mrs Ratsey, wife of a sailmaker, probably an experienced mother who'd recently lost a baby of her own. Mrs Ratsey, a 'fine young woman', arrived at Buckingham Palace by two o'clock in the morning.[58] Unlike her mother, Victoria would not be breastfeeding. She hated the very idea of feeling 'like a cow or a dog . . . so very animal and unecstatic'.[59] And even had she wanted to feed her own baby, it would have hindered her getting pregnant again soon, as now she must.

A few days later, Victoria reported that she was 'recovering fast' and keeping up with international events: 'Albert has been reading to me a Despatch'.[60] The officious Dr Locock tried to prevent these readings-aloud, assuming Victoria would ask to hear a novel and therefore overexcite herself. But Albert in fact stuck to government business, or else read his wife the religious 'lessons for the day . . . as he has done so ever since we were married'.[61] Not even Locock could refuse that. By the end of the month, Victoria was out of bed and, sitting in a chair, was 'rolled into my large sitting room, a great pleasure, & the Baby was moved up into her new Nursery'.[62] Soon Victoria was well enough to make her first visit to church, to give thanks for her survival and that of her baby. This marked a ritual return to the world, and Victoria dressed for it as if for a wedding, 'all in white and had my wedding veil on, as a shawl'.[63]

What did Victoria really think about babies? She did not actually see very much of her daughter. The care of royal babies was so professionalised and outsourced that Victoria, strikingly, only saw Vicky naked in her bath twice in the first five weeks of her life, finding her both times 'amazingly improved' and 'much grown'.[64] The queen thought it was unusual that Vicky sometimes cried, for one of her uncles had told her that his own offspring had never done so. (He meant that he had simply never had to hear them.)[65] Children, Victoria thought, were not terribly interesting, 'mere little plants for the first 6 months'.[66]

And yet in recent years there has been a sea-change in historians' assessment of Victoria's maternal qualities, as scholars who are also mothers have looked at old sources in a new light. Yvonne M. Ward, for example, was rightly amazed that the two earliest editors of Victoria's published correspondence, whose selections heavily shaped later views of her reign, buried the news of Vicky's birth in a footnote, 'several pages after its chronological place'.[67] Very young babies are 'like frogs', Victoria once decreed, in a statement that's often quoted to show her dislike of children, but historian Julia Baird notes that this is an accurate description of the swimming movement a baby makes, if you blow, as any fond mother does, upon its stomach.[68]

And both historians point out that Victoria *did* express enjoyment about her first daughter. 'This day last year I was an unmarried girl,' she wrote, on Christmas Day, 'and this year I have an angelic husband, and a dear little girl five weeks old.'[69] Returning home after a day of engagements, Victoria and Albert would rush 'up to the nursery, where we found dear little Victoria, just out of her bath, looking like such a duck'.[70] The older Victoria's wardrobe contained an apron to tie around the neck, embroidered with a crown, with a pocket for a towel to soak up any spillages: it was intended for bathing or cuddling children.[71] At this stage in her childbearing career, at least, Victoria was happy, interested, involved to the extent that people thought appropriate.

She would be extremely fortunate, as a nineteenth-century mother, never to lose a baby. The average number of children being born to nineteenth-century women was falling fast: between five and six in Victoria's youth, it had dropped to more like three by the time of her death in the early twentieth century.[72] The queen's brood, eventually totalling nine, was unusually large for an upper-class family. Her contemporary, Maria, Queen of Portugal, married to another of the Coburg cousins, exceeded her with eleven. But then, worn out by all this, Maria promptly died at thirty-five. Being so fertile obviously came with risks.[73]

Delighted and relieved after her daughter's birth, Victoria now ordered that it must be 'as soon as possible' that Dr Locock got his fee of £1,000, Dr Ferguson his £800 and Mr Blagden his £500.[74] And once she'd given birth to a child of her own, Victoria now began to see her mother anew. 'Pray <u>don't</u> <u>ever</u> dwell on those sad past times,' she wrote of her childhood. Victoria was belatedly coming to appreciate Victoire's 'love & affection', admitting to her mother that '<u>I</u> was <u>also</u> <u>wrong</u> in my behaviour towards you very <u>often</u> in those miserable days.'[75] Albert, who got on well with his mother-in-law and aunt, is often given the credit for bringing about a reconciliation between mother and daughter. But it seems to me that it was as much due to Victoria's own growing self-knowledge and maturity. In the pleasure of motherhood, much of the unhappiness of her own childhood was washed away.

But all this pleasure came at a price, and it involved Albert.

On the day of his daughter's birth, Albert 'had a late, hurried luncheon, & went to the Council at 4'.[76] His departure to attend the Privy Council while his wife went to sleep was significant. At last he now had the chance to begin to prove that he was more than just the 'parish bull'. In the run-up to Victoria's confinement, it had been necessary to nominate a Regent to take over in the event of the queen's dying but her baby surviving. Albert was selected, in July 1840, a result he took as a great vote of confidence. 'You will understand the significance of the matter,' he told his brother, 'it gives my position here in the country a fresh importance.'[77] In the Council meeting on the afternoon of Vicky's birth, it was also decreed that Albert's name, alongside that of his daughter, should for the first time be included in the liturgy. From now on, the British would pray for him.[78]

For her part, Victoria's devotion to her husband was growing ever deeper. She told Melbourne that she particularly liked the way Albert had no time for other women. 'Damn it, Madam!' was his reply. 'You don't expect that he'll always be faithful to you, do you?'[79] But in fact Victoria did. This was partly because of the tone of the age. Melbourne had grown up in a high society full of scandal and affairs; it's not even certain that he was his father's biological son. But now chivalry had entered the air. Men were committed to the pursuit of just one pure, perfect woman. Victoria and Albert agreed upon this model for their relationship, and in fact modelled it in person when they hosted a costumed ball with a fourteenth-century theme, appearing as Edward III and Queen Philippa (albeit with 1840s corsetry).

This gradual change, from her dominance to his, was taking place not just in ballrooms but more widely in British society. The genders became more clearly and hierarchically distinguished as the 1830s gave way to the 1840s. A successful marriage, thought Sarah Ellis, writing in 1843, was founded on one important truth. 'It is,' she counselled her female readers, 'the superiority of your husband as a man.' 'You may have more talent, with higher attainments,' she advised them, 'but this has nothing whatever to do with your position as a woman, which is, and must be, inferior to his as a man.'[80] In considering her husband to be superior to herself, Victoria only believed what nearly everyone alive held true. The forthcoming campaigns for votes for women would enrage the queen, making her 'so furious that she cannot contain herself'.[81]

After the birth of their child, Victoria wrote, Albert's 'care and devotion were quite beyond expression'. He would happily sit beside her, reading or writing, and 'no one but himself ever lifted her from her bed to her sofa'. His care, she concluded, 'was more like that of a mother, nor could there be a kinder, wiser, or more judicious nurse'.[82] The words ring true, but they were perhaps strange ones to use of a husband: a 'mother', a 'judicious' nurse. In fact, Albert was infantilising his wife. Before their marriage, Albert's letters began 'Beloved Victoria'. But afterwards, he addressed her as 'Dear Child' or 'Dear Good, Little One'.

'Oh! If I only could make him King,' Victoria exclaimed, 'for I do so feel & recognise his superiority, & fitness to be such.'[83] And through his care of her, stealthily succeeding where Conroy had failed, Albert was also establishing himself as her de facto Private Secretary.[84] By 20 December 1840, a month after Vicky's birth, Albert's own secretary, George Anson, noticed 'an important advance in the Prince's position'. Albert now had the keys to the boxes that arrived daily, full of Cabinet documents. This had come about because everyone had got used to him doing 'all the ministerial business during the Queen's confinement'.[85] Albert was thrilled. 'Do not think I lead a submissive life,' he told his brother.[86]

Yet there was a downside. Now that Albert was writing the memos, or at least the drafts of the memos, on official royal business, they underwent a gradual change, a hardening, of tone. Victoria's instincts, claims constitutional historian Vernon Bogdanor, were more conciliatory.[87] But now Her Majesty (or possibly Albert on Her Majesty's behalf) wrote sharply to Lord Palmerston, for example, complaining that the Foreign Office had sent the queen 'drafts to approve when the originals have already been sent away which of course renders her doing so useless'.[88] This was correct, but not charming. Albert, constitutional historians agree, did not really understand the British political situation. He thought that the sovereign was the best placed to determine where the nation's interest lay. But this was not so. The sovereign could only act in tandem with the government.[89] Albert was decisive, and commanded the detail that often eluded Victoria, but he was not acting in the best interests of a monarchy that essentially worked through influence rather than power.

On the same day that his Private Secretary noticed that Albert was now handling the confidential locked boxes of government business, much happier and more comfortable with his role, there was a death in the household.[90] Victoria's little dog Dash passed away in his ninth year. It seems symbolic of a change in the order. On the day of her coronation, Victoria had rushed home to bathe Dash; now she rushed home to bathe her baby. On the day of her coronation, Victoria had delighted in her new role of queen; now she began to shrug it off, and pass it onto her husband if she could. It was almost as if Victoria's early delight in her reign had ended. A baby had been born but, alongside Dash, something else had died.

13

Christmas at Windsor: 25 December 1850

Once Victoria and Albert discovered a working model for their marriage, the years seemed to speed up and blur into each other. Within a decade, Vicky had six siblings. In 1850, at a wintery Windsor Castle, her tenth birthday in November was quickly followed by preparations for her tenth Christmas. By Christmas Eve, George IV's white-and-gold state apartments, hung even in normal times with red silk, were all dressed up for one of Albert's epic celebrations.

On a table stood a fir tree, its branches laden with lighted tapers. Around its base were the artistic presents Albert always chose for his wife: paintings, four bronze statuettes, vases and a bracelet he'd designed especially for her. He led her into the room, as their custom was, to see the spectacular spread. Christmas, for the Victorians, was no longer simply one more religious holiday among many others. It had by now taken on its firmly nineteenth-century form as a super-holiday, an annual blowout with the giving and receiving of presents at centre stage. It had become, in fact, an occasion to warm both the hearts and the balance sheets of a nation of shopkeepers.

'My beloved Albert,' Victoria recorded in her journal, 'took me to my tree & table, covered by such numberless gifts, really too much, too magnificent.'[1] Albert certainly excelled at choosing things both beautiful and meaningful. The bracelet contained a miniature of Princess Louise, now two. Now that they had seven children, the royal family was nearly complete. Its youngest member, baby Prince Arthur, was just eight months old. Victoria was full of gratitude for her family and their continued health. 'The return of this blessed season must always fill one,' she wrote in her journal, 'with the deepest devotion to our Lord & Saviour!'[2]

It was Albert who masterminded Windsor Castle's astonishing Christmases, partly out of nostalgia and regret for his birthplace. 'I must seek in the children an echo of what Ernest and I were in the old time,' he once wrote.[3] As a foreigner in a strange land, it was almost as if he hadn't been truly happy since then. But it wasn't Albert who introduced the ancient German custom of celebrating Christmas with a tree; that had been Victoria's own German forebears. Her grandmother Queen Charlotte, for example, had kept the Christmas of 1800 at Windsor Castle with 'an immense tub with a yew tree placed in it', its branches hung with 'sweetmeats, almonds and raisins in papers, fruits and toys'.[4]

But Albert's trees became celebrated, and much emulated. According to the *London News*, he set up his first one at Windsor Castle in 1841, a year after Vicky's birth: 'a young fir, about eight feet high', with 'six tiers of branches'. Each tier was decorated with a dozen wax tapers, and hanging from the boughs were 'elegant trays' for holding sweets. 'Fancy cakes, gilt gingerbread and eggs filled with sweetmeats' were also suspended straight from the branches by ribbons, while 'toys and dolls of all descriptions' lay on the white damask tablecloth that covered the table upon which the tree stood. And at the very summit stood 'the small figure of an angel, with outstretched wings'. Over the next twenty years, the trees of Windsor Christmases would grow ever more lavish: by 1860, they were 'of immense size', and 'made to appear as if partially covered with snow'.[5] Victoria liked to help Albert to dress the tree 'with her own hands'.[6]

Decorating the tree was an annual ritual to calm and cheer. And it was a welcome change from a family life that was increasingly complex and stormy.

〜

The following morning, Christmas Day of 1850, Victoria woke up much earlier than she'd done before her marriage. Now that she was thirty-one, she spoke 'with such regret' of those 'late hours in the morning' of her youth that she'd wasted lolling in bed, before Albert came along with his reforming ways.[7]

Albert, in fact, got up earlier still. The wardrobe maid called them both at seven, opening the shutters and very often the bedroom window as well. Albert then leapt out of bed at once, in his characteristically German long 'white drawers made with feet'. Putting on his dressing gown and, in winter, an additional shawl, he went into the next room. In the darker months a green oil lamp, imported from Germany, always illuminated his desk. There he read or wrote letters.[8]

Meanwhile Victoria stayed in bed and dozed. 'Her Majesty interests herself less and less about politics,' Albert's secretary noted.[9] Over the ten years since Vicky's birth, her growing number of children, and her responsibilities towards them, had squeezed all that out of her mind. Instead, she deferred to Albert. Politically, domestically, she 'leant on him for all and everything . . . didn't put on a gown or bonnet if he didn't approve it'.[10]

If Albert was away from home for any reason, Victoria could hardly bear it. 'I feel lonely without my dear Master,' she admitted, 'I pray God never to let me survive him.'[11] She loved to be 'clasped and held tight in the sacred hours at night when the world seemed only to be ourselves'.[12] Other people noticed how 'he is King to all intents and purposes . . . while she has the title he is really discharging the functions of the Sovereign.' 'Formerly the Queen received her Ministers alone,' reported 'The Gruncher', but now husband and wife did it together, and 'both of them always said *We* – "We think, or wish, to do so and so".'[13]

The man writing away by lamplight in the hours before dawn was no longer the dashing young hero who'd won Victoria's heart. He was growing portly, and careworn, and looked older than his years. He was never quite comfortable in the Arctic temperatures his wife preferred. 'The weather cold and stormy,' he once wrote to a daughter in one of these early-morning correspondence sessions, 'Mama will be much hurt when she gets up and finds I have had a fire lit.' Sometimes, to keep his head warm, he would wear a wig.[14]

Albert had created a Sisyphean task for himself in becoming king-in-all-but-name. Under his guidance, the Crown now 'constantly desired to be furnished with accurate and detailed information about all important matters'.[15] That way, Albert felt, he could hold ministers to account in an unprecedented manner. Where he really excelled was arts administration; a subject that he loved, understood well and where he won the trust of senior people. He could discuss painting, for example, with a man like Charles Eastlake, President of the Royal Academy, so engagingly that, as Eastlake recalled, 'two or three times I quite forgot who he was – he talked so naturally and argued so fairly'.[16]

For Albert's system to work, though, the reports sent by government departments had to be kept and filed, so that progress could be checked against them. Historian Jane Ridley explains how Albert devised a complicated system of filing the queen's papers by subject, not sender. It was both genius and madness. It meant that an important report might need to be copied out several times, as it could have several relevant homes in the system. Because the reports of government ministers were confidential, Albert believed that he could not delegate this work to anyone else. So, he spent his days copying, writing; writing, copying. The work dominated the time when he wasn't with his wife and children. Over the last decade, since he had first got his hands on the keys to the government boxes, he'd gradually begun to sink under the weight of his self-imposed burden.[17] 'His foreign correspondence alone,' thought one of Albert's friends, 'would have been thought sufficient occupation for one who had nothing else to do.'[18]

And Albert also ran his family as tightly as he ran the nation. 'At a little after eight,' Victoria wrote of their daily routine at Windsor, he'd come back to the bedroom 'to tell me to get up'. She would then check the letters he'd written, correcting the spelling mistakes he still sometimes made in English, while he went to dress.

In his dressing room, Albert kept a caged finch. The original bird, yet another German import, had been stuffed upon its decease, then replaced in turn by numerous successors. One of the birds was successfully trained to say 'Guten Morgen.'[19] Albert probably said 'Guten Morgen' right back at it. When he'd arrived at Windsor he'd also been a German bird in a cage, but now he was king in the castle. His children often came in to watch their papa dress, and to play with his pet. 'What a pity!' said Beatrice, the baby of the family, if she arrived too late and found him fully clothed. 'To see his "drawers" & "trousers" put on was her great delight.'

Albert generally finished his outfit off with the blue ribbon of the Order of the Garter. His wife thought his trousers, checked or otherwise, 'made him look so nice and gentlemanlike', and she records that he '<u>always</u> wore straps to them'.[20] But Victoria was not particularly fashion-conscious – to have been fashionable would have indicated a moral weakness inappropriate in a queen – and was in any case blind to any fault in her husband. Albert's funny trousers were one of the more visible signs of why he would never quite be accepted by Victoria's subjects. Even those who knew him well, and admired him, would say 'he is an excellent, clever, able fellow, but look at the cut of his coat, or look at the way he shakes hands'. He could do nothing – not even sit on a horse – in 'the true orthodox English manner.'[21]

But one of Albert's unorthodox habits – and indeed, his great redeeming feature – was his love of playing with the children whose births he had witnessed. He spent much more time with them than many an aristocratic father, as if taking on some of the mothering that his overburdened wife hadn't time to do. 'He is so kind to them,' Victoria observed, '& romps with them delightfully.'[22] The castle's nurseries were ruled by Sarah, Lady Lyttelton, or 'Laddle', who was beloved by her charges. She had initially been surprised by Albert's hands-on approach. She admired his 'great dexterity and gentle manner' as he managed to get a little glove onto 'Princey's' hand after the nursery staff had given up on the offending article as being too small. 'Princey' was the much-wanted son who'd finally been born a year after Vicky. 'It is not every Papa,' Sarah Lyttelton noticed, 'who would have the patience and kindness' to do such a thing.[23] On Christmas Day, during breakfast, 'the little children would beg to go to the "Presentroom" to fetch a toy to play with', but Albert would not let them go until the meal was finished.[24]

The flipside of the attention Albert paid to his children was his dedication to directing and correcting them. As they by now numbered seven, their mother was rather losing track. 'All the numerous children are as *nothing* to me,' she wrote, 'when *he* [Albert] *is away*; it seems as if the whole life of the house and home were gone!'[25]

This, however, was a very private pronouncement. As the historian Marina Warner notes, any public statements Victoria made about family life always implied that fulfilment and happiness lay at home. What made her glad was not so much her children in themselves, but the delight they gave to Albert.[26] 'I find no especial pleasure or compensation in the company of the older children,' she admitted, 'I only feel properly *à mon aise* & quite happy when Albert is with me.'[27]

Victoria's children could tell that their mother had mixed feelings about them, and in consequence they were growing up to be an unruly and dysfunctional lot. Albert intended them to meet his own high standards of intellectual achievement and self-discipline. When his dullard sons Bertie, the eldest, and his younger brother Alfred (or Affie) did not naturally meet the mark, Albert tried to beat his requirements into them by force. 'Their father decided on whipping them,' explains the ever-supportive Dr Clark, who concluded that the 'effect was excellent'.[28] They were indeed 'rare young toads', in the unguarded words of a Windsor gardener who suffered from their pranks. But other people thought that the boys 'had almost more than their share of corporal punishment from the hands of their father'.[29] Bertie's beatings left him feeling so helpless that he gave way to uncontrollable rages: 'he stands in the corner stamping his legs and screaming in the most dreadful manner.'[30]

With the constant injunctions placed upon the royal children to behave well and to keep quiet, Windsor Castle could have a morgue-like atmosphere. After Albert's reformation of the disorderly and wasteful management he'd uncovered upon taking up residence, it had grown 'almost uncanny, how quiet this enormous building is, and sometimes one could imagine that the Castle was quite empty'. Because of the carpets everywhere, 'one hears nothing at all', and 'people speak very quietly'.[31]

Only at Christmas did the tension lift. 'The younger Royal infants were there during all dinner-time,' wrote one of the maids-of-honour, describing how Princess Vicky and her younger sisters Alice, Lenchen and Louise made a lovely appearance in their 'little wreaths of holly . . . you can't think how simple and happy all the Royalty looked, just like any other family'.[32] The holiday saw a general and much-welcomed relaxation of the usual formality of court life. At Christmas 'people jostle one another', wrote one of the lords-in-waiting. 'Lords, grooms, Queen, and princes laughed and talked, forgot to bow, and freely turned their back on one another . . . little princesses, who on ordinary occasions dare hardly to look at a gentleman-in-waiting, in the happiest manner showed each person they could lay hands on the treasures they had received.'[33]

Albert doted particularly upon his clever eldest daughter. He saw that Vicky had inherited his cerebral, logical nature, rather than her mother's passion and emotion, and he judged her to be 'very intelligent and observant'.[34] He almost worshipped her, to the extent of commemorating the loss of a milk tooth, which he tugged out himself, by setting it into a brooch, where it formed the white flower of a design in the shape of an enamelled thistle. It was a bizarre, and highly Albertian, piece of jewellery.[35] But Vicky, in return, understood that even she could not quite fulfil his desires. Vicky 'never thought he could really care for me', she wrote later. 'I felt so much too imperfect for that. I never dared to expect it.'[36]

Albert had such impossibly high standards. And then, as Victoria told Vicky all too candidly, 'he was disappointed you were not a boy'.[37] Vicky would often get bombshells like this from her mother, bald statements of unpalatable truths, and Victoria placed quite different demands upon her eldest daughter than Albert did. These were urgent claims for affection and attention, very much like those Victoria's own mother had used to make. Just as Victoria had once done herself, Vicky nobly bore her mother's 'anger and reproaches . . . till the poor child . . . is made seriously ill'.[38]

If even brilliant Vicky felt that she couldn't meet her father's expectations, the situation was still graver for her less satisfactory younger brother. Bertie, heir to the throne, was 'uncommonly averse to learning', according to his governess. Laddle thought he showed 'wilful inattention' and made 'constant interruptions' to lessons, 'getting under the table, upsetting the books and sundry other *anti-studious* practices'.

Bertie had been difficult from the start. After the birth of her first child, Victoria had made a swift recovery; not so after her second in November 1841. 'My poor nerves,' she wrote, 'were so battered . . . I suffered *a whole year* from it'.[39] Her doctors began to prescribe further 'soothing draughts', 'draughts for Headache' and 'Draughts for pain'.[40] Victoria started to chafe against the immobility and inconvenience of being pregnant again so quickly: 'men never think, or at least seldom think, what a hard task it is for us women to go through this *very often.*'[41]

But Albert insisted. Not only was it a royal duty, he could perhaps see that having the babies occupied his wife, weighed her down and allowed him to assume more and more of her responsibilities. From Victoria's point of view, though, her concentrated decade of childbearing meant that her initial pleasure in motherhood wore off. Bertie, her second, brought with him an episode of severe postnatal depression. Victoria began to see visions, 'spots on peoples faces, which turned into worms', while 'coffins floated' before her eyes. Even Albert grew worried. 'The Queen is afraid,' he told Dr Ferguson, the obstetrician who took a special interest in psychology, that 'she is about to lose her Mind!' Dr Ferguson was brought in for a consultation, only to find his patient 'lying Down, and the tears were flowing fast over her cheek as she addressed me – overwhelmed with shame at the necessity of confessing her weakness and compelled by the very burden of her mind & her sorrows to seek relief'.[42]

Victoria came to understand that her depression was a distinct malady that came and went, but which affected her particularly during and after pregnancy. In due course, she prepared her own daughter to expect 'lowness and tendency to cry . . . it is what every lady suffers with more or less and what I, during my two first confinements, suffered dreadfully with'.[43] Yet Albert made sure the babies kept coming. 'It is too hard and dreadful what we have to go through,' Victoria complained. Men ought to 'do every thing to make up, for what after all they alone are the cause of'.[44] Victoria eventually told Dr Clark that she could not bear to have any more: 'if she had another Child she would sink under it.'[45]

Witnessing this process of disintegration, the people around her treated Victoria with a toxic mixture of concern and control. There was genuine fear that she would 'go mad' like her grandfather, but this could hopefully be avoided if she were placed under the right sort of regime. Dr Ferguson noted down that Victoria 'is much troubled as to what will become of her when she is dead. She thinks of worms eating her – and is weeping & wretched.'[46] But he believed, as did many of the household, that the solution lay in Albert. 'Providence has shielded her,' Ferguson thought, 'in giving her a husband whose patience and example may perfect those good emotions which he has already called out – nothing else will save her sooner or later from madness.'[47] Dr Clark also thought she must be kept completely calm, 'free from all neural irritation' or 'mental exertion'. 'I feel at times uneasy,' he admitted, 'regarding the Q's mind.'[48]

Surely Victoria's mental health suffered because all the men around her expected it to. But her increasingly negative views about childbirth were also a consequence of the changing emotional climate of her age. During the span of her life, emotion in general became less readily expressed, less openly admitted. Albert's attempts to get her to control her emotional excesses were partly personal, partly part of a wider cultural trend. 'You have again lost your self-control quite unnecessarily,' he would tell her after an argument. 'I do my duty towards you even though it means that life is embittered by "scenes".'[49]

Slowly, gradually, she began to check her feelings, to avoid angering or clashing with Albert. And Victoria began, as a result, to love her children a little less. In her thirties, she had hard words for her own daughter Vicky, when Vicky herself was grown up and about to make her a grandmother. Avoid 'baby worship,' she told the daughter she had once adored so passionately, because 'no lady, and still less a Princess, is fit for her husband or her position, if she does that.'[50] Victoria had once rushed home to see Vicky being bathed at night, but with the younger children it was a ritual she witnessed only 'once in three months perhaps.'[51] 'One is very foolish with one's first child,' she recollected.[52] She came to think of maternity as 'the shadow side' of life.[53]

In their rows over their children, Albert could be bitter, devastating and unfair. Victoria's doctor, he claimed, had not looked after Vicky correctly. 'Dr Clark,' Albert raved, 'has mismanaged the child and poisoned her with calomel and you have starved her. I shall have nothing more to do with it; take the child away and do as you like and if she dies you will have it on your conscience.'[54] There was much to excuse Albert in writing this. He was only twenty-two at the time. He had two children already and a third on the way. He was living in a strange country, and felt he occupied a humiliating, subordinate position both in household and nation.

And yet these are not the phrases of the wise, kind, generous paragon that Victoria paints for us in almost every single one of the many, many words she was to write about her husband. The success of their family life – one suspects the same of so many Victorian families – lay in her seeing only what she wanted to see, and subordinating her own desires to his. She constantly excused him. 'My chief and great anxiety is – peace in the House . . . God only knows how I love him,' she wrote, on the day of Albert's outburst. 'His position is difficult, heaven knows, and we must do everything to make it easier.'[55] She submitted herself to Albert almost as her mother had submitted herself to Conroy, calling him her father, protector, guide, advisor, even 'my mother (I might almost say) as well as my husband'.[56] Her courtiers had once thought her indomitably self-willed, a 'resolute little tit'.[57] 'I suppose,' Victoria now finished, that 'no-one ever was so completely altered in every way'.[58]

One of the prices of her elevation of Albert was the loss of Lehzen, her second mother. Her husband had always seen Lehzen as a rival for Victoria's love and attention and, at the end of 1842, he'd engineered her departure from Windsor. Taking a leaf out of Albert's book, Victoria did not even say goodbye to her old governess. She admitted much 'regret not being able to embrace her once more,' but contented herself with writing a farewell letter instead.[59]

Lehzen went back to her native Germany to live in retirement. Years later, when Victoria was travelling near Lehzen's home, the governess came to the railway platform at Bückeburg station to wave her handkerchief at her former pupil 'in enthusiastic greeting'.[60] The train did not stop.

At Christmas, though, all this was forgotten. For the wider household, the festivities began with the ceremony of gift-giving. Maid-of-honour Eleanor Stanley describes how in December 1843 she was called with her colleagues into the Oak Room at Windsor Castle. Victoria and Albert stood by a table with a tree upon it, handing out gifts 'with the name of each person, written by the Queen on a slip of paper'. Eleanor's own present was a necklace, 'in carbuncles and little diamonds'.[61] Those lower down the social scale got less beautiful, more functional gifts. The queen's dressers, for example, received something like a '*nécessaire*', a little leather case containing thimble, scissors and bodkin.[62]

Windsor Castle under Albert's direction now ran like clockwork. After centuries of inattention and mismanagement by its sovereigns, the royal household as an institution had by Victoria's accession come almost to a creaking halt. One unfortunate guest to Windsor, unable to find a footman to direct him, spent 'nearly an hour wandering about the corridors to try and identify his bedroom. At length, he opened a random door in desperation', only to discover the queen, having her hair brushed.[63] He had happened upon her bedroom.

Now things were much better managed. Another visitor to Windsor, a Madame Bunsen, described what it was like to be invited to stay at the castle. She found that 'a comfortable set of rooms were awaiting me. The upper housemaid gave us tea and bread and butter – very refreshing.' After she'd dressed for dinner, one of the lords-in-waiting showed Madame Bunsen the way along 'the Grand Corridor', which was 'a fairy scene, lights, pictures, moving figures of courtiers unknown'.[64] This wide, curved room – so much more than its name suggests – was described as 'the main street, so to speak, whereon all the rooms in constant use by the Queen's family open, and is in itself a museum of art'.[65]

Madame Bunsen was led onwards, through multitudinous apartments, 'which we passed through one after another till we reached the magnificent ballroom'. There she was joined by a growing gathering of other guests, until two gentlemen entered simultaneously, turned back upon themselves and made 'profound bows towards the open door'. The very moment Victoria appeared, the band began to play 'God Save the Queen'. After dinner and drawing-room chat, it was at half past eleven that Madame Bunsen set back out 'on my travels to my bedchamber'. She could not remember where it was, and 'might have looked and wandered some miles'. But this time there *was* someone to show her the way.[66]

Albert had entrenched himself not only as the paterfamilias of a large family, but also as his wife's financial controller. He cut her dress expenditure down from £5,000 to £2,000 a year.[67] He'd taken it upon himself to save enough money to build up the private fortune that neither of them would inherit. Parliament allowed Victoria nearly £400,000 a year. With her additional income from the Duchy of Lancaster, an estate attached to the monarchy, and with a stripped-down, more stringently run establishment, Victoria had been able not only to pay off her father's debts, but also to start to save.[68] By 1850, Albert had amassed enough money to enable them to think about building a new house of their own, something more to his taste, more cosy and convenient than this vast old castle in which neither of them felt entirely at home.

It was always chilly and draughty at Windsor. Although 'the cold' always made Victoria herself feel 'well and brisk', her household disagreed.[69] 'Three Princesses lame with chilblains, two Princes in disgrace, and Louise ill in her room,' wrote governess Laddle in the midwinter of 1851. 'The Queen has a stiff neck, Mr Wellesley a sore throat, sun not shining, cold wind, all dull and disagreeable enough.'[70] One Christmas Eve Laddle had asked Albert to look over the quarterly accounts she kept for the nursery. 'Yes certainly,' he said, 'if *you* will consent to my doing reel steps all the time to warm myself.'[71] And yet he did love Windsor Castle in the snow, when he took his whole family skating.

The Christmas Day of 1850 at Windsor was spent as always in a simple manner. There was unusually mild weather for the family's walk down through the park 'with the Children to the Kennels'. The princes and princesses there gave presents of toys and dress fabric to the children of a family of Scottish servants. Then it was back to the castle's private chapel for the service at eleven. These walks, to the kennels, to the stables or to the farms to inspect the stock, frequently undertaken at 'Christmastide', were part of the duties of a responsible landowner. They demonstrated the values that Albert was trying to instil in his children.[72] The management of the extensive royal estates was a microcosm for the management of the kingdom, so a visit to the farm was, in effect, an act of good government.

Then came a convivial lunch of foie gras and tapioca pudding, served 'quite in a new style' according to one of the ladies-in-waiting. The children were getting big enough to be considered able to eat 'all together, Queen, prince, children, Gentlemen & ladies & the children's governess – this was an enormous novelty'.[73] In the afternoon Victoria 'went several times to look at my beautiful presents', she notes, before 'the trees were lit up in the evening, & the Children were all playing about so happily'.[74]

Meanwhile preparations were underway for the great Christmas dinner, 'always a gay, merry one'. The sideboard, as ever, held an enormous 'Baron of Beef', served alongside game pie and brawn.[75] This Christmas dinner would be served to Victoria, Albert and twenty assorted household members and guests.[76] The 'table-deckers', a small team responsible for laying the table, checked the silver cutlery out of the Silver Pantry, a small strongroom staffed by some 'veritable giants of men' muscular enough to lift the royal collection's heavier pieces. Either the 'Lion' set of knives and forks, or else the other set marked with the 'Crown', would make its way to the table, each set inscribed upon its handles with its own symbol, and used on alternate nights.[77] The table-deckers also had to prepare centrepieces, flowers and glassware.

Down below in the kitchens, the baron of beef, a huge lump of meat 400 lb in weight, was roasted on a spit turned by 'great iron chains driven round constantly by a machine'. 'That was indeed a roast beef,' exclaimed one of the queen's dressers, who'd never seen anything like it before.[78] Meanwhile, on another spit were 'at least fifty turkeys'.[79] The great kitchens of Windsor were a magnificent sight in all the uproar of roasting, coppers hanging 'like burnished shields' above the two 12-foot closed ranges, and 'six rows of large joints' before the open ranges, revolving on their spits and shielded from view behind 'a meat screen about ten feet high'. Despite Albert's cutbacks, everything about these kitchens was over the top, including the staff list of master-cook, two yeomen, two assistant cooks, two roasting cooks, sixteen apprentices and half a dozen kitchen maids. Even the sand on the floors to soak up spills was not stinted: it was 'swept up and renewed half a dozen times a day'.[80]

Albert had the self-control to follow the occasional fasting day, for the good of an irritable stomach that often plagued him, but for the rest of the family there was always a superabundance of food at the castle. A quiet, low-key dinner for Victoria, Albert and just their eldest daughter, Vicky, for example, served in 1857, consisted of a choice of soups or fish, then between proffered alternatives of roast beef or 'capon with asparagus'. The side dishes were '*vol-au-vents* with *béchamel* sauce and grilled eggs,' followed by apricot flan or waffles '*mit crème*'.[81]

Christmas dinner 1850 was still served in the old-fashioned style with all the dishes laid out at once like a buffet, rather than in separate courses. Service à la Française, as this was called, was predicated on waste: there would be *too much* of everything, that was the point. But there was also a well-established system for dealing with the leftovers, which worked their way down the social scale. For example, after the queen's dinner at around 9.30 p.m., the upper servants sat down to her leftover roast as cold cuts, and what was left after that was given to designated charities. In December 1855, 650 members of the 'poor of Windsor' were fed with the scraps from the Windsor Castle kitchens.

By Christmas 1850, the court was a more sober place than it had been in the past. Albert had forced through reductions so that family and guests were now allowed only a daily bottle of wine per person.[82] The downside of becoming an abstemious, respectable royal family, as Albert wished, was that the court was no longer the centre of scintillating society and intellectual endeavour that some of its predecessors had been. Nor did it have the glamorous, if raffish, qualities of King George IV's. 'The dullness of our evenings,' wrote one maid-of-honour, 'is a thing impossible to describe.' After dinner, the ladies-in-waiting generally made laboured conversation with the queen and whichever bigwigs were sitting at her table while the maids-of-honour quietly plied their needles. At 10.30 Victoria would give the signal that everyone could retire, at which the 'gentlemen make a rush, from the whist table or from the other room, and we gladly bundle up our work, and all is over'.[83]

But at Christmas, at least, a little merriment crept into the proceedings. 'How I lived to tell the tale I don't know,' reports Windsor guest Lord Torrington in 1860. He ate baron of beef, boar's head and a woodcock pie containing 100 birds for dinner, spent the evening playing pool and billiards and finally went to his bed 'near three o'clock'.[84]

Lord Torrington painted a picture of a perfect, convivial, family Christmas in his account of the Windsor festivities of 1860, addressing his account to the editor of *The Times.* Although it was not published, Victoria was pleased, on other occasions, by the attention the press paid to her growing family. 'They say,' she claimed, 'no Sovereign was more loved than I am (I am bold enough to say) and that, from our happy domestic home – wh. gives such a good example.'[85] The *Illustrated London News*, for one, was always hungry for stories both about royalty and about Christmas, depicting the latter as a heart-warming family festival, which reflected the domestic preoccupations of middle-class people. Through its decorations and gift-giving, the Victorian Christmas created a lucrative new opportunity for the members of a capitalist society to sell things to each other. One American journalist, lacking solid information, decided instead simply to imagine what went on at Christmas at Windsor. He gives Albert the (unconvincing) speech, 'Mother, we must have a first-class shindy for the children', to which Victoria (somewhat implausibly) responds: 'Albert, we will just make things whoop.'[86]

A special supplement to one edition of the *Illustrated London News* in 1848 included a highly influential picture of Victoria, Albert, their children and their tree. It showed them enjoying the classic mid-Victorian moment, celebrating both the wonderful new trappings of Christmas and solid family values. Any middle-class family could aspire to live like this, and like them. In talking so proudly about her 'happy domestic home', Victoria was prefiguring the words of John Ruskin, the commentator who'd make the best-known pronouncement on the proper role of a Victorian woman. Home, he thought, was a 'woman's true place and power'. While a husband had to go to brave the rough world's perils, a wife should remain behind, in a private realm where her 'great function is Praise' and her great opportunity the 'sweet ordering' of her household.[87]

Ironically, Victoria herself had little talent for 'sweet ordering', and delegated all that to Albert. And historian Margaret Homans has argued that the royal family's public image, so surprisingly ordinary and middle-class, was in fact nothing more than an illusion. That powerful, relatable image of the family Christmas tree made newspaper readers look twice because everyone who saw it really knew in their hearts that the people in the picture weren't ordinary and middle-class at all.

'Never was there a more tender love, nor so incessant a perform-ance of every conjugal duty,' wrote Laddle of life in the royal family, and the word 'performance' is telling.[88] Normal middle-class families *didn't* live in an ancient castle, or have quite so many Christmas trees. They *didn't* have 100 woodcocks in their pies, or dispense diamond necklaces to ladies-in-waiting. But Victoria's polished 'ordinariness' was a clever – or perhaps even just a completely instinctive – way of ruling over a country that was not comfortable with women in power.[89]

So the happy family Christmas of 1850, drawing to a close with a late bedtime, was not quite what it seemed, and the increasingly stout little woman at the heart of it not quite what she seemed either. Arthur Ponsonby, son of one of Victoria's Private Secretaries, claimed that she was nothing like an aristocrat, or a wealthy middle-class Englishwoman, or a typical princess. He wrote that:

such expressions as 'people like Queen Victoria' or 'that sort of woman' could not be used about her. Her simple domesticity appealed to a vast number of her subjects; she was intensely human, but the unique nature of her personality and position claimed special attention . . . she was simply without prefix or suffix 'The Queen'. [90]

14

A Maharaja on the Isle of Wight, 21–24 August 1854

Early in the afternoon of Monday 21 August 1854, a young Indian prince was steaming across the Solent. This was the Maharaja Duleep Singh, once the ruler of the Sikh Kingdom. Son of Ranjit Singh, the powerful 'Lion of the Punjab', Duleep had not been allowed to occupy his father's throne for long. At the age of ten, after a period of joint rule, he was deposed by the British. Now he was fifteen, exiled from his home and paying his first visit to the Isle of Wight.

Duleep Singh – indeed any visitor – could reach Victoria's holiday home of Osborne House, just outside Cowes on the island's northern tip, in less than three hours from London. Her guests usually made the journey by train and then steamboat. The narrow seas between the mainland and the island were always busy. You could embark for the Isle of Wight at Southampton, where the port was always full of 'merchant ships, many of them bound for America', or else from Portsmouth, packed with 'numerous large warships . . . they bristled with sailors everywhere, up the highest topmast, on ropes and rope ladders'.[1] The Maharaja's steamer probably chugged past ships of Victoria's Royal Navy that were destined for Crimea, where British guns were slowly wearing down the gigantic but ill-equipped army of the Russians.

Osborne House, encircled by wooded hills, seemed remote from such concerns. At Cowes, a carriage waited to take visitors the last mile uphill to the property. Finished only four years before the

Maharaja's visit, Osborne had been Albert's most demanding creative project thus far, and he had put a great deal of himself into it. When the skies were blue, the house looked like a romantic Italian villa commanding a lovely view folding down to azure waters. 'The endless expanse of the sea,' wrote the maidservant who occupied the bedroom right at the top of Osborne's tower, 'looks so smooth that the ships seem to be standing on glass or ice.'[2] On the island's frequent wet days, though, when its cement-covered walls became stained with rain, the Italianate design looked oddly out of place on the Isle of Wight.

As the Maharaja's carriage emerged from the tree-lined drive through the park and drew up before the house, he was met by a 'Footman in scarlet & gold, powdered hair, & silk stockings' before one of the queen's gentlemen conducted him into the main downstairs drawing room.[3] There he waited by himself, until Victoria's arrival into the otherwise empty room was announced by the 'quiet shy opening of the door'. She would slip in unannounced to greet her guests. One visitor found herself 'on my knee kissing the hand which was given to me but I do not know how I came there'.[4] She kept visitors standing up.

A pair of profile portraits dating from this very same year of 1854 reveals that Albert by now had become distinctly jowly, his hair scraped forward to cover his balding forehead, while Victoria was beginning to develop her unique hamster cheeks. But the woman the Maharaja saw before him still looked younger than her thirty-five years. In the photograph, at least, her hair shines, she hardly looks like a mother of eight and her white dress is demure and girlish.[5] Despite Albert's cutbacks, Victoria's spending on her wardrobe had crept up again, to roughly £6,000 annually, or six times a very good annual income for a professional gentleman.[6] But she and Albert – for Albert must approve every outfit – were conservative in their taste. A Frenchman found her frumpy, and laughed at her old-fashioned handbag 'on which was embroidered a fat poodle in gold'. It was probably the work of Princess Vicky.[7]

Although Duleep Singh had once ruled a kingdom, he was only

three years older than Vicky, and Victoria now gave him an informal, maternal welcome. At Osborne, she was completely happy, comfortable and on her own ground. The idea that the royal family needed a rural retreat had first come up in 1843. 'Albert & I talked of buying a place of our own, which would be so nice,' she'd written.[8] 'God knows how willingly I wd. always live with my beloved Albert in the quiet and retirement of private life & not be the constant object of observation and of newspaper articles.'[9] It was the then Prime Minister, Sir Robert Peel, who'd become Albert's ally and friend, who first suggested that they might buy the estate at Osborne. 'It is impossible to see a prettier spot,' Victoria enthused, 'valleys and woods which would be beautiful anywhere; but all this near the sea . . . We have a charming beach quite to ourselves.'[10]

Osborne was restful, and refreshing, but Victoria came to receive her Indian guest straight from a morning's immersion in the business of the Crimean War. She'd spent the time reading telegrams and discussing the progress of the campaign against the Russians. Her officers – to her mind inexplicably – seemed reluctant to attack Sebastopol, and cholera was racing through their men. But now, in one of those switches of gear that Victoria had to make several times a day, she offered the young Maharaja the conventional Osborne afternoon entertainment: a drizzly drive to nearby Carisbrooke Castle.

At dinner later that night, Victoria and Duleep sat next to one another, and she began to talk to him more seriously than had been possible in the carriage. He engaged her at once with his romantic story. 'I observed that he must have seen many terrible things,' Victoria recorded. 'He answered sorrowfully, with a very expressive look. "Oh! Your Majesty," he said, "I've seen dreadful things; when I think of it, it makes me shiver. I am certain they would have murdered me too, had I remained."'[11]

He was referring to his notoriously nasty childhood. In a bloody succession struggle before the British had taken over his lands, Duleep's uncle had been murdered before his eyes and two of his brothers died in mysterious circumstances.

Duleep himself was parted from his mother. The British intention had been to bring him to England and thoroughly to anglicise him, and part of this process included a supposed 'conversion' to Christianity. The first time Victoria had met Duleep Singh, a few months previously in London, his plight had made a profound impression. 'There is something too painful,' she wrote, in the spectacle 'of a young deposed Sovereign, once so powerful, receiving a pension, and having *no* security'. Victoria decided that as the chief of the princes of India, Duleep Singh should come immediately after the royal family in order of precedence. It 'will be a pleasure to us', she wrote, 'to do all we can to be of use to him, and to befriend and protect him'.[12]

The intention may have been good, but the reality was to deprive him of his patrimony and culture. In a gesture towards blending into British society, Duleep's hair was shorn off. It had previously been 'as long and abundant as a woman's', and Duleep's short new style must have been a daily reminder to him that he was no longer a Sikh.[13] His British minders thought it best not to send him to school to get a useful education, for fear that 'he might be thrashed'.[14] It gradually emerged that Duleep's role in his new London life was simply to be present at grand occasions, looking decorative and submissive. It tickled British pride to see the queen's pet Indian prince being led about, glamorous in his Indian clothes. *The Times* admired the way the 'easy and graceful folds' of his attire made 'the garments of civilised Europe' look 'infinitely prosaic and devoid of taste'.[15] He was taken to see the opening of Parliament, while Albert designed him a coat of arms.

The motto Albert chose for Duleep Singh's arms was 'to do good rather than be conspicuous', yet being conspicuous was the unfortunate prince's destiny. At Osborne Victoria now observed that her dinner-table companion was once again 'very handsomely dressed & with his jewels on', and she completed her journal entry with one of her competent little sketches to record his appearance.[16] The Maharaja's jewels were a potent subject, and over the years have become a focus for the resentment his former people still feel towards the British. For the most famous among them was the Koh-i-noor diamond, still displayed in the Tower of London today. And it was very firmly no longer in the possession of this young boy.

Earlier the same summer, Victoria had decided that her pet prince in his silken pyjamas and pearls should be painted by Franz Xaver Winterhalter. (Winterhalter added a few inches to Duleep Singh's height to make him look more imposing.) During the sittings at Buckingham Palace, Duleep had given a masterclass in the art of making a pleasing gesture. One day while Winterhalter was at work, Victoria came into the room and, as a surprise, handed Duleep Singh the Koh-i-noor.[17] It had been given to her as an (inveigled) gift after the takeover of his kingdom.[18] The diamond was displayed in the Great Exhibition of art, science and manufacture that Albert had arranged in 1851, and the queen had worn it herself on her thirty-fifth birthday earlier in 1854.[19] Duleep Singh took some time to recognise it for what it was, because since he'd last seen it, it had shrunk. The great diamond was now cut and polished, in western fashion, to flash in the light.

Once he'd identified it, though, everyone in the room waited anxiously to see how Duleep would react. This jewel was a former prized possession, something he'd worn upon his arm as a child. 'For all his air of polite interest and curiosity,' wrote the lady who'd been looking after the boy, 'there was a passion of repressed emotion in his face.' What might he do? Burst into tears, throw it out of the window? 'It was to me one of the most excruciatingly uncomfortable quarters-of-an hour that I ever passed!'

In the end, though, Duleep had remained inscrutable. He moved quietly over to Victoria and handed it back, claiming that it gave him the 'greatest pleasure', as her loyal subject, to tender 'to *my* Sovereign* the Koh-i-noor!'[20] After all, his pension and position was dependent on his remaining loyal to the British. Lord Dalhousie, governor general of India, later described this piece of theatre as 'arrant humbug'. The diamond, he thought, was not Duleep Singh's to give.[21] But the gesture won Victoria's heart.

She concluded her Osborne evening with Duleep Singh with the soothing notion that removing him from his throne had probably saved him from being murdered like his relatives. 'This thought reconciles me with having had to despoil him of his Kingdom,' she wrote, '& he is convinced of the wisdom of this himself. We were struck by his anxiety to improve himself, his intelligence, & at the same time liveliness & gaiety.'[22]

Winterhalter's portrait, and Victoria's own sketch, show Duleep Singh as westerners saw him: brimming over with exotic romance and an eagerness to please. During this present stay at Osborne, though, Victoria's German secretary Dr Ernest Becker would take a less formal photograph of Duleep, which leaves a very different impression. The young man is sullen, almost miserable, standing awkwardly. He is turbaned, yet wears European trousers. Caught between two cultures as he was, the well-meaning fussing would never solve his problems. Victoria herself recognised that with his new Christianity he was 'for ever cut off from his own people'.[23] Looking at Dr Becker's photograph today, we don't see the innocent, naïve, beautiful boy that Victoria saw. We see an adolescent caught in a terrible trap.

On the second day of Duleep Singh's stay, Victoria and Albert woke in their airy bedroom with views of the sea. Soon after their purchase of Osborne, it had become clear that the existing Georgian house was too small. Privy Council meetings had to take place in the entrance hall, or else outdoors. The Privy Councillors got fed up with being brought from the steamer pier in a one-horsed 'small bathing carriage', designed to take at most two swimmers down to the beach.[24] Osborne was to be a holiday home, but royal business must continue, and it demanded better facilities.

And in truth Albert was attracted to the project of rebuilding the house as much as to the island itself. On visits to Osborne, he enjoyed becoming 'partly forester, partly builder, partly farmer and partly gardener', and relished being 'a good deal upon [his] legs'.[25] Convinced by Albert that he knew far more about it, Victoria deferred to him in all the creative decisions. She 'had no taste', she told third parties, 'used only to listen to him'.[26] It was hard to avoid listening to Albert if he wanted to tell you something, especially something about art or design, as even the Pope discovered. During his brief papal audience in Rome, Albert recorded how 'in spite of his infallibility' he had ventured to put the pontiff right on a point of art history.[27]

In 1845, the foundation stone for Albert's new house was laid. Osborne's architecture divides people today. Some find it institutional and grim. But its many fans see it as the triumphant achievement of Albert's orderly, logical, Renaissance-loving mind, brought to fruition by the Victorian über-builder Thomas Cubitt (the man who'd made his name building Belgravia). The first part of the house to be completed was the pavilion, containing matching suites for both queen and prince. It looks like a Belgravian town house detached from its neighbours, and plonked upon a seaside hilltop.

The family moved in with enormous excitement and some trepidation: this was to be a new kind of royal living. The 'dining room looked very handsome', wrote the children's governess that first night. 'The windows, lighted by the brilliant lamps in the room, must have been seen far out to sea.'[28] When the shutters of these windows were closed, mirrors attached to their insides cleverly magnified the light of the chandeliers. The house was full of ingenious Albertian touches like this, as well as the 'fireproof' structure of iron girders, the bathrooms and the flushing toilets. Albert's own bath was hidden beneath a wooden lid, which makes it look curiously like a coffin, while Victoria's was hidden in a cupboard. A furnace in the basement provided hot water. Victoria's dressing room also had the novelty of a plumbed-in shower, while her commode, off her bedroom, was hidden behind a door discreetly disguised as part of the built-in mahogany wardrobe.

Downstairs on the principal entertaining floor of the pavilion, architectural historian Mark Girouard has noted how the billiard room, drawing room and dining room all flow one into another, round corners. This allowed the court and guests to be present in one space, as politeness demanded, yet able to choose their own entertainments: equerries playing billiards on the special table designed by Albert himself, ladies sewing in the drawing room. Or indeed, Victoria and Albert could send their court out of sight round one of the corners so that its wearier members could simply sit down – something they weren't allowed to do in the royal presence.[29]

But Osborne's interiors were not to everyone's taste. 'You cannot think,' wrote one unusually subversive maid-of-honour, 'how some of the atrocities here strike me. It certainly is the oddest combination of upholstery; hideous presents they have received, and as ill-arranged rooms as I ever saw.'[30] The colours are mauve, maroon, blue and gold, a discordant jangle to modern eyes, while the carpets are luridly flowered. Every surface remains encrusted with ornaments and knick-knacks, as if Victoria and Albert had only just finished arranging their eccentric palace. Their servants found remote Osborne dull and inconvenient. The male servants had to be taken to their own quarters, separate from the main house, by a wagon that departed every night at eleven, and 'the Queen's staff, without exception, dislike staying there'.[31]

While Victoria and Albert began the day in the main pavilion of Osborne House, Duleep Singh woke up in his own separate suite. It lay in an extension, a bulky block in a rather cack-handed classical style. It had been found necessary to add this block to provide enough room for the household. Lofty and gloomy corridors, with icy-white marble statues and the dull gleam of bronzes at intervals, had led him here after his first night's dinner. Victoria's mother also often occupied rooms in this extension. Brought back into sympathy with Victoire by her own experience of childbearing, and the strong relationship that Albert had built up with his mother-in-law and aunt, Victoria now liked to have her mother around.

The Indian prince joined the royal family's outdoor breakfast, during which the queen proudly watched her visitor 'playing so nicely' with her children. Afterwards Duleep was given another Osborne 'treat', a tour of the royal farm.

His hosts noticed that what particularly interested him at the farm was 'the Machinery'. Duleep had grown up in a country of swords, spears and subsistence agriculture, and now he was coming up close to Victorian technology. After lunch, the party set out for the royal yacht (in fact a paddle steamer) named *Victoria & Albert*. They steamed off to the Needles at the western end of the island, to observe the navy testing a new gunboat. It was a further lesson to the Maharaja in how soundly he and his people had been beaten.

On the return journey, the heavy swell made Victoria 'feel rather giddy', but she still managed to have 'a most interesting conversation' with Duleep about Christianity. Duleep's new religion had estranged him from his family. His sister-in-law, for example, would no longer touch or hug him.[32] But Victoria wanted to believe that her protégé's conversion was sincere and lasting. He'd been listening to an account of the stoning of St Stephen, Duleep explained, when he'd found his eyes filling with tears. He'd come to the sudden realisation that 'this religion must be true'. This was exactly what Victoria wanted to hear; she also reassured herself that he was 'aware of the difference & defects of the Catholic Religion'.[33] The merchants of the East India Company who'd first established links with India had not particularly cared about religion; they were more concerned about making money. But in the nineteenth century, a flood of British Christian missionaries to India had brought with them a new sense of moral purpose that had deepened the clashes with Indian indigenous cultures. And what else could Duleep Singh say about religion, anyway? His Christianity was certainly a precondition of his pension.

The third day of Duleep's stay dawned dull, but everyone hoped it would turn fine later. This was the day of the annual Osborne servants' beano in honour of Albert's birthday. After breakfast, Victoria's children took Duleep off her hands, and dragged him along to their Swiss cottage.[34]

This was, and is, a wooden chalet imported from the Continent and only just finished by the time Duleep saw it. The cottage was intended to be an educational facility for the royal children, where they were encouraged to acquire the practical skills of baking and gardening. They were supposed to learn the value of money by selling goods to each other from the miniature counter of Spratt's Grocer. Vicky was now nearly fourteen, and at seventeen she would marry. She'd already known her future husband, a Prussian prince, for three years. After Vicky's wedding, her siblings kept her supplied with the pies they'd once all baked together at the Swiss cottage. The queen's messenger took them weekly to her new home in Germany, a poignant gift from children to a married woman who was still really a child herself.[35]

Life at the Swiss cottage sounds pleasantly domesticated, but the royal children also used it for wickedness and war. It was behind the cottage that they'd meet up for an illicit smoke, something even the girls enjoyed. When they inevitably got detected because of the smell, Alice thought it most unfair that she was punished while her brothers were forgiven.[36] Arthur, the third brother, had made himself master of the wooden cannon defending the fortification at the back of the Swiss cottage.[37] When given a military uniform for Christmas, Arthur got into it at once, seized his 'little rifle' and 'took a pot-shot at his papa'.[38] He would end up as field marshal of the army that expanded his mother's empire to its most bloated state towards the end of her reign.[39]

At mid-morning, the children took Duleep down to the beach.[40] Here, in 1847, Victoria had for the very first time 'bathed in the sea . . . I thought it delightful till I put my head under water.'[41] Her bathing machine, a wooden hut on wheels, would roll her into the waves so that she could emerge through its curtained doorway and descend its five porch steps directly into the water. The queen's machine later spent many years being used as a chicken coop before recently being returned to its original place on the beach. The children, too, learned to swim from this beach, in the safety of 'a well-arranged floating bath' invented for the purpose by Albert.[42] There was no time for swimming today, though, for it was back to the house, where tents for the estate workers, tenants and servants had been erected on the lawn. As Victoria and her children inspected the encampment, greeting the guests, Arthur was seen 'taking the Maharajah's hand.'[43]

The senior members of the household thought the annual Osborne fête a chore. Governess Laddle thought it 'noisy, merry and intensely boring', the 'footmen and housemaids pounding away their ale'.[44] Victoria's journal, though, shows that the children took a less jaundiced view. 'It was very gay,' she says, particularly when the gentlemen of the household 'took part in running races, playing leap frog &c'. There was juggling, blind man's buff, a wheelbarrow race and dipping for oranges. And 'no one enjoyed it more' than Duleep Singh, 'who laughed heartily & was greatly amused. Our Children were constantly near him & chatting with him & he carried little Leopold [the newest baby] who is so fond of him, in his arms.'[45] It seems that after three days in the company of other children, the Maharaja remembered at last that he too was a boy.

Duleep departed from Osborne the next morning, but he left behind some of his wonderful wardrobe so that Affie and Arthur could be photographed in the costume of Sikh princes. Martial little Arthur looks insouciant in his turban, while Affie, always a melancholy soul, adopts the noble, downward gaze of the dispossessed prince himself, while wearing what looks suspiciously like his mother's necklace of pearls.[46]

Victoria was sorry to see Duleep go. 'I take quite a maternal interest in him,' she wrote, and hoped he might 'be kept as good & innocent, as he is at present'.[47] Lord Dalhousie of India, for his part, considered that her compassion for the ex-prince was 'superfluous . . . he will have a good and regular income all his life, and will die in his bed like a gentleman'.[48] Dalhousie thought it was most unfortunate that Victoria had shown the prince such favour. After he'd been so intimate with the royal family at Osborne, how would Duleep Singh stomach taking off his shoes, as he must, as a sign of respect in the presence of India's governor general?

The guests gone, the servants' ball over, Victoria and Albert retreated into their own company: 'We dined alone, read, & played.'[49] Victoria described an evening like this, without the responsibility for entertaining or being entertained, as her ideal. 'I sit on a sofa,' she explains, reading by lamp- and candlelight, with 'Albert sitting in a low arm-chair, on the opposite side of the table with another small table in front of him on which he usually stands his book'.

Their idea of being 'alone', though, did not exclude servants. As she and Albert passed the time 'talking over the company', Victoria also gives details of how her 'maids would come in and begin to undress me – and he would go on talking, and would make his observations on my jewels and ornaments and give my people good advice as to how to keep them or would occasionally reprimand if anything had not been carefully attended to'.[50]

Once you know that Victoria's treasured evenings with her husband involved him castigating the servants who were undressing her, it doesn't sound like quite such a snug domestic idyll. In this closed environment of Osborne, Albert would exert ever greater control over his family and his wife. 'Four weeks of success in the hard struggle for self-control,' he would commend Victoria the following year, praising her for suppressing the emotions and anger that upset him.[51] 'The queen is married just as any other woman is,' Victoria claimed, 'and swears to obey her lord and master'.[52]

Cultural historian Adrienne Munich points out that with his dominance and her submission they were simply acting out the plot of so many mid-Victorian novels, in which a spirited woman is 'humbled by difficulties in her encounters with the world; then, softened by passion, she serves her happy days by submitting to a man'. Dorothea Brooke in *Middlemarch* (1871–2), the heroine of Charlotte Brontë's *Shirley* (1849) and of Mrs Gaskell's *North and South* (1855) all make the same journey.[53]

But rows nevertheless still occurred because Victoria did *not* always quite submit. One of the points of issue was the limited amount of time that they were able to spend together like this. In shielding her from government business by taking so much of it upon himself, Albert kept himself hideously busy, and denied his wife the company she ardently desired. Albert's dedication to his self-perceived duty bordered on the dysfunctional. Wanting to please him, Victoria 'kept every letter and box to tell & show him.' Yet she dreaded showing him 'any foolish draft or despatch' as she 'knew it would distress and irritate him'.[54]

Albert's irritation was a signal of trouble to come. And despite the warm maternal wishes that Victoria expressed when he left the Isle of Wight, the story of Duleep Singh wasn't going to end happily either.

When much of the Indian subcontinent rebelled just three years later, Victoria's government expected Duleep Singh to condemn his countrymen. But instead there came from him only an ominous silence. She was forced to defend him, praising the 'extreme gentleness' he'd displayed when he'd played with her children.[55] Unsuspected by the queen, though, Duleep during his visit to Osborne must have experienced something of the same resentment that lay behind the violence in India. As he grew up, Duleep gradually began to move towards the conclusion that he had – as he put it – 'been cheated out of his kingdom, and out of his private estates'.[56]

In 1884 he returned to India, with the intention also of returning to the Sikh religion, but the British government would not allow him to stay. Before his lonely death, which took place in Paris in 1893, Duleep Singh was heard referring to Victoria, the present owner of his people's diamond, as a receiver of stolen goods. His name for her was 'Mrs Fagin'.[57]

15

Miss Nightingale at Balmoral, 21 September 1856

On 21 September 1856, James Clark was driving along the wooded banks of the River Dee towards Balmoral Castle. He was coming from the nearby valley of Glen Muick, where the queen had lent him a house. Clark's route took him through an ancient forest alongside the river. On a sunny day, the Dee's water runs as brown as tea, but this was a miserably wet autumn. 'Crops much damaged,' Dr Clark recorded in his journal, while the river, usually thigh-high, was five feet deep.[1] It was twenty-one years since he had 'saved' the princess from typhoid in Ramsgate. Despite the unfortunate business of Flora Hastings, Clark was still, at sixty-seven, Victoria's most trusted doctor.

He was accompanied on his journey to Balmoral by his house guest: a tall, angular, dark-eyed woman who was thirty-six years old. Despite being just one year younger than Victoria, now pregnant for the ninth time, Miss Florence Nightingale was childless and unmarried. She had 'a good clear complexion, and pretty mouth and smile', but did not set much store by looking handsome. Her strengths lay elsewhere. Reports had already reached the court that she was 'very quiet and businesslike' yet 'wonderfully clever, full of information on all subjects, a good classical scholar, knowing Greek and Hebrew and those sort of things'.

She could have been cold and formidable, but Florence Nightingale had a knack of winning people over. Despite her 'very quiet, rather stern manner', people said, there was 'an immense deal of fun about her'.[2] Today she wore her customary black, and a 'simple little cap, tied under her chin'. Her dark hair had been cut off because of her work, important work that she wanted to discuss with the queen. For she was an eyewitness to the recent mismanagement of the British forces out in Crimea, and her hair had been shorn 'on account of the insects with which the poor men were covered in the Hospitals!'[3] She was still frequently made nauseous by a mysterious Balkan disease that would plague her for years.

Florence knew Dr Clark well because four years earlier, in 1852, he'd treated her sister Parthenope for another incomprehensible and debilitating illness. Parthenope had at least partially recovered through rainy walks and the sparklingly clear air at Dr Clark's quiet Deeside home. Today we might call Parthenope's condition a nervous breakdown, but Dr Clark had thought her in danger of lunacy, exhibiting 'a total absorption in self, with, at times, chronic delirium'.

According to her biographer Mark Bostridge, though, Florence believed differently: that her sister's condition was all too common among many a well-off spinster, 'condemned to spend her days in a meaningless round of trivial occupations, which ate away at her vital strength'.[4] Parthenope's illness, Florence thought, was simply caused by boredom, 'by the conventional life of the present phase of civilisation, which fritters away all that is spiritual in women'.[5] Watching Parthenope lose her sanity, her strength, even the ability to walk, had left Florence aghast. She observed that all around her women were going 'mad for the want of something to do'.[6] She was determined to avoid this fate for herself.

Her chance had come in 1853 when a dispute broke out between Russia and Turkey. The issue of whether Orthodox or westernised monks should control access to the holy places of Palestine became a trigger both for war and for enormous upheaval in Florence's genteel upper-class life. Soon Russia had invaded Turkey, the French had taken Turkey's side and Britain had followed France into the conflict. Britain and its rich, industrialised allies faced a vast, ill-equipped Russian army whose lack of transport forced its soldiers to walk to the field of conflict. The British were always going to win the Crimean War. But they did so with a surprising amount of pain and ineptitude. At peace for over forty years, the British army was sorely puzzled by the logistics of fighting in a theatre 3,000 miles away. Disease killed more men than enemy action, and the treatment of the British wounded was shockingly bad. Florence Nightingale began to experience a savage desire to do something to help, specifically to lead a team of nurses out to Crimea. Eventually 'Flo's' friends and family accepted the inevitable, gave in and 'allowed' her to go to war.

The Crimean War was the making of the legend of Miss Nightingale, but it was almost the breaking of Victoria. 'Lord John Russell may resign and Lord Aberdeen may resign,' she complained, as the war took a turn for the worse, 'I sometimes wish I could.'[7] It was the most severe test she had yet faced as queen. She herself was deeply frustrated by her government's cautious approach to intervention, which had, she believed, merely encouraged Russian bellicosity. Eventually it became clear that she had to appoint Lord Palmerston as premier, despite her personal dislike of him, as only he had the gumption to lead Britain out of the crisis.[8]

Yet this war, however mis-fought, would bring about a change for the better in the way Victoria ruled. It also illustrated the essential difference between her way of doing things and Albert's. His contribution to the war effort lies in no fewer than fifty bound volumes of correspondence. Training his intellect upon the problem, he compiled detailed plans for drumming up a foreign force to help the British.[9] His plans were rejected, and once they got out, he was pilloried in the press and even accused of treason. Victoria, on the other hand, brought her emotional intelligence to bear. As someone who felt, and suffered, and who could share other people's pain, she revealed herself to be a gifted leader in a way that eluded Albert. It was a 'relief' to write letters of condolence to the parents of the fallen, she explained, as she now so often did, because it allowed her to express 'all that she felt'.[10] In the crisis of the war, through consoling, and rebuilding confidence, Victoria began to show what she might be capable of as a queen. By seeing off her soldiers, receiving the wounded, and publically praising and giving gifts to the troops, she emerged more popular than ever. She managed to make a nation feel that she cared.

This instinct that Victoria had, for entering into the minds of so many of her subjects, had such a subtle, everyday quality that many historians have overlooked it. One of Albert's biographers thought that her diaries 'make very revealing but somewhat depressing reading; there is an artless shallowness about them that reveals not only a selfishness . . . but a melancholy lack of imagination.' 'She was highly emotional and very impressionable,' this historian concludes.[11] Albert could also never be accused of being 'highly emotional' or 'very impressionable'. But he could also never touch the hearts of the British people. It was a later Prime Minister, Lord Salisbury, who claimed that if he heard Victoria's views on any issue, he knew that he was hearing the opinion of the steady, respectable, upper-middle classes. 'She was able to interpret and express the spirit and temper,' wrote someone else who knew her, 'of that class which, throughout her reign, was destined to hold the balance of political power in its hands.'[12]

But it took disaster for this special talent of Victoria's to emerge. On 11 March 1854, she'd been afloat on the Solent to watch her great fleet sailing east. All too soon, 'unsatisfactory accounts' of her soldiers' supplies, welfare and treatment began to arrive.[13] In October, Victoria first heard of a plan to 'send out 30 Nurses for the Hospitals at Scutari & Varna, under a Miss Nightingale, who is a remarkable person, having studied both Medicine & Surgery & having practised in Hospitals at Paris & in Germany'.[14]

'We have now four miles of beds of not 18 inches apart,' Miss Nightingale reported in November from the field hospital at Scutari, 'the dysentery cases have died at the rate of one in two.'[15] Florence's letters home were widely circulated, fanning the flames of an increasingly sordid scandal of army negligence. Victoria was on the side of the nurses and men. 'The Queen trusts,' she wrote, to the rather useless Lord Raglan, that he would 'be *very* strict in seeing that no *unnecessary* privations are incurred by any negligence of those whose duty it is to watch over their wants.'[16]

Victoria followed Miss Nightingale's exploits closely. 'I envy her,' she admitted, 'being able to do so much good & look after the noble brave heroes.'[17] Searching for something that she could do herself, Victoria came up with the idea of the Victoria Cross for soldiers, a medal 'For Valour'. As a personal thank you to Florence, she sent a feminine equivalent, a brooch with a red enamel cross, along with a warmly written letter full of concern for the well-being of Florence's patients at Scutari. Victoria was slightly shocked to discover that Florence had copies of this letter 'stuck up in every ward'. But Miss Nightingale explained that many of the soldiers 'beg for a copy to keep as their greatest treasure, some saying, that they will learn it by heart, & some, how feeling they think it of the Queen to say what she has'.[18] Victoria listened, and learned. She would explore this growing power of her pen.

For her part, Florence Nightingale knew all about the power of propaganda. A mistress of public relations, she jealously guarded her own image. Most Britons didn't know what their national heroine looked like, for she refused to sit for a portrait, citing a dislike of being 'made a show of'. As a Victorian woman determined to play a part in public life, she had to be extra-careful to maintain her respectability, and this meant trying to stay out of the papers. The newspapers, though, were so keen to meet readers' demands to see something of the celebrated Miss Nightingale that they just went ahead and published imaginary images instead. So rare were likenesses of Florence Nightingale that one completely fictional image even ended up being used in a textbook on physiognomy to demonstrate that she was the 'pinnacle of British womanhood'. These made-up pictures in fact made 'the Heroine of Scutari', as the *Weekly News* named her, look extraordinarily similar to the queen.[19]

By 21 September 1856, the war was over, and Dr Clark had suggested that the two women might like to meet face-to-face.

Miss Nightingale accepted his invitation because, as always, she could see a chance to promote the cause of medical reform. She sought advice on how best to influence the queen. The idea emerged that she should suggest a royal commission to investigate the army's medical department. It was relatively easy to improve conditions in barracks and hospitals; harder to change the mentality of the institution that was ultimately responsible for providing such things – and here Victoria might be able to help.

Whatever Victoria might think, Miss Nightingale wasn't coming to Balmoral just to be admired and thanked. She was here to do business.

The queen's castle towards which Florence Nightingale and Dr Clark now drew near contained around seventy rooms, four bathrooms, fourteen water closets and a ballroom. Building work had been completed just twelve months previously. It was quite small for a royal residence, although its turrets, corners and oversized baronial tower made it look bigger than it was. The carriage halted at the porte cochère, where Florence stepped into a tiled entrance hall with antlers lining its walls. It led straight into a sitting room beyond. Balmoral was short of public rooms, because it wasn't designed for large-scale entertaining. It had been created by an Aberdeen architect as a base for Albert to go shooting or stalking, and for Victoria to humour him. The marble coat of arms that surmounted the front door wasn't hers; it was his.[20]

It was the success of Osborne that inspired Victoria and Albert to seek another home even more distant from their London life and responsibilities. Victoria first set foot in Scotland in 1842, having travelled there by sea, and instantly adored it. Albert also liked Scotland because it reminded him of Germany, the towns 'very German-looking' and the people 'like Germans'.[21] 'The people,' he thought, 'are marked by that honesty and sympathy, which always distinguish the inhabitants of mountainous countries.'[22]

As readers of Scott's stirring, chivalric stories from history, they both liked the way that every Scottish spot seemed connected with 'some interesting historical fact, and with most of these Sir Walter Scott's accurate descriptions have made us familiar'.[23] One of the great Scottish lords, welcoming Victoria into his home, gave her such a 'princely and romantic' reception that she was left feeling 'as if a great chieftain in olden feudal times was receiving his sovereign'. This particular host, Lord Breadalbane, conducted the couple through a hall and staircase 'lined with Highlanders', and as dusk fell, the words 'Welcome Victoria – Albert' were spelt out in lamps on the hillside while bonfires blazed on the mountain peaks beyond.[24] For them both, it felt like a spiritual homecoming. At their costume balls at Buckingham Palace, Victoria and Albert had played out the chivalric fantasies they knew so well from Sir Walter. But now, visiting Scotland, they seemed to be stepping into a living world of the past.

It was Dr Clark, already responsible for Victoria's love of fresh air, who introduced the idea that they should acquire a permanent Scottish home. In 1848, Albert opted to rent Balmoral, an estate that had come onto the market after its owner died choking on a fish bone. He made the decision after completing a thorough study of the Scottish weather, which revealed that it rained less on this eastern side of the country. Even so, Dr Clark's own journal, recording autumnal stays at Balmoral and his borrowed home at Birkhall nearby, reads repetitively: 'a drizzly rain . . . a drizzly rain . . . scarcely a day has passed without some rain, some days very wet.'[25]

After purchasing the lease for Balmoral, Victoria and Albert discovered that living there delighted them. The estate, and that of neighbouring Birkhall, encompassed miles of bleak Cairngorm hillside, including the noble peak of Lochnagar and the deep, remote, black loch of Muick.

The new house that Albert now set about building at Balmoral was inspired by the Schloss Rosenau, a much-missed home of his childhood, and he persisted in thinking the wild country of Deeside to be just like Thuringia. (His brother Ernest, however, insisted that it was not.) The completed castle was rather a jumble of architectural styles, and even the loyal Dr Clark secretly admitted in his journal that its colossal tower was 'rather too high for the House, or rather the House too low for the tower'.[26]

Arriving there herself in Dr Clark's carriage, Florence Nightingale was probably surprised – as other visitors were – by the low-key, casual nature of the reception at the castle. There was 'not even a sentinel to be seen', wrote one bemused German count, who was astonished to have been allowed to drive straight up to the door. 'As I entered the hall,' he continued, 'which is ornamented with stags' antlers, I was received by the tones of a bagpipe.'[27]

But Victoria and Albert revelled in the informality of their Highland life. They were protected by just 'a single Policeman . . . who walks about the grounds to keep off impertinent intruders'.[28] Victoria's journal shows the delight she took in covering many miles by foot. Rain gear was highly necessary. The royal family got theirs, made from 'Shetland home-spun Tweed', from the appropriately named Scott Adie, 'Waterproof Cloak and Jacket Maker to Her Majesty'.[29] 'Heavy boots,' wrote one Balmoral visitor, 'and a blue cape . . . with one's skirt hitched up high, and a mighty stick in one's hand – that is how one goes out walking here'.[30]

Once inside the castle, Dr Clark sent Florence on through to the drawing room overlooking lawns down to the Dee. This room made such a striking impression on one visitor that he was heard to say that while he'd formerly thought the drawing room at Osborne the 'ugliest in the world', he'd changed his mind upon seeing its equivalent at Balmoral.[31]

The walls were painted in the 'pale, cold tints which were so fashionable in the '50s', with colour provided by carpets and curtains of Royal Stuart tartan, a theme that ran throughout the whole building.[32] The castle's tartan furnishings made an effect 'more patriotic than artistic', in the words of one of Victoria's grandchildren, while another visitor thought them proof that being Queen of Scotland 'involves painful aesthetic considerations'.[33] Some visitors experienced 'tartanitis', for the ubiquitous checks 'had a way of flickering before your eyes and confusing your brain'.[34] Albert had even designed a special new Balmoral tartan of lilac, red and black. His children went about in plaid kilts, and there was even tartan linoleum in the servants' quarters.

Meanwhile the Highland theme continued in many additional forms: 'the wall-lights are silver antlers, guns or game-bags, and if one's pen needs dipping, one must look for ink in the back of a hound or a boar.'[35] Thistles were important too, sprouting in stone along the castle's roofline, and incorporated into the design of candelabra, dessert plates and wallpaper. The abundance of thistles, claimed one visitor, would 'rejoice the heart of a donkey if they happened to *look like* his favourite repast which they don't'.[36] But Victoria and Albert couldn't care less about the mockery of their guests. The castle for them meant golden days, a less formal, more natural life. Victoria's staff were highly aware of her 'passionate admiration for the Highlands. Leaving them is always a case of actual *red eyes.*'[37]

Victoria and Albert's family and household, however, were far from loving Balmoral with an equal fervour themselves. 'That *most* VILE and *most* ABOMINABLE of places' is what their youngest son Leopold called it, while both upper and lower servants got bored.[38] 'We have no duties to perform to occupy our minds,' they complained, 'and the weather is horribly cold and wet . . . we just exist from meal to meal and do our best to kill time.'[39] 'It is very cold here,' wrote one disgruntled guest. 'I believe my feet were frostbitten at dinner, for there was no fire at all there, and in the drawing room there were two little sticks which hissed at the man who attempted to light them.'[40] Whichever government minister was appointed to be in attendance dreaded the task, for he had no sitting room, and 'was obliged to transact all his work in his bedroom'.[41] This lack of space had been a deliberate ploy to make the house as holiday-orientated as possible.

It was partly because they were bored that the household were now full of excitement at the prospect of seeing Florence Nightingale for themselves. More importantly, though, the heroine of Scutari had long been the subject of admiring letters to and from court. These letters told of her 'knack of getting round people and bringing them to think as she does, in a remarkable degree'.[42] Now it was to be seen if Florence could 'get round' the queen.

Victoria had first met Florence on the latter's presentation at court in 1839 when they were both in their late teens. Florence had then found the young queen 'flushed and tired', but self-possessed, 'not nearly so much frightened as I expected'.[43] But now, nearly twenty years later, their roles were reversed. It was Florence who had the more self-assurance, and the queen who was flustered.

Doubtless Victoria had her usual 'half-a-dozen dogs' in tow, who accompanied her 'when she moved anywhere'.[44] To receive her guest, she was likely wearing something like her surviving day dress of lilac silk from this same year of 1856, which has grey silk ribbons running between waist and hem inside so that the skirt can be drawn up for convenient walking.[45]

During this particular Scottish holiday, though, Victoria hadn't been out walking as much as usual. She was pregnant, again, with Beatrice, her ninth baby. The recent weather had been so rainy, 'without ceasing for a week', all the children had colds, and she hadn't been getting on well with Albert.[46] Both she and he were chagrined that she'd been advised to withdraw her proposal to make him 'Prince Consort', on the grounds that Parliament were most unlikely to allow it.[47]

Victoria now found the woman approaching her across the tartan carpet to be 'tall, & slight, with fine dark eyes, & must have been very pretty', even if she'd become 'very thin & care worn'.[48] Despite the helpful presence of the pets, communication between the two women proved difficult. Victoria was unable to keep up the conversation for more than ten minutes before she resorted to calling Albert into the drawing room to help. Florence began to think, somewhat contemptuously, that Victoria must be 'the least self-reliant person she had ever known'.[49] Dr Clark had earlier that year fretted that the queen was still 'frequently low and nervous', noting that much 'depends on the Prince's management'.[50] Victoria had been encouraged to believe that she was weak, inadequate and unable to cope without him.

And the truth was that she was both tongue-tied and star-struck. Victoria admired Florence immensely, not least because despite her power and charisma she had successfully maintained her maidenly manner, 'travelling under a feigned name, so as not to be known, & refusing all public demonstrations'. Victoria also actively wanted to share the experience of Miss Nightingale with Albert rather than keep it all to herself. 'I had expected a rather cold, stiff, reserved person,' she admitted later, 'instead of which, she is gentle, pleasing & engaging, most ladylike, & so clever, clear & comprehensive in her views of everything.'[51] Victoria sometimes found it difficult to keep the conversation going even in a meeting with her Prime Minister ('fog and rain and [her] coming journey to Italy all did their duty and helped').[52] But Victoria found Florence a particularly daunting conversationalist because the latter simply didn't waste time with small talk. 'Her mind is solely & entirely taken up with the one object,' Victoria noted, 'the subject of medicine.'[53] Florence, then, was the sort of woman of whom Albert had taught Victoria to approve: rational, focused, yet modest.

Now, to both queen and her husband, Miss Nightingale began to expound upon the need for the reform of the army's medical practice. Eighteen thousand men had died in Crimea, but the majority of them were the victims of disease, not the Russians. She 'talked principally of the want of system & organisation which had existed, & been the cause of so much suffering & misery'. And then Florence came on to the meat of her business: 'the necessity for this being improved'.[54] Albert, of course, grew engaged at once, and he and Florence began to discuss the matter thoroughly. Victoria watched and listened, while 'Albert stated in his usual clear, comprehensive way, where, in his opinion, the root of the evil lay.'[55] Florence realised immediately where power lay. 'Albert was really a Minister,' she noticed, 'this very few knew.'[56]

Before she left the Balmoral drawing room, though, Florence did at last find the key to 'getting round' Victoria. She could see that the queen was less interested in the correct placing of hospital beds, and royal commissions, and she found just the right thing to say to put Victoria at ease. 'She thanked me for my support & sympathy,' Victoria proudly recorded in her journal, 'saying, that to a man, the soldiers had all deeply felt & appreciated my sympathy & interest.'[57]

After the sticky start, the afternoon had gone so well that Florence was asked to come back, to stay overnight. During this second visit, everyone under Balmoral's roof fell under the spell of their sombre visitor. Victoria was emboldened to show her a book of photographs she'd commissioned of wounded soldiers, and Florence entreated that their pensions be continued.[58]

Miss Nightingale 'is wonderful', gushed one courtier, praising 'the sweetness of her smile and the grace of her every movement'. Even Victoria's mother was enraptured. 'After dinner,' wrote a lady-in-waiting, 'H.R.H. confided to me that she had wished to propose her health, but was too shy!!! . . . Poor Miss N. would have been tolerably overpowered – it was just as well . . . The servants were all in such a state to see her.' The ladies recorded the conversation at dinner about the hospital at Scutari:

> We asked how many times she went around at night. 'Three', she said (sometimes there were 2,000 patients).
> 'Then when did you sleep?'
> 'Oh! That first winter we did not feel as if we needed much sleep.' I suppose she never went to bed!![59]

Despite the awe of the household, though, the rest of the meal was rather silent, and Miss Nightingale certainly seemed thoroughly out of place at the ball that followed dinner.

It took place in the vast high-ceilinged ballroom added onto the Deeside flank of the house. This room had antlers on its walls, and tall windows with tartan curtains. There was an elevated alcove for the royal family to sit and watch their ghillies and tenants performing reels, but Victoria did not make much use of it. It was only in the Highlands that she felt able to release the pent-up love of late nights and dancing that had caused Albert to despair before he coached her out of making an exhibition of herself before London society. In the privacy of a Scottish ball, though, 'Her Majesty was very much amused throughout the whole evening. She scarcely ceased laughing and kept time with her hands and feet in true Highland style to the music.'[60] Victoria had learned Highland reeling from the Balmoral household dancing master, who would treat her like any other pupil: 'now gently, me deare, try and dance like a lady.'[61]

It was quite a compliment to Florence, then, to have been invited to one of these intimate Balmoral balls, especially as the new ball-room was looking 'extremely pretty' with its lamps 'decorated with wreaths of flowers'. Miss Nightingale was, as usual, 'dressed in black', but Victoria herself would dress for dancing in 'gray watered silk, and (according to the Highland fashion) my plaid scarf over my shoulder'.[62] She was never so happy as when pretending to be Scottish, and the ball came to an end only when refreshments were served at one the next morning.

But Florence had not enjoyed herself. 'Flo says,' recorded a correspondent who heard from her afterwards, that 'Balls are dull affairs & the Queen ought not to dance.'[63] 'Flo' would perhaps have preferred to have spent the evening talking with Albert, who could also be a bit sniffy about the rowdy behaviour of the Highland servants on these occasions, with their 'veritable Witches' dance, supported by whiskey'.[64] Albert was much more engaged by the insights Florence had been able to give him. 'She put before us,' he wrote in his diary, 'all the defects of our present military hospital system, and the reforms that are needed. We are much pleased with her; she is extremely modest.'[65]

Despite her own admiration of Albert, though, Florence could also see that there was something awry with his personality. With his precise, Teutonic rationality, all 'prizes and exhibitions and good intentions', Albert seemed cold, even soulless. He looked, Florence thought, 'like a person who wanted to die'.[66] It was a remarkable intuition, for no one else there that night of the Balmoral ball had an inkling that indeed he might not live much longer.

In the days that followed, Victoria and Albert decided to give Florence their support in trying to get the army's medical service completely overhauled. Victoria instructed Florence to remain as Dr Clark's guest until Lord Panmure, Secretary of State for War, could be summoned to Scotland. Victoria, or possibly Albert drafting in her name, had already been harassing him for change.[67] She now insisted that Panmure come to Balmoral to hear Florence's views 'from her own lips', promising that he would be 'much gratified and struck'.[68] Florence was more sceptical that this would produce any results, but felt herself 'obliged to succumb'.[69]

However, after a couple of meetings with Panmure, she was to be surprised by the warmth of his response to her ideas. 'You fairly overcame Pan,' wrote Dr Clark's son to tell Florence of the impression she had made, claiming that she'd turned the embattled Secretary of State's frazzled 'mane absolutely silky'.[70] Panmure asked Florence to draw up a confidential report on what she felt ought to be done, and she set to work immediately. [71]

'We are delighted,' was Victoria's conclusion on the whole visit, 'I wish we had her at the War Office.'[72] But in fact she had no constitutional power to impose such a thing and nor – according to Nightingale's biographer Mark Bostridge – did she quite share Florence's vision for reform, feeling that a change of personnel should be enough.[73]

And indeed, despite Florence's admirable, masculine grasp of business, and her gleeful anticipation of 'hard work & time spent in London & elsewhere to see men & Institutions' in the cause of reform, something was not quite right with her either. Gradually her health would break down until she was forced to carry on her detailed, almost obsessive written plans for administrative improvement from her bed. But Victoria's admiration remained strong, and in the 1860s she would offer the increasingly sick Florence Nightingale accommodation in her own old home of Kensington Palace.[74]

And Parthenope, the sister whose mental illness and treatment by Dr Clark had introduced the whole encounter at Balmoral, felt sad that her younger sibling's magnificent achievements had effectively broken their family bond. 'Flo,' she wrote sadly, 'is not my sister any more, but the Mother of a great army.'[75]

Neither Victoria, nor Florence Nightingale, both of them 'mothers of a great army' in their different ways, fitted easily into Victorian family life.

16

A Night with Nellie: 6 September 1861

Five years later, at half past nine on the grey morning of 24 August 1861, Victoria was travelling south-west from Dublin by railway. She was going deeper into Ireland, towards a gigantic military camp. More than 10,000 of her soldiers spent each summer practising drill on the long flat plain called the Curragh. This year, they'd been joined by Victoria's eldest son Bertie, Prince of Wales, who was now just short of twenty.

The Curragh Plain was an ancient mustering ground for troops, which had been re-established as a military base in 1855 to train infantry destined for the Crimean War. The soldiers occupied hutments and tents sprawling along a ridge above a plain covered with furze, sheep and no fewer than forty-four prehistoric earthworks.[1] The rich grassland of the Curragh Plain was also grazed by the horses that ran at its famous racecourse. It was 'a splendid position', Victoria thought, with 'an immense amount of turf'.[2] The turf still exists to this day despite the despoliations of the modern world, including a motorway. It is so intensely green in colour that it can only be described as emerald.

The army that had eventually bumbled its way to victory for Victoria in the Crimean War included some 37,000 Irishmen, 40 per cent of its strength. Yet Victoria had markedly different feelings towards Ireland than to her beloved Scotland. Like so many members of the British establishment, she had a deep-rooted suspicion of the Catholic Church.[3] The two countries of Britain and Ireland had been spliced together into a United Kingdom only sixty years previously, a defensive measure on Britain's part to make its colony less vulnerable to insurrection and French invasion. In 1861 Victoria had twice as many Irish as Scottish subjects. But the Irish were easily able to deduce their lesser status from her movements. During Victoria's reign as a whole she spent seven entire years in Scotland, but only five weeks, over four visits, across the Irish Sea.[4] She would also impatiently refuse suggestions that Bertie should become her permanent viceroy and representative in Ireland to give the country's problems some of the attention they so clearly required.[5]

Whenever she did cross the Irish Sea, Ireland's queen found the people and their suffering to be distressing. She made her first visit shortly after the Great Famine, the result of repeated failures of the potato harvest that had seen a million die and millions more emigrate. During this present trip of Victoria's, a whole decade later, its effects could still be seen. Charles Kingsley, writing in 1860, found himself 'haunted by the human chimpanzees I saw . . . if they were black, one would not feel it so much, but their skins, except where tanned by exposure, are as white as ours'.[6] Victoria agreed, finding 'more ragged and wretched people here than I ever saw anywhere else'.[7] Like Kingsley, she found her Irish subjects to be not quite human: 'the more one does for the Irish the more unruly and ungrateful they seem to be.'[8]

Unengaged, absentee landlords who shared these views had exacerbated the problems of the famine, as had the very limited franchise for Irish voters. Despite Victoria's having sent her own charitable contribution to crisis relief funds, many Irish people called her the 'Famine Queen' for the perceived harshness of her government and, by implication, of herself.[9] A newspaper called the *Dundalk Democrat* pointed out that her personal donation had been matched by the Sultan of Turkey and exceeded by the American government.[10]

Everyone knew there was a need for change, but no one could agree on how to bring it about. Victoria's present visit took place three years after the Fenian Brotherhood had been founded in an uneasy Dublin.

And yet, a visit in person by their queen could still bring out the Irish crowds. At Newbridge station, the camp's nearest railhead, Albert and Affie were waiting with a carriage to pick up the female members of the family. Victoria had brought with her Bertie's sisters Alice and Lenchen, as well as her lady-in-waiting Jane Churchill. One newspaper reported that 30,000 spectators had turned out, to see both the queen and the military manoeuvres that her army would perform upon the plain. They arrived in mail coaches, hotel omnibuses, 'shabby-genteel turn-outs of squireen aristocracy', and more than 100 packed railway trains. 'Such a crowd & such a scamper & scramble,' Victoria herself observed, 'people in every direction, ladies, common people &c on foot, & horseback, jaunting cars.'[11] The mood was mixed. The crowds received her with the 'greatest *curiosity*', one Republican newspaper said, but 'with the most marked absence of enthusiasm'.[12]

The royal family now drove across the turf to the camp. It by now consisted of ten squares of huts, each containing 1,000 soldiers. These hutments had been built at extraordinary speed at the height of the Crimean War. Each hut was constructed in a single day by a gang of men who slept in the finished construction that night before starting the next one in the morning. During the 'drill season' from April to September, even this vast number of huts got full up, and some soldiers had to sleep under canvas. It was a veritable city of huts and tents.

The camp gave a strong first impression of order and clockwork military precision. Shooting up at the centre of the site was the 'tall clock-tower' with six cannons before it guarding the Union Jack. There were Catholic and Protestant chapels to right and left, each capable of holding 1,800 men at a time. The schools, the post office, the market: all were 'marvels of neatness and efficiency'. And then, beyond the chapels, stretched the huts. From a distance, wrote a visiting Charles Dickens, they looked 'like a long brown wall . . . you could not suppose that a small army lay quiet behind'.[13]

A closer inspection of the huts would reveal that while they seemed neat enough from the outside, they were not altogether comfortable for the men who slept on straw mattresses within. Wind whistled through the fir planking of the walls, which had only been intended to be temporary, and Victoria's infantry would have to wait until army reforms of the 1870s to get their bedsheets changed even once a month.[14] Twelve infantrymen had to dry their faces on a single shared roller towel, which was only laundered once a week.[15]

In twenty-first-century Ireland, the camp is still the training school for the Irish army, and squads of wheezing youths in black shell suits, both male and female, run back and forth at commands shouted in Irish. But in 1861 it was the British army that now emerged from its hut city to march for its queen. It was the soft and frequent rain that made the grasses of the Curragh grow almost garishly green, and Victoria's visit fell on a typically wet morning with 'most violent' precipitation.[16] 'Two cooling showers,' Victoria said, with her usual nonchalance in the face of bad weather, although she did make the concession of ordering the carriage to be closed.[17] The troops marching past got drenched.

But even the rain could not dampen the ardour of the display. This was one of the great occasions of camp life, and the army relished the chance to show what it could do. All the generals and staff officers came out on a day like this, and 'the artillery thunders in the hollows, the infantry maintain a rain of rattling fire . . . a vast cloud of white smoke, lit up with rapid flashes from the cannon, rolls over the plain.' When the smoke cleared, and the cavalry had been and gone, you could still 'hear their thunder in a distant hollow, or you see one line of steeds and men sweeping, like a wave, above the hills'.[18]

Victoria was growing well used to the thunder crashes of the heavy guns. She had attended reviews of her troops increasingly often as they came shipping back from Crimea. For the purpose, she often wore the superbly tailored outdoor wear that suited her much better than frou-frou evening gowns. Her self-adopted 'uniform' was a scarlet, made-to-measure military-style jacket combined with the skirt of a riding habit. Albert had a matching outfit too, its chest padded out to simulate the muscles that his sedentary lifestyle had failed to give him.

Today, though, as she was travelling by carriage, Victoria wore a dark cloak over her now-customary daywear of the crinolined skirt. She'd held out until the end of the 1850s before adopting this novel steel structure to puff out the skirt, which was widely thought to be an 'indelicate, expensive, hideous and dangerous article'.[19] A crinoline, or 'cage', could swing the skirts out so unexpectedly that they caught fire, or got stuck in carriage wheels. But the stylish Empress Eugénie, whom Victoria much admired, is said to have popularised the crinoline during an 1855 visit to England. 'Carter's Crinoline Saloon' opened soon afterwards, offering London ladies not only the crinoline but also the new 'elastic stays . . . as worn by the Empress of the French'.[20] Victoria nevertheless resisted the fashion until a heatwave three years later made her feel that her customary stiff muslin petticoats were 'unbearable'. 'Imagine!' she wrote, to her married daughter in Germany, 'since 6 weeks I wear a "Cage"!!! What do you say?'[21] Having realised how convenient it was, she now only took her crinoline off to go sailing. There cannot have been much room in Victoria's vehicle today, packed as it was with crinolined princesses.

Meanwhile, outside the carriage windows, the rain and the military manoeuvres continued until at last came the moment that Bertie's mother and sisters had been waiting for: the arrival within sight of the unit being commanded today by the Prince of Wales. Victoria, experiencing an unusual glow of maternal pride, reported that he 'did not look at all so very small'.[22] It was, as customary with her, a backhanded compliment. She constantly worried about her son's disappointing physical appearance. 'Handsome I cannot think him,' she wrote, 'with that painfully small and narrow head, those immense features and total want of chin.'[23]

And Bertie's achievements on the plain were disappointing too. The plan had been that he would march a whole battalion of 800 men past his admiring family, but his skill in drill had been found wanting. Although he was wearing the uniform of a colonel, he'd been given charge of just a single company, of around 100 soldiers.

Once the last soldier had passed by, the family retired for lunch to Bertie's own 'Hut', which in fact belonged to the general with whom he was staying. This was quite an improvement upon the huts of the common soldiers. There were guards outside it, and two tents erected to give extra space. Bertie himself had a 'nice little bedroom' as well as reception rooms and even a 'good sized Dinning room'.[24] In one of those acts of royal patronage intended to support local industry, the furniture was entirely of Irish manufacture.[25] His sisters now had the chance to admire Bertie's quarters, and his martial air. They found him changed, 'a little browner, and certainly more robust and formed in figure' than when he'd left for the camp in June.[26]

And drill wasn't the only new skill that Bertie had been learning in the huts of the Curragh camp.

As Victoria's children grew up, they all understood that they came second best to Albert. When they were young, it was Albert who was the more 'modern' parent at Windsor, who made more of an effort to be 'friends' with the children and who understood that the children were being damaged by their mother's clear preference for him over them.

'It is indeed a pity that you find no consolation in the company of your children,' he once wrote to Victoria, at his most pompous and cruel. 'The root of the trouble lies in the mistaken notion that, the function of a mother is to be always correcting, scolding, ordering them about and organising their activities. It is not possible to be on happy friendly terms with people you have just been scolding.'[27] From the days when her dolls had blindly obeyed her commands, Victoria had been taught that other people would do as she wished in matters both large and small. She extended this habit of command over her children. The downside was a constant sense of strain. 'The Queen really is insane about the maintenance of her maternal authority (tyranny would be a more correct expression),' people said.[28] Yet it must have been difficult to judge. If even normal parents worry constantly about being too lax or too strict, how much harder for a queen to get it right.

It was an almost impossible task. And Bertie suffered from the circumstances of his upbringing perhaps even more than his eight siblings. He was not an academic child, but Albert nevertheless decreed that Bertie should study for seven hours a day, seven days a week. It was light work compared with the programme of nine hours of daily study that Albert had drawn up for himself at fourteen.[29] A letter from Victoria to Uncle Leopold reveals Bertie's greatest – indeed his insuperable – challenge in life: to be as good as his father. 'I wonder very much whom our little boy will be like,' Victoria wrote, 'how fervent are my prayers . . . to see him resemble his father in every respect, both in body and mind.'[30] While Bertie's elder sister Vicky could *almost* live up to Albert's rigorous standards, Bertie could not. At ten, it emerged that Bertie was under the impression that clever Vicky, not he, would inherit the throne.[31]

Eventually, realising he could never live up to expectations, Bertie gave up trying. His mother complained about his 'systematic idleness, laziness – disregard of everything' which was 'enough to break one's heart'. With one of those failures of imagination that seem to be her most lamentable feature as a mother, she did not try to put herself in Bertie's position, but contented herself instead with being indignant at his inadequacies.[32] Bertie did have a streak of creativity, and was genuinely interested – for example – in fashion. But this was not considered acceptable. When Bertie went out shooting, Albert thought that his son paid regrettably little attention to the sport, and was 'more occupied with his trousers'.[33] All in all, Victoria feared that her son would never be 'fit for his position'.[34]

In the year prior to coming to the Curragh, Bertie had sampled university life. The dean of his Oxford college found him good company, 'the nicest fellow possible, so simple, naïve, ingenuous and modest', but he wasn't allowed to stay long.[35] Earlier in 1861, he'd arrived as a student at Trinity College, Cambridge, although he lived in a country house outside the town with his governor, General Bruce. Bertie studied history, and decided – with some irony, given the high-society friends he was starting to gather – that 'the causes of the French Revolution were the luxury and profligacy of the noblesse'.[36]

His mother failed to approve of the raffish friends that Bertie collected at university. The present-day aristocracy, she complained, 'are so frivolous, pleasure-seeking, heartless, selfish, immoral and gambling' that it made her too think of the guillotine.[37] Mother and son, alike in many ways, constantly failed to understand each other. When Bertie's grandmother Victoire died three months before the camp started, a devastated Victoria reproached him for his lack of feeling. 'I did not like to intrude myself,' he wrote back, in a sad little letter, 'because I thought I should be in your way . . . I have ordered some more paper with rather deeper black edges as you wished.'[38]

Bertie had long wanted a taste of military life, but it took some agitation before he was eventually given permission to go to the Curragh camp for ten weeks during his summer vacation. There he would learn how to handle the Enfield Pattern rifle-musket recently introduced into the British army, capable of stopping a galloping horse dead in its tracks.[39] And he was also supposed to learn how to drill infantrymen, shouting the commands to transform columns into a wide line for an attack, or into a closed, defensive square. Provided the men kept their nerve, the square formation was virtually proof against even a cavalry charge.

Bertie was attached to a battalion of the Grenadier Guards for his 'drill season'. His commanding officers hoped that through 'attendance at a daily parade' he would be able to gain a grade each fortnight, climbing through the ranks from ensign to the point of being able to manoeuvre a whole brigade by the time he left.[40]

When he arrived at the Curragh, journalists noted, Bertie 'seemed extremely pleased with the place, and looked around him with evident satisfaction'.[41] His instructor thought that 'certain guarantees for decorum' lay in the presence of Bertie's host, Colonel Percy, and 'the excellent tone among the Officers generally'.[42] In theory, Bertie was to be treated just like every other junior officer, and one day he too arose at half past three to join his colleagues in an eighteen-mile route march.[43] Albert had arranged that his son and heir should be strictly supervised in the evenings. Bertie was to invite his fellow officers to dinner parties twice a week, dine twice a week in the mess of his regiment, and visit other regiments once a week as well. The other two evenings he was to spend quietly by himself, reading.[44] It didn't quite work out like this.

Bertie's presence in the camp did not, of course, go unnoticed. A journalist wrote in July that his quarters could 'be seen by anyone passing on the road'. Passers-by could watch as Bertie 'goes through the routine of military duties every morning with as much exactness as any other officer in the camp'. And after that, everyone could also see that he didn't have much else to do. After lunch, he played 'games of racket', or else cricket, but there were still the long country evenings to get through.[45] A lack of entertainment might still be a problem for the occupants of Curragh camp today, to judge by the bins throughout the camp crammed with empty bottles once containing vodka.

And as the weeks went by, Bertie failed to make the progress expected. General Bruce reported that the goal had been over-ambitious, and that there was no chance the prince would be able to command a battalion by the end of August. 'You are too imperfect in your drill,' Colonel Percy told Bertie, 'your word of command is not sufficiently loud and distinct.' Colonel Percy declined to try to make anyone 'think you more advanced than you are'.[46]

Whatever Victoria may have thought privately about Bertie's lack of progress towards his target, she thanked Colonel Percy in public for 'treating Bertie as he did, just as any other officer'.[47]

Albert, on the other hand, was openly dissatisfied, and complained about the 'idle tendencies of English youth'.[48]

After their lunch in Bertie's hut on the day of the manoeuvres, his family went off back to Dublin again, leaving behind just Affie, who was to spend the night in the camp as a treat. By the end of the week, Victoria and Albert were en route, by yacht, for Scotland and Balmoral. There is no record of how Bertie felt after his disappointing drill performance, but his fellow officers in the Grenadier Guards were only too keen to help him deal with any lingering sense of inadequacy. There were other ways in which he could be made to feel more manly.

All of Victoria's children had been kept in ignorance of the mechanics of human reproduction. When Affie, aged fifteen, encountered a pregnant lady, he commented on how ugly her dress was. 'She is expecting an addition,' he was told. 'What for?' he asked, surprised.[49] Bertie's biographer Jane Ridley explains how his Latin tutor, discovering that Albert had not explained sexual inter-course and reproduction to his son, found himself doing the job instead.[50] And Bertie then improved his theoretical knowledge through fieldwork. At sixteen, he was sent on a mini-version of the conventional aristocratic Grand Tour, and in Germany he managed to snog a girl. This was something that the future Prime Minister William Gladstone heard all about, and referred to as a 'squalid little debauch'.[51] Next Bertie succeeded in falling in love with one of his mother's married ladies-in-waiting, Jane Churchill.

Belatedly coming to realise that Bertie was experiencing disruptive hormonal urges, Albert decided that the solution was to get him married as quickly as possible. He and Victoria began to look around for a suitable bride, someone royal, healthy, good-looking and docile. Vicky, now living in Berlin as the wife of the Crown Prince of Prussia, was asked to scout about. 'God knows!' Victoria told her daughter, 'where the young lady we want is to be found!'[52]

The answer, as it turned out, was Denmark. Vicky's parents

approved her recommendation of Alexandra, or Alix, daughter of the Danish king. While she had the qualifications of youth and birth, her disadvantage was the conflict between her native country and the Germany that Victoria and Albert loved. But she seemed of good character, and with her long nose and tiny waist she was beautiful. When he was shown a picture of Alix, Albert announced that 'from that Photograph I wd marry her at once'.[53]

Bertie, though, was less than enthusiastic about being hustled into marriage, and asked if he could think it over.[54] In fact, he was thinking harder about someone else. Bertie rarely filled in the pages of his printed engagement diary, and in June 1861 his entries petered out altogether, one day being much like another at the camp. On 6 September, though, with his mother safely out of Ireland, Bertie's diary kicks back into life. He records just the words 'Curragh' and 'N.C. 1st time.' But Jane Ridley has deduced that this laconic comment was code for having taken the major life step of losing his virginity.

Bertie's first time with 'N.C.' was an encounter with a lady called variously Nellie or Nelly, Clifden or Clifton, although her most likely surname was Clifford. He climbed out at night through the window of his quarters to enjoy 'intercourse with her at another officer's hut'.[55]

Historians usually describe 'Nellie' as an 'actress', though a friend of Bertie's pronounced her to be 'a well known "London Lady" much run after by the household brigade'.[56] The decade that would become known as 'The Gay Sixties' had just begun, with its language of 'swells' and 'houris'. The best places to find yourself a 'London Lady' (also known as a 'soiled dove') were the dining and dancing clubs like Mott's in Foley Street, named for its proprietors, who 'had some connection with the ballet depart- ment of the Opera' and where 'one generally found some pretty members of the corps among the dancers'.[57] Between two and three in the morning, the riotous crowd at Mott's would call for cold fowl, ham and champagne to fuel the 'revelry fast and furious'.[58] Many of the 'London ladies', sniffed the *Daily Telegraph*, were merely the daughters of stablemen, who sold their 'miserable bodies' to 'wealthy profligates' so that they could 'dress splendidly, and drive handsome equipages'.[59] Their number included the celebrated 'Baby Jordan', 'Shoes' and 'Skittles' and, indeed, Nelly Clifford. She was present at Mott's the legendary night that Lord Hastings, after ordering six cases of champagne, released 200 sewer rats into the ballroom as a joke.[60] Bertie obviously liked 'N.C.' enough for two further appointments recorded in his diary on the nights of 9 and 10 September.[61]

But Nellie was not an uncommon name. Bertie and his friends were also in thrall to another 'London Lady' called Nellie Fowler, and then there was also Nellie Farren, a variety actress who sang her songs in the 'purest and most delicious Cockney'. She had the secret of eternal youth, people thought, and 'dances in tights on the Gaiety stage, and she, a grandmother!'[62] This profusion of 'Nellies' has caused some confusion, and in recent years another intriguing possibility has emerged. Perhaps Bertie's 'Nellie' wasn't a 'London Lady' shipped over from the nightspots of London after all, but instead one of the Irish camp followers of the Curragh known as the 'Wrens'. The lives of this community of women who existed alongside the British army have come into focus as historians search harder for those whom the official records have forgotten.

Communities entirely made up of men, from palaces to army bases, have always been accompanied by a shadow, transient, female version of themselves, and the Curragh camp was no different. Its female camp followers – some of them common-law wives to the soldiers, others who might sometimes support themselves through prostitution – inhabited makeshift, shanty-like structures that resembled nests. That's why the respectable folk of the Curragh Plain called them after birds. 'Wrins!' said one local. 'That's the name ov 'em! Wrins! . . . and a dridful life they lade. Most distressing, believe me!'[63]

The army authorities did little to stop prostitution within the camp's bounds. In just six months of 1866, there were 556 cases of prostitutes being caught trespassing. Each time a woman got caught, she had to pay a fine of a shilling to the Newbridge magistrate. But this was no deterrent and appears to have been regarded simply as a tax on business. 'If I turn them out one end of the camp,' complained the camp's sergeant in 1866, 'in ten minutes they are at the other.'[64]

These prostitutes and other camp followers, roughly 100 in number, inhabited burrows constructed out of 'rough, disshapen domes of furze' strengthened with pieces of corrugated iron. The 'nests' were hard to spot at first among the hillocks at the edge of the Curragh Plain until you had seen one of them for what it was. After that you noticed that you were standing amid an entire village of them. 'The smoke of the fire which burns on the floor of the hut has to pass out of the door,' we hear, which itself is 'a slit . . . kept open by two rude posts, which also serve to support the roof'. The 'Wrens'' homes therefore resembled nests, 'big, rude birds' nests compacted of harsh branches, and turned topsy-turvey on the ground'. Space within was so limited that 'suspended against the prickly sides' of the 'nests' you might see a crinoline, 'an article so bulky and intractable that it could not well be got inside'. It was 'put on or taken off, as occasion required, at the hole that served for a door'.[65]

This description of shanty-type dwellings forged from nature is the work of a sensationalist journalist and must be treated with care. At the very least, it must be exaggerated or romanticised. Yet it does remain true, even today, that the rolling hills of the Curragh grasslands continue to bristle with clumps of prickly furze, beneath which it is possible to creep and to make out a shelter. The evidence of empty food cartons and Jameson whiskey bottles even suggests that the Wrens' 'nests' are sometimes still occupied.

It was an article in Dickens's publication *All the Year Round* that first exposed the difficulties of the lives of these women of the Curragh camp. It recounted the tale of a priest who encountered one of the 'Wrens' on the street of the local town, and 'threw her down, tearing from off her back the thin shawl and gown that covered it, and with his heavy riding-whip so flogged her over the bare shoulders that the blood actually spirted over his boots'. The same writer also saw 'four women lying in a bit of a hole they had scooped out . . . wet, cold, and perishing from want of exposure', and was taken aback when they spent his alms on whiskey.[66]

There is no denying that these women had hard lives, but care needs to be taken with these articles about them because they were written in a Victorian genre known as 'slumming', a semi-salacious relishment of the misfortunes of lower-class people. In 1867 another investigative journalist, James Greenwood, wrote the account of the lives of the Curragh Wrens that secured their lasting recognition. Greenwood's special selling point was that he would spend the night with his subjects, in a workhouse, for example, observing their lives at first hand. He was writing for large amounts of money, and doubtless overstated the horror and squalor of what he saw. He described the Wrens as frighteningly independent, with a look of 'hard depravity . . . determined and defiant wickedness'.[67]

Despite their melodrama, though, Greenwood's works had a colour and immediacy that brought the plight of poor people more vividly to life in the minds of his middle-class readers than any government report could do.[68] And Greenwood also paints a picture of a real community among the Wrens. Living as a cooperative of women, they enjoyed freedoms that would have been unavailable to them in a traditional family, subordinate to a husband, or within a religious community subordinate to the Church. Some of the Wrens might eventually end up in the care of the Magdalene nuns who specialised in the redemption of 'fallen women'.[69] Their modern historian, Maria Luddy, points that the Wrens and the nuns were flipsides of the same image: a woman defined mainly by her sexual habits. Whether by having sex outside marriage or abstaining altogether, both groups had placed themselves beyond society's control.

Greenwood more precisely quantifies the Wrens' community as about 'ten bushes' containing roughly sixty inhabitants, mainly aged between seventeen and twenty-five. The Wrens, he says, pooled their resources and labour: the older ones stayed behind and looked after the babies, while the younger ones were dressed up and sent out for sex work. Greenwood met one young lady who was, despite the living conditions, 'a perfectly neat-looking girl, washed, combed, and arrayed in a clean starched cotton gown, and with bright white stockings and well-fitting boots'.[70]

And among these Wrens of the Curragh is another candidate for the role of the deflowerer of the Prince of Wales. An Irish family historian has pointed out that an 'Ellen Clifton' was baptised in County Waterford in 1844, which would have made her seventeen if she really was Bertie's first sexual partner.[71] She appeared in poor law payment records. Perhaps 'Nellie', then, was really an Irish girl, orphaned by the Great Famine, whose bright white stockings caused her to be picked up by Bertie's friends to entertain the son of the Famine Queen.

Whoever Nellie really was, Bertie's romantic future lay in a very different direction. On 11 September, he made a farewell speech to his regiment. 'I shall ever look back to my intercourse with yourselves,' he said, 'with feelings of unmingled pleasure.'[72] That night he attended a grand ball at the Mansion House in Dublin, before leaving Ireland. He was off to Germany, to attend a review of the Prussian army.[73] Then it was on to Speyer Cathedral, supposedly for a bit of sightseeing, but really to take part in a carefully contrived 'accidental' meeting with Alix. This encounter was his chance to play his princely part and to fall in love. He did his best. 'I can now candidly say,' Bertie wrote the next day, 'that I thought her charming and very pretty.'[74]

The pressure placed upon Bertie to marry Alix was dramatically increased a few weeks later when his father had the misfortune to hear, through London clubland gossip, what had really happened in the huts of the Curragh. As ever, under stress, Albert picked up his pen. He tackled his son on the subject, writing him an astonishing, enormously long and highly intemperate letter laden with reproach and regret. Albert had always known, he claimed, that Bertie was 'thoughtless & weak', but he now understood that the reality was much worse. His son, he thought, had 'sunk into vice & debauchery . . . deception & profligacy'. The knowledge that his twenty-year-old son had become sexually active had given Albert, he claimed, 'the deepest pain' he'd yet experienced in the whole of his life.[75]

What was worse, Albert feared that Bertie's 'vice' hadn't been a one-off. Albert's letter also outlined rumours that Nellie had actually come to Windsor Castle for an assignation on Bertie's birthday the week before (becoming known, in consequence, as 'The Princess of Wales'). In fact the 'lady' who visited Bertie at Windsor Castle that autumn looks like one Mrs Green, a successful black-mailer, who got £60 a year for keeping quiet and going to live in New Zealand.[76] It looks as if Nellie Clifford perhaps spread the scandal of her seduction round London because she too was unhappy with her side of whatever financial deal had been done. Once the secret was out, and had done its damaging work, she was certainly paid off more handsomely and effectively. By 1862, a 'Nelly Clifford' had a glamorous new life on the other side of the Atlantic, as a star of the Metropolitan Concert Saloon in Wilmington, Delaware.[77]

Albert's letter revealed just how disgusted, shocked and hurt his son's immorality had made him feel. On a more practical note, he thought Bertie had stupidly put himself into a woman's power. Nellie, Albert thought, would 'probably have a child' and pursue Bertie as the father through the courts: 'she will be able to give before a greedy Multitude disgusting details of your profligacy for the sake of convincing the Jury, yourself cross-examined by a railing indecent Attorney and hooted and yelled at by a Lawless Mob!! Oh horrible prospect, which this person has in her power, any day to realise!'[78]

Given that Bertie's actions were not particularly out of place for his class and time, it does seem that there was something over-the-top, unhinged, almost hysterical, about Albert's reaction. Victoria was spared the details, but she too found it agonising. She decided that the best story for public consumption was that 'wicked wretches' had seduced a 'poor, innocent boy into a scrape'. What really concerned her, though, was 'the agony and misery' that Albert himself experienced when he 'first heard of poor Bertie's misfortune!' 'Oh!' Victoria wrote, that had been 'so dreadful to witness!' And Bertie's shame in the huts of the Curragh would place a lasting strain upon his relationship with his mother. He was tainted, and she could never again look at him, she thought, 'without a shudder! Oh! that bitterness – oh! that cross!'[79]

Why did Albert, and therefore Victoria, react quite so strongly? Benjamin Disraeli, for example, thought the incident 'undignified', but 'not seriously discreditable'.[80] It was Albert's upbringing that explains his violent reaction to even the slightest sexual incontinence. 'You know well the events and scandals that had always happened in Coburg Castle,' Albert once wrote to his brother Ernest, regretting the many and lurid affairs of their father, and the single but catastrophic dalliance of their mother.[81] Albert had never been able to process the consequences of his parents' divorce. He was locked in a state of cognitive dissonance: he loved his mother, he missed his mother, but he'd lost her because she'd done wrong. But he could also see that his father was unbearable, indulging his appetites for women with seigneurial swagger.

Albert had good reason to suspect that Bertie would be black-mailed, because that was exactly what had happened to his father too. One of his mistresses had published her memoirs after he'd failed to pay her off. This woman, Pauline Panam, was 'scarcely fourteen' when the Duke of Coburg seduced her and left her pregnant. 'Never,' she claimed afterwards, 'did a woman fall more blindly into the abyss.'[82]

And in fact, it wasn't just Albert who thought that the pleasures of the 1860s were deeply, utterly wrong. His view that the loss of virtue meant falling into an abyss was typical of the binary way in which the respectable Victorian family considered morality. Albert's reaction shows how the royal family had once again fallen into alignment with the slice of their subjects who'd become their most important supporters.

If Bertie was not good, then he must be wicked. And his mother would come to believe that Bertie's wicked night with Nellie had fatal consequences. One might almost see it as Ireland's revenge upon its Famine Queen.

17

The Blue Room: Windsor Castle,
14 December 1861

It was one o'clock in the morning of 14 December 1861, just a month after Albert had learned about 'N.C.', and Victoria was feeling very, very slightly better. She had just received a message from her husband's doctors that he was doing well. Albert had been seriously ill for weeks, but his condition seemed finally to have stabilised. In the hope of quickening his heartbeat and slowing his breathing, his medical team were giving him brandy every half an hour.

Victoria was spending the night in her Windsor Castle dressing room. She'd been sleeping there ever since Albert had moved, some days ago, out of their private suite. Doctors brought her updates at intervals throughout the night. Their news continued fair at 2 a.m., and at three as well. By sunrise, the spirits of the whole household were definitely on the rise. 'We are allowed again *a hope*,' Albert's Private Secretary informed the Prime Minister, Viscount Palmerston, by telegram. 'The Prince has had a quiet night and all the symptoms are somewhat modified.'[1]

Victoria even managed a little sleep before being woken at 5.30 to be told that there 'is ground to hope that the crisis is over'. Her husband, the doctors said, had even been strong enough to get out of bed and walk across the room to answer a call of nature.[2] Victoria's daughter Alice, now eighteen, was lying on a little bed next to her mother's. They learned in their dressing gowns that Albert's breathing was still far from normal, but that 'if he could get over that day . . . he might recover'.[3]

The relief was enormous. Albert had been raving and talking nonsense in his delirious sickness. Feeling courage return, Victoria began in her mind to store 'up all the things he had said and done . . . to amuse him on his return to health'.[4] 'My Husband won't die,' Victoria explained to Dr Clark, 'for that would kill me.'[5]

Victoria had not yet seen him, but at three that morning, Bertie had arrived at Windsor from Cambridge, summoned by telegram by his sister. She hadn't contacted Bertie herself, for she blamed him for his father's illness. Albert's discovery of 'that dreadful business in the Curragh', Victoria believed, had burdened his mind so heavily that his resistance to illness was reduced.[6] 'Albert has such nights since that great worry,' Victoria complained, 'it makes him weak and tired.'[7] Albert himself admitted in November that he'd 'scarcely closed' his eyes 'for the last fortnight'.[8] Victoria was therefore reluctant to let Albert see Bertie, 'lest it should excite or agitate him'.[9]

But now, thank God, the prognosis was different. At seven, Victoria went along the corridor, as usual, to where Albert was lying in the 'Blue Room'. Situated in the Clarence Tower and named for its silk hangings, the Blue Room looked east over the gardens towards the sunrise. It was, however, a place of ill omen, for it was here that both George IV and William IV had died.

Albert had occupied a great many beds around the castle during the course of the last week, before settling here. He had been extremely restless, moving from one room to another in the night. The Blue Room's great state bed – 'in which the kings had died'[10] – had now been taken out and replaced by two little ones for easier nursing. As Victoria entered, she noticed that 'the room had the sad look of night-watching, the candles burnt down to their sockets, the Doctors looking anxious'.[11]

Victoria and Albert's second daughter, Alice, had been a constant presence during his illness. Albert once mentioned to Alice that he liked to lie near the window that 'he might see the sky, and watch the clouds sailing past.'[12] And now, in Victoria's words, 'it

was a bright morning . . . the sun just rising and shining brightly
. . . never can I forget how beautiful my Darling looked lying
there with his face lit up by the rising sun'. He was wearing a
special white jacket that he always put on when he wasn't well,
and his hands were clasped on his chest just as they were when
he fell asleep while sitting in the drawing room after dinner. Albert's
eyes, though, were unusually bright, and he was gazing 'as it were
on unseen objects', taking no notice of Victoria or anyone else
the Blue Room contained.[13]

While Alice had played her part in watching, waiting and
attending on her father, Victoria herself hadn't been much use. It
was generally agreed that she was 'not the best nurse in the world'.[14]
'Poor mama!' wrote Alice, 'she wants to help as much as she can.'[15]
Victoria was delighted when she was allowed to feed Albert some
soup, but she did sometimes manage to annoy him, for which he
'quite slapped' her hand.[16] Alice wasn't a trained nurse either, but
she had an instinct for it, and tradition and convention insisted in
any case that a daughter was better than the most professional nurse
available. (Tradition and convention were wrong about this, as
Victoria herself later admitted.)[17]

The one thing Victoria *could* do for Albert was to read aloud
to him, and she reached for Sir Walter Scott, who'd brought them
together so long ago. The Royal Library's copy of Scott's novel
Peveril of the Peak still contains a note in Victoria's hand, saying
'This book was read up to the mark in Page 81 – to my beloved
Husband during his fatal illness.'[18] Literature, like music, had always
'seemed to take him into a dream-world, in which the anxieties
of his life were for the moment forgotten', where 'the pressure on
a brain often too severely taxed was for the moment removed'.[19]

But now the dazzling morning, the good news, dispelled something
of the gloom of the castle. 'I cannot ever feel the slightest affection
or tendre for this fine, dull place,' Victoria claimed, 'I think I dislike
it more and more.'[20] At Windsor Castle the drains had long posed
problems. Even after improvements had been carried out in the

1840s, Victoria's Lord Chamberlain still complained that noxious smells from 'the old drains and numerous cesspools' were 'so exceedingly offensive as to render many parts of the castle almost uninhabitable'.[21] The courtiers sighed at the irony that a palace could be so nasty. 'There are more stinks,' wrote one of them, 'in Royal Residences than anywhere else.'[22] People were also surprised to encounter the penny-pinching ways at Windsor, including the ration of one lump of sugar only in one's morning tea, and the newspaper squares in the lavatories.[23]

Just three years before Albert's present illness, the whole town of Windsor had suffered a particularly virulent outbreak of typhoid fever. Three or four hundred people had been affected, 'even in the comparatively well-appointed houses of the middle and upper classes'.[24] This was unusual because a disease like typhoid generally respected class and was hungrier for victims in poorer homes with inferior sanitation. A report published in 1842 revealed that in Manchester life expectancy at birth for a child from a working-class family was seventeen, while a 'gentleman' or member of the professional classes, with his better plumbing, could expect to live to thirty-eight.[25]

Albert's valet, Rudolf Löhlein, had taken the Windsor typhoid outbreak very seriously. 'Living here will kill your Royal Highness,' he'd said. Löhlein was a fellow Coburger, thought by some to be Albert's illegitimate half-brother by his promiscuous father the Duke.[26] Albert, his valet thought, must 'leave Windsor and go to Germany for a time to rest and recover strength'. But Albert refused to listen, and Löhlein's warnings 'passed unheeded'.[27]

Earlier in 1861, a new doctor had been appointed to the household. Dr William Jenner seemed a good choice for a royal residence situated in an insanitary town, as he'd become celebrated for his work at the London Fever Hospital. There he'd worked out that typhus and typhoid fever are in fact slightly different illnesses. Typhus is carried by lice, while typhoid fever is picked up from food or water.[28] But Jenner and Albert's other doctors could not agree on exactly what was wrong with him now. Dr Jenner, this supposed specialist in fevers, had named Albert's ailment as 'gastric' or 'low' fever, and reassured Victoria that it would run its course in a month.[29] No one mentioned typhoid.

When Victoria talked over the possible causes of her husband's illness with Doctors Jenner and Clark, their conclusions were 'worry, & too hard work'.[30] Dr Clark had been saying for a decade that Albert's declining health was to do with lifestyle and stress. 'For years,' Dr Clark considered, he'd 'worked his brain so much' that it had damaged his nervous system.[31]

And those closest to him had known for a long time that Albert was incapable of managing his time and energy effectively. 'I am more dead than alive from overwork,' he'd claimed, back when he had staged his Great Exhibition in 1851.[32] In 1844, his secretary had warned Albert 'most seriously' that he must adopt 'some plan of fixed hours' instead of working late into every night.[33] In 1861, though, Albert was still at it. 'His nervous system is easily excited and irritated and he's so completely overpowered by everything,' Victoria admitted. She found him 'often very trying – in his hastiness and over-love of business'.[34] Albert developed what was referred to as 'rheumatism' in his right shoulder, a pain he described as 'frightful torture' that left him unable to hold a pen.[35] It sounds like repetitive strain injury from too much writing.

Historian Helen Rappaport points out that the talk of fever from Albert's doctors is confused and inconsistent. Having made a remarkably thorough study of the evidence for his symptoms, she suggests the intriguing possibility that he really had Crohn's disease, with its stomach and joint pains. It's a disease that can be made worse by stress, and it was certainly apparent that Albert's malaise both pre-dated his fever and had a mental component.[36] 'God have mercy on us!' Baron Stockmar had said. 'If anything serious should ever happen to him, he will die.'[37] And then, of course, Albert had been terribly put out by Bertie's sexual awakening. 'Mental anguish' about this, wrote Dr Clark, 'acting on him for weeks' before the fever set in, had greatly increased its severity.[38]

And the year of 1861 had been full of trouble for the royal family even before Bertie's 'fall'. Victoria's mother died in March after suffering terribly for some years from the skin disorder erysipelas. 'What agony, what despair was this!' Victoria wrote.[39] Despite having reached a better understanding with Victoire in recent years, she was poleaxed to discover from looking through her mother's papers 'how very very much she and my beloved Father loved each other. Such love & affection . . . Then her love for me – It is too touching; I have found little Books with the accounts of my Baby-hood, & they show such unbounded tenderness! Oh!'[40]

But Victoria's grief helped blind her to her husband's growing weakness, disguised as it was behind his stern, withholding attitude towards her. She wished that Albert would 'listen to and believe me', yet simultaneously not 'believe the stupid things I say like being miserable I ever married and so forth which come when I am unwell'.[41] But he continued to accuse her of self-indulgence. In October, when she was still deeply grieving for her mother's death only seven months before, he told her, in one of his pitiless letters, to be 'less occupied with yourself and your own feelings'.[42] 'If you will take increased interest in things unconnected with personal feelings,' he added, 'you will find the task much lightened of governing those feelings in general which you state to be your great difficulty in life.'[43] Cold comfort, for a bereaved and lonely woman.

Their very worst rows stemmed from parenting disagreements, Victoria unable to express her concerns and Albert retreating into silence, supposedly to allow her space to 'calm' herself. She expressed distress, or at least tried to; he withdrew. 'I never intend or wish to offend you,' he wrote, 'I try to be patient.' But deep down he felt that listening to her 'recriminations' was 'the dreadful waste of a most precious time & of energies which ought to be turned to the use of others'.[44] There was the whole issue in a nutshell: Victoria, who lacked a father, had long sought mentors or alternative fathers in Uncle Leopold, Melbourne and then in Albert himself. Yet she couldn't get him to listen to her. It was, in any case, a vain hope. A Victorian man was failing in his masculinity if he failed to control his wife, and Albert could never quite control a wife who was also a queen. So they were doomed to clash.[45]

Despite her general inattention to her husband's health, Victoria did notice a link between stress and Albert's long-standing digestive problems. If he were annoyed by badly done paperwork, for example, it would 'affect his poor dear stomach'.[46] Albert himself believed – in characteristically ascetic manner – that when his stomach gave him trouble he should fast. Putting no food into it would 'rob' it 'of the shadow of a pretext for behaving ill', he claimed.[47] In October 1861, he purchased a new travelling medicine chest, packed with drugs particularly suitable for disorders of the belly, including a powder of rhubarb and cinnamon, to be 'taken when the bowels are disturbed, & disposed to diarrhoea,' and another mixture 'to be taken after every action of the bowels'.[48] Victoria's accounts show that her doctors were gearing up for trouble as well, with the acquisition of 'a new stomach pump' and a 'syringe in case'.[49] The royal chemist – Peter Squire of Oxford Street – delivered a standing monthly order for rhubarb pills, calomel, senna and bicarbonate of soda. Helen Rappaport notes that in the autumn of 1861, there were disturbing new additions to this list: belladonna and sulphuric acid. It looks as if Albert's stomach was getting worse, and the strength of the medicines required was increasing.[50]

Albert, then, had long been unwell, though Victoria could not bear to see it. She also believed Dr Clark to be infallible. His medical method lay in jollying along and encouraging his patients to think that they were improving, so that matter would follow mind. He put this into practice by, for example, taking the trouble to disguise the nauseating taste of medicine with flavouring, which was a small but significant thing to do.[51] 'Your position is constantly exposing you to the risk of having your health deranged,' he warned the prince.[52]

Dr Clark told Albert to slow down, but he was constitutionally incapable of doing so. On 1 December, despite being ill, Albert wrote a paper advising the government how to respond to the growing crisis of the American Civil War. A British ship had been intercepted and the situation was dangerous, but Albert's intervention in favour of reconciliation reminded everyone how helpful he could be when he trained his mind upon a problem. Yet the effort had cost him dearly. 'I could hardly hold my pen,' he told his wife as he gave her the draft to copy.[53]

And Clark's optimistic approach failed, utterly, in convincing Victoria that Albert's condition was serious. On 9 December she was even still complaining that his sickness was a bore: 'you know he is always *so* depressed when anything is the matter with him . . . it is extremely vexatious.'[54] As a household insider later revealed, 'she could not bear to listen, and shut her eyes to the danger.'[55]

And so, it was only with his gentle, nurturing daughter Alice that Albert shared his belief that death was drawing near. Albert understood that he lacked the inner resources for a severe struggle. 'I do not cling to life,' he'd said, previously. 'If I had a severe illness I should give up at once.'[56]

'I have told my sister that you are very ill,' Alice now said to him, having written to Vicky in Germany.[57] 'You have done wrong,' was her father's reply, 'you should have told her I am dying, yes I am dying.'[58]

This seemed a remote possibility, though, on the sunny morning of Saturday 14 December. Dr Clark 'was very hopeful, so was Dr Jenner, & said it was a decided rally.'[59] Victoria was shown a draft of the news bulletin that the royal doctors were to issue. Based on his progress over the previous night, they announced at 9 a.m. that Albert's condition was improving.

Victoria left the Blue Room after her early-morning visit to breakfast with Bertie, who then went in at Albert's own request to see his father. All was going to be well. Victoria decided she could risk taking 'a breath of fresh air.' She went out on the terrace with Alice, for half an hour, and they heard the military band playing in the distance. But she could not fully relax into her feelings of relief; there was too much at stake. 'I burst out crying,' she recalled later, 'and came home again.'

Victoria's premonition was correct. Returning to Albert's room that afternoon, she found an unexpected deterioration. 'The breathing was the alarming thing,' she wrote, '<u>so</u> rapid, I think 60 respirations in a minute . . . there was what they call a dusky hue about his face and hands, which I knew was not good.' Victoria was perturbed to find that Dr Jenner had not himself noticed this. She also observed that 'Albert folded his arms, and began arranging his hair, just as he used to do when well and he was dressing . . . Strange! As tho' he were preparing for another and greater journey.'[60]

At half past four, the doctors issued another bulletin, contradicting their earlier optimistic statements. Now, they were forced to admit, the prince was in a 'most critical state'.[61] At five, his bed was moved from its place near the window and into the middle of the room. Victoria asked Dr Jenner if any hope remained. It did, he said, but only just: it was 'not impossible' that Albert should live.[62]

The room was beginning to grow crowded with a considerable number of people. The Victorians generally died, as they were born, at home, and in the presence of their families. What can appear to us twenty-first-century people to be an unhealthy fascination with death and mourning in Victorian culture may in fact have been a source of powerful mental resilience. They were 'in touch' with birth and death. Today grieving and mourning are perceived as weaknesses, almost sicknesses, to be conquered and overcome. It might be better to accept bereavement, as the Victorians did, as an integral part of life, and to say a collective farewell to family members as they died in their own familiar bedrooms.

So now, at their father's unexpected decline, Bertie, Helena, Louise and Arthur came trooping into the darkening sickroom as the afternoon wore on, each to take in turn his or her father's hand. Missing were Vicky, who was in Germany with her husband, Affie, at sea with the navy, Leopold, sick with an illness of his own in the South of France and Beatrice, who at four was thought too young.

Also in attendance were the doctors, three gentlemen of the

household and the Dean of Windsor. His presence was an augury that the time for prayer was coming. 'Oh how can I govern the Country without him?' Victoria asked the Dean while they were both taking a brief break in the room next door, 'her hair in disorder burying her face in her hands'. He told her that she'd done it before Albert and could therefore do it again. 'Oh how badly I did it, I did nothing right,' was her response.'[63]

At about half past five, Victoria continues in her own account, she went back into the Blue Room, 'and sat down beside his bed'. Albert's body was by now bathed in perspiration. This encouraged the doctors, because they thought it meant he was going to throw off his fever.

And now he recognised Victoria. '*Gutes Frauchen*,' he said, German for 'good little wife'. In Victoria's words, he 'kissed me, and then gave a sort of piteous moan or rather sigh, not of pain, but as if he felt that he was leaving me, & laid his head on my shoulder'.[64] So they sat, and waited, and prayed. Albert 'seemed to wander and to doze' as the winter afternoon grew dark, and sometimes he said things that didn't make sense.[65] He was heard to mutter the name of 'General Bruce', Bertie's governor and commanding officer, which suggested that his mind was still wandering painfully through the hutments of the Curragh camp.[66]

But even if he wasn't making much sense, Albert still lived. As the clock in the Curfew Tower chimed out the quarters of the hour, and as the afternoon stretched into evening, 'things went on, not really worse'. Then, in another heart-stopping reversal of fortune, Albert showed remarkable signs of improvement. 'It was thought necessary to change his bed,' Victoria continues, 'and he was even able to get out of bed and <u>sit up</u>'. Albert's digestive system was still functioning, and although no one liked to state clearly what had happened, he'd obviously experienced a bowel movement. 'I observed to Dr Jenner,' writes Victoria, 'that this was surely a good sign.' Dr Jenner said it was no good a patient's having a functional digestive system if he couldn't breathe, but so long as air was passing through the lungs, 'there was still hope'.[67]

It was hope that was misplaced. Some time between ten and eleven that night there was another change in Albert's breathing. The doctors gave up trying to dose him with alcohol to raise his heartbeat. They'd resorted to using a sponge to dribble it between his lips, but he'd 'cried out and resisted the brandy so much that they did not give it any more'.

By this point, in the late evening, Victoria was in the Red Room next door, where she 'sat down on the floor in utter despair'.[68] But Alice was still at her post, and noticed a new rasping note in her father's throat. 'That is the death rattle,' she whispered.[69] It was essential to call Victoria back in. She was there at once. She 'started up like a Lioness', wrote one of her ladies, 'rushed by every one, and bounded on the bed imploring him to speak and to give one kiss to his little wife'.[70]

Then, as Victoria tells us,

> two or three long but perfectly gentle breaths were drawn, the hand clasping mine and (oh! It makes me sick to write it) all, all, was over . . . I stood up, kissed his dear heavenly forehead & called out in a bitter & agonising cry 'Oh! my dear Darling!' and then dropped on my knees in mute distracted despair, unable to utter a word or shed a tear![71]

'Oh yes,' people heard her say. 'This is death. I know it. I have seen this before.'

Now other people have to take up her story. In the gloomy Blue Room everyone knelt down on the floor: the queen and her elder children, 'the Leiningens, Phipps, Grey, Biddulph, Robert, the Dean, the Duchess, Miss Hildyard and I', wrote Lady Augusta Bruce. They all watched 'in agonised silence, the passing of that lofty and noble soul'.[72] They had to experience the harrowing sight of Victoria falling upon Albert's body and calling him 'by every endearing name'.[73] She was seen 'throwing herself with both her arms extended on the corpse'. She 'almost screamed Oh! Duchess! he is dead! he is dead! Oh! Albert! and gave way to a fearful but short paroxysm of agony.'[74]

Victoria stayed there for some time, clasping Albert's body, and refusing to let go. Finally, 'it was thought better by the Dean and one of the Physicians to remove her by force' and to take her next door.[75] Her pharmacist had earlier provided four stoppered bottles of smelling salts.[76] Victoria now lay on the Red Room's sofa, and gathered her children round her, hugging them, and telling them 'she would endeavour, if she lived, to live for them and her duty'.[77] Even Bertie was pitifully contrite. 'Mama I will be all I can to you,' he said.[78]

Then Victoria went to see her sleeping baby Beatrice. Her dresser, Annie Macdonald, a witness to so much of the queen's private life, said later that 'it was an awful time — an awful time. I shall never forget it. After the Prince was dead, the Queen ran through the ante-room where I was waiting. She seemed wild. She went straight up to the nursery and took Baby Beatrice out of bed . . . she cried for days. It was heart-breaking to hear her.'[79] As she went along the passage, Victoria was heard calling 'Oh! Albert, Albert! are you gone!'[80]

Only very late at night did Victoria give her intimate staff permission to undress her. 'Oh, what a sight it was,' wrote one of them, 'to gaze upon her hopeless, helpless face, and see those most appealing eyes lifted up.'[81] Victoria herself later recalled how her maids, Sophie Weiss, Emilie Dittweiler and Mary Andrews, 'strove kindly to soothe her', while Lady Augusta Bruce helped her into bed.[82] There she did at last have 'two hours of good sound sleep — worn out, I suppose, with tears and anxiety'.[83] From this night on, Victoria would still always sleep with Albert in the form of his clothes: 'his dear red dressing-gown beside her and some of his clothes on the bed'.[84]

Victoria's former governess Laddle perceptively noticed that the queen's grief would be worse because 'she has *no* friend to turn to'. 'The worst, far the worst,' Laddle continued, 'is yet to come — the numberless, incessant wishes to "Ask the Prince," to "Send for the Prince", the never-failing joy, fresh every time, when he answered her call . . . her greatest delight was in *obeying* him.'[85]

'She is worse off than ordinary persons,' thought Lord Clarendon, because 'she is isolated.'[86]

She had clasped his cold body because she could not bear to let him go. And something else Victoria could not easily bear to relinquish was the hold Albert had had over his wife's life.

PART THREE

The Widow of Windsor

18

'Sewer-poison': Sandringham, 13 December 1871

'This really has been the worst day of all,' wrote Victoria.[1] It was ten years later, ten terrible years, a whole lost decade of mourning and despair. Outside Sandringham House, the grounds were white and grey, and the weather was 'miserable and depressing, sloppy, snowy, windy and rainy'.[2] Inside, Dr William Jenner was once again attending a royal patient who appeared to be suffering from typhoid fever. It was 13 December, just one single day before the dreaded anniversary of Albert's death, and now Victoria's eldest son and heir Bertie seemed likely likewise to die. The coincidence of the dates, Victoria told her journal, 'filled us & believe the whole country with anxious forebodings and the greatest alarm'.[3]

The previous weeks had been awful, full of warnings that 'at any moment dear Bertie might go off, so that I had better come at once'.[4] Victoria had been summoned several times to Sandringham, the comfortable, modern house that Bertie, now a married man, had built for himself in the middle of a flattish, northern Norfolk estate with excellent shooting.

Since her arrival two weeks ago, Victoria had spent long hours watching and waiting in her eldest son's blue and white bedroom, 'the candles burning, & most dreary, Poor dear Bertie was lying there breathing heavily'.[5] His condition was now so critical that at one o'clock in the morning of 13 December his doctors issued a bulletin to waiting journalists and well-wishers saying there was no change from the four updates they'd issued the previous day.[6]

At 3 a.m. he was breathing between forty-four and fifty times a minute, his pulse 'quick' and 'feeble'. At 4.30 he was heard 'moaning' and 'muttering'. 'The strength is failing,' his doctors' notes admit.[7]

Relationships within the royal family had grown so strained that Bertie's doctors thought the sight of his relatives might upset him. So when Victoria visited her son's bedroom, she had to remain 'sitting behind the screen'. She sat there, silently, listening for long hours to his painful, ragged breathing. It sounded like he 'must choke at any moment'.[8] Dr Jenner's opinion was that 'the breathing had all along been the one thing that caused anxiety'. For Victoria, it was more than distressing. She was reminded 'so vividly and sadly of my dearest Albert's illness!'[9]

In this year of 1871 it wasn't just the Prince of Wales who was in desperately poor health. So, too, was the monarchy itself. Earlier in the year an anonymous pamphlet called *What Does She Do With It?* had caused a sensation. The work, probably written by radical politician George Otto Trevelyan, accused the queen of squirreling away public money from the Civil List to build up a private fortune. This was indeed an accurate accusation – she'd by now saved half a million pounds – though Trevelyan overstated his figures. The previous month of November had actually seen Charles Dilke making a speech calling outright for the monarchy's abolition.[10]

The situation had come about because some people thought Victoria had grown incapable of doing her job. In the years following Albert's death, she'd been paralysed, almost incoherent with grief. 'But oh!' she wrote to her Uncle Leopold, that Albert should be 'cut off in the prime of life . . . CUT OFF at forty-two – when I *had* hoped with such instinctive certainty that God never *would* part us . . . is too awful, *too cruel*!'[11] She had lost the confidence to appear in public, retreating behind the walls of Windsor to the disappointment, and the increasing disrespect, of her subjects.

Lord Clarendon, for one, believed that without sensible Albert, Victoria was utterly lost. 'No other woman,' he wrote, 'has the same public responsibility or the same motive for being absolutely guided by the superior mind of her husband.'[12] Once again, insiders began to worry that she would fall prey to the Hanoverian family madness. Florence Nightingale heard that the widowed Victoria was wasting away physically, 'half the size she was', and was unable to see more than one person at a time for fear of going insane.[13] Dr Jenner, who had by now replaced the kindly Dr Clark as the queen's chief medic, did not mince his words. 'A species of madness' had come upon her, he claimed, and it was 'hopeless to contend' with it. Her withdrawal from public appearances was due to 'nervousness', he thought. Meanwhile Lord Halifax considered that there was considerable 'evidence of insanity'.[14]

Part of this was genuine concern and pity for the queen's grief; part was the perceived threat of the royal family's hereditary 'madness' coming out in a new generation. But these fears were greatly amplified by the fact that Victoria was approaching that time of life when Victorian women in general were believed to lose control of themselves: the menopause.

One Victorian doctor thought that forty-two, the age at which Victoria lost Albert, was the precise moment the period of danger began. Forty-two, he thought, was a significant milestone on the road 'from the cradle to the grave'. From forty-two, wrote another doctor, 'climacteric mania' would begin, with its accompanying 'nervousness', 'improper explosions of temper' and 'frantic feeling of delirium and loss of self-control'.[15] Around 1865 Victoria did experience 'flushings' and 'distressing restlessness'.[16] Menopausal women, contemporary doctors hinted, would become sex maniacs. It is true that Victoria found herself physically bereft, desperately missing the touch of another human. There were so few people who could place consolatory hands upon a queen. 'I could go mad from the desire and longing,' she wrote.[17] Victoria had a life-sized carving of Albert's hand in marble, taken from a cast of his dead hand upon the day he died.[18] Perhaps she grasped it still.

But her daughter Alice believed that Victoria's greatest challenge was the lasting sense of subordination she still felt she owed to Albert. Victoria once admitted to Alice that 'she was afraid of getting too well — as if it were a crime & that she <u>feared</u> to begin to like riding on her Scotch poney etc.'[19] Now Bertie's illness, and the unfinished business of his presumed responsibility for Albert's death, threatened to make matters still worse.

Victoria had never taken the trouble to visit her son's home at Sandringham until 29 November, when reports of Bertie's worsening condition had brought her to Norfolk. It was a four-hour train journey to the railway station only a mile and a half away from the house. Today Sandringham feels much more remote, as the station has closed and it's necessary to drive there through a flat forest of fir, bracken and birch.

Alice, the natural nurse whose ministrations had eased her father's last days, had suggested that her mother should *not* be summoned. She had experience of the unhelpful drama and tension that Victoria could bring to a sickroom. Victoria came nevertheless, but when Bertie seemed to improve, she left. An urgent telegram from his doctors, announcing a relapse, brought her back on 8 December.[20] 'If he lives until Her Majesty comes I shall be satisfied,' said Dr Jenner, giving up on his patient's life.[21] 'She looked so small and miserable — poor poor thing,' wrote Augusta Bruce, who saw Victoria arriving at the house through the snow.[22]

Victoria was physically much smaller than she'd been even two years before. Earlier in 1871, she had suffered a serious illness, probably a swelling of the arm following a bee sting. Dr Jenner had brought in the shy but brilliant Professor Joseph Lister to drain the abscess and spray the wound with carbolic acid, a pioneering technique he had developed to prevent infection.[23] A surviving mourning dress from 1862, the year following Albert's death, reveals that even after nine children her waist was still a slender thirty-two inches. During her illness of 1871, an additional throat infection left Victoria unable to eat, and she lost two stones in weight after several days of being 'fed like a baby'.[24] In 1871, she must have, at fifty-three, once again been very slight. It's sometimes believed that Victoria gained weight in an immediate emotional response to

Albert's death, but her well-known late-life rotundity in fact dates from much later.

As she arrived at Sandringham House, Victoria was of course dressed in black. Any widow would have been expected to wear mourning for a full year after her husband's death. But after that Victoria made the unusual decision never to wear colour again. 'My dress is always the same,' she explained to Vicky in Germany. Now Vicky was married, and safely distant across the sea, Victoria confided in her as if her daughter were an adult friend. And in one letter to Vicky, she claimed mourning as 'the dress which I have adopted for ever, for mine'.[25]

There were many good reasons why the Victorians embraced mourning. People wearing black were instantly identifiable as needing special consideration for their bereaved status. Then again, an increasingly consumerist society pressurised people into thinking that they constantly needed to buy new clothes for each new situation. And mourning clothes were themselves becoming easier and cheaper to make: the Courtauld firm of crêpe-makers achieved astonishing commercial success with a 'secret' industrial process for producing the crêpe that weighed down widows' weeds.[26]

Yet Victoria was extraordinary in her dedication to black. If wearing mourning was a demand for greater-than-usual understanding, it's certainly true that she felt entitled to it for the rest of her life. Mourning was turned into a sort of disguise for her. It indicated that she was a victim, bereaved, which was a way of pre-empting criticism. And within the conventions of black, Victoria insisted that her clothes be cut in a way that she found comfortable and convenient: a bodice with only light boning, a skirt with capacious pockets. She no longer followed fashion; she had created a fashion all her own.

Victoria's black clothing also had terrific 'brand value' in creating a recognisable royal image. Although she rarely appeared in person, Victoria's physical appearance was more widely known than ever before. In 1860, she and Albert had taken the decision to allow photographs of themselves to be published on *cartes de visite*, highly collectible little rectangles of illustrated cardboard. Within two years, between three and four million of these cards depicting the queen had been sold.[27] The people who bought them understood that they were in possession of something more potent than a lithograph or an engraving. The effect, in terms of making the queen's subjects feel they 'knew' her, has been compared by the Royal Collection's photography curator to the sensational 1969 television documentary series, *Royal Family.*[28] So even if Victoria had been bodily absent from public life for the last decade, in paper form she had been more present than ever.[29]

Bertie was also a very popular subject for the purchasers of *cartes de visite*, especially the ones that showed him with his beautiful Danish wife, Alix. He had, in the end, been unable to avoid marrying her. During Victoria's stay at Sandringham, Alix too was constantly in and out of his bedroom.

The first medical update sent to Victoria after she woke up on the miserable morning of 13 December indicated that Bertie 'seemed very weak' and his 'breathing very imperfect & feeble'. He'd had 'no rest all night, from the constant delirium'. Victoria got up quickly, 'taking a mouthful of breakfast before hurrying to Bertie's room'. As usual, she sat on a sofa behind a screen so he couldn't see her.[30]

Bertie was beleaguered even before he'd fallen ill. The 1870s hadn't begun well for him. This was a decade characterised beyond the palace walls by a roaring economy and swanky excess. Despite his marriage, Bertie was still running around with the womanising 'swells' who'd introduced him to Nellie. The previous year had seen him drawn into the scandalous divorce of Sir Charles Mordaunt, and he'd even been forced to appear in court as a witness. In the end, nothing could be proved against Bertie beside having written a few innocuous letters to Sir Charles's estranged wife. (This poor woman, Harriet, spent most of the rest of her life in a lunatic asylum.) But while Bertie may have been innocent of adultery, he was certainly guilty of bad judgement. His behaviour did not play well with public opinion. 'In rude and general terms,' wrote Prime Minister William Gladstone, the monarchy's image problem lay in the fact that 'the Queen is invisible and the Prince of Wales is not respected.'[31]

Earlier in his illness, Bertie had admitted in a lucid moment to his sister Alice that he'd 'led a very difficult life, but it was <u>too late</u> now' to reform.[32] His disease – the dreaded typhoid once more, with its high fever and convulsions of the bowels – had begun at his friend Lord Londesborough's new seaside villa in Scarborough, Yorkshire. Londesborough had packed his rather badly built house with upper-crust guests. The drains could not cope. The two cesspools in the basement overflowed at high tide. A later investigation discovered that a pipe linked one of the cesspools directly to the water closet provided for Bertie's use. Members of the medical profession later concluded that 'the sewer-poison', as they called it, must have come creeping up that pipe and into Bertie's bathroom.[33] Doctors still held that you could 'inhale' infection by breathing in a bad smell, the so-called miasmatic theory of disease. In reality, Bertie must have drunk water containing bacteria. On 1 December, news had reached Sandringham that a fellow guest of Bertie's at Scarborough had died. So too had a stable boy employed in the house. It was chilling news for the family of the heir to the throne.

And Sandringham itself was not a happy or healthy house. Within the encircling ginger-coloured sandstone wall of the estate, a great many tense people had gathered. Alix's lady-in-waiting Lady Macclesfield found that Princess Alice was among the more trying guests. Chief nurse at her father's death, Alice had now been supplanted by two professionals. There was much to do for Bertie: making his bed, helping him relieve himself, feeding him orange jelly, barley water, beef tea and 'gravy from chicken'.[34] Lady Macclesfield thought that Alice, excluded from this important bustle, showed her resentment by being 'meddling, jealous and mischief-making'.[35]

At least Alice had been allowed to come to her brother's bedside; others had not. There was no room for Vicky, or Lenchen, despite their wishes, and Louise and Beatrice were sharing a bed through lack of space. The unmarried men were packed off to Bachelor's Cottage, through the gardens, past the lake and across the stream. It was 'quite impossible to keep a house quiet as long as it is swarming' with so many visitors, complained one onlooker, who was shocked by the way the queen's children 'squabble and wrangle and abuse each other'.[36] There was nothing for the anxious house guests to do, apart from take wet walks, or else pace up and down the saloon.

Victoria might have been expected to take pleasure in the presence of her children, but as ever she did not. Her Private Secretary Henry Ponsonby had a most un–courtier-like eye for the amusing. He described how, finding himself in Sandringham's garden one day, he was 'suddenly nearly carried away by a stampede of royalties, headed by the Duke of Cambridge and brought up by Leopold, going as fast as they could'. 'We thought it was a mad bull' that had caused the exodus, Ponsonby wrote, 'But they cried out: "The Queen, the Queen", and we all dashed into the house again and waited behind the door till the road was clear'.[37]

The house itself was spanking new, completed just a year previously. At the time of his death, Albert had been thinking about purchasing a country estate for Bertie as a twenty-first-birthday present. The search continued without him, and Sandringham was settled upon in 1862. Bertie brought his young Danish bride home to it three weeks after the wedding. They soon decided that the existing twenty-nine-bedroom house was too small and rebuilding ensued.

The result, completed in 1870, was not entirely a work of beauty. The new house had a peculiarly long and narrow plan, and rather dark reception rooms shaded by the thorn, elm and larch trees preserved from the garden of its predecessor. Alix tried to lighten the murky interiors by installing a multitude of mirrors.[38] Bertie's architect, Albert Jenkins Humbert, was an expert in ecclesiastical work, and his qualifications for the job lay chiefly in his well-received designs for the royal mausoleums at Windsor. At Sandringham, Humbert borrowed gables and pinnacles from the nearby Jacobean Blickling Hall, but the red-brick block he finally produced rather calls to mind a seaside hotel. Insofar as a house that eventually grew to 360 rooms can be so described, Sandringham was unpretentious. Guests thought it odd that one entered straight into the 'saloon', a Victorian version of a Great Hall, with no cloakroom or waiting room, but this was supposed to create cosy informality. During happier times, Bertie's parrot would welcome his guests with squawks, while Bertie himself would record their weight upon a set of jockey scales kept near the door.[39]

The chief attraction of Sandringham was the shooting, enabled by fifty or sixty beaters, and the whole estate regularly rang with the sound of gunfire. The beaters, dressed alike in 'blue blouses' and 'black chimney hats', looked like a small army that 'divides, and sweeps . . . scouring the country'.[40] Bertie's purpose-built game carriage had space for 250 dead birds, and was so heavy it required two enormous Suffolk Punch horses to pull it. When the guests returned to the house for tea, Alix herself served them in the saloon beneath the stuffed noses of antlered deer and moose. The floor was made treacherous with slippery 'Persian carpets & skins of wild animals . . . their enormous stuffed heads stuck up'. 'Take care you don't fall over them,' Prince Affie warned newcomers.[41]

Dinner took place in the small dining room, which could seat only twenty-two. Bertie expected his male guests to wear informal smoking jackets, precursors of the modern dinner jacket, instead of the conventional tailed coat.[42] Alix, thin and fashionable, would hobble in, showing off her waspish waist. The house was supposedly fireproof with its iron girder construction (it wasn't, and would twice be severely damaged by flames) and sported a final eccentric addition that was Bertie's pride and joy: his private bowling alley.[43]

But once Victoria was in residence, she issued a whole string of orders for changes. There was to be no smoking; windows were to be opened; the clocks were to be put back to normal time.

Bertie kept his timepieces half an hour fast in order to gain maximum daylight for winter shooting expeditions. Whenever she wasn't in her son's sickroom, Victoria tried to entertain herself by inspecting his stables, kennels and cottages.[44]

A further source of worry came with the news that a Sandringham servant, a groom named Charles Blegg, had also succumbed to the same sickness as his master. Was it possible that Sandringham, not Scarborough, was the origin of Bertie's disease? And might his own home also be tainted with typhoid? There had been long-standing concerns that the house was somehow unhealthy, and now 'quite a panic among the servants' began. They began to whisper to each other that 'the place is never free from fever'.[45]

It was true that in 1867 Alix had suffered a severe attack of fever that left her with a lifelong limp. There was one theory that her illness was caused by foul air from the Sandringham lake. This water feature had since been moved further away from the house as a precaution, but even so, Victoria believed her son's home 'very unhealthy – drainage and ventilation – bad; bad smells in some rooms – of gas and drains'.[46] Her cousin the Duke of Cambridge, another house guest during Bertie's illness, upset everyone by conversing 'on nothing but drains'. He spent the short dark days prowling round the house detecting odours and proclaiming Princess Louise's room uninhabitable. 'This afternoon the Duke thought there was a bad smell in the library,' records one courtier. Paranoia was setting in. He 'jumped up and said "By George, I won't sit here."'[47]

Twenty-seven-year-old Alix loved riding, and in normal times she would happily introduce guests to her favourite mare, Vera.[48] She was far too anxious to be able to do so now. Victoria found her daughter-in-law's state utterly pitiable. 'Poor dear Alix,' she wrote, 'was in the greatest alarm & despair & I supported her as best I could.' Another symptom that 'frightened' both mother and daughter-in-law 'dreadfully' was Bertie's 'clutching at his bed clothes & seeming to feel for things which were not there'.[49]

Alix, Princess of Wales, has not emerged well from the accounts of historians, some of whom have almost excused her husband's playboy activities on the grounds of her coldness, her icy beauty, her deafness. 'Are you aware,' Victoria once wrote, in acid ink, 'that Alix has the smallest brain ever seen?'[50] But Alix's personal friends and servants were vocally devoted to her. Lady Macclesfield thought that 'she never thinks of herself – but is always with him . . . as gentle & considerate to everybody as ever. Poor little darling.' Alix had grown even thinner, and even whiter, during Bertie's illness: 'it goes to one's heart to see her going about like a ghost.'[51]

Alix had come to Sandringham as a beautiful eighteen-year-old upon her marriage in 1863. She quite liked the flat countryside of Norfolk because it reminded her of her native Denmark. She'd been taught to think that her beauty was her greatest achievement, and at heart she was a simple, straightforward person. 'I always think I was intended for a nursery maid,' she said.[52] Earlier in 1871, she'd lost a premature baby son, John, who'd lived for only twenty-four hours.

The doctors tried to exclude Alix from the sickroom partly because of the bizarre things that her husband now did and said in his delirium. Upon Victoria's arrival at the house, she'd found Bertie 'wandering dreadfully' in his mind, and 'talking incessantly'.[53] On the darkest day of 13 December, it remained 'very distressing to hear him calling out & talking incessantly quite incoherently', at the same time 'picking at things in the air and playing with his fingers.'[54] Bertie's brothers Affie and Arthur found this funny; their mother did not. 'Too much giggling,' she said, 'and the way in which you both *listened* to poor Bertie's wanderings grieved me.'[55]

And it really was no laughing matter. As her husband raved, the doctors attempted to keep Alix away lest she learn 'all sorts of revelations' and hear 'names of people mentioned'.[56] Bertie, his inhibitions quite gone, was revealing his sexual secrets. At other times, he pelted Alix with pillows. His speech was 'thick . . . much of the character of a drunk man'.[57] No wonder, for even when he couldn't swallow food Bertie could still drink. On 13 December, for example, he was given wine in his water at 10.30 a.m., more wine at 1.40 p.m., champagne at two and champagne seltzer at three.[58] He yelled at another of his doctors, Dr Gull, to give him more: 'that's right *old Gull* . . . that's good, two or three more spoonsful, old Gull.'[59] 'I can't breathe,' he was heard to pant in his more lucid moments, 'I shall die.'[60]

Bertie also – apparently – denied his marriage bond. 'That was once,' Bertie said to Alix when she came in to see him, 'but is no more. You have broken your vows.'[61] The words imply that at some point Alix had broken off sexual relations in the light of his own repeated infidelities. All this was very scandalous to the household. Yet perhaps the worst among Bertie's delirious ravings was a 'great secret' that Henry Ponsonby nevertheless passed on to his wife: that Bertie 'thinks he has succeeded & is King'.[62]

Victoria had briefly been out during the morning for a stroll in Sandringham's dripping pleasure gardens. They featured fake rock formations made from Pulhamite, a new type of concrete named for its inventor James Pulham, but they were so new that the plants had barely got going. She came back in, though, to discover that the midday medical bulletin revealed no improvement in Bertie's symptoms.[63] Victoria and Alice began to prepare them-selves for the end. 'There can be no hope,' they said to each other through their tears.

In the afternoon, Victoria remained indoors, and was 'so terribly anxious' that she hardly left Bertie's room.[64] Yet he did not know that she was there. His doctors continued to argue that Bertie should be shielded from the knowledge of the presence of his family. Alix crawled on hands and knees 'to be near him & he not see her', while Victoria lurked behind her screen.[65] Eventually, though, Victoria overcame her scruples and the medical advice about not bothering him. 'I went up to the bed,' she writes, '& took hold of his poor hand, kissing it & stroking his arm.'

But Bertie failed to recognise his mother. He 'turned round', Victoria writes, '& looked wildly at me saying "Who are you".'[66]

Even though he had disappointed her so badly, even if she

believed that he'd killed Albert and even if she had essentially given up on him and cast him off, it must still have stabbed her to the heart.

Throughout 13 December, the nation hourly expected Bertie's death. 'Many millions,' claimed *The Times*, are 'watching at a distance by this bedside.'[67] The bell-ringers of St Paul's were called into work to be ready to sound the death knell for his passing.[68] The newspapers prepared special announcements. Reporters in hired gigs waited at the Sandringham estate's Norwich Gates, its point of exit nearest to the telegraph office at Dersingham.[69] No one could fail to notice the eerie coincidence of dates: 'it is now ten years tomorrow since the Prince Consort died of a familiar affliction . . . there is real anxiety.'[70] 'We were getting nearer & nearer to the 14th,' Victoria noticed. Sickeningly, events 'seemed more & more like ten years ago'.

Throughout the course of that dark and dreadful afternoon, though, the grasp of the bitter cold upon the Norfolk countryside had gradually been relaxing. It was 'raw' outside, but also 'damp', and it had been 'thawing all day'. When Victoria had taken her son's hand, he'd been too confused to recognise her. Yet, as evening came, everyone began to hope that 'dear Bertie was really a little better'.[71] 'The Prince is sleeping,' reads a boldly scrawled, excited note in pencil among his medical team's papers, dated 8.45 p.m. This was the first time he had dozed in many days.[72]

And later in the evening, Bertie at last seemed to come to himself. 'That lady,' he whispered, 'is very like the Queen.'

'It is the Queen,' said Dr Gull.[73]

'It's Mama,' she said, 'Dear child.'[74]

'Don't sit here for me,' Bertie wheezed, and 'the gasping between each word was most distressing' to Victoria. But he'd known her, he'd understood that his mother was present and he'd spoken sanely. Everyone was 'so thankful'.[75]

After Victoria eventually felt able to leave to go to her own room, one of the doctors made an urgent call for 'two bottles of old brandy'. Bertie's body was rubbed with the spirit, which seemed to restore some further measure of life.[76] Midnight passed, and still Bertie lived, with just Alix, now, sitting by his bed. Finally, at four o'clock in the morning of 14 December – that date of all dates, the very anniversary of Albert's death – Bertie finally managed to fall into a deep slumber and, at last, to grow quiet.

By eight the following morning, another doctors' bulletin was issued to the press, and, remarkably, this time 'there was no decrease of strength to be chronicled'. Thirty-six painful hours 'of the wildest, loudest, incessant talking, in all languages – whistling, singing, began to subside'.[77] Dr Jenner and Dr Gull now told the world that Bertie had 'slept quietly at intervals during the night', with 'some abatement of the gravity of the symptoms'.[78]

At 8.45 a.m., Bertie managed to swallow some milk.[79] His brother Affie, himself a serious drinker, suggested a glass of pale ale. The patient drank it off quickly, 'which seemed to revive him'.[80] And then he thrilled everyone by asking for another. 'It seemed hardly possible to realize,' his mother wrote, '& to feel that on this very day our dear Bertie is getting better instead of worse! How deeply grateful we are for God's mercy!'[81] At 5 p.m., Bertie even 'wanted to leave his bed to go out!'[82]

But no one felt able to celebrate too much. While Bertie was getting better, a Sandringham kitchen maid was simultaneously falling ill with the same fever. And in his distant little bedroom above the stable, Charles Blegg the groom lost his own fight for life. A chastened Alix attended Blegg's funeral at Sandringham Church, and commissioned him a memorial that said: 'One is taken, and the other left.'[83]

Victoria had realised that perhaps after all she did love her wayward child. And her subjects likewise surprised themselves by how much they minded so nearly losing their Prince of Wales. 'There have been daily beautiful articles in the papers,' Victoria wrote.[84] People seemed to realise that despite their complaints about Bertie they would not quite like to do without him. The politician responsible for noticing this, and capitalising upon it, was a man whom Victoria hated: William Gladstone. Despite her animosity, though, Gladstone was deeply devoted to the monarchy, and had been sincerely concerned for Bertie's health.

Victoria was much more personally inclined towards the policies of Gladstone's Tory enemies than his own Liberal Party, and she didn't like his manner either. She found the man who possessed the greatest political brain of her reign to be cold, verging on disrespectful. She considered that he had 'a strange lack of know-ledge of men and human nature . . . which does not give me the idea of his having any great grasp of mind'.[85] To Victoria's evident distaste, Gladstone made no concessions to her femininity. He treated her just like a man, or else 'as a competent and intelligent head of state', as historian Paula Bartley puts it, speaking to her plainly and without flattery.[86]

If Gladstone earned Victoria's dislike by neglecting to treat her as a Victorian upper-class woman, he also displeased her by telling her straight out when he thought she was wrong. He considered that her withdrawal from public life during her decade of bereave-ment had been deeply damaging to the monarchy. It would perhaps have been forgiveable in an ordinary woman, but not acceptable in a queen. He felt that her persistent failure to turn up to ceremonies such as the opening of Parliament, for example, in the years since Albert had died, was harmful, indeed distressing: a 'smaller and meaner cause for the decay of Thrones cannot be conceived'.[87]

He now argued that Victoria should capitalise on Bertie's recovery. There must, he decreed, be some public act of thanks-giving. The Prince of Wales's seemingly miraculous salvation had been enormously good for the monarchy as an institution. Indeed, Gladstone wrote, it had 'worked in an extraordinary degree to the effect of putting down that disagreeable movement with which the name of Sir C. Dilke had been connected.'[88] It's one of Gladstone's typically prolix and trying sentences, but you can certainly see his point.

Eventually, with poor grace, Victoria agreed to Gladstone's proposal that she should attend a service at St Paul's Cathedral to give thanks for the saving of her son. On 25 January 1872, his mother was pleased to hear that Bertie had been 'placed on the sofa' rather than his bed. By February he was well enough – though 'very lame' – to travel with her to St Paul's for the service.[89] Thirteen thousand people were accommodated in the building in specially constructed galleries, with queen and prince taking pride of place under the dome.[90] The scandals of his past, the disappointment of her seclusion, was forgotten. The nation was simply glad to have them both back. 'The deafening cheers never ceased the whole way,' Victoria recorded. 'I saw the tears in Bertie's eyes and took and pressed his hand! It was a most affecting day.'[91]

It sounds like a happy ending. But historians in recent years have downplayed the significance of Gladstone's intervention. Victoria did not take the criticisms of Dilke and others as seriously as Gladstone himself had done. In truth, the complaints of the republicans, while disturbing, weren't really that effective. The criticism came not because people wanted to *abolish* the monarchy, but because they wanted *more of it*.[92] 'They want to see a Crown and a Sceptre and all that sort of thing,' wrote Lord Halifax. 'They want the gilding for their money.'[93]

The historian Margaret Homans argues that in fact there was nothing unconsidered, or foolish, about Victoria's withdrawal from public life. For a queen, for Victoria, 'being is a form of doing'.[94] In 1862, she was discovered to be in arrears to the vast number of 16,000 signatures on officers' commissions for the army and navy. She'd simply failed to get it done. But Britain hadn't been invaded, there had been no terrible consequences and an Act of Parliament was passed to excuse her from doing it in the future.[95] When a queen appeared at the opening of Parliament, even if she remained silent, it was reported in *The Times*. When a queen did absolutely nothing more significant than going for a pony ride, that too got reported in *The Times*. If the queen was still alive, and if the life of the nation was going on regardless, then all would be well. 'Her absence,' Homans argues, made the monarchy 'unthreatening'. To the political classes, anxious about the upheaval of the Second Reform Act of 1867, a queen who was out of sight but not out of mind was perfect. To them, 'the best possible occupant of the throne was a widow'.[96]

And in time it would turn out that being a widow might suit Victoria too. Before the twentieth century, to be a widow was perhaps to be in the most potent of a woman's life stages. For the first time, a widow was answerable to no one. For the first time, she could own property. For all women other than the queen, a woman's worldly goods, and even her children, had up to that point been not hers but her father's or her husband's. Gladstone's contribution, then, must be downplayed in Victoria's emergence into the third stage of her life. Her most decisive political interventions would begin to be made as she began to re-possess her power.

And even at rock bottom, when her doctors had thought she would go mad with grief, Victoria had spoken of endurance. She was '*determined*', she wrote, that as a widow '*no one* person, may *he* be ever so good . . . is to lead, or guide, or dictate *to me*'.[97] In other words, she was saying that no one would ever again have the mastery over her that Albert had possessed. And she was right. From now on, she stood, and ruled, alone. Lord Clarendon came to think that being queen was in fact the saving of her. 'The best thing for her,' he thought, 'is the responsibility of her position & the mass of business wh: She cannot escape from & wh: during a certain portion of the day compels her to think of something other than the all-embracing sorrow.'[98]

Bertie's illness had also, in an unexpected way, done them all good as a family. It had brought Alix's husband back to her. Their household noticed that she was 'so affectionate, tears in her eyes talking of him, and his manner to her so gentle'.[99] Victoria also noticed a new maturity in her son. 'There is something different which I can't exactly express. It is like a new life . . . he is constantly with Alix and they seem hardly ever apart!'[100] And Victoria herself was affected for the good. 'How it touches one,' wrote Augusta Bruce, 'to read of the poor dear Queen sitting holding the P. of W.'s hand! Is it not affecting? I quite long to see Her thus, Her best self, by being taken out of herself – taken out of Doctors and maladies (I mean her own) and nerves.'[101]

With Bertie's illness, Victoria's return to her best self, the self she had lost in Albert, had begun.

19

Lunch with Disraeli: Hughenden Manor, 15 December 1877

On 15 December 1877, Europe was at war, and Victoria was at work. In the foggy early morning, a telegram from Constantinople reached Windsor Castle.

'Very interesting,' she thought as she read it. Telegrams like this one passed across her desk every day, and she consumed the most important immediately before consigning them to the 'dainty silk-lined waste-paper basket'. The daily contents even of her bin 'would be more interesting than a year's file of *The Times*,' people said.[1] This particular morning, her hawkish ambassador to the decaying Ottoman Empire, a former archaeologist named Sir Austen Henry Layard, used his telegram to pass on a personal message from the Sultan. The Sultan requested that Victoria should in turn request the Russian Emperor to come to an armistice in the ongoing conflict with the Turks.[2]

This was the so-called 'Eastern Question' bursting dangerously back into life. The peace treaty at the end of the Crimean War had marked only an intermission, not a conclusion. Tsar Alexander II, Emperor of All Russia, still believed that he could grab more land and influence in the Ottoman Empire's troubled Balkan regions. Earlier in 1877, Russia had destabilised Bosnia, Herzegovina and Bulgaria by supporting a rebellion against the Sultan.

The Sultan had failed to quash his discontented subjects, but not for want of trying. Back in England, the *Manchester Guardian* reported on a stream of Turkish atrocities in Bosnia: villages burned, people slaughtered. Britain's Liberal Party, under Gladstone, were disgusted by the way the Turks had treated their Balkan Christian subjects. *Bulgarian Horrors* was the title of an inflammatory book Gladstone had published denouncing Turkey. But although his book had been a wildfire success, Gladstone was now out of power, and the governing Tories under Benjamin Disraeli took the opposite view. Disraeli feared that if Britain failed to intervene to help Turkey, the Russians would do what they liked in the Balkans, moving on eastwards towards British India, amassing lands and threatening Victoria's global dominance.

In Britain, impassioned debate had resulted in stalemate. Both 'sides', Gladstone and his peacemongers, Disraeli and his warmongers, were growing angry. Back in Constantinople, Layard was getting desperate simply to be told what the British position was. 'I am in very great anxiety,' he admitted to a friend. 'We have no policy, no definite views, consequently no influence, no power.'[3]

Victoria, however, knew exactly what she wanted, which was to support the Sultan and to act against Russia. 'It maddens the Queen,' she told Disraeli, that Britain had not yet intervened.[4] She was too laissez-faire, too Tory at heart, to engage with projects to better the social conditions of her people. And while she was personally charitable, she did not believe in anything approaching a welfare state. But foreign affairs were the one part of her job guaranteed to get her feeling fanatical.

By holding and acting upon such violent personal views, Victoria was in fact behaving unconstitutionally. British foreign policy was now the business of Parliament, not the monarch. Yet diplomacy was still nevertheless a personal business. Not only had Victoria, at twenty, danced with Tsar Alexander II during a visit of his to London, but also her son Affie had recently married his daughter.

Victoria's desk, then, stood right at the nexus of power in Europe. And despite her ties of family and friendship with Russia, Victoria instinctively understood what her subjects really wanted, which was war.

∽

'We don't want to fight,' they were singing in pubs and music halls,

> . . . but, by Jingo, if we do,
> We've got the ships,
> we've got the men,
> we've got the money too . . .

> 'The Dogs of War' are loose
> and the rugged Russian Bear,
> Full bent on blood and robbery,
> has crawl'd out of his lair.

Victoria was with them all the way. But immediately after reading Layard's telegram, she made one of her surprising switches from world leader to housekeeper. She now picked up a 'violet ink-pencil' to correct the proposed menus for Windsor Castle's meals that day, which had to be sent 'back to the kitchens, confectionary, and other departments, before ten o'clock'.[5]

And after that the casual observer might have thought that politics were over, and that the rest of the queen's business for 15 December was the simple matter of going out to lunch. She had an engagement with Disraeli himself, at his Buckinghamshire home of Hughenden Manor. The writer of an editorial in *The Times* believed that Victoria, now just short of sixty, had grown passive through age and inactivity, a mere meddler in constitutional affairs. Today would be a nice jaunt for her, ran its rather patronising editorial. 'We may be sure that it was literature rather than politics' that monarch and Prime Minister would discuss during their lunch together, *The Times* pronounced, and that 'the wars of nations may for a season be forgotten'.[6]

But they could not have been more wrong. As she prepared to leave for her lunch, Victoria had a clear foreign policy objective to achieve. No one in Britain wanted more than she did to put the Russian Bear back in his lair. Unlike her predecessors, she could not give the order for war. But she could create the right conditions for such an order to be given. Never had she been more experienced, nor more committed to acting as sovereign.

Over at Hughenden Manor, two counties away, Disraeli would have been up since his habitual half past seven. The first sight he saw as he opened his eyes was the queen. In his bedroom were pictures of Victoria's children Bertie (two different ones), Louise, Arthur (again two versions), Leopold, Affie and Beatrice; and her daughters-in-law, Russian Marie and Danish Alix. There were pictures of Victoria with Albert, of Victoria and Albert separately, of Victoria on horseback, of Albert in Highland dress and finally a statuette of the queen. It was a shrine to the royal family, and no royal stalker could have been more assiduous. 'I love the Queen,' Disraeli once admitted to her lady-in-waiting Jane Ely, 'perhaps the only person in this world left to me that I do love.'[7]

When he was at home at Hughenden for the day, Disraeli off duty usually wore his 'rustic hat' and his velveteen breeches. Today, though, he was more formally dressed. He'd been a dandy in his youth, and even in old age he was fond of white coats, and lavender kid gloves. When he was about to make a striking statement, which happened very often, he would 'give a nervous cough' and pass a 'handkerchief lightly under his nose, hardly touching it'.[8] He was vain about his figure, and it was sometimes possible through the back of his coat to discern the outline of 'an unquestionable pair of stays'.[9] This morning he was doubtless going through his corre-spondence at his standing desk as usual before his customary 'saunter on the terrace' and review of his peacocks.[10] He found being Prime Minister a heavy burden. He was seventy-two and in poor health, and the constant crises in the east made it impossible for him 'to do anything but attend to them and brood over them'.[11]

'He is very peculiar, thoroughly Jewish looking,' Victoria had thought upon first meeting Disraeli properly in 1852, 'a livid complexion, dark eyes and eyebrows and black ringlets. The expres-sion is disagreeable, but I do not find him so to talk to.'[12] He and she took to each other, and enjoyed lengthy conversations about 'poetry, romance and chivalry'. When he knelt to kiss her hand, he would seize it in both of his and embrace it, as he said, 'in loving loyalty'.[13] Disraeli presented himself as Victoria's swain, promising her that it would be 'his delight and duty to render the transaction of affairs as easy to your Majesty, as possible'.[14]

This was a careful strategy on Disraeli's part. He had seen how Gladstone had fallen foul of her socially as much as politically, and worked out a more effective means of handling his boss: 'I never deny; I never contradict; I sometimes forget.' Only occasionally did he remind her that their joint powers were not limitless. 'Were he your Majesty's Grand Vizier,' Disraeli once wrote of himself, 'instead of your Majesty's Prime Minister, he should be content . . . but, alas! it is not so.'[15] Victoria adored all this flattery, and perhaps did not realise just how much he was manipulating and talking down to her. Her Private Secretary Henry Ponsonby had much less time for Disraeli, thinking him 'bright in sparkling repartee but indolent and worn out . . . how anyone can put faith in Dizzy is what I don't understand.'[16]

Yet Victoria particularly liked Disraeli's energetic colonial policy, which had seen him smooth the way to her becoming empress of India in 1876, and which would see Britain pursue a multitude of conflicts in Africa. Victoria thought that the high cost of ambition overseas was worth it in terms of security for the existing empire and for global prestige. Britain and its colonies must, she considered, 'be *prepared* for *attacks* and *wars, somewhere* or *other,* CONTINUALLY'.[17]

Her aim today, then, was to hasten yet another conflict, in the Middle East, and to stiffen Disraeli's will to bring it about. But 15 December 1877 was not an auspicious day for doing so. In Disraeli's post that morning was a letter that Victoria had written first thing and sent over from Windsor ahead of her visit. It was a note of apology, begging his pardon for a mistake she'd made. She'd only just realised that she was coming to lunch on a day of 'sad recollections', the fifth anniversary of the death of Disraeli's much-mourned wife, Mary Anne.[18] And a good deal of Disraeli's affectation and whimsy can be forgiven in the light of his deep love of this rather extraordinary woman he'd lost. Another bond that queen and Prime Minister shared was their bereavement.

Back at Windsor, after writing her letter of apology, Victoria would have made a substantial breakfast. A sample menu from the 1870s lists 'sausages with potatoes, grilled whiting, poached eggs in stock, hot and cold roast fowl'.[19] She did not, however, eat it all. She liked to have alternatives 'to see about her and to know are there'.[20]

After breakfast, Victoria told her daughter Beatrice to get ready to leave. Beatrice was reluctant, for she had a cold and 'was suffering much from her head & throat, & again feverish'.[21] But the queen's unmarried daughters who lived at home were essentially permanent ladies-in-waiting whose personal circumstances must always give way to duty. At half past twelve it was inevitable that both queen and sniffing princess set off together for Windsor railway station.

It was now thirty-five years since Victoria had taken her first trip by train. In June 1842, she'd walked along a crimson carpet laid on the platform at Windsor station to climb aboard and travel to Paddington with the engineer Isambard Kingdom Brunel himself driving the engine. There was 'great applause' when, twenty-five minutes later, they 'reached the terminus'.[22]

Although rail travel was by now well established, Victoria remained slightly nervous of it. She'd first seen what she called a 'Rail road' when she was seventeen, the 'steam carriage' passing with 'startling quickness . . . enveloped in clouds of smoke, and making a loud noise'.[23] In 1861, a member of her medical staff had been killed in an accident while travelling towards Osborne. The train had just been pulling out of the platform when it stopped especially for Dr Baly to board. During some miscommunication it moved off too soon, and he was crushed to death.[24] From her purpose-built saloon car Victoria had access to a lever to operate a signal on the roof commanding the train driver to 'go slow' or even to 'stop'.[25] There was supposedly a speed limit of forty miles an hour for royal train travel, though Victoria's recorded actual journey times suggest that it wasn't observed.[26]

Her train took forty-five minutes to make this particular journey to High Wycombe, Hughenden's nearest station. On the crowded station platform, a military band played 'God Save the Queen'.[27] Victoria now had to endure an address from the mayor, and receive a bouquet from his daughter.[28] The mayor must have enjoyed himself, though, as greeting the queen made a pleasant change from his overriding preoccupation, the town's new sewerage works.[29]

Victoria then drove slowly along High Wycombe's high street in a landau, a carriage with very low sides to allow its occupants to be seen. She was accompanied by Beatrice and her lady-in-waiting Jane Ely. The road was lined with schoolchildren and the church bells ringing. The landau passed under several specially constructed 'triumphal arches', the most curious of them 'entirely composed of chairs, which is the staple industry of the town'.[30] It was such an odd sight – a 'unique and artistic structure', according to a proud local historian – that Victoria 'stopped her carriage to inspect and admire it'.[31]

High Wycombe had become a furniture town because of the fine local beech, which was so abundant that people called it 'The Buckinghamshire Weed'.[32] The town's woodturners were known as 'bodgers', and High Wycombe was capable of fulfilling enormous orders, such as the 19,200 chairs required in 1874 for the vast audience expected when a pair of celebrated American evangelists visited England. Many a bodger was married to a 'caner' or maker of cane seats, and their offspring were perhaps polishers or packers. Working at its hardest, the little town could produce an astonishing 4,700 chairs each day.[33] The biggest arch now erected across the high street consisted of a carefully calibrated hierarchy of seats. At the bottom were common Windsor chairs, the town's biggest seller. Then came drawing-room, library and rocking chairs, topped by the state chair of the mayor.[34] All along the high street the bodgers and caners cheered Victoria. They cheered too for their own chair arches, one with a banner reading 'HAIL, EMPRESS OF INDIA', another spelling out 'LONG LIVE THE QUEEN'.

∽

Now the landau passed through Disraeli's park, climbed a hill and set the queen down outside the red-brick front of Disraeli's manor. It had become 'a fine day, and with some gleams of sunshine'.[35]

In the eighteenth century, a monarch visiting her Prime Minister would most likely have found herself at the estate of a great landed peer, but Disraeli was a new type of more meritocratic politician. Hughenden was 'the pleasant but modest home', as The Times put it, 'of a country gentleman of literary tastes'.[36] Disraeli had borrowed thousands of pounds to purchase it, a debt he thought worth incurring because owning property was an essential qualification for achieving his ambition of becoming leader of the Conservatives. His home was an ugly eighteenth-century house made even uglier by changes he and his wife had carried out in the 1860s. The architectural historian Nikolaus Pevsner found the house 'excruciating, everything sharp, angular and aggressive', while Disraeli's own guests described the interiors as 'very gaudy'.[37]

Yet Benjamin and his Mary Anne didn't care. He was extraordinary in so many ways, a Jew of Italian background who'd converted to Anglican Christianity at twelve. He regretted not being sent to one of the great public schools, but nevertheless considered himself a classical scholar: 'in the pride of boyish erudition, I edited the Idonisian Eclogue of Theocritus, wh. was privately printed.' After stints as a solicitor's clerk and a speculator, he made his mark as the author of sensational novels about high society. Yet eventually he decided that politics interested him more. He campaigned as a Radical before settling down as a Conservative.

A flamboyant, contradictory man, Disraeli had drawn great support from his wife. Twelve years older than him, wealthy, if slightly disreputable, Mary Anne picked Disraeli from among her suitors not least because of his gracious way with words. The odd couple were deeply devoted. 'More like a mistress than a wife' was how he described her. 'Dizzy married me for my money,' Mary Anne admitted, as she entered old age, yet 'if he had the chance again, he would marry me for love.'[38] But she'd died in 1872, leaving Disraeli, like Victoria, in the position of having lost the great love of a lifetime.

As soon as she arrived, Disraeli invited Victoria into the 'pretty Italian garden' behind the house to plant a commemorative tree.[39] Disraeli proudly kept and cherished the commemorative spade she used. He loved inviting his friends to plant special trees. He did it so frequently that the trees' foliage eventually darkened all the downstairs rooms of his house, and the forest had to be felled.

But then it was back inside, to the library, and to business, namely the crisis unfolding in the East. 'Be bold,' Victoria had enjoined her Prime Minister, 'call your followers together . . . tell them . . . that Russia is as barbarous and tyrannical as the Turks. Tell them this, and that they should rally round their sovereign and country.'[40] But Disraeli was finding it hard, in the light of the atrocities they'd committed in Bulgaria, to get his colleagues to agree to a policy of intervention in favour of the Turks. 'In a Cabinet of twelve members,' he explained, 'there are seven parties or policies.'[41]

Now Disraeli gave Victoria a detailed account of the previous day's 'very stormy' Cabinet meeting. When he'd proposed that British should step up and mediate between Russia and Turkey, his words had fallen into 'a dead silence'. Then Lord Derby 'spoke with unusual fire' against the proposal and 'hard remarks were made'.[42] Victoria wished they would just get their act together. 'Oh, if the Queen were a man,' she groaned on another occasion, 'she would like to go and give those Russians . . . such a beating!'[43] But she was pleased to discover that Disraeli was 'determined to bring things to an issue' at the next meeting, in two days' time. Only having dealt with international affairs did they go 'in to luncheon.'[44]

This lugubrious meal, just Victoria, Beatrice, lady-in-waiting and Disraeli, took place in the Gothic dining room. There was a ten-minute break between each course for the benefit of Disraeli's notoriously disarranged digestion.[45] According to Hughenden tradition, he'd had the barley-sugar legs of one of his chairs specially shortened for his tiny sovereign to sit upon, and indeed one member of the set is still smaller than the others.

But Disraeli was not noted for such domestic thoughtfulness. Hughenden had long held a poor reputation among High Wycombe's tradesmen, who were disappointed by the meanness of the grocery orders they received.[46] There's no doubt, though, that the Prime Minister of Jewish background and his older, childless wife were considered a little odd by the locals. After lunch, Disraeli showed Victoria his pictures, which included a gallery of portraits of dead relatives and friends.[47] Disraeli noted afterwards that 'The Faery' (his private name for Victoria) 'seemed to admire, and be interested in, everything.'[48]

She departed from Hughenden at half past three and was back at Windsor soon after four, one of those astonishingly quick Victorian journeys that simply wouldn't be possible today except by helicopter.[49] She left laden with a small statue of her host. 'The Faery took away my statuette,' he says, implying that it had been seized rather than proffered, while Beatrice walked off with 'the most beautiful *bonbonnière* you ever saw, or fancied: just fresh from Paris.'[50]

According to that pompous *Times* editorial, its readers 'will scarcely, perhaps, think that the visit was paid for the purpose of determining any question of domestic or foreign policy'.[51] But Victoria's journal entry for the day, as she completed it that evening, is in fact completely dominated by politics and the Eastern Question, in much more detail than quoted here. And her visit to his house *was* read by some as a political action. It was seen, as she'd intended, as a vote of confidence in Disraeli and therefore in the policy of intervention. Some anti-Semitic supporters of Gladstone sniffed that she 'gone ostentatiously' to eat 'in his ghetto'.[52] They took the lunch party as it had been meant: as an attack upon their ambitions.

And as politics, Victoria's lunch at Hughenden worked. 'The great struggle is over,' Disraeli reported to a friend four days later, 'and I have triumphed.' He persuaded his Cabinet colleagues that Britain should take a more forceful role: Parliament was to be summoned, £6 million was to be committed, action was to be taken. 'The Faery,' he claimed, 'is delighted.'[53] Two months later, Britain agreed to send ironclad ships to the Dardanelles to deter the Russians from invading Constantinople. The tottery Ottoman Empire was kept intact, and the 'atrocitarians' (as Disraeli termed Gladstone and his friends) were beaten. Victoria was so delighted she made Disraeli a Knight of the Garter.[54]

It's customary among historians to suggest that Victoria's greatest achievement was to negotiate the last stages of the monarchy's transformation from absolutist to purely constitutional. That's what contemporary writers such as Walter Bagehot truly believed had happened. But it's not quite that simple. Even in the very earliest days of her public life, Victoria was already making ceremonial appearances and 'popularity tours' just like a symbolic, constitutional monarch. And even in these later years she could still exert enough influence to act a little like a tyrant.[55]

For indulging Victoria's jingoism like this came with a cost attached. Working so closely with Disraeli, she'd occasionally – and quite wrongly – negotiated with the Tsar behind the backs of the Cabinet. Disraeli was a false friend in failing to challenge her when she did this. The ultimate pragmatist, to the point of cynicism, he was storing up future trouble by letting her think she had more power than she really did.

In Disraeli's Hughenden hallway, there still stands a small statue of Victoria's favourite pony. He'd positioned it there, where his Faery would see it, because it also features the figure of her favourite Scottish servant. And in the matter of this man, John Brown, Victoria could also have done with some tough love.

20

John Brown's Legs: 6 March 1884

Six years later, on 23 February 1884, Victoria asked her Private Secretary Henry Ponsonby for help with a book she had been 'trying to write'. Progress had been slow, the queen explained, because she got so 'continually disturbed and interrupted'.[1] This book was a 'memoir' of a deceased friend, and Victoria had taken the story as far as 1865. The subject was her celebrated 'Highland servant' John Brown. He'd initially been employed at Balmoral as a guide for expeditions on the moors and mountains. But he'd gradually become such a favourite that he was given indoor duties too. Over time, he started to join the household when it travelled back down south to Windsor, and indeed ended up accompanying the queen everywhere she went.

Ponsonby was known among his fellow courtiers for holding particularly liberal views. But even he concluded at once that Victoria's proposition for a book was a terrible idea. It would open her to ridicule and worse. Like everyone at Windsor, though, he was all too aware of the difficulties involved in going against the queen's increasingly eccentric and imperious commands. She'd been aided and abetted by Disraeli, her officials muttered, to the extent that there was 'extreme difficulty' in contradicting her even in 'the slightest degree'.[2] 'The Queen,' grumbled one of her politicians, 'is enough to kill any man.'[3]

Henry Ponsonby, an appealing character, was tall, quiet, bearded and slightly scruffy in his tailcoat and elastic-sided boots. Despite his loyalty to his queen and the exceptional service he gave her, he secretly took pleasure in the occasional absurdities of court life.[4] Victoria's self-confidence, her indomitable refusal to countenance any gainsayer, was rather magnificent. But for well-intentioned men like Ponsonby it was also rather troubling.

On the frosty morning of 6 March, then, he went walking round the battlements of Windsor Castle with a trusted colleague, the Dean of Windsor, Randall Davidson. They talked about the business of the biography of John Brown and, together, they made a plot to defy the queen.

Victoria herself spent the morning quietly in the Upper Ward, unaware of the intrigues going on in the outer castle below the Norman Gateway. Life at Windsor ran along an unvarying and increasingly narrow course. 'Everything else changes,' wrote one of the maids-of-honour, returning to duty from a spell in the outside world, 'but the life here never does, and is always exactly the same from day to day and year to year.'[5] Many of her household's members might never even see the queen except on Sunday mornings, when she attended St George's Chapel.

On Sunday afternoons, every week like clockwork, she was rolled in her chair among the flower beds of the private East Terrace to the strains of the military band that played (and still plays) for the inhabitants of castle and Windsor town alike.[6] She could reach the gardens unobserved along an underground tunnel to the orangery from her private suite in the Victoria Tower.[7] She was wheeled in a chair because she now, at sixty-four, had great difficulty in walking. She complained constantly about her ill health, but there was much debate in her household about how far she was genuinely ill, and how much of her malaise lay in her mind.

It was, however, perfectly true that her body had never quite recovered from giving birth to nine children. Although nobody but her dressers knew it, she suffered pain from a painful ventral hernia, a condition where the internal organs force their way through a point in the stomach wall weakened, in her case, by multiple childbirths. Her serious illness of 1871, and a subsequent fall down stairs at Windsor, had certainly contributed to her increasing immobility, which meant that she was now gaining weight. Victoria was never parted from her green-velvet-lined medicine chest, which her pharmacist kept filled with 'opium pills' for pain and 'rhubarb pills' to stimulate the digestive system that opiates clogged up.[8]

But she still believed in the power of fresh air. On the cold morning of 6 March, while Ponsonby paced his battlements, Victoria went out into the park in her little pony cart. Her youngest, stay-at-home daughter Beatrice walked dutifully beside her. They sat for a while 'in the old summer house by the water', but the outing's real destination was 'the dear Mausoleum' containing Albert's remains.[9] This was a white, Italianate, cross-shaped building. Inside there lay – and still lies – the sculpted figure of a sleeping Albert, modelled from a single piece of granite. Wearing bulky and uncomfortable-looking robes, he nevertheless occupies a delightfully soft-looking bier.

Victoria paid him almost daily visits. 'After the Prince Consort's death,' she once said, 'I wished to die.'[10] And in many ways, it was as if all the clocks at Windsor Castle had stopped in 1861. She carefully kept her boudoir in exactly the same state as it had been at the time of his illness. On its door, a plaque recorded the fact that 'every article in this room my lamented husband selected for me'. Within, Miss-Havisham-like, 'the Queen's bridal wreath and the first bouquet which the Prince presented to her lie withered in a glass case'.[11]

The isolation of her position, her lack of friends and equals, a lifelong feeling that she could not afford to trust other people, helps to explain why Victoria turned instead to the consolation of objects. She also kept the Blue Room itself preserved as a sort of shrine to Albert. Two days after his death, the favoured royal photographer William Bambridge of Windsor had been called in to photograph it, not least as a record of the layout so that the furniture could be put back in precisely the same positions after cleaning.[12] Bambridge had also experienced a huge demand for memorial photos of Albert's corpse, and during the short winter days of December 1861 he'd had to race to fulfil a deluge of orders. One of these photos of her husband's dead body hung on the headboard of Victoria's bed.[13] It seems macabre to us, in an age when we like to pretend death doesn't exist, but this was the Victorian way.

Yet, as the years went by, there began to be something unusual and particularly extreme about Victoria's mourning. So rarely did she experience denial from the people around her that she thought that she might countermand even death, and a wraithlike version of life continued still in Albert's suite.

This maintenance of the scene of a death was a German tradition, although Victoria wrote that the Blue Room was not to be a 'Sterbe-Zimmer' or 'death-room', but instead 'a living beautiful monument'. 'On the table in the ante-room,' reported one visitor, 'there were laid out his gloves and his white wide-awake hat as on the day when he had last used them'.[14] A painting from 1864 shows that the Blue Room was kept full of fresh flowers. In the evenings, if the door was open, people passing in the passage could glimpse the ghostly gleam of the white marble bust of Albert's head, placed just about at standing height upon a column. As many as forty years later, a visitor to the room could still see 'all his things – uniforms, walking sticks, the bed he died in . . . the palms laid on his coffin, and casts of his hand and foot'.[15] The Blue Room became a kind of long-running work of performance art dedicated to Albert's memory, and Victoria had his favourite artistic advisor, Ludwig Grüner, decorate its ceiling with angels.[16]

Hot water was still delivered to Albert daily, not because Victoria had ordered it, but simply because she had never given the order for it to stop. Her servants did not dare to challenge her. 'Two of the old pages' of the castle wished that someone would have the courage to bring it up. 'Such a pity Her Majesty does not give us orders to stop this,' they said, 'it makes people mock, and yet nobody likes to say anything to her about it.'[17]

Since Albert's death there had been just one person within the walls of Windsor who *did* have the gumption to 'say anything'. That had been the queen's Scottish servant John Brown. The gift he'd possessed for treating Victoria like a normal human being had brought him both great power, and great unpopularity, within the royal household. Even now, despite his death, Brown's spirit lived on as the cause of the kerfuffle that had brought Ponsonby and Davidson to their anxious conference.

Despite the intensity of Victoria's grief, it was not possible that it could remain at the same high pitch for ever. And slowly, gradually, she began to recover. Some years later, she told a lady-in-waiting that although she'd once wished that she could die too, '*now* I wish to live and do what I can for my country and those I love'.[18] Brown's greatest achievement had been to help bring about this change.

He'd begun to make a good impression upon Victoria even during Albert's lifetime. In 1861, during the couple's last stay together at Balmoral, she noticed that Brown was 'invaluable' and '*so* handy about cloaks and shawls'. 'He always leads my pony,' she explained, and 'attends me out of doors.'[19] When in 1864 Brown began to travel with the queen beyond Scotland's borders, she tried to describe his uniquely sympathetic qualities. His constant presence was 'a real comfort', she wrote, 'for he is so devoted to me – so simple, so intelligent, so unlike an ordinary servant'.[20]

Those final four words held the lasting key to his charm: he wasn't like an ordinary servant, but more like an equal. He was plain-speaking, fitted by temperament to perform the ancient court role of a jester, or fool, with the capacity to speak truth to power. One insider account tells us that the queen's servants had 'the strictest possible orders on no account to look at Her Majesty'.[21] But John Brown was permitted to look, even to speak, without the usual royal rigmarole. Many examples survive of his reported words, and perhaps some of them are real. 'Hoots, then wumman,' he was supposed to have said to her, along with 'Take me arm, 'tis slippery.' What provisions did he and the queen take on their picnic expeditions onto the moors around Balmoral, Brown was once asked. Did they drink tea? 'Well, no,' he replied. 'She don't much like tea. We tak oot biscuits and speeruts [spirits].'[22] Brown was a drinker, and neither was Victoria abstemious: 'she drinks,' reported William Gladstone, 'her claret strengthened, I should have thought spoiled, with whiskey.'[23] Brown was also – and this was significant in her canine-heavy household – the only person who could keep Victoria's terrifying and bad-tempered pet dog Sharp 'in some sort of order'.[24] In short, such was the bond between them that Brown was 'the only person who could fight and make the Queen do what she did not wish'.[25]

In 1865, Brown was given a special job title of 'The Queen's Highland Servant'. Gradually his extended family also began to creep into positions of influence within the royal household, at their native Balmoral but also at Windsor. Certain long-serving families developed over the decades into household dynasties, with the Scottish Grants, Browns and Clarks being increasingly common below stairs.[26]

But in 1866, Victoria's special favour towards Brown began to cause serious and lasting damage to her reputation. That year, a Swiss newspaper printed a report that she and her favourite servant had secretly married.[27] Scurrilous slanders like this would dog the queen for the rest of her reign. In July 1866, the satirical magazine *Punch* went so far as to produce a Brown-related spoof of the *Court Circular*, as if he were a member of the royal family:

Mr. John Brown walked on the Slopes [of Windsor Castle]. He subsequently partook of a haggis.

In the evening, Mr. John Brown was pleased to listen to a bagpipe.

Mr. John Brown retired early.[28]

The reason that Brown caused such a scandal was the unspoken belief that a widowed woman of middle age, as Victoria was, must inevitably become sexually insatiable. 'Many women,' claimed one medical authority, 'even those of the most irreproachable morals and conduct, – are subject to attacks of ovario-uterine excitement approaching to nymphomania.'[29] 'The Queen was insane,' ran one magazine's round-up of British society gossip, 'John Brown was her keeper.'[30] She did indeed find herself desperately missing the touch of another human. 'I am alas! not old,' she wrote, 'and my feelings are strong and warm.'[31] But human touch need not have been sexual to give her comfort. Brown helped her, lifted her, gave her a strong arm to lean on. It was an important relationship, even if it wasn't the full-blown torrid affair that some modern historians may have hoped for.

Biographer Jane Ridley points out that the queen's relationship with Brown seems to us to stand out as unique, but that's partly because other intimate relationships between Victoria and her servants, particularly her dressers, have been obliterated by time and propriety.[32] When Victoria's daughter Beatrice came to transcribe her journals, destroying many of the originals as she went, she often missed out the names of servants, thinking it improper or unnecessary to include them. For example, Victoria's original entry for 9 August 1845 mentions by a mixture of surnames and forenames her maids Singer, Peneyvre, Rebecca, Dehler, Skerrett and Margaret. These were people the queen knew well. She was more truly intimate with them than with her upper courtiers or members of her extended royal network. Beatrice, though, brutally summarises them all in her version of the journal as just 'the maids'.[33]

When it came to Brown, Victoria's relationship was not just physical. It also came to be emotional. She described him as her 'dearest & best friend' who 'for 18 years & a ½ never left me for a day'.[34] He never *left* her, he was always there: it was servants who gave her the continuity their social superiors could not provide. Victoria took care not to become dependent upon the aristocratic maids-of-honour and ladies-in-waiting who rotated on and off duty. They had their own lives and, often, to her annoyance, they took themselves off to get married or look after their children.

Some of them wrote indiscreet letters; others kept indiscreet diaries. She could not afford to become too close to them. With Brown, though, it was different. In some respects, Ridley concludes, their relationship resembled a marriage. He devoted his life to her, and their partnership 'was healthier than her marriage to Albert. Brown did not undermine Victoria's confidence, he never infantilized her in the way that Albert did.'[35]

Brown also helped his mistress by acting as a sounding board on political issues. He'd interested himself in the Eastern Question, for example, causing Disraeli once to joke that all new legislation should have 'the approval of the two J.B.s'. These were John Brown and that shorthand name for the great British public: John Bull.[36]

And John Bull loved hearing about the domestic detail of Victoria's life. One of the ways in which she marked her return to something like normal life was with a commemoration and celebration of her and Albert's mutual love of the Scottish Highlands. She published some selections from the daily journals she'd kept on visits to Balmoral, and Scottish tours further afield, in a book called *Leaves from the Journal of Our Life in the Highlands, from 1848 to 1861* (1868). Its contents were pretty innocuous, heavy on descriptions of picnics and scenery. But it became a huge bestseller, a fact that pleased Victoria enormously. She proudly sent copies to friends and relatives. 'The book has been wonderfully well received by the public,' wrote Dr Clark, one of the recipients.[37] 'The publication of my book,' she claimed, 'did me more good than anything else.'[38] It benefitted not only Victoria's sense of achievement, but also her reputation. A woman who wrote so rawly about having loved and lost seemed sympathetic, relatable. Although her subjects now rarely saw her in public, the queen's book kept her alive. It showed that she enjoyed simple pleasures: hot tea and a rug on a cold day. But it was also blunt and sincere about her real grief and devastating sense of loss. In short, it made her human.

But then, in 1883, John Brown's role in bringing the queen back to life came to a sudden end. He died, of a skin disease but also, it's been suggested, of complaints related to alcoholism.

Victoria was devastated, yet it's doubtful that his fellow household members shared her feelings. Her favour had caused him to rise to an almost untouchable position within the royal establishment. No one had felt able to challenge him on his notorious drinking, and he'd taken to issuing orders and commands to his fellow servants. He'd also been highly unpopular with the royal children. They resented his privileged access to their mother, and joined in the general mockery. Among themselves they called him 'Mamma's Stallion'. Prince Leopold, for example, who was frequently ill and required physical help, hated the 'dreadful Scotch servants', by which he meant Brown and his family. He found John Brown 'fearfully insolent to me, so is his brother, hitting me on the face with spoons for fun'.[39]

Victoria later described Brown's death in 1883 as being as cataclysmic as the loss of a husband: 'one of those shocks like in 61 when every link has been shaken & torn'. It affected her physically. She described how (in the third person) 'The Queen can't walk the least & the shock she has sustained has made her very weak – so that she can't stand.'[40] She was already in a poor physical condition that year because of her accident on the stairs at Windsor Castle on 17 March. Because Brown was himself ill at the same time, he wasn't available to help rehabilitate her, and after spending a week on a sofa, her mobility was greatly reduced.[41] Brown's death later the same year removed not only someone Victoria had trusted to give her physical support, but also the one person who had been able to cajole her into taking exercise. From 1883 onwards, the queen's visitors could expect to 'see Her Majesty enter either leaning on one side on a stick', or else she might be 'slowly propelled into the room in an amply-cushioned wheel chair'.[42] 'I presume all the Family will rejoice at his death,' wrote Sir William Knollys, 'but I think very probably they are shortsighted.'[43] Brown had, after all, been keeping her young. Without him, she began to grow old.

At the end of the year of Brown's death, Victoria commemorated him in the same way she'd commemorated Albert: by publishing a second book. It was called *More Leaves from the Journal of a Life in the Highlands*. As she put the finishing touches to the text, she dedicated it to 'the memory of my devoted personal attendant and faithful friend John Brown'. This second volume contained even more than its predecessor about her servants, including personal notes on each one as if they were high-born lords and ladies. Readers are introduced, for example, to Löhlein (Albert's valet), Mayet (the second valet) and Nestor Tirard ('the Queen's hair-dresser'). The three of them were included in the list of names present at the unveiling of a statue of Albert, a list that also included Prince Leopold. This sort of thing appealed to her wider audience, making them feel that she was really 'one of them'. But the court circle found it regrettable. It left the impression that there really was very little difference between the queen's son and her hairdresser.

Leaves had been a huge success in terms of sales, and so too was *More Leaves*. But this second book exposed Victoria to slander and malice in a way that the first had not. She showed a certain naivety in publishing, for example, her distress upon learning that on a rainy day 'poor Brown's legs' had been 'dreadfully cut by the edge of his wet kilt'.[44] John Brown appears perhaps too often in *More Leaves*: he suggests that everyone 'ought to drink the health of Princess Beatrice'; he is 'so distressed' at the death of a French prince; he dances a reel with Princess Louise; he begs the queen to drink whisky-toddy.[45] When given an oxidised silver biscuit box he is pathetically grateful, weeps and says 'it is too much.'[46] Just like Albert, Brown is given the privilege, when the queen is signing papers, of 'always helping to dry the signatures'.[47]

John Brown, in Victoria's book, becomes a second consort. This explains the rumours of a covert marriage, or indeed the obsession, which still exists in the present day, with trying to prove that queen and servant also had a conventional sexual relationship. Historian Dorothy Thompson has pointed out the double standard at work here. A king's having a mistress was regrettable, but ultimately acceptable. The possibility, though, of a female ruler having a sexual relationship outside marriage, causes dismay and prurient ridicule.[48]

After the wet-kilt injury, John Brown's 'poor' legs make a second appearance in the text when he suffers 'a severe hurt on the shin' while travelling on a boat.[49] This unfortunate coincidence led to the publication of a spoof of the queen's second book, called *John Brown's Legs*. It was dedicated, its satirical author declared, 'to the memory of those extraordinary Legs – poor bruised and scratched darlings', those 'inexpressibly lovely' appendages, 'which bore their Sovereign through many a rushing, mountain torrent (often as deep as an inch and a half)'.[50]

Clearly, Henry Ponsonby thought, if the queen published any more of her artless recollections of John Brown's physical body, there would be further trouble. But then, in February of 1884, she'd sent him a *third* work of her pen, a memoir specifically about the life of John Brown, and with it a proposal to print Brown's private diary.

Ponsonby's immediate reaction was to equivocate. Before coming to court he'd been a soldier, and had fought in Crimea. He hadn't survived fourteen subsequent years of palace life without developing a good sense of which battles were worth fighting. He pronounced that literary matters were beyond his sphere of expertise. When pressed, he was forced to admit to the queen that he had a sense of unease. 'There are passages,' he wrote, delicately, 'which will be misunderstood if read by strangers.' He concluded that the 'feeling created by such a publication would become most distressing and painful to the Queen'.[51]

Henry Ponsonby's reaction *against* publication, his instinct to protect, and to preserve the monarchy's mystique, is understandable but not entirely correct. As so often when it came to members of the establishment of Victorian Britain, there were things that she could see that he could not.

All the time that officials like William Gladstone or Henry Ponsonby were imploring her to appear more often in public, Victoria had in fact bypassed them with the immensely powerful, simple and popular appeal contained in her books about life in

Scotland, or through the occasional article she published in 'worthy' media organs like *Good Words*.[52] Trivial details of picnics, trite letters to the papers, made her real to her millions of subjects in a way that attending countless openings of Parliament in person could not. But this fact the court and government elite could not grasp.

Even so, there's no doubt that Victoria inspired devotion from people like Henry Ponsonby, whose respect for her underlaid his jokes. Those whom she trusted sometimes witnessed what the wider world did not: that the queen has 'an enormous appreciation of any fun'. The photographs through which her subjects knew her did not do justice to this side of her character. Her whole life, she looked her best in motion. When she started to talk, 'the kind, sad eyes light up, the nostrils distend, the cheeks glow, the curves of the mouth turn up in smiles'.[53] Victorians generally felt that they ought to look serious during the serious business of having a photographic portrait taken. But some smiling photos of the queen *do* exist, and in them she is almost unrecognisable. Those images of her animated face help explain why – despite her demanding, irrational behaviour – clever and capable people devoted their lives to her service.

As Private Secretary, Ponsonby operated from a plainly furnished suite leading off the Marble Hall at Windsor. He had a staff of clerks 'always at work', and access to the 'telegraph office through which pass in cipher the secrets of all nations'.[54] 'Don't Knock – Walk In', said a sign on Ponsonby's door, and within he ran a relaxed regime alongside his younger assistant Arthur Bigge. (Bigge was discretion embodied, to the extent that his colleagues called him 'Better NOT'.[55])

Whenever he could, though, Henry Ponsonby escaped from his office to his home in the Norman Tower, a suite of rooms hollowed out from the medieval fabric of the castle's walls. This was an excitingly Gothic place to live, with its steep garden, 'deepset windows' and 'narrow winding passages . . . like the linked exca-vations of a mine'.[56] Ponsonby was extremely uxorious, and people believed that 'his chief joy, relaxation and refreshment' was to 'steal half an hour' with his wife Mary.[57] 'Your advice is worth more than anyone's,' he told her. Being apart, as they often were when he was required to travel to Osborne or Balmoral, 'is the unhappiness of my life and makes me often long to give up everything'.[58]

Henry was very open with his wife, and he 'told her everything and consulted her about everything'.[59] The walls of the Norman Tower must therefore have witnessed some discussion of the proposed Brown biography. Mary was small in stature but had an enormous brain. She was considered almost 'alarmingly' intelligent.[60] Henry Ponsonby sometimes got on the wrong side of Victoria because he did not quite share her straightforwardly conservative instincts, and it was the same with his wife. The essential fault that Mary was thought, in royal circles, to possess was that of being a 'clever woman'.[61] As the Ponsonbys' biographer William Kuhn points out, Mary was a member of the Society for Promoting the Employment of Women, a student of Nietzsche and a proponent of medical training for females (Victoria found this one utterly inimical). It's funny to think of such a woman living in a home from which so many details of the queen's life across the courtyard – her coming in, her going out, her lights being extinguished – could be observed.[62]

Mary was thought by a friend to have a 'feverish longing for a wider sphere of action than has been allotted by circumstances'.[63] And yet, living quietly here at Windsor, she was actually playing a significant role in the history of the monarchy. 'Do burn my letters,' she would implore correspondents, knowing that she had been indiscreet.[64] This was advice that was often ignored, meaning that her words survive as witnesses to the ludicrousness, as well as the splendour, of the queen's later court. Mary and Henry between them, in their correspondence and published writings, show us the richly ridiculous side of life at Windsor. Although Victoria would certainly not have approved, they actually did their queen a service by making her sound so intriguing.

In all their many surviving words, though, Henry and Mary are naturally silent on the super-sensitive topic of Brown. Doubtless

Mary, decisive and energetic, encouraged Henry to take positive action. But he argued it wasn't that simple. 'People constantly say "Why don't you advise The Queen?"' he once explained. 'One can do so once, but she takes care you shan't press unwelcome advice upon her by preserving strict silence on the subject.'[65] He resorted to dodges such as drafting letters for her to consider, including sentences he'd crossed out as if he'd had second thoughts. Sometimes she'd do exactly what he had intended, which was to reinstate them.[66] Sometimes she couldn't even be bothered to put pen to paper, and would send verbal messages instead, through servants. Never strong on verbal communication, Victoria was growing increasingly lazy about talking face-to-face to people she didn't like. Her officials believed that this 'odious practice of doing everything through a third person makes endless difficulties and misunderstandings'.[67]

Just a year prior to this conundrum of the John Brown memoir, a new person had walked into this claustrophobic community at Windsor Castle. Randall Davidson, the recently appointed Dean of Windsor, had first become Ponsonby's colleague, and then his firm friend.

When she'd started the search for a new Dean, Victoria had stipulated that she wanted someone 'whom she can confide in'.[68] Upon meeting the thirty-four-year-old Randall Davidson, with his smooth, egg-shaped head and receding hairline, she at once found him 'sympathetic and evidently very intelligent'.[69]

In return, Davidson could see something that for all their virtues the urbane, sophisticated Ponsonbys could not. He had a firm appreciation of what he called Victoria's 'common sense', which 'enabled her (though not in the ordinary sense of the words a really clever woman) to do far more than most clever women could have accomplished'.[70] Unlike Albert, unlike even the Ponsonbys, Davidson appreciated her talent for identifying how mainstream opinion among her subjects would respond to almost any issue. Elsewhere in Europe, when revolutions succeeded, it was because middle-class people and the oppressed workers made common cause. In Britain, though, this never quite happened. Perhaps it was because the middle classes somehow believed that the middle-brow queen was 'on their side'.

Randall Davidson, a future Archbishop of Canterbury, was himself an excellent temperature-taker of public opinion. He arrived in 1883 at the castellated Deanery hidden behind St George's Chapel, a little way down the hill from Ponsonby's place. He at once felt at home. Before Davidson had been at Windsor a year, he and Ponsonby would 'pace up and down in the Castle walks discussing most things in the Castle and out of it'.[71] 'My dear Dean,' Henry wrote, in one of the frequent letters that flew between the Private Secretary's office and the Deanery, 'Do we officially believe in Purgatory?'[72]

But although Davidson was perhaps more in tune with Victoria's intentions than Ponsonby was, in the matter of the John Brown memoir they came to an essential agreement that the publication should not proceed.

The difference between them was that they had contrasting ideas of how to stop it. Ponsonby now explained that he lacked the courage to confront the queen. 'When she insists that two and two make five,' he said, 'I say I cannot help thinking they make four. She replies there may be some truth in what I say, but she knows they make five. I drop the discussion.' What she couldn't abide was 'proofs, arguments'.[73]

For his part, Davidson thought that Ponsonby lacked rectitude, and 'would cleverly try to get her out of doing wrong things' when 'he might have done far more sometimes by a direct appeal'.[74] The queen's most trusted courtiers understood that she respected them for the occasional intransigence. 'If I lacked all moral courage,' wrote Marie Mallet, one of her particularly favoured women-of-the-bedchamber, 'the Queen would be the first to despise me.'[75]

However, Ponsonby was right that it was genuinely hard to change Victoria's mind. Once her household were discussing the possibility of her attending a social gathering at Buckingham Palace. 'But H.M.,' Ponsonby records, 'in sad and mournful tones said to me she was damned if she would.'[76] She didn't confront people who disagreed with her; she just excluded them from her presence. Or she simply snubbed them, staring through them unseeingly, like a silent ghost, 'pale and statue-like'.[77] At state occasions in her sixties, Victoria appeared in a black dress, black velvet train, pearls and a small diamond crown. She was quite capable of looking 'straight in front of her . . . not even the flicker of a smile on her face'. The effect, the lack of interaction, could be terrifying, 'the very embodiment of majesty'.[78]

So if Victoria wouldn't talk to Ponsonby about John Brown, he could not make her. And he'd previously experienced periods of icy silence in punishment for having said the wrong thing. She'd once put him firmly in his place after a row by sending Miss Norèle, the royal children's French governess, to tell him that a government minister had resigned.[79]

But with Randall Davidson it was different. It became clear that Victoria could unburden herself to him with ease. Davidson's predecessor as Dean had noticed that she *did* need someone to talk to. It was a basic human requirement. Her position had made her distrustful until she knew a person well, but then 'there is no one with whom more is gained by getting her into the habit of inter-course with you'.[80] In the gap between Deans before Davidson's arrival at Windsor, wrote lady-in-waiting Horatia Stopford, 'the Queen had literally no one whom she ever spoke' to about personal matters. As well as befriending the queen, Davidson had quickly learned the ways of the wider castle, and built up valuable allies among the female staff. He knew, as one of the ladies-in-waiting put it, 'everything from the shape of the kitchen-maids' new caps to some of the deepest padlocks of my soul!'[81]

Eventually, on the evening of 6 March, after discussing the matter at length with Ponsonby, Davidson sat down in his Deanery to write Victoria a long, long letter. He had decided to go where Ponsonby feared to tread, and directly to address the issue of her John Brown book and advise her not to publish it. He wrote page after page, most of it fulsome gratitude and praise. The surviving draft contains crossings-out, insertions and revisions.[82] But among the fulsomeness he threw in a few stingers. Davidson said that most of her subjects had enjoyed the confidences she'd shared with them from her Highland journals. But, he continued, there were some Britons, perhaps it would be true to say *many* Britons, 'who do not show themselves worthy of these confidences, and whose spirit, judging by their published periodicals, is one of such unappreciative criticism as I should not desire your Majesty to see'.[83] By this, Davidson probably meant the satirical pamphlet *John Brown's Legs*. A copy of it remains filed right next to the draft of his letter of 6 March among his private papers at Lambeth Palace Library.[84]

Having finished his explosive letter, and having sent it up the hill into the Upper Ward, Davidson must have been anxious for an answer. But none came.

When she wanted to chastise a member of her household or family, Victoria had a habit of writing a letter, putting it in a box labelled 'The Queen' and ordering a footman to take it to the person in question. Her later Prime Ministers, like it or not, might expect to receive 200 letters and almost as many telegrams from the queen in a year.[85] Albert had taught her that paper was the best way to wage a war of words. But the disadvantage of carrying out a quarrel by this means was that 'it did not give the poor culprit much chance of a personal explanation', words could be misinterpreted, and it all made for bad feeling.[86]

And on this occasion, Davidson's letter caused such grave offence that he couldn't even be told off by letter. The queen's most trusted ladies-in-waiting were the unfortunate messengers often selected to convey their mistress's rebukes. 'We are,' said one of them, 'sheets of paper on which H.M. writes with words as less trouble than using her pen and we have to convey her words *as a letter* would do.'[87] They had become accustomed to being her bearers of bad news. Jane Ely, one of the two ladies who lived all the time with Victoria, was the chosen favourite for ticklish tasks. Jane Ely would pass on royal reprimands in a 'mysterious whisper'.[88] Now she was deployed for the task of chastening Davidson. Jane Ely herself came down from the Victoria Tower to the Deanery to ask Davidson, verbally, to withdraw his words.

But Davidson refused to do so. He surprised everyone, and possibly even himself, by writing straight back to the queen, suggesting that he should resign.

It was a bold move in palace politics, and Davidson must have had an apprehensive time sitting it out, waiting to hear if his resignation would be accepted. Sunday morning came, and another preacher took his place in chapel. But no letter of acceptance ever arrived at the Deanery from the Victoria Tower.

Eventually, two whole days later, on 8 March, a gnomic missive at last arrived, in the hand of Horatia Stopford. 'I have had a hard fight I assure you the last 48 hours,' it read, 'but I believe I have conquered, for which I thank God! I think you will be pleased at what I shall tell you.'[89]

The news, whatever it was, was conveyed verbally, but it seems that behind the closed doors of the queen's suite, Davidson's allies among her female staff had waged some kind of skirmish on his behalf against the John Brown memoir. It was as if the castle and court was a living organism. Almost like a snake digesting a swallowed mouse, there had to be a period for dissent to be processed before equilibrium could return. And Davidson ultimately triumphed. A whole fortnight passed until he again saw Victoria, but then nothing was said about his offer of resignation, and she was 'more friendly to him than ever'.

Davidson had learned something very valuable: that Victoria 'liked and trusted best those who incurred her wrath provided that she had reason to think their motives good'.[90] He now shared the secret of John Brown's own hold over the queen: not to be afraid.

After the tense stand-off of March 1884, the plan to publish the life of John Brown fizzled out. Ponsonby quietly disposed of Brown's diary, and thus the story seemed to end.

But not quite. The Brown business went on causing trouble

even after Victoria's death. Bertie, as King Edward VII, had to deal with a case of attempted blackmail from a Balmoral connection who had come into the possession of some 300 letters from Victoria, which were said to be 'most compromising' on the subject of John Brown. Eventually, after negotiation, the letters were handed over and, it is believed, destroyed.[91] Mary Ponsonby, meanwhile, went on writing articles for the press, and her children in due course published books that did much to illuminate the Windsor their parents both loved and loathed. And court myth tells that Ponsonby's authentic nature was revealed in his final interview with the queen, which took place just before his stroke and eventual death in 1895. She is said to have rung the bell, and dismissed him, with the words, 'Sir Henry you cannot be well.'

This had been in response to something that he'd said to her, his true views expressed at last. His words had been: 'What a funny little old woman you are.'[92]

21

Baby Gets Married: Osborne House, 23 July 1885

'The day splendid,' wrote Victoria at Osborne House, 'a very hot sun, but a pleasant air.'[1] As usual she breakfasted outside beneath the trees. The sight of the breakfasting queen beneath her 'large green-lined and green-fringed parasol', a Scottish piper playing, was eccentrically magnificent.[2] She'd eat a boiled egg from a golden cup, and her empire was usually present in human form. 'Two Indian *Khitmagars* in scarlet and gold remained motionless behind her chair,' wrote one witness, while 'a page and a Scotchman in a kilt waited till she rang.'[3]

This particular morning Beatrice was also present at the breakfast table with its view of the sea, and the meal was heavy with emotion. As it finished, Victoria handed her daughter a ruby ring of great sentimental value, a wedding present she'd been given forty-five years previously. Victoria 'could hardly realise the event that was going to take place'.[4] But this, at long last, was her youngest child's own wedding day.

Victoria had long treated Beatrice as a human crutch. As a baby, Beatrice stood out among her stolid, Hanoverian-looking siblings. She'd been a beautiful infant, with blue eyes and a satin skin. 'Quite the prettiest of us all,' one of Beatrice's sisters said, 'she is like a little fairy.'[5] 'Such a delight to kiss and fondle,' Victoria wrote upon Beatrice's first birthday, regaining a bliss in babies she hadn't experienced since her firstborn. 'If only,' Victoria added, Beatrice 'could remain, just as she is.'[6]

The empty conventional words – 'remain, just as she is' – would have cruel significance as the beautiful baby grew up.

Beatrice was not only pretty but also precocious. Albert called her 'the most amusing baby we have had'.[7] At three, she had golden hair and high spirits, 'a most amusing little dot, all the more so for being generally a little naughty'.[8] She wanted to read a letter written by one of her mother's ladies-in-waiting. 'You can't, it is French – you must learn,' the lady said. Oh, but Beatrice already had: 'I can say "bonne jour and wee".' When asked why she had not completed a chore, Beatrice always had a ready excuse: 'I was very busy, too busy blowing soap bubbles.'[9]

But then this privileged childhood as her parents' pet came to a sudden end. On the ghastly night of Albert's death, there are persistent tales that Victoria took the baby Beatrice into her own bed, and wrapped her little body in the nightshirt of the man who had just died. 'Though this story is most probably apocryphal,' writes Princess Beatrice's biographer, Matthew Dennison, it 'stands as a metaphor' for Victoria's treatment of her youngest child and favourite daughter.[10] After Albert's death, Victoria diverted much of her love and her clinginess to Beatrice instead.

In the early years of Victoria's widowhood, it was Beatrice, still not yet ten, who 'mothered' her mother. Beatrice 'spends an hour with Her' each morning, we're told, 'and is in agonies when She sees Her cry. "Dear Darling" as She calls Her, hugging and kissing her so tenderly.'[11] The youngest daughter in any well-off Victorian family understood that she would be expected to remain at home, unmarried, to be her parents' companion and carer. Beatrice was no exception. At six, she was asked if she would like to be a bridesmaid? 'Oh, no, I don't like weddings at all,' she replied at once, 'I shall never be married. I shall stay with mother.'[12]

When Beatrice was old enough to be launched upon the marriage market, Victoria avoided the subject. She forbade her household from even mentioning weddings in conversation if Beatrice was present. Isolated from her contemporaries, the 'amusing little dot' began to lose her self-confidence, and grow shy and withdrawn. Henry Ponsonby noticed Beatrice's 'want of interest, which I believe comes from fearing to care for anything the Queen hesitates about'. He suspected that her nervous, tongue-tied manner would never change unless 'a good husband stirs her up'. But that was an unlikely prospect. 'Poor girl,' Ponsonby concluded, 'what chance has she?' Someone else who sat next to Beatrice at dinner reported that there was hardly any safe topic to talk about. 'What with subjects tabooed, the subjects she knows nothing about, and the subjects she turns to the Queen upon, there is nothing left but the weather and silence.'[13]

Beatrice was also losing the blonde beauty of her babyhood. Victoria's latest doctor, James Reid, naughtily referred to her in private as 'Betrave', a pun on the French word for beetroot.[14] Matthew Dennison describes Beatrice in her late twenties as a 'dumpy, despairing figure, too overwhelmed by boredom even to look up'.[15] Albert had noted Victoria's tendency to fret and sweat over small domestic matters. 'Your fidgety nature,' he'd complained, 'makes you insist on entering, with feverish eagerness, into details about orders and wishes which, in the case of a Queen, are commands.'[16] The adult Beatrice bore the brunt of this, acting as an unpaid maid whose life was micromanaged by her mother.

However, in 1884, a remarkable thing happened. Beatrice, who'd just turned twenty-seven, accompanied her mother to the quiet German town of Darmstadt. They were attending the marriage of one of Victoria's many nieces to Prince Louis of Battenberg. Also present was the groom's brother, Prince Henry.

Henry, often known as 'Liko', was the third son of Alexander of Battenberg. The Battenberg brothers were dashing young princes-about-Europe, multilingual, and martial in their interests. Their mother was only morganatically married to their father, which meant that Henry wasn't properly royal. But this did not prevent him and Beatrice from secretly falling in love. During the Darmstadt trip, other wedding guests noted that Victoria 'alarmed and tyrannized over her family'.[17] And when she discovered what had been going on behind her back, she was horrified. 'The dreadful engagement', she called it. She felt the fact that her permission hadn't been asked beforehand amounted to a grave deception.[18]

What was worse, Prince Henry was an army officer, serving in the royal household of Prussia. In the normal course of things, any wife would go to live with him in the Prussian royal palace of Potsdam.[19] Victoria was adamant that there was to be no engagement, not least because Beatrice could never leave her mother.

On 23 July 1885, though, Victoria spent the morning resting in her Osborne bedroom while Beatrice used her dead father's room nearby to get dressed for her long-awaited wedding. She had to be cruelly corseted to fit into her wasp-waisted white dress, with orange blossom at the bosom and all down its long lace skirt. 'I came in,' Victoria recorded in her journal, 'whilst her veil & wreath were being fastened on. It was <u>my</u> dear wedding veil which I wore at all my Children's christenings.'[20]

Beatrice must often have thought that this day would never come. She later told her eldest son that from May to November 1884, after she'd announced her intention to marry, her mother simply refused to speak to her. Any communication took place in the form of notes. Given Beatrice's previous closeness to her mother, this seven-month estrangement must have been hard to bear.[21]

Beatrice's exact statement, that her mother never addressed a word to her, must have been exaggerated by hindsight, for Victoria's journal does record at least *some* conversation. On 8 July, for example, Victoria notes that 'Beatrice came early to my bedroom to wish me goodbye' before going on a visit.[22] And yet, this particular page of the journal only survives at all in Beatrice's own later transcript. It must have been tempting for Beatrice, as she decided what to copy and what to leave out, to massage the evidence here and elsewhere to minimise the record of her mother's nastier behaviour. Perhaps she even did it unconsciously.

And it is undeniable that Beatrice's name, which had previously

The sexy 'secret' picture Victoria commissioned as a surprise gift for Albert. He liked to see her like this, with loose hair and open mouth. In this image she is not his queen but his wife.

Victoria became pregnant straight after her wedding, 'in for it at once,' she said, '& furious I was.' The birth of her children had to be witnessed by various dignitaries; here they inspect the new-born Vicky, Victoria's eldest daughter.

RECOGNITION OF THE ROYAL PRINCESS.
BY THE PRIVY COUNCILLORS OF ENGLAND.

Dr Ferguson later treated Victoria for what we might today call post-natal depression. His sketch of the bed from the side shows how a screen shielded Victoria's lower body from the witnesses during childbirth, but they could see her head, and hear her.

Albert reformed the wasteful royal household, and masterminded magnificent Christmases at Windsor Castle including the German tradition of the tree.

Albert helped reconcile Victoria to her mother. Victoire, Victoria, Albert himself and seven of the couple's nine children stand outside Osborne House, their spanking new Italianate palace on the Isle of Wight.

Victoria and Albert grew addicted to the new artform of photography. Candid shots like these made them look like a normal middle-class couple, thus delighting their middle-class subjects.

Albert quickly lost his looks and put on weight. Logical and intellectual where his wife was emotional and passionate, he worked himself too hard and took himself too seriously.

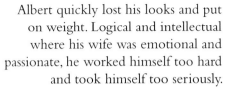

The Maharaja Duleep Singh was exiled from his kingdom in the Punjab by the British. Queen Victoria took him into protection as a kind of human pet.

Victoria was gratified when the Maharaja came to the Isle of Wight and played with her children. Here at Osborne her sons Arthur and Alfred dress up in some of the deposed Indian prince's clothes.

The room at Windsor Castle in which Albert died was kept 'alive' as a sort of shrine. His daily jug of hot water continued to arrive, and years later his possessions still lay where he'd left them.

A marble carving of Albert's hand as it was the day he died. Perhaps Victoria commissioned it so that she could continue to hold hands with her late husband. She loved the hand so much she even had a cast of it buried with her in her coffin.

Albert on his deathbed. His mysterious illness was exacerbated by stress, over-work and insomnia, partly caused by his extreme anxiety about his eldest son's losing his virginity.

Victoria's daughter Louise, a talented artist even as a little girl, imagines a heart-breaking scene of her mother asleep, and dreaming of a reunion with Albert.

Victoria let her daughter Beatrice ('Baby') get married only after a huge row. But once she'd given in, she lent Beatrice the very same treasured lace veil she'd worn at her own wedding.

During the Crimean War, Victoria came greatly to admire Florence Nightingale. But when the two finally met, Victoria was star-struck and tongue-tied.

John Brown, a Scottish servant from Balmoral, was the only servant who could tell the queen what to do. Their closeness sparked rumours of a secret marriage.

Victoria's oldest son Bertie and his wife, the elegant Danish princess Alexandra. Bertie nearly died of typhoid fever here at his Norfolk home of Sandringham.

A bizarre 'triumphal arch' made entirely out of chairs. It was erected in celebration of High Wycombe's furniture-making industry when Victoria visited the town in 1877.

Abdul Karim, Victoria's 'Munshi' or teacher, became her trusted servant in later life. But other household members sought to discredit this unexpected favourite.

One of the reasons for Victoria's enormous appeal in later life was her unthreatening, grandmotherly appearance. See how this official portrait has been heavily touched up to make her look a little younger, notably about the hair, chin and waist.

A grinning Victoria with her daughter, granddaughter and great-granddaughter. Those who knew the queen well often saw her smiling or laughing, but she grew ever more eccentrically reclusive with age.

Victoria died in the home Albert had built for her,
Osborne House on the Isle of Wight, in 1901.

This photograph of the late queen laid out in her bedroom shows that she
still slept with Albert to the very end of her life, in the form of a picture
hanging over what had once been his pillow.

peppered their pages, practically disappears from the queen's letters. Exceptions are made only when Victoria writes, for example, 'of the pain it has caused me that my darling Beatrice should wish . . . to marry'. 'What agonies, what despair,' she wrote, what 'horror and dislike of the most violent kind' she felt, 'for the idea of my precious Baby's marrying at all'.[23]

The problem lay not so much with Prince Henry; Victoria had a host of unrelated reasons for wanting her youngest daughter to remain single. As she told one of her sons-in-law, 'mine is a nature which *requires* being loved, and I have lost almost all those who loved me most.'[24] She felt she was owed company, attendance, attention from her children, and from an unmarried daughter most of all.

By this stage in her life, if Victoria was thwarted in anything, she would say that her health was at risk. Her physical fitness had become something of a smokescreen behind which she would hide. The queen 'is roaring well and can do everything she likes and nothing she doesn't', wrote one perceptive courtier in 1869.[25] The same year the historian Thomas Carlyle described her as 'plump and almost young', with a waddling walk; she 'sailed out as if moving on skates, and bending her head towards us with a smile'.[26] A less friendly German source from the Darmstadt wedding, though, described her as looking 'like a cook' with a 'bluish-red face'. This gentleman believed the rumours that she was 'more or less mentally deranged'.[27]

Yet it *was* indisputably the case that Victoria's eyesight had begun to fail. And here the role of Beatrice, the person who read the queen's correspondence aloud, was vital. Frederick Ponsonby, son of the magnificent Henry, joined his father in the royal household, and described the role of unofficial Private Secretary that Beatrice attempted – but ultimately failed – to fill. 'The Queen is not even *au courant* with the ordinary topics of the present day,' wrote the younger Ponsonby, 'imagine B[eatrice] trying to explain . . . our policy in the East.' He, or Arthur Bigge, would write long reports setting out what they thought the queen needed to know, 'but they are often not read to HM as B[eatrice] is in a hurry to develop a photograph or wants to paint a flower'. As a result, 'hideous mistakes' sometimes occurred. The saddest aspect of the situation, according to young Ponsonby at least, was that it was only Victoria's eyes that were wearing out. 'Her memory is still wonderful, her shrewdness, her power of discrimination as strong as ever.'[28]

Victoria had also grown increasingly squeamish. She'd once been notably at ease with bodies and biology and matters of the flesh. But she'd come to think of her daughter as a pure, perfect, untouched lily. She therefore experienced deep distress when she imagined Beatrice losing her virginity. 'That thought – that agonizing thought,' Victoria wrote, that 'is to me the most torturing thought in the world.'[29] The queen would not have been so concerned in her more robust youth. But this was nine babies later, and it also reflects how women were seen more widely in high Victorian culture.

Yet Beatrice, perhaps realising that this was her only chance, persisted in her rebellious insistence that she *would* marry. By December, her mother's silent disapproval could not be sustained. Beatrice *could* marry, Victoria conceded, but there was one condition. Prince Henry would have to give up his army career, and come to live with his mother-in-law. While Victoria would reluctantly allow the marriage, it was '*quite out of the* question' that Beatrice should ever 'have left the Queen'.[30]

It was an unusual stipulation, but Prince Henry agreed. And once Victoria knew that he was 'willing to come & live in my house', she could resist no longer. It was at the very end of the year, on 29 December 1884, that she called Beatrice and her betrothed into Albert's room at Osborne. There, in the presence of her dead husband's spirit, Victoria gave them her blessing.[31]

She might have reconciled herself to the thought that she was gaining a son rather than losing a daughter, but even so Victoria dreaded the couple having children. She was relieved to find that the courtship had included 'no kissing, etc.', which she believed that 'Beatrice dislikes'. (One suspects that Beatrice may have failed to express her true opinion on the subject.) 'The wedding day,' Victoria groaned, 'is like a great trial and I hope and pray there may be no *results!*'[32]

This royal wedding, indeed any royal wedding, was bound to be good for the monarchy. To a constitutional commentator like Walter Bagehot, who observed the phenomenon at work, a royal family was simply much more palatable 'to the common mind' than a republic. 'One person doing interesting actions,' he thought, was a hundred times more attractive than scores of elected represen-tatives, all doing the same boring things. He believed that women in particular 'care fifty times more for a marriage than a ministry'.[33] And Beatrice was a quietly popular figure in the press and with the public, who appreciated her selflessness. 'Many daughters have acted virtuously, but thou excelleth them all,' ran the inscription on a silver tea and coffee service among her wedding gifts.[34]

To make it entirely clear that Beatrice would never leave Osborne, she was to be married there, and the first royal wedding to take place in a parish church was planned. It soon became clear that the pressure upon the Isle of Wight's accommodation would be immense. Some guests were to stay on board the royal yachts. Forty-four witnesses would sign the register, in an order that Victoria had carefully worked out in advance, to avoid any demeaning squabbles about precedence.[35]

After a good deal of confusion caused by Victoria's customary detailed but unclear directions, it emerged that guests were to wear *demi-toilette*, which meant jewels and elbow-length sleeves.[36] One guest noticeably absent from the list was the Prime Minister, William Gladstone, who was back in office after Disraeli's death. Victoria had not been able to bring herself to invite the man she called a '<u>half-mad</u> <u>firebrand</u>', even though it would have been politically expedient.[37]

By late morning, in hot sun, Victoria and Beatrice were finally ready to leave by carriage for the short drive to the church of St Mildred's in the nearby village of Whippingham. 'The whole way crowds of people,' Victoria noted with satisfaction.[38] St Mildred's was a 'little ivy-clad village church', and this was supposed to be 'an ideally perfect village wedding'.[39]

It was one o'clock, and the bride was late, by the time they arrived. Outside St Mildred's stood a guard of honour of Highland soldiers and a band of 'Pipes & drums'. Bertie was waiting at the gate, along with 'the sweet young Bridesmaids' wearing white dresses and white carnations.[40] Ten in number, they were all Beatrice's nieces. The radical MP Henry Labouchère thought they possessed a 'decided absence of beauty'. He also considered that Bertie 'seemed ill at ease and out of sorts', while Victoria 'looked exceedingly cross'.[41]

Feeling the pressure of the occasion, Beatrice and her mother now moved along a red-carpeted covered way lined with people.[42] The church interior was filled with 'ivy and ferns' and a 'pyramid of flowers in pots'.[43] The choristers from St George's Chapel, Windsor, had been brought down for the occasion, but they were feeling miffed because no one had remembered to arrange for them to have any refreshments.[44]

Waiting patiently at the altar was the stunningly handsome Prince Henry, in his brand-new blue sash of the Order of the Garter. Beneath it, at the queen's own request, he was wearing his glittering white Prussian military uniform.[45] The music was German too. Beatrice's walk up the aisle, orange blossom in hand, was accompanied by Wagner, 'beautifully played on the organ by Mr Parratt'.[46]

Beatrice could only squint at her groom-to-be through the folds of the very same Devon lace veil her mother had worn when she'd married Albert. This was hugely significant. Victoria attached great importance to clothes, and a well-informed source tells us that 'almost without exception, her wardrobe woman can produce the gown, bonnet, or mantle she wore on any particular occasion.'[47] The veil was one of the most precious items in the Albertian reliquary. 'I look upon it as a holy charm,' Victoria wrote, 'as it was under <u>that veil</u> our union was blessed forever.'[48] Her loan of it to Beatrice was an important act of blessing.

And the queen seemed to have relented. 'A happier looking couple could seldom be seen kneeling at the altar together,' she wrote. 'Though I stood for the 9th time near a child . . . at the altar, I think I never felt more deeply than I did on this occasion.'[49] Even so, those present noted her impatience with the Archbishop of Canterbury's lengthy homily: 'Her Majesty commenced to tap with her foot in a very ominous way.'[50] Then the veil was lifted, and with it much of the tension, and Beatrice was married at last.

Matthew Dennison reads the lending of the veil as the closing of a circle, as redemption.[51] Yet I see it more as an action of control. Yes, Victoria had allowed Beatrice to marry. But only on her own terms.

Back at Osborne, after the signing of the register, it was time for a sumptuous lunch. The wedding breakfast took place on the lawn in tents filled with ferns and flowers.[52] Victoria's meals were notoriously quick affairs, by now served in a succession of courses rather than from common serving plates: 'when you finish one dish you get the next, without a pause for breath.'[53] A visitor who often dined at Osborne in the 1880s recorded how dinner lasted exactly fifty minutes, 'too much put on each plate by the servants' and all the food 'thoroughly British'.[54]

This kind of large-scale, outdoor entertaining was something that grew more common as Victoria's reign progressed. The late-night balls of her youth were giving way to the garden parties that survive as a fixture of national life to this day. When such parties were held at Buckingham Palace, Victoria would be driven slowly round the lawns in her landau before entering a 'large black tent banked up with flowers; it was wide open – all the front – and her faithful subjects could see her taking tea and having her toast buttered by the Indian servant.'[55] There's even jerky surviving film footage of the elderly Victoria being handed, with great difficulty, out of her vehicle.

At Beatrice's wedding luncheon, the guests feasted to the accompaniment of ten bagpipers from a Highland regiment, who marched round the table 'playing splendidly'.[56] Victoria had a long-standing, highly inconvenient habit of listening to military music while eating. Once, the younger Ponsonby recalled, he had the job of reading some documents aloud to her during a dinner performance of Wagner by the Royal Marines band, bellowing so that she could hear. The other guests found it hilarious when the music came to an unexpected stop, leaving Ponsonby 'shouting' into silence.[57]

After the lunch, and a photograph, the mother-of-the-bride's mask began to slip. At four, she went upstairs with Beatrice, who was to change into her going-away dress of cream crêpe de Chine. The awful moment of parting was approaching. Prince Henry was also summoned, and now Victoria broke down in tears. She took leave of 'my darling "Baby" . . . I felt utterly miserable when they left my room, & had not the heart to go down & see them drive away.' She would, in fact, see her daughter in just two days' time, but even this short break seemed unendurable.

After dinner that night, the guests spilled out into the sweet-smelling air of the gardens. The evening sky was bright with fireworks, and the yachts in the bay below 'were lit up & sent off rockets'.[58] The great fountain in the middle of the Osborne lawns was 'hung with many-coloured lamps' and while 'the fireworks gleamed and paled, and died out in the darkness . . . the sounds of laughter made pleasant echoes in the night'.[59]

Yet Victoria could not enjoy it. She felt old, and tired, and lonely. She circulated dutifully among the guests on the lawn, '& tried to speak to people'. But she was so weary, and 'so low, that it was an effort, & I escaped quietly to my room. My dear child was never out of my mind.'[60] Even on peaceful days it was usually one o'clock in the morning before Victoria nodded off.[61] After a trying day like this one, perhaps it was even later before the lady-in-waiting appointed to read the queen to sleep found that her work was done.

After Beatrice had driven triumphantly off with her gorgeous husband, through crowds and past massed bands, her first thought had been of the mother she'd left behind.[62] Arriving at nearby Quarr Abbey for the night, Beatrice immediately sat down to write a letter to say that she'd arrived safely.[63] She could then with a clear conscience try to enjoy her forty-eight-hour honeymoon.

Beatrice regretted her mother's histrionics. 'When I took leave of her,' she told a friend, Victoria had 'got very upset, poor thing'. But Beatrice also now experienced, perhaps for the first time, the pleasure of having had her own way. 'What rest & peace I feel,' she admitted, 'now that all is accomplished, my heart has so long desired'.[64]

Beatrice would in due course give birth to four children, and her husband became a valued member of Victoria's family circle. With his love of theatricals and singing, Prince Henry's lively company meant that 'several of the Queen's lonely habits of life have gradually disappeared'.[65] One of the rare photographs of Victoria smiling was taken at Osborne the year after the wedding, the queen's podgy face a butter-ball of pleasure. In the picture Beatrice stands behind her, and Victoria has a granddaughter and a great-grand-daughter at her side. Four generations, and her own grin, encouraged the queen to pronounce the sitting 'very successful'.[66]

But there is a sad coda to Beatrice's story. Henry eventually got bored with jollying along his mother-in-law on the Isle of Wight, and finally won grudging permission to go to fight in Africa. He was observed to be 'bursting with excitement' at the prospect of being a soldier once again.[67]

His mission was to destroy the Ashanti Kingdom and – purportedly – to end its traditions of slavery and human sacrifice. In reality, the expedition was part of the unseemly 'Scramble' for Africa that was taking place between the various European powers, who used gunboats and machine guns against native populations armed with muskets.[68]

Yet the continent of Africa also had its own natural defences. Henry was travelling through modern-day Ghana when he succumbed to the malaria that attacked no fewer than half of the British forces. He died on board the ship bringing him home, and his corpse was preserved in rum in a makeshift coffin run up out of biscuit tins.[69] He was laid to rest in St Mildred's Church, where he'd been married just ten years before.

Regardless of her initial reluctance to accept Prince Henry into her family, Victoria was inconsolable, mourning him as 'a bright sunbeam in My Home'.[70] And Beatrice, having loved, and lost, had no choice but to return to being her mother's closest companion and assistant. She devoted her fifty-year widowhood to writing, copying, checking and labouring away as the queen's most trusted and intimate secretary.

Despite her valiant struggle, Beatrice failed, in the end, to escape.

22

Munshi-Mania: Excelsior Hotel Regina, French Riviera, 4 April 1897

It was 4 April 1897, and Victoria was on holiday among the cicadas and the palm trees on the Côte d'Azur. She'd often visited Nice before, but this time she was trying out a spanking new hotel named in her honour as the Excelsior Hotel Regina. A new suite, its balconies overlooking the slow heave of the Mediterranean far below, had been completed specially just three weeks before her arrival. Victoria had observed the construction of this hotel – 'the new enormous erection', as she called it – during a stay the previous year in the Grand Hotel. The Grand was now completely over-shadowed by the hulking Regina.[1]

The 400-room Regina, which still stands today, is a belle-époque wedding cake of a building, loved and loathed in equal measure. One of Victoria's courtiers called it 'a monstrous stage decoration, with grotesque pinnacles and ugly, bloated, white-domed towers'.[2] It is so large that it stands atop an entire street of shops. At the time its doors opened, it was the very pinnacle of luxury, with electric lighting throughout, 'steam pipe heating' and an omnibus service that could get you to Nice's casino in fifteen minutes.[3]

Victoria even had a private lift 'with artistic ironwork' to take her up to her first-floor rooms.[4] She could now 'only walk a few steps with the greatest difficulty, supported by an Indian attendant'.[5] Her suite, all on one level, included a bedroom with rose silk hangings and a 'yellow plush' rug.[6] Victoria's rooms were furnished, as usual, with familiar pieces brought with her from Windsor, although the hotel management had somehow rustled up locally a portrait of George III for the queen's dining room. It was worth their trouble, for Victoria's household occupied no fewer than seventy rooms in the hotel's entire western wing, at a cost of 80,000 francs for two months.[7] She preferred staying in a big hotel rather than a private rented villa because even the biggest villa couldn't accommodate her whole party.

'I am a terribly modern person,' Victoria had written in her journal at the age of seventeen. Regarding her holiday habits at least, this was still true.[8] Today it takes less than two hours to fly from London to Nice, but in the year of Victoria's birth the journey had involved sixteen days of continuous travel. With the coming of the railway to Cannes in 1863, the voyage was slashed to just forty-eight hours.[9] Victoria's household, like her still clad in mourning for Albert, would get off the train blinking and disorientated by the speed of the transition. 'The weather is glorious,' wrote woman-of-the-bedchamber Marie Mallet, 'everyone in white dresses and flowery hats, I feel like a little black mole and a dowdy one too.'[10]

Michael Nelson, historian of the French Riviera, points out that after Albert's death Victoria made almost annual visits to the Mediterranean, spending 332 nights, or nearly a year of her life, on its sunny shores. Where their queen led, other Brits followed. A French innkeeper, upon being asked where his guests came from, got the reply that 'they were all English, but he was not sure if they were Germans or Russians'.[11] If they were tourists, they *must* come from England. Even today, the Hotel Westminster, Le Royal and Queenie's Brasserie jostle each other for space on Nice's Promenade des Anglais.

And Victoria herself was enjoying something of an Indian summer beneath the long-trunked, cloudy-headed pines that looked so picturesque against a Mediterranean skyline. The pattern of her hotel days in Cimiez, an upmarket suburb on a hill behind Nice, was undemanding. She was dressed by the servants who were almost a second family. One of her wardrobe maids spent the night on call in the dressing room just next door to her bedroom.[12] At half past seven, the maid on the next shift would come into Victoria's bedroom to open the green silk blinds and shutters. Her silver hairbrush, hot water, folded towels and sponges were all laid out by these wardrobe maids. Her pharmacist's account book records the purchase of beauty products such as 'lavender water', 'Mr Saunders' Tooth Tincture' and 'cakes of soap for bath'.[13]

Victoria's clothes were handled by the dressers, who were better paid than the maids. Their duties, ran Victoria's instructions, included 'scrupulous tidiness and exactness in looking over everything that Her Majesty takes off . . . to think over well everything that is wanted or may be wanted'.[14] Her black silk stockings with white soles had for decades been woven by one John Meakin, while Anne Birkin embroidered the garments with 'VR'.[15] Victoria grew fond of faithful servants like Anne, and even had Birkin's portrait among her collection of photographs. Despite their sombre aspect, even her mourning gowns were finely made. She had settled into a series of very minor variations upon a square-necked bodice and skirt, customised with quirky little pockets for keys and seals, all cut pretty much the same to save her the trouble of fittings. On her head went a white cap, with streamers of lace, and round her neck a locket containing miniatures of two of her children: Alice, now lost to diphtheria, and Leopold, to haemophilia.[16]

She ate her 9.30 breakfast in the garden beneath her open-sided green-fringed tent. She had two cups for her coffee, and her servants observed a habit of pouring the drink from one to the other until it was the right temperature.[17] The menu included 'rolls, eggs, fried fish, grilled bacon and Cambridge sausages', and she would graze among the dishes, trying different things each day.[18]

Meanwhile the wardrobe maids were cleaning her rooms. Among their duties was the task of putting away the journal in which Victoria had invariably completed an entry the night before.[19] The maids used photographs, like those taken of Albert's death-chamber, to guide them in putting the furniture and knick-knacks back in place.[20]

In former times, it had also been a maid who signed for the red leather boxes – brought by a messenger with his badge of a silver greyhound – that contained the day's government business.[21] But now the boxes were handled by Abdul Karim, employed by the queen as her confidential Indian clerk.[22] Even at the Regina he went about this business just as usual, laying the boxes on her table. Towards eleven, Victoria opened them up and began the work of going through them, seated in her 'capacious writing-chair' with footstool and back cushion.[23]

Each morning she read reports and, if the topic interested her, sent her own detailed commands back to her ministers. Extra police patrols must be sent out, she insisted, when the supposed serial killer 'Jack the Ripper' was on the loose. The next draft of a bill outlining the punishments for homosexuality must omit all mention of females; it was unnecessary for 'women don't do such things'.[24] Any threat to Britain's status abroad was guaranteed to get her excited. Domestic affairs bothered her less, as did the whole concept of democracy. She could not see, she complained, why an admirable government like Lord Salisbury's (a Prime Minister with whom she shared a great rapport) should fall 'merely on account of the number of votes'.[25]

Much to the disgust of Arthur Bigge, now promoted from Assistant to Private Secretary, Victoria abhorred the typewriter, and insisted on everything being handwritten. As her eyesight grew ever worse, she complained ever more loudly that the ink was not 'as black' as formerly. This had caused Bigge's predecessor Henry Ponsonby (now deceased) to obtain 'a sort of little spirit stove' to cook the paper and therefore darken his writing. Meanwhile, Victoria's own handwriting became notoriously difficult to read, not least when her words strayed into the black borders of her mourning notepaper, and there became completely invisible.[26]

As she read or wrote, Turi, or Turri, a little white dog acquired in Florence, would usually sit at her feet, and the spirits of dead dogs lived on in the marble or bronze effigies of them that crowded her rooms. 'One of the worst signs of wickedness in human nature,' she thought, was cruelty to animals.[27] The local street musicians, knowing that she would reward them generously, gathered to play and sing just below her balcony. They were watched with anxiety by her Head of Security.[28] Living in a public hotel like this, Victoria was closely guarded by detectives, who 'generally adopted the dress and manners of tourists'.[29]

From her balcony, Victoria could look out over a marvellous view of five kilometres of beaches below. Her servants found her more relaxed, more easily pleased, on these Mediterranean holidays. She was delighted by the 'masses of olives . . . orchards laden with lemons . . . eucalyptus as high as elms', and above all, the 'deep blue sky and the calm sea from which you have delicious breezes'.[30] After work, she would roll in her wheelchair along the smooth paths between the cypresses, palms and urns overflowing with flowers that crammed the Regina's paradisical garden. Some afternoons she would drive out, followed by children calling out 'Madame la Reine!' On one such drive, her pony trap raced Charles Alberique, Nice's celebrated one-armed beggar, in his own tiny cart pulled along by two dogs. The funny scene happened to be sketched by a newspaper artist, and was reproduced round the world.[31]

Victoria would climb into her little carriage up carpeted steps, accompanied by 'an infinity of rugs, shawls, parasols', and leaning upon the arm of her new favourite servant: her clerk, Abdul Karim. She trusted him to help, lift and handle her. People observed him getting in close enough to use 'his delicate brown hands' to lower 'the Queen's gauze veil over her face'.[32] Karim had been promoted to the extent that Victoria now considered him the equal of the gentlemen of the household. They, for their part, disliked him, which meant that he had no friends among them, and had to sit in solitary splendour when he went out for a drive of his own.

The local Niçois believed that Abdul Karim was 'a captive Native prince, attached, as it were, to the chariot-wheels of the Empress of India'.[33] In reality he was very far from royal. Twenty-four years old when he entered the queen's service in 1887, tall, bearded and

Muslim, Karim came from a family living in Agra. He was a fine physical specimen. 'Six feet in height', according to *The Times*, he spoke 'broken English in a melodious voice'. He clearly had enormous personal charisma. 'To look upon his face and hear his voice,' continued this entranced reporter, one would think that he 'could tame lions and silence tigers'.[34]

Karim, along with a colleague named Mohammed Bakhsh, had first come to Britain to play a part in the celebrations for Victoria's Golden Jubilee in 1887. In 1886, Victoria had opened the spectacular Indian and Colonial Exhibition at the Royal Albert Hall, which brought Indian architecture and costume – and indeed Indian faces – to London. She was increasingly drawn to all things Indian, and wanted her new status as Empress of India to be visually reflected in the composition of her household. After the Jubilee, Karim and Bakhsh did not return home, but instead stayed in royal service as table waiters. The two men continued a long royal tradition of employing exotic-looking servants to add visual drama to the court.

Soon the two Indians were serving the queen as intimately as John Brown had once done: 'so clever when they help me out of my chair or into a carriage . . . they never pinch me.'[35] Yet just as Brown had been distrusted by the rest of the household, so it was with Karim and Bakhsh as well. They formed their own 'little set apart from the others'. They were described as 'impenetrable, impassive and supercilious persons', attentive and silent in their 'big turbans and wonderful cashmere garments of dazzling hues'.[36]

Victoria's courtiers generally shared the views of her administrators and colonial staff in India, which were that Indians were decidedly inferior to Europeans. Victoria, however, perhaps having less cause to worry about her status being challenged, was less prone to this. 'There is no hatred to a brown skin – none,' she wrote, even in the wake of the Indian Rebellion of 1857.[37]

Wanting to know more about the India of which she was now the titular head, Victoria began in 1887 to take language lessons from Karim. She decided to learn a few words of Hindustani, or

Urdu, she explained, as 'it is a great interest to me for both the language and the people'.[38] The Empress of India, who could not travel to visit her dominions, could nevertheless welcome something of the subcontinent into her own home.

Two years later, Karim entirely gave up his duties as a waiter and was promoted to the position of 'Munshi', meaning teacher or secretary. Victoria called him her *Personal Indian Clerk* with the job of looking after her 'boxes, letters, papers'.[39] When they travelled to Nice, the French papers called him *'le professeur de la reine'*, or else 'Le Munchy', which incensed the other members of the household who were themselves rarely mentioned in the press.[40]

Some of the household suspected that Karim's level of literacy and skill in Urdu was not as great as he claimed. Indeed, in his own private journal, recently analysed and partially published by historian Shrabani Basu, Karim admitted that as his mother's favourite he had been 'rather over-indulged', and that his youthful studies had been 'very irregular'.[41] Whatever his precise educational attainments, he was well-attuned to the subtle clues to status that were so important in court society. He was certainly ambitious. As time went on, he asked for, and was given, better accommodation, including furnished cottages at Balmoral and Osborne. This annoyed those who had to make way for him. 'I hear the Queen has given Abdul not only my old room but also the large central sitting room off it, which she declined to give me last year!' complained the latest royal doctor, James Reid. He felt that this reflected 'the relative estimation in which Abdul and I are held!!'[42]

When the queen granted Abdul Karim the right to go into the billiard room of an evening with the other gentlemen, there was an outcry. Henry Ponsonby, before his death, had experienced great difficulty in controlling it, and indeed admitted sharing personally in the racism that motivated his fellow household members. 'As long as it was English or European work I got on fairly,' he wrote, 'but these Injuns are too much for me.'[43] Victoria also had to reprimand Lord Salisbury for describing the Indian servants as 'n—rs.'[44]

Early in 1897, when the queen's spring holiday to the South of France was being planned, it was announced that the Munshi was to come too. This further annoyed the household, for if he stayed in the Regina with them, they would be expected to eat with him. This was a recognition of his status they were not willing to make.

Dr James Reid was particularly annoyed. Having joined the household in 1881, he was by now reaching the height of his influence as Victoria's trusted physician. Son of a puritanical and hard-working local physician, Dr Reid came from the 'small, grey, granite' town of Ellon in Aberdeenshire.[45] Having studied in Vienna, Reid had first encountered the royal household when a 'resident medical attendant' was required for Balmoral. His plain speaking was highly valued by his colleagues. He had a notable 'absence from the Royal Culte and a delightful way of stripping the leaves from the trees', wrote a colleague. He was short, balding, mous-tachioed and pince-nez'd, and his colleagues came to think that Victoria 'was guided more by him than anyone else' in this last decade of her life.[46] One of them went so far as to say that 'she takes advice from no one else'.[47]

Dr Reid now compiled a long list of grievances against her other favourite, the Munshi. Abdul Karim had requested that his photograph for the newspapers be retouched to make him look 'thinner and less dark'. Dr Reid did not approve. In a small hotel, Abdul Karim had 'deprived H.M.'s maids of bathroom and W.C.' by insisting 'on having it entirely reserved for himself'. Dr Reid was furious.[48] His reaction was not only racist. It also encompassed a courtier's atavistic jealousy of a rival for the position of royal favourite. The fact that Karim was a handsome young man and Victoria an older woman made it all seem doubly wrong.

And there was worse to come. On 20 February 1897, just before they all left for Nice, Dr Reid had some distasteful news to pass on to Victoria. Karim was ill again. When her Munshi had been sick previously, she'd been greatly concerned, visiting him twice a day and spending time 'in his room taking Hindustani lessons . . . examining his neck, smoothing his pillows, etc.' Reid had previously treated Karim for venereal disease, and now, he told the queen, the gonorrhoea had returned.[49] Was this true? We do not have a record of whether Victoria believed him or not. Dr Reid's colleagues certainly admired him for his integrity. But maybe he wanted to think the worst of Karim.

Yet Victoria refused to listen to any suggestion that the Munshi be left behind. On 10 March 1897, when Victoria departed for Nice, Karim went too. Dr Reid, though, had not exhausted his arsenal of weapons to use against the Munshi. Despite the queen's seemingly endless litany of complaints – her knee, her nerves – she was in fact in fairly robust health in her late seventies. Yet Dr Reid would now once again resurrect the spectre of Hanoverian 'madness'.

The passage to Cimiez was planned by Ernest Dossé, who had the enviable job title of 'Director of Her Majesty's Continental Journeys'. The train that took Victoria south through France included two custom-made coaches that belonged personally to her. Her sleeping car lacked the usual brakes, as they might shriek in the night and wake her up.[50] Her daytime saloon was decorated in pearl-grey silk brocaded with roses, thistles and shamrocks.[51] The train also transported Victoria's own carriage and pony cart, her mobile hospital and her 'mahogany bedstead, that old-fashioned, high, narrow bedstead that had accompanied her on all her journeys over the past forty years'.[52] The food on board was Irish stew, brought from Windsor and kept warm(-ish) in cushions made of red flannel. A footbath filled with ice provided rudimentary air conditioning.[53] Her Head of Security described the royal train as a 'rolling palace', everything in it 'heavy, large and comfortable'.[54]

Karim, meanwhile, travelled in his own private saloon, and when the President of France came aboard the train to welcome her, Victoria seized the opportunity to introduce him to her Munshi.[55] Although she was travelling incognito, which meant that the ceremonies normally paid to a sovereign need not be observed, the station at Nice was nevertheless carpeted in crimson when she descended on Karim's arm.

The trainload of courtiers driving in her wake up the long wide boulevard to the Regina conferred and complained about Karim's presence. Victoria knew what was going on, and sent her grand-son-in-law, Prince Louis of Battenberg, to instruct them that they must include Karim in their social activities. But the rest of the household agreed that if she forced the matter they would resign en masse.

It all came to a head on 4 April. The day at Cimiez dawned as fine as usual, if 'not very bright', as Victoria recorded in her journal. She described a church service at eleven, to which her sons Bertie and Affie both came, and a visit to the beautiful Liserb garden near her hotel. After lunch, she drove out with two of her grand-daughters. She dined with a small party of three, meeting the Bishop of Ripon after dinner. It sounds like a normal, quiet, pleasant holiday day.[56]

Nothing in Victoria's journal suggests the terrible storm that broke at the Regina that evening. But this should serve as a reminder of how deceptive the journals can be. Not only did Victoria know that they would be read, but the actual surviving text mostly consists of what her daughter Beatrice thought it appropriate for posterity to know. She sometimes condensed her mother's words, which had the effect of deleting details and reducing pungency. Beatrice has sometimes been accused of censoring Victoria's journals, but she was more probably motivated by the wish to preserve them, and to simply to get through the gargantuan job of transcribing them.

Either way, other sources reveal that the quiet Sunday in Cimiez had also seen a blistering confrontation between Victoria and her household. It began when Dr Reid came in to report new information about the misdeeds of the Munshi. A telegram had arrived from India with damaging details about the family history of the Karims. Reid and others had been asking questions in order either to confirm or challenge the background Karim had himself supplied. Karim had said, or at least implied, that he was the son of a doctor. But now this inflammatory message from India revealed that Karim's father was merely employed in the 'Subordinate Medical Service' as a hospital assistant, paid sixty rupees a month.

Karim had also claimed to have worked as a clerk or paper-pusher in India, rather than in a lowly job like that of table waiter, as he had on his arrival at Windsor. He had indeed been a clerk, Reid discovered, but only an inferior sort of 'vernacular clerk in Agra Gaol at 10 rupees a month'. In a final twist, the telegram concluded that there was 'no information about wife or there being more than one'.[57] Karim had a wife in England, so obviously someone had also been hoping to find out that he was a bigamist.

Reid now pounced with glee on the fact that he appeared to have caught the Munshi out. Karim's father was not a qualified doctor. To my mind, though, the telegram can also be read the other way: as proof that the senior Karim certainly *was* associated with medicine, and that Abdul Karim himself *had* held a job as a clerk. Reid and the household simply made the least generous possible interpretation of the data.

But what Reid forgot, as he now confronted her with this 'evidence', was that Victoria didn't really care about the social class of her servants. After all, she'd known 'two Archbishops who were the sons respectively of a Butcher and a Grocer'.[58] And Karim was obviously more to her than 'just' a servant. In the written records of their Urdu lessons, it's clear that he taught her how to say phrases such as 'You will miss the Munshi very much', and she signed notes to him as 'Your loving mother'.[59] She was in need of someone to love, and in Karim she'd found a substitute son.

Like others before him, Dr Reid didn't understand that this feeling could not be destroyed by logical argument. Just as when she'd ignored John Brown's drinking, Victoria was determined to believe the best of Abdul Karim. At Windsor Castle Karim now occupied the very room formerly used by Brown himself. He'd inherited the same protected status.[60]

But Dr Reid was undaunted. He came back to the fray in Victoria's private rooms at the Regina with further ammunition. He'd also received, he claimed, additional worrying news from government sources. On 2 April, information had come in that Karim was suspected of associating with the Muslim Patriotic League, an organisation that sought to undermine British rule in India. Karim had a raffish friend: a journalist, and possible spy, named Rafiuddin Ahmed. He'd also been staying at the Regina until the household managed to get him expelled. Ahmed was suspected of espionage on behalf of the Amir of Afghanistan, and was certainly associated with the Muslim Patriotic League.[61] In other words, he was someone who wanted the British out of India. Could it be, Reid now asked, that Karim was not only low-born, but a traitor?

It is true that her closeness to Karim had made Victoria damagingly over-partial to his fellow Muslims at the expense of the Hindus. She thought Islam 'when well known and understood, contains so much that is fine and to be respected and admired'.[62] It was a valid viewpoint, but it had the downside of making her, unfairly, less keen on her Hindu subjects.

But this was hardly treachery, and straight-talking Dr Reid did not have the subtlety of a Randall Davidson in putting his case. In stating things so baldly, in using logic so harshly, he caused grave offence. He then tried to excuse his conduct with perhaps the cruellest accusation of all.

Many people, he said to Victoria, in increasing desperation, 'say to me that the only charitable explanation that can be given is that Your Majesty is not sane'.[63] This was a low blow, and a hurtful one. 'The time will come,' Dr Reid warned, 'when to save Your Majesty's memory and reputation it will be necessary for me to come forward and say so.' What's more, he told her that Bertie was also worried about the same thing.

Victoria's son and heir, then, and her trusted medical advisor, and other unnamed 'people in high places', appeared to be in league to tell Victoria that unless she laid off her Munshi-mania, they would reveal to the world that she had gone mad. The fear that the queen might lose her mind had been at its greatest in the years of her early widowhood and menopause, then it had died away. Victoria must have been horrified to hear the words 'not sane' once more.

Interestingly, it wasn't just the highly placed who were involved in the bullying. Also present in the room during this epic row was Victoria's long-time dresser, Annie Macdonald. 'Your Majesty sits there,' Macdonald said, 'and hears nothing of what is being said. No one tells you the truth about this.'[64] It's a fascinating glance under the bonnet of Victoria's life, included among newly published selections from Reid's diary by historian Kate Hubbard. Here was the queen being harangued by both her doctor and her dresser. Yet from Beatrice's edited version of Victoria's journal, you would never know it. Dr Reid described the harrowing scene as a 'very painful interview', and not the only one at that hotel during that holiday to conclude with 'the most violent passion'.[65]

Victoria was distressed, and her household were greatly distressed, but ultimately Reid's arguments, ranging from snobbery to treason to madness, were all in vain. As John Conroy had discovered long ago, it had always been hopeless to try to coerce Victoria. She would not dismiss Karim, and in her service he remained. She simply issued a memorandum that her gentlemen must stop 'talking about this painful subject'.[66]

Abdul Karim's biographer, Shrabani Basu, points out that he may have lied about his family origins. He may have had venereal disease. He may have been overfond of reading about himself in the newspapers. But all this was worth it to Victoria. Like John Brown, Karim gave a grieving, ageing woman a new lease of life. In the wake of Brown's death, she'd raged against her immobility: 'How can I see people at dinner in the evening? I can't go walking about all night holding on to the back of a chair.'[67] For all his drawbacks, Karim gave the Empress of India an insight into this empire she governed, he encouraged her to move about and take physical exercise and he rejuvenated her in the final decade of her life. And in the end even the Prime Minister, Lord Salisbury, was forced to admit after making a personal investigation that there was no evidence for Karim's supposed treason.[68]

It was only after Victoria's death that her household and family were able to take their revenge. Then, her daughter Beatrice and daughter-in-law Alix went down to Karim's cottage at Windsor, burned all the queen's letters to him and sent him back to India.[69] 'They will be the sufferers thereby!' Bertie threatened, should the Munshi or his family attempt to keep any letters back from the blaze.[70] However, Karim did indeed successfully smuggle a personal diary out of Windsor and off to India. It would have been tragic if it had been destroyed, for it completely redeems him from any charge of treason, and reveals him to have been faultlessly devoted to his queen.

Because of the terrible argument about her Munshi on 4 April 1897, Victoria spoke later of the 'dislike' she had taken against her room at Cimiez, 'from the scenes I had there . . . and from the pain I suffered'.[71] Yet Lord Salisbury had a sneaking suspicion that she enjoyed rows. He told Dr Reid that 'she really likes the emotional excitement, as being the only form of excitement she can have'.[72]

The Regina still stands today, impressively enormous, like a slightly seedy ocean liner beached on the top of a mountain. Despite Victoria's patronage, it never quite 'succeeded in attracting a very aristocratic *clientele*', perhaps because its size and ostentation was just a little bit vulgar.[73] Today its 400 rooms have been divided into 100 flats, many of them occupied by workers from the nearby hospital. Yet while Victoria may have turned against the Regina, the French Riviera in general remained her happiest place. 'Alas!' she wrote of it, 'I grieve to leave . . . I shall mind returning to the sunless north.'[74] In 1901, as she entered into her final illness, she felt she would surely recover 'oh, if only I were at Nice.'[75]

23

Apotheosis: London, 22 June 1897

Midsummer's Day 1897 ended in a warm, close night. Londoners slept poorly, their city clamped under clouds. Their queen also tossed and turned. Her private rooms at Buckingham Palace were hung with red silk. Every piece of furniture was crowded with reminders of the past, tables completely hidden under a 'fascinating confusion of books, photo-frames, and *bibelots* of all kinds',[1] In her bedroom the subject matter was Albert, Albert, Albert. 'Photographs and pictures' of him buried each surface, standing 'conspicuously on every hand'.[2]

Lying amid the nostalgic clutter, Victoria was 'rather restless' and 'very hot'.[3] She'd become a poor sleeper, often fussing about 'the shawls and the cushions – then the lamps to put out – then again, it felt too hot . . . Annie [her dresser] was called many a time – to bring her something to drink.'[4] This particular night, there was 'such a noise going on the whole time' outside the palace that it was almost impossible to sleep. Thousands of people did not go to their homes, 'but slept and ate in the places which they had secured along the pavements' to see the following day's Diamond Jubilee procession.[5] Victoria did snatch some rest before the dull dawn of 22 June finally arrived.[6]

If she'd had any doubts about the burden that the coming events would place upon her, *The Times* that morning was keen to remind her. 'To-day the eyes of the whole Empire,' its editorial ran, 'will be fixed upon London, and upon the great and inspiring ceremony in which we celebrate the sixty years of the Queen's reign.' At the heart of it all was an overheated, tired old lady of seventy-eight.

Rising from her bed, Victoria dressed, as always, in black. The crowds who saw her today would consider her 'dress of black silk' to be modest and widowly, almost dingy. Her taste in clothing had become ever more subdued. Departing from Windsor Castle to travel to Buckingham Palace for these few days of the Jubilee, she'd been worried about the stains the sooty train to Paddington might leave on her outfit. 'I could have cried,' said the woman who ran the draper's shop in Windsor, 'to see Her Majesty start for the Jubilee in her second-best "mantle" – after all the beautiful things I had sent her.'[7]

If you'd had the chance to examine the queen's outfit closely, though, you'd've seen that it was in fact sombrely splendid, her black cape embroidered with swirling silver sequins, huge pearls hanging from each ear and upon the gown itself decorative 'panels of grey satin veiled with black net & steel embroideries, & some black lace'.

Round her neck now went a 'lovely diamond chain', a Jubilee present from her younger children, while her 'bonnet was trimmed with creamy white flowers & white aigrette'.[8] This bonnet, worn with resolution, had caused some upset. Her government had asked its queen to appear more . . . queenly. 'The symbol that unites this vast Empire is a Crown not a bonnet,' complained Lord Rosebery. But Victoria stoutly refused, and 'the bonnet triumphed'. She would wear it today, just as she'd worn it at her Golden Jubilee a decade before.[9] The queen looked just like a 'wee little old lady'. The only touch of colour about her black-clad figure was her 'wonderful, blue, childlike eyes'.[10]

Once dressed, Victoria tottered through to breakfast with her daughters Vicky, Lenchen and Beatrice. The meal took place in the Chinese Room, dead centre in the front of the palace and part of Edward Blore's wing that Victoria had added to provide extra space. It's the room still used today for royal balcony appearances at Buckingham Palace, every twitch of its net curtains closely analysed by expectant crowds. From it, Victoria and her daughters were now able to watch a procession of the 25,000 colonial troops who had come to London for the Jubilee, most of them camping in Hyde Park. It took forty minutes for them all to pass by. She'd missed a good number of them because they'd already been and gone before she got to breakfast, 'but there were still a great many, chiefly British' still passing.[11] Masticating mournfully upon omelettes, fried soles, beef fillets and cold fowl, Victoria 'watched them for a little while'.[12]

The Chinese Room was decorated with exotic oriental furnishings, recycled in the 1850s from the bizarre seaside pavilion built in Brighton by George IV. Since Albert's death, a gloom had fallen over Buckingham Palace and its magnificent gilded state apartments were opened up only when Victoria felt she really couldn't avoid it. At one family wedding Alix, Princess of Wales, found that the Chinese Room had not been prepared, and quickly ripped the covers off the furniture herself. The dust made her gloves 'black as coal'.[13]

The frozen palace came back to life only when Victoria could be coaxed out of Windsor, Balmoral or Osborne to make an appearance in the capital, and Bertie thought the place a 'sepulchre'. Toys from his youth still crammed the attics, including a stuffed lion that swallowed a Russian soldier when its tail was pulled.[14] 'There are naturally many things lying about on tables, chairs, and on the floor,' noted one palace denizen, 'books, for instance, shawls and old envelopes.' The servants picked them up for cleaning purposes, then put them all back in their exact places according to chalk marks 'made upon the carpets'.[15]

When the elderly queen did make the effort to entertain guests at Buckingham Palace, the balls of her youth had by now given way to sedate afternoon garden parties. But the celebration of sixty years on the throne required something grander than a picnic. 'Now comes my swan song,' she claimed.[16] No one knew quite how to celebrate the occasion, as no previous monarch had ever lived or reigned for so long. People didn't even know what to call it. It was Victoria's Private Secretary, Arthur 'Better NOT' Bigge, who came up with the term 'Diamond' to signify sixty years.[17]

The true anniversary of her accession fell on Sunday 20 June 1897, but the Sabbath wasn't appropriate for a celebration. Instead, Tuesday 22 June was selected to become a special Bank Holiday, and a year-long process of planning had begun.[18]

One of the parameters was cost. The celebrations for Victoria's Golden Jubilee ten years previously had left her £50,000 out of pocket, and she was determined that this should not happen again.[19] The Jubilee of 1887 had been marked by an influx of royal guests. Since then, though, some important relationships, including with Germany, had turned sour. Victoria was adamant that in 1897 her eldest grandson, Vicky's son Wilhelm, or Willy, should *not* attend. She thought him a 'hot-headed, conceited' young man, strutting around in his ridiculous military uniforms. If he came to London, her courtiers warned, he 'would arrive with an enormous suite & would try & arrange things himself and endless trouble would arise'.[20] A clever solution to the problem of how to get out of inviting Willy was presented by the Colonial Secretary, Joseph Chamberlain. He suggested that instead of foreign royalty, delegations from far-flung corners of Victoria's own empire should take centre stage.

This was agreed, and festivities were planned not just for a queen but for an empress. After breakfast, Victoria 'touched an electric button' that set off a starburst of telegrams to destinations all round the world. In Grant Land, an island east of Greenland, in the Punjab and in Victoria, Australia, her subjects received her message, and 1,310 of them sent telegrams of congratulation straight back again. 'From my heart,' Victoria's message had said, 'I thank my beloved people, may God bless them.' At the very moment she sent it, 'the sun burst out'.[21]

By quarter past eleven, the morning had become bright and hot: 'The Queen's Weather', people called it. Victoria got into her low-sided landau by shuffling up a 'green baize plank slanting up from the doorstep' with the help of one of her Indian servants.[22] The windows of the Buckingham Palace courtyard and even the roofs of the building were precariously packed with servants and household staff who wanted to see their mistress drive off.

This landau was the very same one Victoria had used to travel to St Paul's in 1872 to give thanks for Bertie's recovery from typhoid fever. It had no driver, as such, and the eight cream horses were managed by a team of red-jacketed, buckskin-breeched postillions on horseback and on foot. Just as Victoria had refused to wear her crown, she'd also declined to use the golden state coach. But no one would be left in any doubt that her landau would provide the climax of the procession, coming as it did after a seemingly endless succession of marching and mounted troops, an escort of Indian princes on horseback, then an entourage of other members of the royal family. The landau's creams were 'very nervous animals, and exceedingly delicate and restive'. They'd been specially trained for the procession by being driven 'day after day past every kind of military band'.[23] Even so, 'I felt a good deal agitated,' Victoria admitted, as her driverless carriage moved off, 'for fear anything might be forgotten or go wrong.'[24]

Her nerves were for the stage management of the occasion, rather than her personal safety. This was despite the fact she'd been attacked seven times in her sixty-year reign by would-be assassins. Some of them were clearly mentally ill rather than politically motivated, but during the previous thirty-two years, the Tsar of Russia, the Presidents of America and France and the Prime Minister of Spain had all been assassinated.[25] Victoria herself possessed a green parasol with a lining of steel mesh, to deter murderous bullets.[26] It must have been an inventor's gimmick rather than something of practical use, for it is enormously heavy. Today she was holding instead a black chiffon parasol. It was a gift from the House of Commons, presented to her two days earlier by its oldest member, who was ninety-five.

More than three million people had poured into London to see this Jubilee parade, and they all wanted a good view. The newspapers advertised a novelty item: 'a cork galosh', 4½ inches high, to be worn over the shoes of 'short persons, who wish to view the procession and find themselves in the back rows'.[27] The route had been closed to vehicles three days earlier so that seating, bunting, banners and a host of other decorations could be installed. (The novel electrified decorations attempted in St James's, though, had been taken down after catching fire.)

By eleven, the galleries and stands of seats had been occupied for some time by happy crowds, while the windows of the houses and offices along the way were 'as snugly packed as boxes in a theatre'.[28] The spectators had, for the most part, brought provisions with them, 'coffee, claret and champagne, cold meats, salads, cake and sandwiches'. Opening their lunch baskets and chatting to their neighbours, they were thought 'a remarkably decorous crowd'. This was something that could not be taken for granted in a century of violent, street-based revolutions. The alternating soldiers and policemen who lined the route 'almost touching elbows' would not tolerate any pushing or shoving.[29] They must have been mindful that through the mismanagement of the coronation of the Russian Tsar, the previous year in Moscow, more than 1,000 people had been crushed to death.

The procession was led by the tallest man in the British army, all 6 feet 8 inches of him. Spectators could follow the various troops who followed by the means of a printed programme identifying each unit. Mark Twain, watching from a seat in the Strand, came to the conclusion that 'this procession could not be described. There was going to be too much of it, and too much variety in it, so I gave up the idea. It was to be a spectacle for the kodak, not the pen . . . the Chinese, the Japanese, the Koreans, the Africans, the Pacific Islanders – they were all there.'[30] 'Up they came, more and more,' wrote one journalist, 'new types, new realms at every couple of yards an anthropological museum – a living gazetteer of the British Empire. With them came their English officers, whom they obey and follow like children. And you begin to understand, as never before, what the Empire amounts to.'[31]

The spectators were intended to feel that the whole world had come to their city to honour their queen. Yet some of them may have detected something rather desperate in this parading of British might. Earlier in her reign, Victoria's empire been expanding in a manner that seemed inexorable. When Disraeli had won Victoria the title of Empress of India, it had merely set the seal upon an informal colonisation of the subcontinent that the East India Company had carried out for mercantile reasons. In the last decade, though, Victoria's government had pursued more of a policy of 'Empire for Empire's sake', snapping up territories simply so that other great powers could not have them. Germany, now subject to Victoria's personal animosity, and America too, were threatening Britain's previously unchallenged economic dominance. At Victoria's Golden Jubilee in 1887 there'd been no need to celebrate her empire; it was taken for granted. Now, in 1897, Britain's empire was beginning to seem both more precious and more precarious.[32] Many of its subjects were fed up of being described, and treated, as 'children'.

After the soldiers, and the gorgeously attired phalanx of Indian princes, the royal family started to appear. One spectator noticed that some of Victoria's grandchildren, while 'bowing their little best', were already 'beginning to look as if they had had almost enough of it'. It was awfully hot. Then came five carriages, each with four horses, 'filled with the well-known Princes and Princesses', and then, at last, behind her eight horses, came the queen. Much of the warmth of the occasion was reserved for her personally. 'We beheld the dear old Queen – and what a cheer they gave her, it made the tears come to my eyes. She was sitting quite upright and brisk in the carriage not looking flushed or overcome, but smiling.'[33] Victoria carried her parasol high, so the crowds could see her face; her outriders were her field marshals Lord Wolseley (veteran of the Indian Rebellion, and reliever of the besieged garrison at Khartoum) and Lord Roberts (who'd served in Afghanistan, and who'd go on to serve in the Second Anglo-Boer War). The message was clear: this was not just a queen but an empress.[34]

But the doubts of those who did not quite believe in the empire were partly assuaged by the fact that its empress did not look like one. She may now have ruled over a quarter of the globe's landmass, but the woman the crowds cheered was not physically impressive. 'She is short, stout, and her face rather red,' remembered one person who met the queen in later life.[35] 'A big round ball on wobbly legs,' recorded Tsar Nicholas II.[36] 'I had pictured to myself a dazzling apparition arrayed in sumptuous robes,' recalled another, who was desperately disappointed when she turned out to be just 'a middle-aged lady, simply dressed in widow's "weeds" and wearing a widow's cap'.[37]

It was, in fact, Victoria's very ordinariness that was extraordinary. Her lack of 'stately or splendid appearance' constituted its own sort of charm, 'because of the very way in which it took people by surprise'.[38] 'A Queen in a bonnet cuts a very different figure from a commoner so dressed,' writes historian Margaret Homans; 'in Victoria's case, the crown is visible by its absence.'[39] That an empress should wear a bonnet does make complete sense if you remember that the Victorians liked to see domesticity as the highest achievement of their age. With this kindly-looking empress/grandmother at its head, Adrienne Munich argues, then surely the empire itself must be just 'one happy family'? With its troops as obedient children? It was a pleasing construct, even if it was not one that could last much longer.

Victoria may have succeeded at least in part simply because she looked no more threatening than your own loving grandmother. But, in a passive way, she did change things for other women too. After experiencing decades of female rule, no one, wrote the journalist W. T. Stead, 'could honestly repeat the old rubbish about the natural incapacity of woman'. He thought that Victoria's silent example, simply sitting there in her landau being looked at, had ushered in an age when it was normal to see 'Woman' as well as 'Man . . . in the playing-field and the park, on the cycle and the street, on the platform, in business, in hospital and at the university'.[40]

And Victoria brought other women with her into the public eye. Sitting opposite her, their backs to the horses, were her daughter Lenchen and daughter-in-law Alix. Vicky had been sent ahead in her own carriage, for royal etiquette suggested that the Empress of Germany must, like the Empress of India, travel facing forward.

Alix was doing what she did best, which was 'looking very pretty in lilac'.[41] Her dress, immensely narrow, and as always immensely chic, had leg-of-mutton sleeves and her usual high collar. Alix's necklines, originally serving the purpose of covering up a scar, had created a widely adopted fashion.

Unfortunately, the rapprochement between Alix and Bertie after his illness had not lasted. He'd become captivated in 1891 by 'The Babbling Brooke', a nickname given to the loquacious and indiscreet Daisy, Lady Brooke, who would end up as Countess of Warwick. Bertie was embroiled in a notorious altercation with one of Daisy's previous lovers, Lord Charles Beresford. There were rumours that Lord Charles had actually thrown a punch at the Prince of Wales.[42] Alix had retaliated by taking a long holiday in her native Denmark, missing her husband's fifty-fifth birthday. 'I was so angry about Lady Warwick,' she explained. Giving up on her marriage, she told her husband 'once and for all that he might have any woman he wished'.[43]

Bertie himself was riding elsewhere in the procession. His main challenge in life was boredom. He consoled himself for a certain lack of purpose with cigars, his numerous women and enormous meals (his waist now measured forty-eight inches, and his friends called him 'Tum-Tum'). His mother still lacked confidence in him, and excluded him from many matters of business. She was unable, or at least unwilling, to see that he had a flair for public relations and image management. It was something that they had in common, and which Albert had lacked. If allowed to, Bertie could do a perfectly good job of running a court. 'He never missed saying a word to the humblest visitor, attendant or obscure official,' said one witness. 'He would enter a room and, with the skill of an accomplished billiard player, look forward several strokes ahead, so that no one was left out.'[44] He had a real gift for 'setting others at ease'.[45] Along with his social grace, and the sense of style he'd always manifested through his clothes, Bertie could also see that events like today's would blossom into a whole new branch of monarchical business. Well-rehearsed, well-funded royal pageantry, a sort of performance art in its own right, would become fundamental to the monarchy in the next century.

Bertie had chaired the organising committee for his mother's Diamond Jubilee procession, but the loudest cheering today was reserved for her.[46] It was, she reported, 'quite deafening, & every face seemed to be filled with real joy. I was much moved & gratified.' As her landau inched down the Strand, she encountered the Lord Mayor of London on a runaway horse, and passed a house into which were packed the 'survivors of the Charge of Balaclava'.[47] Her only regret was not being able to view the procession as a whole: 'I had a very bad place and saw nothing.'[48]

Towards St Paul's, 'the crowds broke out into singing God save the Queen.'[49] Fifteen thousand people, including a choir of 500, had crammed themselves into the square before the cathedral. As Victoria approached, ran a breathless account in the *Daily Mail*, 'the roar surged up the street'. When her carriage reached 'the very steps of the Cathedral; cheers broke into screams and enthusiasm swelled to delirium . . . and there . . . and there . . . so very quiet, so very grave, so very punctual, so unmistakeably and every inch a lady and a Queen'.[50]

Now a special service took place, right there in the street in front of the church, to avoid the need for Victoria to go through the lengthy and undignified process of getting out of her carriage. It was a neat solution to the problem of her immobility, and indeed every aspect of the day had been carefully considered. Even the question of whether the horses might defecate during the more spiritual parts of the service had been discussed.[51]

Then it was time to start moving again, crossing London Bridge and going south, 'along the Borough Road'. Victoria noted that even though there was a 'very poor population' down here on the other side of the river, they were 'just as enthusiastic & orderly as elsewhere . . . festoons of flowers, on either side of the street'.[52]

To route the procession through the poorer quarters of south London like this was unprecedented. As long ago as 1843, the radical papers had been calling for her to 'put down the glass of the Royal carriage when passing the Town Common-side' to 'judge the real condition' of her subjects.[53] Victoria had indeed travelled more, seen more, than previous monarchs, but despite this, there was no question that she was anything other than a deep social conservative. She didn't even see the point of educating people 'for *themselves*'. 'To be labourers and house-servants,' she thought, 'was as good and necessary as being clerks.'[54] So it was with a grateful eye for their loyalty, but with no real eye to bettering their condition, that she passed through the Borough.

It would be different in her children's generation. Even while the procession unspooled, halls and community centres throughout the city were being set up to give a 'Jubilee Feast' for 400,000 London paupers. Alix, acting in the role of the bountiful princess, had set up a charitable fund to pay for their dinners. This was a precursor of the way that the philanthropy of Victoria's grandchildren would come to define the monarchy in a way that Victoria's own charitable giving had not.[55] The idea for the feast, part of a wider conception that the monarchy should 'do good', had remained a vague royal dream until made real by the Scottish grocer Thomas Lipton. Famous for both his yellow-labelled tea and his grasp of logistics, he'd calculated that 700 tons of food and 10,000 waiters were required, and coughed up £25,000 to pay for it all.[56] The newly rich, so long as they were as generous as Lipton, would consequently become welcome at Bertie and Alix's court in a way they weren't at Victoria's.[57]

Philanthropy on a smaller scale was also taking place as Victoria got to the bottom of the Borough. St George's Church at the final twist of the High Street had rented out its roof to spectators, raising enough money to pay for the new ceiling inside, which survives to this day. The church was also the station of one of the forty camera operators from twenty different commercial firms who'd positioned themselves along the route.[58] When Victoria was later shown some of their footage, she described it as 'very wonderful' if 'a little hazy & rather too rapid'.[59] These films nevertheless proved wildly popular over the following days in variety programmes in provincial theatres.[60] The research of film historian Luke McKernan has revealed that the cameraman sited at St George's was R. J. Appleton of Bradford. Later that afternoon, Mr Appleton rushed back to Bradford by train, developing his film en route. That very same evening he showed it on an outdoor screen erected by the local newspaper. As he'd caught Victoria in the act of smiling, it's particularly sad that Appleton's film doesn't survive. But the story shows how technology now allowed many thousands more people who hadn't even been physically present to join in the day.[61]

At last it was time to head back towards Buckingham Palace, everyone by now rather desperate to get out of the sun. One senior courtier riding alongside Victoria 'fainted, & had a bad fall', and she herself admitted that 'the heat during the last hour was very great'.[62] She had a quiet lunch of lamb cutlets with Vicky and Beatrice, then rested before tea in the garden.[63] There is a charming, humanising description, of how she would 'carefully remove her gloves, untie her bonnet strings, and fling them over her shoulders', preparatory to drinking her cup.[64] She spent the afternoon gathering herself for a big dinner that night, and changing into 'a black & silver dress'.[65]

The grand dinner, including '*bernoise à l'imperatrice*', or 'chicken soup of the Empress', was served upon plate worth a million pounds specially brought up from Windsor Castle in a large, discreet, dark-coloured wagon.[66] The 108 diners in the Buckingham Palace ballroom (250 further household members ate in the Garden Pavilion) included numerous children and grandchildren.[67] Victoria was well on the way to becoming, as she would be at the end of her life, foremother of nine children, thirty-six grandchildren and thirty-seven great-grandchildren.[68] The grandson who was missing,

Kaiser Willy, found his exclusion 'deeply mortifying'.[69] Although Victoria disliked him in principle, his skilful flattery usually won her round when they met in person. This evening, though, she did not miss him. She 'tried to speak to most of the Princes & Princesses' but 'felt very tired' and went to bed early at eleven.[70]

Five days later at Osborne, Victoria had an official Jubilee photograph taken, wearing her Jubilee dress and, of course, her wedding lace.[71] The whole royal family was becoming familiar with manipulating its photographic image. In 1863, *The Times* reported that Vicky and Alice had themselves retouched their brother Bertie's wedding photos.[72] (The princesses really preferred sitting to an old-fashioned artist, like a sculptor, who excelled in 'making them look like ladies, while the Photographs are common indeed'.[73]) After each new photographic sitting, Victoria 'carefully criticised' the results.[74] In her later photographs, like this Diamond Jubilee portrait, she was heavily retouched, a double chin removed, inches shaved off her waist. The *Photographic News* criticised a photo from her Golden Jubilee for making her look as if she had 'oedematous disease', a condition where the body bloats up with excess fluid. Her skin had been smoothed to the extent that she looked like a waxwork.[75]

This, for a queen, wasn't vanity, but part of her job. Uncle Leopold in her youth had conceptualised monarchy as a craft, almost as a trade: to remain in business, you had to work at it. Victoria did not make many public appearances, but photographs were doing that on her behalf, so she took them seriously. She was, in her mind, the hard-working head of a hard-working, entrepreneurial empire.[76]

The Jubilee showed that her subjects generally agreed. Victoria was exhausted, but satisfied by her day. Of course, not everyone had been pleased to see her. Letitia Whitty, six years old, refused to wave 'at that ugly woman', and another unwelcome comment came from 'a ribald voice in the crowd which shouted, "Ullo! 'Ere comes the Queen's cook!"'[77] But Victoria felt she'd lived through 'a never to be forgotten day. No one ever I believe, has met with such an ovation as was given to me, passing through those 6 miles of streets.'[78]

She was probably right. The admiration, the affection, were for the person as much as the office, for someone who'd become the nation's grandmother, and a focus for the feeling that Britain was somehow better than other countries.

And yet the Diamond Jubilee would linger on in many people's minds as both the apogee of her reign, and the beginning of its end. 'Scarlet and gold, azure and gold, purple and gold, emerald and gold . . . always blinding gold,' wrote one witness of the procession, but 'it was enough. No eye could bear more gorgeousness.'[79] There was a sense of surfeit, that the empire was a fine thing but a costly one, threatened on all sides not just by qualms about its moral mission, but also by Britain's rivals on the world stage. William Gladstone had predicted as long ago as 1878 that America would inevitably become 'what we are now, the head servant in the great household of the World, the employer of all employed'.[80] This growing sense of the ephemerality of power is perhaps the underlying but overwhelming feeling from the Diamond Jubilee. It was most powerfully expressed in a poem that Rudyard Kipling had published in *The Times* that morning.

> Far called, our navies melt away;
> On dune and headland sinks the fire:
> Lo, all our pomp of yesterday
> Is one with Nineveh and Tyre.

Victoria was not the only person to suspect that her Diamond Jubilee, for all its colourful triumph, had been, as she put it herself, her 'swan-song'.

24

Deathbed: Osborne, 22 January 1901

As the New Year of 1901 began, Victoria still slept with Albert. On his side of the bed hung a memorial wreath of china flowers, surmounting a photograph of Albert's corpse. Wherever his widow had travelled, these two items came along as well.[1] But now, at eighty-one, Victoria was too frail to leave the Isle of Wight. In fact, she could hardly leave her bedroom at Osborne House.

The last twelve months had been hard. In July 1900, her son Affie died after an unhappy marriage, the suicide of his own son and years of smoking and drinking. In October her favourite grandson, Lenchen's son Christian Victor, followed Beatrice's husband Henry in dying of malaria in Africa. The two blows almost crushed Victoria. One of her ladies, Marie Mallet, described how the queen's majesty was ebbing away. When she 'lets me stroke her dear hand', Marie wrote, 'I quite forget she is far above me and only realise she is a sorrowing woman who clings to human sympathy.'[2]

'The greatest change had taken place,' wrote someone who was shocked to find her losing weight as well as spirits; she 'had lost much flesh and had shrunk so as to appear about one half the person she had been.'[3] Victoria now had the smallest appetite of her lifetime, eating just 'a tiny slice of boiled chicken' or 'a cut from the sirloin, which is sent from London every day'.[4] As many older people do, she had grown shorter, losing three inches from her adult height. Her surviving dresses from this late period reveal adaptations to accommodate an osteoarthritic hump to the upper back. Dr Reid did not know it, for Victoria had never confided it to him, but she was still suffering from that ventral hernia, or painful stomach.[5]

Victoria found it hard, in old age, to remain engaged with the more distant branches of her enormous family. She was simply losing track. When grandchildren 'come at the rate of three a year', she admitted, 'it becomes a cause of mere anxiety . . . and of no great interest'.[6] Her grandchildren could themselves detect her lack of enthusiasm. 'I well remember Grandmama's shocked yet amused little exclamations of horror when it was reported that one or the other of us had not been good,' wrote one of them. 'I have a sort of feeling that Grandmama as well as ourselves was secretly relieved when the audience was over.'[7] But her daughters were as firmly captive as ever. 'Had a fair night,' Victoria wrote, on 13 January 1901:

> . . . but was a little wakeful. Got up earlier & had some milk. — Lenchen came & read some papers. — Out before 1, in the garden chair, Lenchen & Beatrice going with me. — Rested a little, had some food, & took a short drive with Lenchen & Beatrice. — Rested when I came in & at 5.30, went down to the Drawingroom, where a short service was held, by Mr Clement Smith, who performed it so well, & it was a great comfort to me. — Rested again afterwards, then did some signing & dictated to Lenchen.[8]

This was the very last entry in the journal that Victoria had kept for so many years. The next day she simply . . . did not write.

Those close to her could see that she was in a steep decline, with no specific cause, just old age. Yet the news of her condition was not allowed to pass beyond the estate walls of Osborne. This was partly the wish of Bertie. Unwilling, or perhaps unable, to confront reality, he chose to believe that his mother was perfectly well, and his wishes had to be respected. But even while 'all the news published from her court was calculated to cheer her people', the best-informed London gossip had it that 'a heavy cloud was darkening the sky – the Queen was failing'.[9]

Three days after that last journal entry, on 16 January 1901, Dr Reid had a novel experience. He'd seen Victoria often, sometimes four times a day, for the last twenty years of his service as her doctor. But this was the first occasion, he recorded, that he'd 'ever seen the Queen in bed'. 'She was lying on her right side,' he observed, 'all huddled up and I was struck by how small she appeared.'[10] For decades, she'd been very particular about her privacy, and not even her own children were allowed to see her unwell.

The room in which she lay, vulnerable at last to other eyes than those of her trusted dressers, was the one in Osborne's private pavilion designed all those years ago by Albert. Since 1893, Victoria had been able to ascend to her bedroom in a new lift. The room had salmon pink walls, and on its mantelpiece was the small ivory thermometer that helped her servants keep the temperature steady.[11] The lavatory, bath and shower hidden behind the door-disguised-as-a-wardrobe had been luxurious, up-to-date fittings when they were installed in the 1850s. It was a sign of the prosperity that Britain had experienced in the latter half of her reign that these were things you could now find in many well-off households.

Despite her wishes, it was going to prove difficult to keep Victoria's privacy intact. Although neither she nor Bertie wanted anyone to know of her decline, Dr Reid in fact had a private arrangement with her eldest grandson, Kaiser Willy. Willy was anxious – rightly – that his English relatives would try to stop him from being called to his grandmother's deathbed. It wasn't just that they disliked him, although that came into it; it was also a matter of international politics. Everyone sensed that Willy saw himself and the German nation as successors to his grandmother's leading role in Europe. Willy wanted some of her glamour to rub off on him. Bertie's sisters, whatever private opinions they may have held on the capabilities of their brother as a future king, knew that this was not in the best interests of Britain.

And yet, there was no denying that Willy was the queen's eldest grandson, and Dr Reid, at least, thought he had the right to be kept informed. 'Disquieting symptoms,' Reid telegraphed to Berlin from Cowes, on Friday 18 January, 'this is private.'[12] In fact, historian Tony Rennell has revealed that the German envoy in London had already picked up the gossip at a club in Pall Mall, telegraphing the previous day to warn his kaiser. On Saturday 19 January, the news could no longer be contained, and the queen's ill health was on the front page of the *Daily Express*.[13] On Sunday, prayers were said for her at St Paul's.

That same day, 20 January, a screen was brought into Victoria's bedroom at Osborne so that workmen could wheel in a small bed without seeing her or being seen. Once the little bed was prepared, she was rolled into it from the big double she'd shared with Albert, abandoning the marital bed at last.[14] As in Albert's final days, the scene was being set for a deathbed gathering. The cast were assembling too, jostling for a ringside seat at the moment of succession. Also on the Sunday, Willy commandeered a mailboat to bring him across from Flushing to Sheerness. He persevered in coming to Britain in the face of telegrams from his aunts at Osborne asking him to stay away. Bertie felt compelled to go and meet Willy's train when it arrived in London. 'I hope urgently the royal family will not get on the wrong side of the Kaiser with their usual lack of consideration,' the German Foreign Office telegraphed to their envoy in London.[15]

That Sunday night the doctors down at Osborne panicked that the queen might not survive until morning. Should they telegraph to Bertie to come from London to the Isle of Wight immediately? Intense discussion ensued, because they realised that if his mother was going to die before he arrived, it would be better if Bertie remained in the capital, in order to summon the Privy Council to begin the new reign. 'Nobody is clear,' recalled eyewitness Randall Davidson, 'for lack of any precedents within people's memory or knowledge.'[16] The queen was the only one at Osborne who had been through the death of a monarch before, and she wasn't talking.

Davidson, Victoria's old friend and confidant from Windsor

Castle, had by 1901 been promoted from Dean of Windsor to Bishop of Winchester. He'd taken a chance and rushed to the Isle of Wight upon hearing that she was ill, despite 'not exactly' having been summoned. This involved crossing to Cowes in a storm, making the passage on a late-night boat incongruously packed with journalists and a noisy 'great company of footballers'.[17] Although he was a pompous man who could sometimes take himself rather too seriously, Davidson did have a firm sense of the momentousness of what would now unfold. It drove him, usefully to historians, to record every detail both in private notes and in letters to his wife.

Davidson put down on paper the great fear, felt by many of the courtiers – and to a certain extent by Victoria herself – that there might be a long and uncertain period when she was dying but not dead. A regency, in other words. 'They will want me to give in,' she'd said a few days previously, '& to have a Regency to do my work. But they are wrong. I won't, for I know they would be doing things in my name without telling me.' Now it looked like death was near enough to avoid such a situation. 'How splendid that she should just <u>end</u> like this,' Davidson thought, 'without even putting off her armour . . . & full of all her old fire & pluck & independence.'[18] Princess Louise's husband, also attending the deathbed gathering, described the waning of the queen as rather magnificent, like 'the sinking of a great three-decker ship'.

At 1.30 in the morning of Monday 21 January, Davidson wrote to his 'beloved wife' to tell her that having arrived at Osborne, and having seen the evidence of how seriously ill the queen really was, he'd experienced 'one of the most solemn hours I am ever likely to spend in my life . . . the thoughts that rush in are overwhelming'.[19] During the course of that Monday, though, Victoria seemed to recover a little. According to the official medical bulletin issued by Dr Reid and his colleague Sir Thomas Barlow, she'd 'slightly rallied'. Sir Thomas was 'a special authority on diseases of the brain', called into attendance because Dr Reid suspected his patient had an 'obstruction in the brain circulation'.[20] The 'right side of the face' wasn't working and moving normally, which made it look like she'd had a stroke. But Barlow determined that wasn't 'an apoplexy', just a 'failure of the vessels of the brain'.[21]

By the end of Monday, both Bertie and Willy were at her bedside. They'd arrived together on the royal yacht. Characteristically, Bertie spent the journey across the Solent lounging in the saloon, while Willy occupied himself by annoying the ship's captain on the bridge. Upon reaching Osborne, Willy cleverly disarmed his aunts by his humble behaviour. 'I should like to see Grandmama before she dies,' he said, 'but if that is impossible I shall quite understand.'[22] After that, Lenchen, Louise and Beatrice did not have the heart to forbid him, so Willy wormed his way in.

Bertie's optimistic presence now changed the tone of the medical bulletins: a second hopeful one was issued, even in the face of a returned decline, shifts of emphasis closely analysed by Tony Rennell. Desperately afraid of what his mother's death meant for him, Bertie was praying that she might live as long as possible. Willy, though, had the better grasp of how the situation would play politically, and how the possibility of her lingering on inca- pacitated could damage both her legacy and the monarchy as an institution. Willy 'poured out' his views to anyone who'd listen, including Randall Davidson, saying 'what a splendid life hers had been,' and wishing that there might be no 'mean or unfitting' physical close.[23]

On 22 January, the Tuesday morning, Randall Davidson was summoned early and urgently from the house near Osborne where he'd been sleeping. Osborne's beds were all full, and there'd been no room for an uninvited guest like him. He nevertheless managed to get to Victoria's bedroom soon after eight. There he found, at the doctors' request, that 'the Family were assembling, some of them not fully dressed. They knelt round the bed, the Prince of Wales on the Queen's right, the German Emperor on her left . . . about 10 or 12 others were there. The Queen was breathing with difficulty . . . the nurse was kneeling behind her in the bed, holding up the pillows.'[24] It was an extraordinary scene. Ironically, Victoria had been determined that such a public palaver should never take place. 'That I shall insist is never the case if I am dying,' she once wrote of a similar hullabaloo at the deathbed of a Prussian relative.[25]

Gradually, as Victoria's spirit sank still further and the tension grew, the friction between Willy and his aunts was once again felt. The room was crowded, rather too much so, and occasionally some of the relatives were persuaded to take a break from watching for the death. Victoria was not fully conscious, but seemed to understand that the end was near. Louise clearly heard her mother say, 'I don't want to die yet. There are several things I want to arrange.'[26] Those present called out their names so that their mother, who was now fully blind, would know they were there – 'Lenchen, mama' – 'and Baby's here' – and 'Louise'. But no one gestured to Willy to speak.

'Wouldn't it be well to tell her that her grandson the Emperor is here too?' Dr Reid whispered to Bertie. 'No,' the answer came, 'it would excite her too much.'[27]

After this apparent climax, though, Victoria once again rallied. Dr Reid cleared the room, and the family members went off to get dressed. Now Willy saw his chance for a quiet word. 'Did you notice that everybody's name in the room was mentioned to her except mine?' he asked Dr Reid.

Dr Reid relented. He asked Bertie directly for permission to let Willy go into his grandmother's room on his own. It was granted. 'Your Majesty,' Dr Reid said to Victoria, 'your grandson the Emperor is here. He has come to see you as you are so ill.'[28] She smiled, and for five minutes they seemed to talk.

But Willy's triumph was perhaps empty. Some observers thought that Victoria, wandering in her mind, had in fact mistaken Willy for his dead father, Frederick, the greatly loved son-in-law who'd been husband to her eldest daughter Vicky. 'The Emperor is very kind,' she was heard to say, words that could have applied to the late Emperor Frederick as much as her own grandson.

Surely, if any human being had occupied her mind that afternoon as it grew dark outside, it would have been Albert. At one point,

Davidson spoke aloud the words of John Henry Newman's poem, which seemed almost unbearably appropriate:

> And with the morn those Angel voices smile,
> Which I have loved long since, and lost awhile.

One popular writer, an unauthorised insider who'd convincingly described the queen's life and homes in 1897, and whose work would soon be rushed out as a new memorial edition, believed that Victoria's fingers told the story of everything that really mattered about her. She still wore a plain gold ring of marriage, and memorial rings containing Albert's hair. 'In them,' this writer claimed, 'you will read all the homely romance of a happy wife, a fond mother, and a sorrowful but resigned widowhood, which are the greatest attributes of a good woman.'[29]

This is perhaps Queen Victoria's achievement: to have convinced her subjects that she wasn't just their queen. More importantly, she was what they believed to have been an ordinary 'good woman'. This part she played – utter theatre in some ways, but in others essentially true to her real self – might have been the magical ingredient that left the institution of the monarchy strong enough to thrive in twentieth-century Britain while crowns tumbled else-where. In this book I have questioned, sometimes undermined, the story of Victoria and Albert's endlessly, superbly, unquestionably happy marriage. But for Victoria, his charm had never failed. For her, the bewitchment of the 'angel' to whom she had proposed marriage sixty-one years previously at Windsor Castle still held strong. I hope that she did dream now of meeting him again soon, if it made her happier.

After five o'clock, there was another decline. Now Willy simply refused to budge. 'My proper place is here,' he told Randall Davidson, 'I could not be away.'[30] He remained there for two hours and more, supporting his grandmother with his one strong arm, the other having been weakened by a birth defect.[31] Davidson, who had been asked to step outside and leave off praying, was called back in, at 6.25, just in time to begin the final prayers. Those present thought that Victoria fixed her eyes upon a painting of Christ over the fireplace. Lenchen described how 'a look of radiance' appeared on her mother's face. Eyes open quite wide, she 'saw beyond the Border land and had seen and met all her loved ones'.[32]

But this is what Lenchen wanted to imagine. Others believed that the queen was not thinking of her human family at this final moment. One 'very confidential channel' revealed that her last words were to request that 'her little dog should be allowed to jump up on her bed'. Perhaps it was Turi, successor to Dash, the dog who symbolised her bold and carefree side, who was by her side and on her mind as she died.[33]

As Randall Davidson finished the blessing, Dr Reid was holding Victoria's wrist, taking her pulse, and he finally let it drop at 6.30. The queen's corpse remained supported by the arms of Dr Reid and Willy. 'At 6.30 she breathes her last,' Bertie later wrote in his diary.[34] At least he, rather than his nephew, got to close his mother's eyes.[35]

Randall Davidson now left the room and, clearly distraught, scrawled in urgent red ink that a mere twenty-five minutes previously, 'I was present at her death.'[36] The paper is extraordinary, bringing us as close as possible to witnessing the ending of a long life. She'd been in her eighty-second year, and her sixty-fourth as queen.

Outside the gates of Osborne, the gathered journalists, talking among themselves, did not at first notice Superintendent Charles Fraser, the late queen's personal detective. Fraser had been told to wait until the Lord Chancellor, the Prime Minister, the Lord Mayor of London, the Archbishop of Canterbury and the sovereigns of Europe had all received the news by telegram. But finally, in the deep January dark, Fraser stepped out to say 'Gentlemen . . . I grieve to say Her Majesty passed away at half-past six.'[37] The journalists dashed, in a crowd, for East Cowes Post Office, with an undignified amount of jostling and scrumming. One of them described his fellow hacks as a 'yelling stampede', like a fox hunt in full cry.[38] They were ravenous for statements and accounts of exactly what had happened. Randall Davidson, who was now preparing to officiate at the queen's funeral, received an unseemly telegram:

> could you greatly oblige with 1600 words on Queen Victoria by Monday Honorarium ten Guineas.

It was from the editor of *Sunday at Home*.[39]

In 1897, seeing a certain amount of confusion and disagreement when the Duchess of Teck died without having made a proper will, Victoria decided to put her own wishes on paper. She left instructions 'for my Dressers to be opened directly after my death and to be always taken about and kept by the one who may be travelling with me'.[40]

Unbeknown to her family, these instructions listed a veritable jumble-sale of items she wanted to be placed with her in her coffin. Now Dr Reid, with the help of the dressers Victoria had trusted so much, faithfully carried out her final commands. The items were so many and varied that Reid had some difficulty fitting them all in. First of all, in went a cloak and dressing gown of Albert's and a model of Albert's hand in plaster. Then came the multitude of photographs she'd requested. After that, a coffin-shaped cushion hid them from sight before her body was placed on top of it.[41] The list is intensely characteristic, revealing Victoria's love of photographs, and of Albert. It also included the man who had, to some extent, been Albert's successor. At the end of the list came a 'photo of Brown and his hair in a case', which Dr Reid wrapped in tissue paper before positioning them, as requested, in Victoria's cold left hand.[42] And later that day, before the coffin lid was screwed down, Bertie even allowed Abdul Karim to come to say goodbye.

Once the coffin was sealed, it was transported by sea and land back to London, through the capital and on to the mausoleum near Windsor, where it was placed beside Albert's. But that story is for Bertie's reign, as King Edward VII. Our twenty-four days with Queen Victoria have come to an end.

She lived a life of extraordinary privilege, experiencing great events and a magnificent lifestyle. Yet Victoria would rarely have said that she was happy, and my lasting feeling about her is pity. Many people envied her position as the winner of the Baby Race and the wearer of the crown. But when she discovered she was to be queen, Victoria already knew that it was the breaking, not the making, of her life. 'I cried much,' she said.[43] Her mother had prepared her for the lonely royal trap in which both of their lives would be lived, a trap that tightly clasped so many Victorian women but which squeezed and nipped at a queen perhaps most damagingly of all. 'You cannot <u>escape</u> your <u>own feelings</u>,' Victoire told Victoria, all those years ago, 'you cannot <u>escape</u> . . . <u>from</u> the <u>situation</u> <u>you</u> are born in'.[44] You cannot escape. It was true. You cannot escape.

Acknowledgements

I would like to acknowledge with thanks the permission given by Her Majesty Queen Elizabeth II to quote from material in the Royal Archives at Windsor. Julie Crocker and staff at the Royal Archives could not have been more welcoming and helpful. In addition, I received much-appreciated advice from Terry Wheeler of Ramsgate Historical Society; Vivienne and Hilary Crane at the Royal Glen Hotel, Sidmouth; Michael Hunter, curator of Osborne House; Brian Golding of Sidmouth Local History Group; Karin Fernald, who likes Lehzen as much as I do; Felix Lancashire at The Royal College of Physicians; Matt McNamara of the Curragh History Forums; Mario Corrigan and James Durney from the Local Studies Department of Newbridge Library, County Kildare; Daisy Hay, Claire Isaacs, Beatrice Behlen and of course from my fellow Historic Royal Palaces curators Matthew Storey, Joanna Marschner, Claudia Williams and Deirdre Murphy. It was particularly rewarding to work closely for the summer of 2017 with Matthew on our joint article about Queen Victoria's wardrobe. My entire text was read by Peter Mandler and Jane Ridley, and I am immensely grateful to both of them for saving me from many errors. In the world of publishing, I love working with Felicity Bryan and her agency, and at Hodder & Stoughton with Veronique Norton, Caitriona Horne, Juliet Brightmore and especially editor Maddy Price. For putting up with me during the writing of this particular book I would like to thank my friends Jenni Waugh, Jamie Wallace, Isla Campbell,

343

ACKNOWLEDGEMENTS

Alan Gardner and Katherine Ibbett, with apologies for my regrettable tendency towards spending my time with dead people rather than having fun with them. Finally, I dedicate my work to the best putters-up of all, Mark Hines and Ned Worsley.

Sources

Archives

Balliol College Archives
Lambeth Palace Library
Museum of London, especially former curator Kay Staniland's files,
including her transcription of the journal of Thomas Sully (1838)
The National Archives
Royal Archives
Royal College of Physicians
Royal Pharmaceutical Society
Wellcome Library

Printed

I must begin this section by gratefully acknowledging the authors
whose books listed here were particularly helpful for the relevant
chapters. Each of them would be the obvious place to turn for
more detail on that particular period of the queen's life. These
titles include Lynne Vallone's *Becoming Victoria*, New Haven and
London (2001) for Chapter 4; Katherine Hudson's *A Royal Conflict*,
London (1994) for Chapter 5; Kathryn Hughes's *Victorians Undone*,
London (2017) for Chapter 9; Helen Rappaport's *Magnificent
Obsession: Victoria, Albert and the Death that Changed the Monarchy*,

London (2011) for Chapters 13 and 17; Mark Bostridge's *Florence Nightingale: The Woman and Her Legend*, London (2008; 2009 edition) for Chapter 15; Jane Ridley's *Bertie: A Life of Edward VII*, London (2012; 2013 edition) for Chapters 17 and 18 and her *Victoria: Queen, Matriarch, Empress*, London (2015) for Chapter 20; Daisy Hay's *Mr and Mrs Disraeli: A Strange Romance*, London (2015) for Chapter 19; Kate Hubbard's *Serving Victoria*, London (2012) and A. N. Wilson's *Victoria: A Life*, London (2014) for Chapter 20; Matthew Dennison's *The Last Princess: The Devoted Life of Queen Victoria's Youngest Daughter*, London (2007) for Chapter 21; Shrabani Basu's *Victoria and Abdul*, Stroud (2010, 2011 edition) for Chapter 22; Greg King's *Twilight of Splendor*, Hoboken, N (2007) and the lecture notes on the Diamond Jubilee uploaded by film historian Luke McKernan to his personal website for Chapter 23, and Tony Rennell's *Last Days of Glory: The Death of Queen Victoria*, London (2000) for Chapter 24.

Printed sources used more generally include:

Robert C. Abrams, 'Sir James Reid and the Death of Queen Victoria', *The Gerontologist*, vol. 55, issue 6 (December 2015) pp. 943–50

Alison Adburgham, *Shops and Shopping, 1800–1914*, London (1964)

R.A.L. Agnew, 'Clark, Sir James, first baronet (1788–1870)' *Oxford Dictionary of National Biography* (2004)

Harold A. Albert, ed., *Queen Victoria's Sister: The Life and Letters of Princess Feodora*, London (1967)

W. L. Alden, *Shooting Stars as observed from the 'Sixth Column' of The Times*, New York, NY (1878)

Michael Alexander and Sushila Anand, *Queen Victoria's Maharajah*, London (1980)

Anita Anand, *Sophia: Princess, Suffragette, Revolutionary*, London (2015)

William James Anderson, *The Life of . . . Edward, Duke of Kent, illustrated by his correspondence with the De Salaberry Family*, Ottawa (1870)

Percy Andreae, trans., *Memoirs of Ernest II*, 4 vols., London (1888–90)

Anon., 'A Lady', *Anecdotes, Personal Traits, and Characteristic Sketches of Victoria*, London (1840)

Anon., 'One of the Old Brigade' [Donald Shaw], *London in the Sixties*, London (1908)

Anon., 'The Queen's Bedroom', *Woman's Life* (23 May 1896) p. 431

Anon., 'One of her Majesty's Servants', *The Private Life of Queen Victoria*, London (1897; 1901 edition)

Anon., 'Queen Victoria and the Medical Profession', *The British Medical Journal* (26 January 1901)

Anon., *New Margate, Ramsgate and Broadstairs Guide*, Margate (1821 edition)

Anon., *The Thanet Itinerary*, Margate (1823 edition)

Anon., *Isle of Thanet Illustrated Visitors' Guide*, n.p. (1887)

Anon., *Costume*, London Museum Catalogues no. 5, London (1934)

Harriet Arbuthnot, *The Journal of Mrs. Arbuthnot, 1820–1832*, London (1950)

Theo Aronson, *The Kaisers*, London (1971)

L. J. Ashford, *The History of the Borough of High Wycombe*, London (1960)

A. Aspinall, ed., *The Letters of George IV, 1812–30*, Cambridge (1938)

Walter Bagehot, *The English Constitution*, London (1867)

Julia Baird, *Victoria: The Queen*, London (2016)

Peter Bance, *The Duleep Singhs: The Photograph Album of Queen Victoria's Maharajah*, Stroud (2004)

George Barnett Smith, *Queen Victoria*, London (1887)

Paula Bartley, *Queen Victoria*, London (2016)

Shrabani Basu, *Victoria and Abdul*, Stroud (2010, 2011 edition)

Georgina Battiscombe, *Queen Alexandra,* London (1969)

G.K.A. Bell, *Randall Davidson, Archbishop of Canterbury*, Oxford (1935)

Daphne Bennet, *King Without a Crown*, Philadelphia, PA (1977)

Arthur Christopher Benson and Viscount Esher, eds., *The Letters of Queen Victoria: A Selection from Her Majesty's Correspondence Between the Years 1837 and 1861*, first series, 3 vols., London (1907, 1908 edition)

A. C. Benson, *Memories and Friends*, New York, PA (1927)

E. F. Benson, *As We Were: A Victorian Peep Show*, London (1930)

——, *King Edward VII, An Appreciation*, London (1934)

Wilfred Scawen Blunt, *My Diaries: Being a Personal Narrative of Events, 1888–1914*, New York, NY (1921)

G. C. Boase, 'Portman, Edward Berkeley, first Viscount Portland (1799–188)', revised H. C. G. Matthew, *Oxford Dictionary of National Biography* (2004)

Hector Bolitho, ed., *The Prince Consort and His Brother: Two Hundred New Letters*, London (1933)

——, ed., *Letters of Queen Victoria from the Archives of the House of Brandenburg-Prussia*, New Haven (1938)

Mark Bostridge, *Florence Nightingale: The Woman and Her Legend*, London (2008; 2009 edition)

Sarah Bradford, *Disraeli*, London (1982; 1996 edition)

Maurice V. Brett, ed., *Journals and Letters of Reginald Viscount Esher*, London (1934)

Clifford Brewer, *The Death of Kings*, London (2005 edition)

George Earle Buckle, ed., *The Letters of Queen Victoria*, second series, 3 vols., London (1926–8)

——, *The Letters of Queen Victoria*, third series, 3 vols., London (1930–2)

William Budd, 'On Intestinal Fever', *The London Lancet*, vol. 1, New York, NY (1860) pp. 387–92

Thomas Bull, *Hints to Mothers*, London (1837)

Charles Bullock, *The Early Days of Queen Victoria*, London (1887)

Charles Busson, *The Book of Ramsgate*, Buckingham (1985)

Christy Campbell, *The Maharajah's Box*, London (2000; 2001 edition)

David Cannadine, 'The British Monarchy, c.1820–1977', in Eric Hobsbawm and Terence Ranger, eds., *The Invention of Tradition*, Cambridge (1983), pp. 101–64

Miranda Carter, *The Three Emperors*, London (2009; 2010 edition)

Sarah Carter and Maria Nugent, eds., *Mistress of Everything, Queen Victoria in Indigenous Worlds*, Manchester (2016)

Caroline Chapman and Paul Raben, eds., *Debrett's Queen Victoria's Jubilees*, London (1977)

Monica Charlot, *Victoria: The Young Queen*, Oxford (1991)

Malcolm Chase, *1820: Disorder and Stability in the United Kingdom*, Manchester (2013)

Ronald Clark, *Balmoral: Queen Victoria's Highland Home*, London (1981)

J. B. Conacher, *Britain and the Crimea, 1855–56*, London (1987)

A. A. Cormack, *Two Royal Physicians*, London (1965)

Con Costello, *A Most Delightful Station*, Wilton, Co. Cork (1996; 1999 edition)

Virginia Cowles, *Edward VII and His Circle*, London (1956)

Norman Cramp, 'Regency Ramsgate' in *Thanet Panorama, A Modern Guide to the Island*, Isle of Thanet Geographical Association (n.d.)

Jean Crane, *Queen Victoria and the Royal Glen*, Exmouth (1984)

Julia Creeke, *Life and Times in Sidmouth*, Sid Vale Association (1992)

Dormer Creston, *The Youthful Queen Victoria*, London (1952)

J. Mordaunt Crook and M. H. Port, *The History of the King's Works*, vol. 6, London (1973)

Allan Cunningham, *The Life of Sir David Wilkie*, London (1843)

M. C. Curthoys 'Davys, George (1780–1864), bishop of Peterborough', *Oxford Dictionary of National Biography* (2004)

William Dalrymple and Anita Anand, *Koh-i-noor: The History of the World's Most Infamous Diamond*, London (2017)

Arthur Dasent, *John Thadeus Delane: His Life and Correspondence*, London (1908)

David Daniel Davis, *The Principles and Practice of Obstetric Medicine*, London (1836; 1841 edition)

Frances Dimond and Roger Taylor, *Crown and Camera*, Harmondsworth (1987)

Ralph Disraeli, ed., *Lord Beaconsfield's Correspondence with His Sister*, London (1886 edition)

Thomas Dixon, *Weeping Britannia*, Oxford (2015)

Martyn Downer, *The Queen's Knight*, London (2007)

David Duff, *The Shy Princess*, London (1958)

——, ed., *Victoria in the Highlands*, London (1968)

——, *Victoria Travels*, London (1970)

——, *Alexandra, Princess and Queen*, London (1980)

——, *Queen Mary*, London (1985)

Ethel M. Duff, *The Life Story of HRH The Duke of Cambridge*, London (1938)

Mountstuart Elphinstone Grant Duff, *Notes from a Diary*, London (1905)

Maria Edgeworth, *Moral Tales for Young People*, London (1910 edition)

Sarah Ellis, *The Wives of England*, London (1843)

Nina Consuelo Epton, *Victoria and Her Daughters*, New York, NY (1971)

Rowland Ernle, ed., *Life and Letters of Dean Stanley*, London (1909)

Beatrice Erskine, ed., *Twenty Years at Court: From the Correspondence of the Hon. Eleanor Stanley, 1842–1862*, London (1916)

Frank Eyck, *The Prince Consort: A Political Biography*, London (1959)

John Feltham, *A Guide to Watering and Seabathing Places*, London (1813 edition)

Lacy Fidler, 'Newspaper Representations of Queen Victoria's Agency During the Hastings Scandal and Bedchamber Crisis of 1839', MA thesis, University of Alberta (2009)

Olivia Fryman, ed., *Kensington: Palace of the Modern Monarchy*, New Haven, CT, and London (forthcoming, 2019)

Roger Fulford, *Royal Dukes: Queen Victoria's Father and 'Wicked Uncles'*, London (1948)

——, *The Prince Consort*, London (1949)

——, ed., *The Greville Memoirs*, London (1963 edition)

——, ed., *Dearest Child: Private Correspondence of Queen Victoria and the Crown Princess of Prussia, 1861–1864*, London (1964; 1981 edition)

——, ed., *Dearest Mama: Private Correspondence of Queen Victoria and the Crown Princess of Prussia, 1861–1864*, London (1968)

——, ed., *Your Dear Letter: Private Correspondence of Queen Victoria and the Crown Princess of Prussia, 1865–1871*, London (1971)

——, ed., *Darling Child: Private Correspondence of Queen Victoria and the Crown Princess of Prussia, 1871–78*, London (1976)

——, ed., *Beloved Mama: Private Correspondence of Queen Victoria and the German Crown Princess, 1878–1885*, London (1981)

John Galt, ed., *Diary Illustrative of the Times of George the Fourth, Interspersed with Original Letters from the Late Queen Caroline*, Paris (1839)

Mollie Gillen, *The Prince and His Lady*, London (1970)

Madeleine Ginsburg, 'The Young Queen and Her Clothes', *Costume*, vol. 3 (Spring 1969) pp. 39–46

Mark Girouard, *The Victorian Country House*, London and New Haven, CT, (1979; 1990 edition)

W. E. Gladstone, *Bulgarian Horrors and the Question of the East*, London (1876)

The Hon. F. Leveson Gower, ed., *Letters of Harriet, Countess Granville*, London (1893)

Annie Gray, *The Greedy Queen*, London (2017)

Abigail Green, *Moses Montefiore*, Cambridge, MA (2010)

Grace Greenwood, *Queen Victoria, Her Girlhood and Womanhood*, London (1883)

James Greenwood, *The Wren of the Curragh*, pamphlet reprinted from the *Pall Mall Gazette*, London (1867)

Charles Grey, *The Early Years of His Royal Highness the Prince Consort*, London and New York, NY (1867)

Susanne Groom and Lee Prosser, *Kew Palace*, London (2006)

Philip Guedalla, *The Queen and Mr Gladstone*, London (1933)

——, *Idylls of the Queen*, London (1937)

Janice Hadlow, *The Strangest Family*, London (2014)

Walter Phelps Hall, *Mr Gladstone*, London (1931)

Lord Frederic Hamilton, *The Days Before Yesterday*, London (1920)

Dan Harvey, *Soldiers of the Short Grass: A History of the Curragh Camp*, County Kildare (2016)

Daisy Hay, *Mr and Mrs Disraeli: A Strange Romance*, London (2015)

Benjamin Robert Haydon, *The Diary of Benjamin Robert Haydon*, Cambridge, MA (1960)

Edna Healey, *The Queen's House*, London (1997)

Olwen Hedley, *Queen Charlotte*, London (1975)

Percy Fitzgerald Hetherington, *The Good Queen Charlotte*, London (1899)

Christopher Hibbert, *The Court of St James*, London (1979)

——, *George IV*, London (1988)

——, *George III: A Personal History*, London (1998)

——, *Victoria: A Personal History*, London (2000; 2001 edition)

——, *Disraeli: A Personal History*, London (2004; 2005 edition)

James O. Hoge, ed., *The Letters of Emily Lady Tennyson*, University Park and London (1974)

Richard R. Holmes, *Queen Victoria, 1819–1901*, London (1901)

——, *Edward VII*, London (1910)

Edward Holt, *The Public and Domestic Life of His Late, Most Gracious Majesty, George III*, London (1820)

Margaret Homans, '"To the Queen's Private Apartments": Royal Family Portraiture and the Construction of Victoria's Sovereign Obedience', *Victorian Studies* vol. 37, no. 1 (1993) pp. 1–41

——, *Royal Representations, Queen Victoria and British Culture, 1837–1876*, Chicago, IL (1998)

Pamela Horn, 'Lord and Lady of the Manor: The Disraelis at Hughenden', *Records of Buckinghamshire*, vol. 51 (2011) pp. 205–13

Richard Hough, ed., *Advice to a Grand-daughter: Letters from Queen Victoria to Princess Victoria of Hesse*, New York, NY (1975)

Kate Hubbard, *Serving Victoria*, London (2012)

Katherine Hudson, *A Royal Conflict*, London (1994)

Kathryn Hughes, *Victorians Undone*, London (2017)

Robert Huish, *The Public and Private Life of George III*, London (1821)

Leigh Hunt, *The Old Court Suburb*, London (1855)

Horace G. Hutchinson, *Portraits of the Eighties*, London (1920)

Kurt Jagow, ed., *Letters of the Prince Consort, 1831–1861*, London (1938)

Robert Rhodes James, *Prince Albert*, London (1984)

Roy Jenkins, *Gladstone*, London (1995; 2002 edition)

Louis A. Jennings, ed., *The Croker Papers*, New York, NY (1884)

Clare Jerrold, *The Heart of Queen Victoria*, London (1897)

C. Rachel Jones, *Sandringham, Past and Present*, London (1888) p. 12

Jasper Tomsett Judge, *Sketches of Her Majesty's Household*, London (1848)

William Judson, *A Local Guide and Directory for the Town of High Wycombe*, High Wycombe (1875)

A. L. Kennedy, ed., *'My Dear Duchess': Social and Political Letters to the Duchess of Manchester, 1858–1869*, London (1956) p. 183

Sarah Kilby, ed., *Victoria Revealed*, London (2012)

Greg King, *Twilight of Splendor*, Hoboken, NJ (2007)

Maurice Kingsley, ed., *Charles Kingsley, His Letters and Memories*, New York, NY (1899)

John van der Kiste, *Childhood at Court, 1819–1914*, Stroud (1995)

Seth Koven, *Slumming: Sexual and Social Politics in Victorian London*, Princeton, NJ (2004)

Mary Hannah Krout, *A Looker on in London*, New York, NY (1899)

William M. Kuhn, *Henry and Mary Ponsonby*, London (2002)

Felix Lancashire, 'Royal Doctor's Diaries', blog post (2 October 2016) rcplondon.ac.uk

Jeffrey L. Lant, *Insubstantial Pageant: Ceremony and Confusion at Queen Victoria's Court*, London (1979)

Ernest Law, *Kensington Palace*, London (1899)

Arthur Gould Lee, ed., *The Empress Frederick Writes to Sophie Her Daughter*, London (1955)

Sidney Lee, *Edward VII*, n.p. (1925)

C. R. Leslie, *Autobiographical Recollections*, London (1860)

Louis Loewe, ed., *Diaries of Sir Moses and Lady Montefiore*, London (1890)

Lena Campbell Login, *Lady Login's Recollections, 1820–1904*, London (1916)

Elizabeth Longford, *Victoria R.I.*, London (1964)

——, 'Queen Victoria's Doctors', in Martin Gilbert, ed., *A Century of Conflict, 1850–1950*, London (1966) pp. 75–87

——, ed., *Darling Loosy*, London (1991)

Marquis of Lorne, *V.R.I., Her Life and Empire*, New York and London (1901)

Anabel Loyd, *Picnic Crumbs*, Clifton-upon-Teme (2012)

Mary Lutyens, ed., *Lady Lytton's Court Diary*, London (1961)

Anne M. Lyden, *A Royal Passion: Queen Victoria and Photography*, Los Angeles, CA (2014)

Philip Magnus, *King Edward the Seventh*, London (1964; 1975 edition)

Victor Mallet, ed., *Life with Queen Victoria: Marie Mallet's Letters from Court 1887–1901*, London (1968)

Marie Louise, Her Highness Princess, *My Memories of Six Reigns*, London (1956; 1979 edition)

Marie, Queen of Romania, *The Story of My Life*, New York, NY (1934)

Jonathan Marsden, ed., *Victoria & Albert: Art & Love*, London (2010)

Emma Marshall, *In Four Reigns: The Recollections of Althea Allingham, 1785–1842*, Leipzig (1887)

Robert Bernard Martin, *Enter Rumour*, London (1962)

Theodore Martin, *The Life of His Royal Highness the Prince Consort, 1819–1861*, 5 vols., London, (1875–80)

——, *Queen Victoria as I Knew Her*, London (1901)

Harriet Martineau, *Autobiography*, Boston, MA (1877)

John Matson, *Dear Osborne*, London (1978)

H.C.G. Matthew and K. D. Reynolds, 'Victoria (1819–1901)', *Oxford Dictionary of National Biography*, Oxford University Press, (2004)

Herbert Maxwell, ed., *The Creevey Papers*, London (1904)

L. J. Mayes, *Chair making in High Wycombe*, Local History Essays, High Wycombe Library Local Studies Collection, (n.d.)

Charles Meigs, *Females, Their Diseases and Remedies*, Philadelphia, PA (1848)

Wilfred Meynell, *Benjamin Disraeli: An Unconventional Biography*, London (1903)

W. F. Monypenny and G. E. Buckle, *The Life of Benjamin Disraeli*, London (1929)

F. Max Müller, ed., *Memoirs of Baron Stockmar*, London (1873)

Harriot Georgiana Mundy, ed., *The Journal of Mary Frampton*, London (1885)

Adrienne Munich, *Queen Victoria's Secrets*, New York, NY (1996)

William Munk, *The Roll of the Royal College of Physicians of London*, London (1878)

Deirdre Murphy, '"I like this poor palace": Victoria's Childhood', in Olivia Fryman, ed., *Kensington: Palace of the Modern Monarchy*, New Haven and London (forthcoming, 2019)

Michael Nelson, *Queen Victoria and the Discovery of the Riviera*, London (2007)

Michael De-la-Noy, *Windsor Castle, Past and Present*, London (1990)

Marilyn Bailey Ogilvie and Joy Dorothy Harvey, eds., *The Biographical Dictionary of Women in Science*, London (2000)

Osbert Wyrdham Hewett, ed., '. . . and Mr Fortescue', A Selection of Diaries from 1851 to 1862 of Chichestor Fortescue*, London (1958)

Maurice Paillon, *Guide-Joanne pour Lyon et ses environs*, Paris (1905)

Hannah Pakula, *An Uncommon Woman, The Empress Frederick*, New York, NY (1995; 1997 edition)

Pauline Panam, *Memoirs of a Young Greek Lady*, London (1823)

Xavier Paoli, *My Royal Clients*, London (1910)

Charles Stuart Parker, ed., *Sir Robert Peel: From His Private Papers*, London (1899 edition)

John Parker, *The Early History and Antiquities of Wycombe*, Wycombe (1878)

Hesketh Pearson, *Labby*, London (1936)

John Plunkett, *Queen Victoria, First Media Monarch*, Oxford (2003)

Arthur Ponsonby, ed., *Sir Henry Ponsonby, Queen Victoria's Private Secretary: His Life from His Letters*, London (1942)

Doris Almon Ponsonby, *The Lost Duchess: The Story of the Prince Consort's Mother*, London (1958)

Sir Frederick Ponsonby, *Side Lights on Queen Victoria*, New York, NY (1930)

Magdalen Ponsonby, ed., *Mary Ponsonby: A Memoir, Some Letters and a Journal*, London (1927)

Mary Ponsonby, 'The Character of Queen Victoria', *The Quarterly Review*, vol. 193, London (1901)

McKenzie Porter, *Overture to Victoria*, London (1961)

Frank Prochaska, *Royal Bounty: The Making of a Welfare Monarchy*, New Haven and London (1995)

Lee Prosser, 'Apartments for the Royal Family, 1790–1848', in Olivia Fryman, ed., *Kensington: Palace of the Modern Monarchy*, New Haven and London (forthcoming, 2019)

Peter Quennell, ed., *The Private Letters of Princess Lieven*, London (1937)

Helen Rappaport, *Queen Victoria: A Biographical Companion*, London (2003)

——, *Magnificent Obsession: Victoria, Albert and the Death that Changed the Monarchy*, London (2011)

Henry Reeve, ed., *The Greville Memoirs: A Journal of the Reigns of King George IV, King William IV and Queen Victoria*, London (1874 onwards)

Michaela Reid, *Ask Sir James*, London (1987)

Tony Rennell, *Last Days of Glory: The Death of Queen Victoria*, London (2000)

Eustace A. Reynolds-Ball, *Mediterranean Resorts*, London (1908)

Norman Rich, ed., *The Holstein Papers*, Cambridge (1959)

Christopher Thomas Richardson, *Fragments of History pertaining to . . . Ramsgate*, Ramsgate (1885)

Jane Ridley, *Bertie: A Life of Edward VII*, London (2012; 2013 edition)

——, *Victoria: Queen, Matriarch, Empress*, London (2015)

Andrew Roberts, *Salisbury: Victorian Titan*, London (1999)

John Robert Robinson, *The Last Earls of Barrymore, 1769–1824*, London (1894)

John Ruskin, a lecture 'Of Queens' Gardens', published in *Sesame and Lilies*, London (1865)

Thomas Ryan, *Queen Charlotte's Lying-In Hospital*, London (1885)

Giles St Aubyn, *Edward VII, Prince and King*, London (1979)

Walter Scott, *The Bride of Lammermoor*, London (1819; 1858 edition)

R. W. Seton-Watson, *Disraeli, Gladstone and the Eastern Question*, London (1935)

George Edgar Sheppard, *George, Duke of Cambridge*, London (1906)

S. Ganda Singh, 'Some Correspondence of Maharaja Duleep Singh', *Journal of Indian History*, vol. 108 (April, 1949) pp.1–23

G. Barnett Smith, *Life of Her Majesty Queen Victoria*, London (1887)

Ethel Smyth, *Streaks of Life*, London (1921)

——, *As Time Went On*, London (1936)

Ivan G. Sparkes, *Wycombe Chairmakers In Camera*, Buckingham (1989)

Sally Stafford, *Disraeli and Hughenden: Buckinghamshire: a Souvenir Guide*, The National Trust (2010)

Kay Staniland and Santina M. Levey, 'Queen Victoria's Wedding Dress and Lace', *Costume*, vol. 17 (1983) pp. 1–32

——, *In Royal Fashion*, London (1997)

W. T. Stead, *Her Majesty the Queen*, London (1887)

George Warrington Steevens, *Things Seen*, London (1900)

Richard Henry Stoddard, ed., *The Greville Memoirs*, New York, NY (1875 edition)

Benita Stoney and Heinrich Weltzien, eds., *My Mistress the Queen: The Letters of Frieda Arnold, Dresser to Queen Victoria, 1854–9*, London (1994)

Lytton Strachey, *Queen Victoria*, London (1922)

Lytton Strachey and Roger Fulford, eds., *The Greville Memoirs, 1814–1860*, London (1938)

Roy Strong, *Coronation*, London (2005)

Dorothy M. Stuart, *The Daughters of George III*, London (1939)

——, *The Mother of Victoria*, London (1942)

Lord Sudley, ed., *The Lieven-Palmerston Correspondence 1828–1856*, London (1943)

G. B. Tennyson, ed., *A Carlyle Reader*, Cambridge (1969)

Hallam Tennyson, ed., *Alfred Lord Tennyson: A Memoir*, London (1899)

Dorothy Thompson, *Queen Victoria, A Woman on the Throne*, London (1990; 2001 edition)

F.M.L. Thompson, ed., *The Cambridge Social History of Britain, 1750–1950*, Cambridge (1990)

Nathan Tidridge, *Prince Edward, Duke of Kent*, Toronto (2013)

E.E.P. Tisdall, *Queen Victoria's Private Life, 1837–1901*, London (1961)

Sarah Tooley, *The Personal Life of Queen Victoria*, New York, NY (1897)

Peter Underwood, *Queen Victoria's Other World*, London (1986)

Lynne Vallone, *Becoming Victoria*, New Haven and London (2001)

Bruce Vandervort, *Wars of Imperial Conquest in Africa, 1830–1914*, London (1998)

Queen Victoria, *Leaves from the Journal of Our Life in the Highlands, from 1848 to 1861*, London (1868)

——, *More Leaves from the Journal of a Life in the Highlands, from 1862 to 1882*, London (1885)

Mary King Waddington, *Letters of a Diplomat's Wife, 1883–1900*, New York, NY (1903)

Helen Walch, *Sandringham: A Royal Estate for 150 Years*, Norwich (2012)

Edward Walford, *Life of the Prince Consort*, London (1862)

Yvonne M. Ward, 'The womanly garb of Queen Victoria's early motherhood, 1840–42', *Women's History Review* vol. 8:2, (1999) pp. 277–94

——, *Censoring Queen Victoria*, London (2014)

Vera Watson, *A Queen at Home*, London (1952)

Stanley Weintraub, *Victoria: Biography of a Queen*, London (1987, 1988 and 1996 editions)

Gerald Wellesley, ed., *Wellington and his Friends: Letters of the first Duke of Wellington*, London (1965)

Klaus Weschenfelder, 'Prince Albert: Early Encounters with Art and Collecting', *Essays from Study Day Held at the National Gallery, 2010*, London (2012)

Henry Wheatley, ed., *The Historical and Posthumous Memoirs of Sir Nathaniel Wraxall*, London (1884)

Tyler Whittle, *Victoria and Albert at Home*, St Lucia, QLD, Australia (1980)

Kate Williams, *Becoming Queen*, London (2008)

A. N. Wilson, *Victoria: A Life*, London (2014)

Robert Wilson, *Life and Times of Queen Victoria*, London (1891–3)

The Dean of Windsor and Hector Bolitho, eds., *Letters of Lady Augusta Stanley*, London (1927)

———, *Later Letters of Augusta Stanley*, London (1929)

Cecil Woodham-Smith, *Florence Nightingale*, London (1951)

———, *Queen Victoria, Her Life and Times*, vol. 1, 1819–1861, London (1972)

Lucy Worsley, *Courtiers*, London (2010)

The Hon. Mrs Hugh Wyndham, ed., *The Correspondence of Sarah Spencer, Lady Lyttelton, 1787–1870*, London (1912)

Edmund Yates, *His Recollections and Experiences*, London (1884)

Charlotte M. Yonge, *The Victorian Half Century*, London (1887)

The Duchess of York with Benita Stoney, *Victoria and Albert: Life at Osborne House*, London (1991)

Philip Yorke, ed., *Letters of Princess Elizabeth of England*, London (1898)

Charlotte Zeepvat, *Prince Leopold*, London (1998)

Marquis of Zetland, ed., *The Letters of Disraeli to Lady Bradford and Lady Chesterfield*, 2 vols., London (1929)

Philip Ziegler, *King William IV*, London (1971)

———, *Melbourne*, London (1976)

Internet

The Royal Archives/Bodleian Library/Proquest website Queen Victoria's Journals (qvj.chadwyck.com)

Lee Jackson's Victorian London (victorianlondon.org)

Turtle Bunbury's Irish history website (turtlebunbury.com)

The blog 'Researching the House of Commons, 1832–1868' (victoriancommons.wordpress.com)

The Crimean War Research Society's website (cwrs.russianwar.co.uk)

Film historian Luke McKernan's website (lukemckernan.com)

The blog of the Royal College of Physicians blog (rcplondon.ac.uk)

Notes

Introduction

1. For example, Cecil Woodham-Smith, *Queen Victoria, Her Life and Times*, vol. 1, 1819–1861, London (1972); Monica Charlot, *Victoria: The Young Queen*, Oxford (1991); Katherine Hudson, *A Royal Conflict*, London (1994); Lynne Vallone, *Becoming Victoria*, New Haven and London (2001); Kate Williams, *Becoming Queen*, London (2008)
2. For example, Greg King, *Twilight of Splendor*, Hoboken, NJ (2007) but particularly A. N. Wilson, *Victoria: A Life*, London (2014)
3. RA VIC/MAIN/M/5/80 (2 August 1835)
4. Paula Bartley, *Queen Victoria*, Abingdon (2016) p. 10
5. Ibid., p. 64
6. Sarah Kilby, ed., *Victoria Revealed: 500 Facts about the Queen and Her World*, London (2012) pp. 146–7
7. Stanley Weintraub, *Victoria: Biography of a Queen*, London (1987) p. 643
8. E. F. Benson, *As We Were: A Victorian Peep Show*, London (1930) p. 8

1. Double Wedding: Kew Palace, 11 July 1818

1. Susanne Groom and Lee Prosser, *Kew Palace*, London (2006) p. 87
2. Philip Yorke, ed., *Letters of Princess Elizabeth of England*, London (1898) p. 88
3. The Prince of Wales: unknown, but several rumoured. Duke of Clarence: 10. Duke of Kent: 1. Duke of Sussex: 2. Princess Sophia: 1
4. Henry Wheatley, ed., *The Historical and Posthumous Memoirs of Sir Nathaniel Wraxall*, London (1884) vol. 5, p. 379
5. F. Max Müller, ed., *Memoirs of Baron Stockmar*, London (1873) vol. 1, p. 50
6. Quoted in Olwen Hedley, *Queen Charlotte*, London (1975) p. 296
7. Percy Fitzgerald Hetherington, *The Good Queen Charlotte*, London (1899) p. 255
8. RA GEO/MAIN/36817–36818, Queen Charlotte to the Prince Regent (10 April 1818)

9. RA GEO/ADD/24, Establishment of Her Majesty's Household (1817)
10. Müller, ed., (1873) vol. I, p. 50
11. Hedley (1975) p. 297; RA GEO/ADD/15/0843, R. Grenville to General de Budé (7 August 1818)
12. Dorothy M. Stuart, *The Daughters of George III*, London (1939) pp. 99–105
13. Charles Greville, quoted in the *Spectator*, vol. 163 (1939) p. 520
14. Lytton Strachey and Roger Fulford, eds., *The Greville Memoirs, 1814–1860*, London (1938) p. 272
15. Hedley (1975) p. 297
16. 'The Royal Marriages' in *The Times*, issue 10407, London (13 July 1818) p. 3
17. Quoted in Hudson (1994) p. 75
18. Philip Ziegler, *King William IV*, London (1971) p. 121
19. Charlot (1991) p. 22
20. Ziegler (1971) p. 123
21. 'The Royal Marriages' in *The Times*, issue 10407, London (13 July 1818) p. 3
22. Richard R. Holmes, *Queen Victoria, 1819–1901*, London (1901) p. 17
23. Quoted in Ziegler (1971) p. 122
24. Müller, ed. (1873) vol. I, p. 75
25. Nathan Tidridge, *Prince Edward, Duke of Kent*, Toronto (2013) p. 31
26. Müller, ed. (1873) vol. I, p. 51
27. RA GEO/MAIN/45412-3 (9 July 1790)
28. Tidridge (2013) p. 51
29. Müller, ed. (1873) vol. I, p. 76
30. Herbert Maxwell, ed., *The Creevey Papers*, London (1904) vol. I, p. 277
31. Yorke, ed. (1898) p. 70
32. John Wolcot, writing as 'Peter Pindar'
33. Christopher Hibbert, *George III*, London (1998) p. 102
34. Müller, ed. (1873) vol. I, p. 76
35. Quoted in Tidridge (2013) p. 58
36. Elizabeth Longford, 'Edward, Prince, Duke of Kent and Strathearn (1767–1820)', *Oxford Dictionary of National Biography*, Oxford University Press, (2004)
37. RA GEO/MAIN/46659 (23 November 1790)
38. Quoted in Mollie Gillen, *The Prince and His Lady*, London (1970) p. 20
39. Quoted in Tidridge (2013) p. 159
40. RA GEO/MAIN/44165 (13 December 1800)
41. Arthur Christopher Benson and Viscount Esher, eds., *The Letters of Queen Victoria: A Selection from Her Majesty's Correspondence Between the Years 1837 and 1861*, London (1907) vol. I, p. 7
42. Woodham-Smith (1972) p. 10
43. Maxwell, ed. (1904) vol. I, p. 271
44. Ibid., p. 269
45. Müller, ed. (1873) vol. I, p. 77, quoted in Dorothy M. Stuart, *The Mother of Victoria*, London (1942) p. 5
46. *The Ladies' Monthly Museum*, quoted in McKenzie Porter, *Overture to Victoria*, London (1961) p. 175
47. Anon., *Costume*, London Museum Catalogues no. 5, London (1934) pp. 151–2
48. Weintraub (1987) p. 33
49. 'The Royal Marriages' in *The Times*, issue 10407, London (13 July 1818) p. 3

50. RA GEO/ADD7/1345, account of the Duke of Kent's 'necessary arrangements for his marriage' (11 January 1819)
51. Quoted in Woodham-Smith (1972) p. 15
52. RA VIC/MAIN/M/2/25 (25 January 1818)
53. Weintraub (1987) p. 32
54. Leopold to his sister Countess Mensdorff-Pouilly, quoted in Dormer, Creston, *The Youthful Queen Victoria*, London (1952) p. 54
55. RA VIC/MAIN/M/2/68 (11 July 1818)
56. Hedley (1975) p. 293
57. RA VIC/MAIN/M/2/70 (1818)
58. Maxwell, ed. (1904) vol. 1, p. 283

2. Birth: Kensington Palace, 24 May 1819

1. RA VIC/MAIN/M/3/6 (22 June 1819)
2. Lee Prosser, 'The Duke of Kent' lecture at the Tower of London (13 January 2017), forthcoming article in *Architectural History*
3. TNA LC 9/369 fo. 131r
4. Roger Fulford, *Royal Dukes: Queen Victoria's Father and 'Wicked Uncles'*, London (1948) p. 299
5. Anon., 'A Lady', *Anecdotes, Personal Traits, and Characteristic Sketches of Victoria*, London (1840) p. 13
6. RA VIC/MAIN/M/3/3 (24 May 1819)
7. RA VIC/MAIN/M/2/43 (5 May 1818)
8. RA VIC/MAIN/M/2/43 (31 December 1818)
9. Ibid.
10. RA VIC/MAIN/Z/484/36 (1854)
11. RA GEO/ADD7/1345, account of the Duke of Kent's 'necessary arrangements for his marriage' (11 January 1819)
12. RA GEO/MAIN/1349, Duke of Kent to General Weatherall (11 January 1819)
13. RA VIC/MAIN/M3/3 (24 May 1819); Prosser, p. 217
14. RA VIC/MAIN/Y/63/47
15. RA GEO/MAIN/ADD7/1353 (29 January 1819)
16. Marilyn Bailey Ogilvie and Joy Dorothy Harvey, eds., *The Biographical Dictionary of Women in Science*, London (2000) vol. 2, p. 1193
17. David Daniel Davis, *The Principles and Practice of Obstetric Medicine*, London (1836; 1841 edition) p. xviii
18. RA GEO/MAIN/45344–5 (8 June 1819)
19. Quoted in Porter (1961) p. 175
20. *The Annual Register For the Year 1819*, London (1820) p. 35; Müller, ed. (1873) vol. 1, p. 78
21. RA VIC/MAIN/M/3/3 (24 May 1819)
22. Müller, ed. (1873) vol. 1, p. 78
23. RA VIC/MAIN/Z/484/40 (2 March 1854)
24. Woodham-Smith (1972) p. 30
25. Edward's letter, quoted in Porter (1961) p. 183

26. The Hon. Mrs Hugh Wyndham, ed., *The Correspondence of Sarah Spencer, Lady Lyttelton, 1787–1870*, London (1912) p. 64
27. Quoted in Lee Prosser, 'Apartments for the Royal Family, 1790–1848' in Olivia Fryman, ed., *Kensington: Palace of the Modern Monarchy*, New Haven and London (forthcoming, 2019)
28. Information provided by Lee Prosser, the accounts are at TNA LC 9/369, fos. 120–147
29. Kay Staniland, *In Royal Fashion*, London (1997) p. 82
30. RA VIC/MAIN/M/3/3 (24 May 1819)
31. *The Times*, London (26 May 1819) p. 3
32. RA VIC/MAIN/M/3/3 (24 May 1819)
33. The Hon. F. Leveson Gower, ed., *Letters of Harriet, Countess Granville*, London (1893) p. 169
34. Sarah Tooley, *The Personal Life of Queen Victoria*, New York, NY (1897) p. 8
35. RA VIC/MAIN/M/3/5 (22 June 1819)
36. RA VIC/M/4/26

3. Wet Feet: Sidmouth, 23 January 1820

1. Malcolm Chase, *1820: Disorder and Stability in the United Kingdom*, Manchester (2013) p. 10
2. Ibid., p. 9
3. Emma Marshall, *In Four Reigns: the Recollections of Althea Allingham, 1785–1842*, Leipzig (1887) p. 228
4. RA VIC/MAIN/Z/286 (7 January 1820)
5. Marshall (1887) p. 229
6. Ibid., p. 225
7. Ibid., (1887) p. 225
8. A print of the drawing room is reproduced in Jean Crane, *Queen Victoria and the Royal Glen*, Exmouth (1986) p. 37
9. RA VIC/MAIN/Z/286 (15 January 1820)
10. A. Aspinall, ed., *The Letters of George IV, 1812–30*, Cambridge (1938) vol. 2, p. 304
11. Müller, ed. (1873) vol. 1, p. 77
12. For example, TNA WORKS 19/16/1/29, Edward, Duke of Kent, Kensington Palace (30 July 1815)
13. Marquis of Lorne, *V.R.I., Her Life and Empire*, New York and London (1901) p. 13
14. RA VIC/MAIN/M/3/20 (19 November 1819)
15. Crane (1986) p. 13; John Feltham, *A Guide to Watering and Seabathing Places*, London (1813 edition) p. 365, (1824 edition) p. 374
16. Julia Creeke, *Life and Times in Sidmouth*, Sid Vale Association (1992) p. 39
17. RA GEO/ADD7/1345, account of the Duke of Kent's 'necessary arrangements for his marriage' (11 January 1819)
18. RA GEO/MAIN/45391–2 (6 January 1820)
19. Quoted in William James Anderson, *The Life of . . . Edward, Duke of Kent, illustrated by his correspondence with the De Salaberry Family*, Ottawa (1870) p. 233
20. RA VIC/MAIN/Z/286 (7, 11 January 1820)

21. RA VIC/MAIN/M/3/3 (24 May 1819)
22. RA VIC/MAIN/Z/286 (7 January 1820)
23. Balliol College Conroy Papers 14B+.5 (an account of Sir John Conroy's background)
24. Anderson (1870) p. 284
25. Quoted in Hibbert (2000; 2001 edition) p. 14
26. Müller, ed. (1873) vol. 1, p. 78
27. 'Item Description: Woolbrook Cottage, [Sidmouth,] 10 January, 1820. 'Captain Conroy is commanded by Their Royal Highnesses . . . to Invite Mr. Mrs. and Miss le Merchant to Tea, on Friday evening next.' Offered for sale on Abebooks.co.uk, 17 November 2016.
28. RA VIC/MAIN/Z/286 (10 January 1820)
29. Anon., *The Annual Register For the Year 1820*, London (1821) p. 6
30. Robert Huish, *The Public and Private Life of George III*, London (1821) p. 700
31. RA VIC/MAIN/Z/286 (11–12 January 1820)
32. Harold A. Albert, ed., *Queen Victoria's Sister: The Life and Letters of Princess Feodora*, London (1967) p. 34
33. RA VIC/MAIN/Z/286 (16 January 1820)
34. RA VIC/MAIN/Z/286 (19 January 1820)
35. Louis A. Jennings, ed., *The Croker Papers*, New York, NY (1884) vol. 1, p. 141
36. RA GEO/ADD12/359, Princess Mary to the Prince Regent (25 January 1820)
37. *The Annual Register For the Year 1820*, London (1821) p. 82
38. See Gillian Gill, *We Two*, New York, NY (2009) pp. 38–9
39. Müller, ed. (1873) vol. 1, p. 79
40. Benson and Esher, eds. (1907, 1908 edition) vol. 1, p. 9
41. Marshall (1887) p. 229
42. Holmes (1901) p. 19
43. Albert, ed. (1967) p. 34
44. Creeke (1992) p. 40
45. RA GEO/MAIN/46640 (1820)
46. Creeke (1992) p. 40
47. Balliol College Archives Conroy Papers 11 [6F] memorandum of Edward Conroy
48. RA VIC/MAIN/Z/286 (1 February 1820)
49. Benson and Esher, eds. (1911 edition) vol. 1, p. 258
50. RA VIC/MAIN/Z/286 (10 February 1820)
51. Quoted in Hudson (1994) p. 127

4. 'I will be good': Kensington Palace, 11 March 1830

1. Leigh Hunt, *The Old Court Suburb*, London (1855) vol. 2, p. 195
2. Benson and Esher, eds. (1907, 1908 edition) vol. 1, p. 14
3. RA VIC/MAIN/Y/36/132 (15 April 1843)
4. Charles Bullock, *The Early Days of Queen Victoria*, London (1887) p. 11
5. G.K.A. Bell, *Randall Davidson, Archbishop of Canterbury*, Oxford (1935) p. 1045
6. Melbourne described her so, Hudson (1994) p. 18
7. Quoted in Hudson (1994) p. 64
8. RA VIC/MAIN/Y/203/79 (6 September 1867)

9. Ibid.

10. Benson and Esher, eds. (1907; 1908 edition) vol. 1, p. 10

11. The story can be traced back to Victoria's daughter Lenchen, who told Lord Esher. Michael De-la-Noy, *Windsor Castle, Past and Present*, London (1990) p. 101

12. RA VIC/MAIN/Y/203/79 (6 September 1867)

13. Gower, ed., (1893) p. 169

14. Rev. G. Davys' diary (28 May 1823), quoted in Lorne (1901) p. 55

15. RA VIC/MAIN/3/6 (22/23 June 1819), translated in Woodham-Smith (1972) p. 33

16. Quoted in Staniland (1997) p. 85

17. Ibid, p. 86

18. John Galt, ed., *Diary Illustrative of the Times of George the Fourth, Interspersed with Original Letters from the Late Queen Caroline*, Paris (1839) p. 53

19. Marquis of Zetland, ed., *The Letters of Disraeli to Lady Bradford and Lady Chesterfield*, New York, NY, (1929) vol. 1, pp. 404–5

20. TNA WORKS 19/16/1/163 (1 December 1837); Deirdre Murphy, '"I like this poor palace": Victoria's Childhood', in Olivia Fryman, (forthcoming 2019)

21. RA VIC ADDO/57/B (1823)

22. Benson and Esher, eds. (1907; 1908 edition) p. 13

23. Quoted in Annie Gray *The Greedy Queen*, London (2017) p. 24

24. Ibid., p. 26

25. RA VIC/MAIN/ADDA/7/1a

26. Richard Henry Stoddard, ed., *The Greville Memoirs*, New York, NY (1875 edition) vol. 2, p. 220

27. Quoted in Kate Hubbard, *Serving Victoria*, London (2012) p. 26

28. Hunt (1855) vol. 2, p. 264

29. Quoted in Woodham-Smith (1972) p. 75

30. RA VIC/MAIN/Z/111

31. Rev. G. Davys' diary (17 April 1823), quoted in Lorne (1901) p. 53

32. 'The Queen's Minute' (1897), quoted in Arthur Ponsonby, ed., *Sir Henry Ponsonby, Queen Victoria's Private Secretary*, London (1942) p. 51

33. Anon., 'One of Her Majesty's Servants', *The Private Life of Queen Victoria*, London (1897; 1901 edition) p. 22

34. Tooley (1897) p. 31

35. Quoted in De-la-Noy (1990) p. 84

36. Written by Victoria in the margin of RA VIC/MAIN/Y/203/81 (2 December 1867)

37. RA VIC/MAIN/QVJ/1838: 22 March

38. Quoted in Ponsonby (1942) p. 85

39. Hudson (1994) pp. 11, 86

40. Duchess of Kent to Conroy (26 December 1838), quoted in Hudson (1994) p. 16

41. RA VIC/MAIN/Z/484/36/10 (18 February 1854)

42. Sir John Conroy to Edward Conroy (9 March 1848), quoted in Hudson (1994) p. 17

43. RA QVJ/1870: 12 September

44. Hanmer Papers, quoted in Hudson (1994) p. 19

45. Lord Holland, quoted in Edna Healey, *The Queen's House*, London (1997) p. 121; RA QVJ/1838: 3 February
46. Maria Edgeworth, *Moral Tales for Young People*, London (1910 edition) pp. 351–2
47. Jennings, ed. (1884) vol. I, pp. 155–6, Mr Peel to Mr Croker (23 March 1820)
48. Quoted in Woodham-Smith (1972) pp. 86–7
49. Ethel M. Duff, *The Life Story of HRH The Duke of Cambridge*, London (1938) p. 108
50. Benson and Esher, eds. (1907, 1908 edition) vol. I, p. 10
51. Tooley (1897) p. 31
52. Randall Davidson in Bell (1935) vol. I, p. 83
53. M.C. Curthoys 'Davys, George (1780–1864) bishop of Peterborough', *Oxford Dictionary of National Biography (2004)*
54. Tooley (1897) p. 20
55. RA VIC/MAIN/Z/111
56. Benson and Esher, eds. (1907, 1908 edition) vol. I, p. 256
57. Weintraub (1987) p. 77
58. Mary Ponsonby, 'The Character of Queen Victoria', *The Quarterly Review*, London (1901)
59. Tooley (1897) p. 52, letter of Baroness Lehzen (May 1831)
60. Kilby, ed., (2012) p. 25
61. See annotation to RA VIC/MAIN/M/5/8; Vallone (2001) p. 44
62. Tooley (1897) p. 37
63. RA VIC/MAIN/M/2/8 (10–11 March 1830)
64. RA VIC/MAIN/Y/203/81 (2 December 1867)
65. Ibid.
66. RA/VIC/MAIN/2/8 (10–11 March 1830)
67. RA VIC/MAIN/5/9/28, Duchess of Kent to the Bishop of London (13 March 1830)

5. The Three Missing Weeks: Ramsgate, October 1835

1. Anon., *The Thanet Itinerary*, Margate (1823 edition) p. 69
2. Anon., *New Margate, Ramsgate and Broadstairs Guide*, Margate (1821 edition) p. 42
3. Anon., *The Thanet Itinerary*, Margate (1823 edition) p. 57
4. Louis Loewe, ed., *Diaries of Sir Moses and Lady Montefiore*, London (1890) vol. I, p. 96; Abigail Green, *Moses Montefiore*, Cambridge, MA (2010) p. 105
5. Quoted in Hudson (1994) p. 93
6. RA VIC/Y/63/5 (7 October 1836); Vallone (2001) p. 14
7. Quoted in Woodham-Smith (1972) p. 63
8. RA VIC/MAIN/Z/485/6, pp. 13, 17 (September 1878)
9. Royal College of Physicians, MS 4973, journal and reminiscences of Dr Ferguson, p. 12
10. RA VIC/MAIN/5/78 (30 July 1835)
11. Balliol College Archives Conroy 11 [6F] memorandum of Edward Conroy
12. Anon., *The Annual Register For the Year 1835*, London (1836) p. 136
13. Vallone (2001) p. 157
14. Ibid., pp. 156–7; 218

15. RA QVJ/1835: 22 September
16. RA QVJ/1835: 25 September
17. RA VIC/MAIN/5/9/84 (2 September 1835)
18. Royal College of Physicians, MS 4973, p.2
19. RA VIC/MAIN/5/9/84 (2 September 1835)
20. RA QVJ/1835: 29 September
21. Robert Edward Hunter, *A Short Account of the Isle of Thanet*, Ramsgate (1815) p. 39
22. Anon., *The Thanet Itinerary*, Margate (1823 edition) p. 64
23. James Jones, *Isle of Thanet Guide* (n.d.), quoted in *The Ramsgate Millennium Book*, The Ramsgate Society (2000) p. 46
24. A nameless contributor to *Fraser's Magazine* (1823), quoted in *The Ramsgate Millennium Book*, The Ramsgate Society (2000) p. 544
25. Charles Busson, *The Boot of Ramsgate*, Buckingham (1985) p. 133
26. Ibid., p. 66
27. 'Map of the Town and Royal Harbour of RAMSGATE From an actual Survey made in the Year 1849', reproduced in *The Ramsgate Millennium Book*, The Ramsgate Society (2000) p. 8.1.5
28. Anon., *Isle of Thanet Illustrated Visitors' Guide*, n.p. (1887) p. 40
29. RA QVJ/1832: 1 August
30. Benson and Esher, eds. (1907, 1908 edition) vol. 1, p. 11
31. Albert, ed., (1967) p. 40
32. Christopher Thomas Richardson, *Fragments of History pertaining to . . . Ramsgate*, Ramsgate (1885, 1999 edition) p. 18
33. RA VIC/ADDA/11/22, Baroness Lehzen to King Leopold (n.d.)
34. RA QVJ/1835: 18 September
35. Notebook belonging to Dr William Mason quoted in Gray (2017) p. 27
36. Gower, ed. (1893) p. 169
37. Maxwell, ed. (1904–5) vol. 2, p. 326; *Private Life* (1897; 1901 edition) p. 140
38. Quoted in Woodham-Smith (1972) p. 92
39. Gray (2017) p. 28
40. RA VIC/ADDA/11/22, Baroness Lehzen to King Leopold (n.d.)
41. Hunter, (1815) p. 2
42. RA QVJ/1835: 4 October
43. Benson and Esher, eds. (1907, 1908 edition) vol. 1, p. 72
44. RA VIC/MAIN/Z/482/1, John Conroy to the Duchess of Kent (15 July 1837)
45. RA VIC/ADDA/11/22, Baroness Lehzen to King Leopold (n.d.)
46. RA QVJ/1835: 7 October
47. R. A. L. Agnew, 'Clark, Sir James, first baronet (1788–1870)' in *Oxford Dictionary of National Biography* (2004) (accessed 2 June 2017)
48. A. A. Cormack, *Two Royal Physicians*, London (1965) p. 17
49. RA VIC/ADDA/11/22, Baroness Lehzen to King Leopold (n.d.)
50. Quoted in Hudson (1994) p. 106
51. RA VIC/ADDA/11/22, Baroness Lehzen to King Leopold (n.d.)
52. RA QVJ/1838: 26 February
53. RA VIC/MAIN/Z/485/11 (15 November 1879)
54. RA QVJ/1838: 26 February
55. Quoted in Woodham-Smith (1972) p. 70

56. RA VIC/MAIN/Y/65/37, Leopold to Victoria (12 March 1839)
57. RA VIC/MAIN/4/16 (12 January 1830)
58. RA VIC/ADDA/11/22, Baroness Lehzen to King Leopold (n.d.)
59. Ibid.
60. *Kentish Gazette* (14 October 1834) (14 November 1837), England, Wales & Scotland Census (1851)
61. RA VIC/ADDA/11/22, Baroness Lehzen to King Leopold (n.d.)
62. RA QVJ/1835: 31 October
63. RA QVJ/1838: 17 October
64. RA QVJ/1835: 31 October
65. RA VIC/MAIN/Y/88/4 (3 November 1835)
66. Walter Scott, *The Bride of Lammermoor*, London (1819; 1858 edition) p. 5
67. Warner (1979) p. 68
68. Balliol College Conroy Papers 11 [6F] Edward Conroy's memorandum
69. Quoted in Hudson* (1994) p. 83
70. RA VIC/ADDA/11/2 (1 May 1836)
71. Royal College of Physicians, MS 4973, pp. 6, 12
72. RA QVJ/1838: 17 October
73. RA VIC/ADDA/12, part three (8–13 June 1837)
74. Lady Elizabeth Grosvenor, quoted in Weintraub (1987) p. 69

6. Albert: Kensington Palace, 18 May 1836

1. RA QVJ/1836: 18 May
2. Deirdre Murphy, '"I like this poor palace": Victoria's Childhood', in Fryman, ed., (forthcoming, 2019)
3. Ibid.
4. RA VIC/MAIN/Y/88/33 (14 March 1837)
5. Sir John Conroy to Lord Durham (6 February 1836), quoted in Hudson (1994) p. 114
6. TNA WORKS 19/16/1/655, 'Kensington Palace Inventory' (18 February 1862)
7. RA VIC/MAIN/5/9/86, James Clark (29 January 1836)
8. RA QVJ/1837: 24 May
9. Quoted in Hudson (1994) p. 114
10. Ibid., p. 114; Anon., 'A Lady', *Anecdotes, Personal Traits, and Characteristic Sketches of Victoria*, London (1840) p. 472
11. Thomas Sully, *Journal* (22 March 1838), transcribed in Kay Staniland files, Museum of London (consulted August 2017)
12. Edward Boykin, ed., *Victoria, Albert and Mrs Stevenson*, New York, NY (1957) p. 57
13. Gray (2017) p. 40
14. Sully (22 March 1838)
15. Boykin, ed. (1957) p. 104
16. Ibid; Maxwell, ed. (1904–5) vol. 2, p. 326
17. E.E.P. Tisdall, *Queen Victoria's Private Life, 1837–1901*, London (1961) p. 15
18. Henry Reeve, ed., *The Greville Memoirs*, London (1896 edition) vol. 4, p. 81
19. Boykin, ed. (1957), p. 57

20. Benson and Esher, eds. (1907, 1908 edition) vol. 2, p. 49
21. Staniland (1997) p. 92
22. Scott (1819; 1858 edition) p. 368
23. RA QVJ/1836: 1 November
24. Benson and Esher, eds. (1907, 1908 edition) vol. 1, pp. 48–9
25. Charles Grey, *The Early Years of the His Royal Highness the Prince Consort*, London and New York, NY (1867) p. 90
26. Doris Almon Ponsonby, *The Lost Duchess: The Story of the Prince Consort's Mother*, (London, 1958) p. 151
27. Arthur Gould Lee, ed., *The Empress Frederick Writes to Sophie, Her Daughter*, London (1955) pp. 199–200
28. Klaus Weschenfelder, 'Prince Albert: Early Encounters with Art and Collecting', *Essays from Study Day Held at the National Gallery, 2010*, London (2012) pp. 12, 7
29. Benson and Esher, eds. (1907, 1908 edition) vol. 1, p. 49
30. Quoted in Theodore Martin, *The Life of His Royal Highness the Prince Consort 1819–1861*, London (1875; 1879 edition) vol. 1, p. 2
31. Quoted in Martin (1875; 1879 edition) vol. 1 pp. 2–3
32. RA QVJ/1836: 18 May
33. Grey (1867) p. 90
34. RA QVJ/1836: 23 May
35. RA QVJ/1836: 24 May
36. Percy Andreae, trans., *Memoirs of Ernest II*, London (1880) vol. 1 p. 69
37. Müller, ed. (1873) vol. 2, p. 7
38. RA VIC/MAIN/Y/34/51 (16 April 1836)
39. RA QVJ/1836: 10 June
40. RA VIC/MAIN/M/4/55, Palmerston to Conroy (13 May 1836)
41. RA VIC/MAIN/M/4/57, Albert's notes on a memorandum of Charles of Leiningen
42. RA QVJ/1836: 10 June
43. RA VIC/MAIN/M/4/57
44. RA VIC/MAIN/M/4/57, memorandum of Charles of Leiningen, translated in Woodham-Smith (1972) p. 116
45. Quoted in Woodham-Smith (1972) p. 122
46. Benson and Esher, eds. (1907 1908 edition) vol. 1, p. 49
47. RA VIC/MAIN/QVLB/24 January 1838

7. Accession: Kensington Palace, 20 June 1837

1. Lorne (1901) p. 61
2. *Private Life* (1897; 1901 edition) p. 153
3. RA VIC/MAIN/Z/294, fo. 3r
4. RA QVJ/1836: 13 January
5. RA QVJ/1837: 24 May
6. Lord Palmerston (26 May 1837), quoted in Christopher Hibbert, *Victoria*, London (2000; 2001 edition) p. 50.
7. W. F. Monypenny and G. E. Buckle, *The Life of Benjamin Disraeli*, London (1910) vol. 1, p. 370

8. Quoted in Ziegler (1971) p. 289; Clifford Brewer, *The Death of Kings*, London (2005 edition) pp. 238–9
9. RA ADDA/11/12 (8–13 June 1837), translated in Woodham-Smith (1972) p. 136
10. Benson and Esher, eds. (1907, 1908 edition) vol. 1, p. 72
11. RA VIC/ADDA/15 (16 June 1837)
12. RA VIC/MAIN/M/4/57, memorandum of Charles of Leiningen, translated in Woodham-Smith (1972) p. 137
13. Quoted in Hudson (1994) p. 130
14. TNA PRO 30/29/423, Palmerston to Granville (26 May 1837)
15. RA VIC/MAIN/M/7/67, memorandum of Charles of Leiningen, translated in Hudson (1994) p. 121
16. Benson and Esher, eds. (1907, 1908 edition) vol. 1, p. 70
17. RA QVJ/1837: 19 May
18. RA VIC/MAIN/Z/294, fo. 3v
19. Ibid, fo. 3r–v
20. Woodham-Smith (1972) p. 138
21. RA VIC/MAIN/Z/294, fo. 3v
22. Tooley (1897) pp. 70–2. The evidence given by Dean Stanley records that the duchess advised that her daughter must go in alone, rather than, as some historians have said, Victoria ordering her mother to remain behind
23. Anon., *The Annual Register and Chronicle for the Year 1837*, London (1838) p. 61
24. Tooley (1897) pp. 70–2
25. Peter Quennell, ed., *The Private Letters of Princess Lieven*, London (1937) p. 200
26. Tooley (1897) p. 72
27. Thomas Dixon, *Weeping Britannia*, Oxford (2015) pp. 177–9
28. Theodore Martin, *Queen Victoria as I Knew Her*, London (1901) p. 65
29. RA VIC/MAIN/QVLB/19 June 1837
30. Anon., *The Annual Register and Chronicle for the Year 1837*, London (1838) p. 65
31. Benson and Esher, eds. (1911 edition) vol. 1, p. 72
32. RA VIC/MAIN/QVLB/20 June 1837
33. Sir John Clark, Sir James Clark's son, made this claim; Elizabeth Longford, 'Queen Victoria's Doctors', in Martin Gilbert, ed., *A Century of Conflict, 1850–1950*, London (1966) p. 84
34. Philip Ziegler, *Melbourne,* London (1976) p. 123
35. RA QVJ/1838: 30 December
36. RA QVJ/1837: 20 May
37. Anon., *The Annual Register and Chronicle for the Year 1837*, London (1838) p. 63
38. Reeve, ed. (1899 edition) vol. 3, p. 415
39. Quoted in Bartley (2016) p. 42
40. Tooley (1897) pp. 70–2
41. De-la-Noy (1990) p. 101
42. Barratt (2000) p. 45, quoted in Gray (2017) p. 279
43. Eyewitness Barrett Lennard, quoted in Ernest Law, *Kensington Palace*, London (1899) p. 37; Allan Cunningham, *The Life of Sir David Wilkie*, London (1843) p. 229
44. Anon., *The Annual Register and Chronicle for the Year 1837*, London (1838) p. 63
45. Quoted in John Plunkett, *Queen Victoria, First Media Monarch*, Oxford (2003) p. 89
46. Deirdre Murphy, '"I like this poor palace": Victoria's childhood', in Fryman, ed., (forthcoming, 2019)

47. Reeve, ed. (1899 edition) vol. 3, p. 415
48. Marshall (1887) p. 301
49. Reeve, ed. (1899 edition) vol. 3, p. 415
50. Quoted in Woodham-Smith (1972) p. 140
51. Anon., *The Annual Register and Chronicle for the Year 1837*, London (1838) p. 63
52. Law, (1899) p. 37
53. Vernon Bogdanor, *Gresham College History Lecture* (20 September 2016)
54. RA VIC/MAIN/4/28 (23 April 1831)
55. Cunningham, (1843) p. 229
56. The Bishop of London, quoted in Lorne (1901) p. 67
57. RA VIC/MAIN/M/7/68, memorandum of Baron Stockmar (1847); RA MP/116/89, memorandum of Sir John Conroy
58. RA VIC/MAIN/M/7/68, memorandum of Baron Stockmar (1847)
59. RA VIC/ADDA/11/4 Stockmar to Leopold (3 April 1837), translated in Woodham-Smith (1972) p. 131
60. RA QVJ/1837: 20 May
61. RA VIC/MAIN/Z/294, fo. 3r
62. RA VIC/MAIN/Z/294, fo. 3v
63. RA QVJ/1839: 8 January
64. Quoted in Vallone (2001) p. 199
65. RA QVJ/1837: 20 May
66. Adrienne Munich, *Queen Victoria's Secrets*, New York, NY (1996) p. 16
67. Reeve, ed. (1896 edition) vol. 4, pp. 16–17

8. Coronation: Buckingham Palace, 28 June 1838

1. RA QVJ/1838: 28 June
2. Lady Wilhelmina Stanhope, quoted in Lorne (1901) p. 82
3. Staniland (1997) p. 114
4. *Private Life* (1897; 1901 edition) p. 62
5. Plunkett (2003) pp. 18–19
6. *Caledonian Mercury* (1 July 1837) p. 5, quoted in Bartley (2016) p. 39
7. Benson and Esher, eds. (1907, 1908 edition) vol. 1, p. 86
8. Ibid., p. 106
9. Ibid., p. 115
10. Anon., *The Annual Register For the Year 1838*, London (1838) p. 135
11. Charlot (1991) p. 115
12. Weintraub (1987) pp. 112, 650
13. Reeve, ed. (1896 edition) vol. 4, p. 113; Plunkett (2003) p. 23
14. Anon., *The Annual Register For the Year 1838*, London (1838) p. 96
15. Harriot Georgiana Mundy, ed., *The Journal of Mary Frampton*, London (1885) p. 404
16. Ibid., pp. 404–5
17. Anon., *The Annual Register For the Year 1838*, London (1838) pp. 96–7
18. RA QVJ/1838: 28 June
19. Roy Strong, *Coronation*, London (2005) p. 406
20. Mundy, ed., (1885) p. 406
21. Ibid., pp. 407–8

22. Anon., *The Annual Register For the Year 1838*, London (1838) p. 97
23. Felix Mendelssohn, quoted in Charlotte M. Yonge, *The Victorian Half Century*, London (1887) p. 9
24. RA QVJ/1838: 28 June
25. Yonge (1887) p. 9
26. Ibid.
27. Lord Beaconsfield's letters, published in *New Outlook*, New York, NY (1886) vol. 33, p. 24; Rix (2013)
28. TNA LC 2/67, pp. 23–4
29. Lady Wilhelmina Stanhope, quoted in Lorne (1901) p. 82
30. RA QVJ/1838: 28 June
31. Grace Greenwood, *Queen Victoria, Her Girlhood and Womanhood*, London (1883) p. 117
32. Ralph Disraeli, ed., *Lord Beaconsfield's Correspondence with His Sister*, London (1886 edition) p. 109
33. RA QVJ/1838: 28 June
34. Lady Wilhelmina Stanhope, quoted in Lorne (1901) p. 82
35. RA QVJ/1838: 28 June
36. Quoted in Yonge (1887) pp. 10–11
37. C. R. Leslie, *Autobiographical Recollections*, London (1860) vol. 2, p. 239
38. Quoted in Yonge (1887) pp. 10–11
39. Warner (1979) p. 84
40. Quoted in Yonge (1887) pp. 10–11
41. RA QVJ/1838: 28 June
42. Benjamin Robert Haydon, *The Diary of Benjamin Robert Haydon*, Cambridge, MA (1960) p. 350
43. Strong (2005) p. 381
44. Kilby, ed. (2012) p. 35
45. TNA LC 2/67, p. 66
46. Reeve, ed., (1896 edition) vol. 4, pp. 111–12
47. Lady Wilhelmina Stanhope, quoted in Lorne (1901) pp. 83–4
48. TNA LC 2/68 (22 June 1838)
49. RA QVJ/1838: 28
50. Mundy, ed., (1885) p. 408
51. Ibid.
52. Harriet Martineau, *Autobiography*, Boston, MA (1877) p. 422
53. RA QVJ/1838: 28 June
54. TNA LC 2/68 'Coronation of Her Most Sacred Majesty'
55. Newspaper account, quoted by Kathryn Rix, blog post, 'MPs and Queen Victoria's Coronation' victoriancommons.wordpress.com/2013/06/28_
56. Rix (2013)
57. Quoted in Yonge (1887) pp. 10–11
58. RA QVJ/1838: 28 June
59. Balliol College Conroy Papers 14.B.A.(a).10, Basil Hall to Sir John Conroy (29 June 1838)
60. Lady Wilhelmina Stanhope, quoted in Lorne (1901) pp. 83–4
61. Lord Beaconsfield's letters, published in *New Outlook*, New York, NY (1886) vol. 33, p. 24

62. RA QVJ/1838: 28 June
63. Anabel Loyd, *Picnic Crumbs*, Clifton-upon-Teme (2012)
64. Martineau (1877) pp. 421–3
65. RA QVJ/1838: 28 June
66. Leslie, (1860) vol. 2, p. 239
67. Reeve, ed. (1896 edition) vol. 4, p. 22
68. RA QVJ/1838: 28 June
69. Quoted in Strong (2005) p. 417
70. Martineau (1877) pp. 421, 424
71. F. M. Mallalieu, 'The Coronation', *The Times* (28 June 1838)
72. Anon., *The Annual Register For the Year 1838*, London (1838) p. 107
73. Plunkett (2003) p. 68
74. Ibid., p. 70

9. In Lady Flora's Bedchamber: Buckingham Palace, 27 June 1839

1. Sully (22 March 1838)
2. Benita Stoney and Heinrich Weltzien, eds., *My Mistress the Queen: The Letters of Frieda Arnold, Dresser to Queen Victoria, 1854–9*, London (1994) p. 52
3. Ibid., p. 51
4. Jasper Tomsett Judge, *Sketches of Her Majesty's Household*, London (1848) p. 97
5. Sully (22 March 1838)
6. Stoney and Weltzien, eds. (1994) p. 52
7. J. Mordaunt Crook and M. H. Port, *The History of the King's Works*, vol. 6, London (1973) p. 274
8. Ibid., p. 287
9. Ibid., p. 290
10. Judge (1848) p. 62
11. Crook and Port (1973) vol. 6, p. 376
12. Boykin, ed. (1957) p. 83
13. RA QVJ/1839: 25–27 June
14. Crook and Port (1973) vol. 6, p. 287
15. Martin (1962) p. 67
16. RA QVJ/1839: 25–27 June
17. RA MRH/MRHF/MENUS/MAIN/BP/1839 (28 June 1839)
18. RA QVJ/1839: 25–27 June
19. Martin (1962) p. 67
20. *The Age* (7 July 1839), quoted in Martin (1962) p. 67
21. RA QVJ/1839: 18 March
22. *The Chronicle*, quoted in Martin (1962) p. 70
23. *Morning Post* (4 July 1839), quoted in Lacy Fidler, 'Newspaper Representations of Queen Victoria's Agency During the Hastings Scandal and Bedchamber Crisis of 1839', MA thesis, University of Alberta (2009) p. 90
24. RA QVJ/1839: 16 May
25. Reeve, ed. (1896 edition) vol. 4, p. 23
26. Ziegler (1976) p. 106
27. Reeve, ed. (1896 edition) vol. 4, p. 136

28. RA QVJ/1837: 3 October
29. RA QVJ/1838: 4 September
30. Roger Fulford, ed., *The Greville Memoirs*, London (1963 edition) p. 156
31. RA VIC/MAIN/M/7/65, Duchess of Kent to Victoria (n.d., June 1837)
32. RA QVJ/1838: 20 February
33. RA VIC/ADDV/2, translation of VIC/ADDA/14/66 (6 March 1838)
34. Woodham-Smith (1972) p. 161
35. RA QVJ/1839: 25–27 June
36. Quoted in Robert Bernard Martin, *Enter Rumour*, London (1962) p. 49
37. RA QVJ/1839: 25–27 June
38. Quoted in Woodham-Smith (1972) p. 162
39. Wyndham, ed. (1912) p. 285
40. RA QVJ/1838: 14 October
41. RA QVJ/1838: 4 August
42. Beatrice Erskine, ed., *Twenty Years at Court: From the Correspondence of the Hon. Eleanor Stanley, 1842–1862*, London (1916) p. 57
43. RA MRH/MRHF/GOODSREC/SPICE/WC, fo. 13 (21–30 June 1837)
44. Maxwell, ed. (1904) vol. 2, p. 325
45. For example, RA MRH/MRHF/MENUS/MAIN/MIXED/24, fo. 191r (29 September 1837)
46. RA QVJ/1838: 30 December
47. RA QVJ/1838: 17 December
48. Sully (24 February 1838)
49. Brewer (2005 edition) p. 244
50. Quoted in Hibbert (2000; 2001 edition) p. 61
51. RA QVJ/1839: 25–27 June
52. Statement by Lady Flora Hastings published in *The Times* (16 September 1839), issue 17148, p. 3
53. RA QVJ/1839: 2 February
54. G. C. Boase, 'Portman, Edward Berkeley, first Viscount Portland (1799–188)' revised H.C.G. Matthew, *Oxford Dictionary of National Biography* (2004)
55. RA VIC/MAIN/Z/486/2 (17 February 1839)
56. TNA PRO 30/29/9/4, fo. 547v (5 March 1830)
57. Charles Mansfield Clarke, 'Notes on lectures on Midwifery and the Diseases of Women and Children' (1815), Wellcome Library MS 5605, quoted in Kathryn Hughes, *Victorians Undone*, London (2017) p. 42
58. Quoted in Martin, (1962) p. 37
59. Hughes (2017) p. 45
60. *The London Medical and Physical Journal* (1819) vol. 42, p. 26
61. Hughes (2017) p. 56
62. Reeve, ed. (1896 edition) vol. 4, p. 178
63. Balliol College Conroy Papers 14B.A.(a).4 Lady Flora Hastings to Sir John Conroy (October 1837)
64. RA QVJ/1839: 2 February
65. Hughes (2017) p. 27
66. Jennings, ed. (1884) vol. 2, p. 117
67. Reeve, ed. (1896 edition) vol. 4, p. 240
68. RA MP/116/95, Lord Duncannon to Lord Melbourne (11 December 1837)

69. Quoted in Plunkett (2003) p. 19
70. Royal College of Physicians, MS 4973, p. 10
71. Reeve, ed. (1896 edition) vol. 4, p. 209
72. Quoted in Robert Rhodes James, *Prince Albert*, London (1984) p. 75
73. Vernon Bogdanor, *Gresham College History Lecture* (20 September 2016)
74. Jane Ridley, *Bertie: A Life of Edward VII*, London (2012; 2013 edition) (2015) p. 19
75. RA MRH/MRHF/MENUS/MAIN/BP/1839 (28 June 1839); RA QVJ/1839: 27 June
76. Martin (1962) p. 65
77. Quoted in Martin (1962) p. 64
78. Ibid., p. 50
79. RA QVJ/1839: 5 July
80. Sir James Clark, statement in *The Times* (6 October 1839)
81. RA QVJ/1839: 15 June, 6–7 July
82. Fulford, ed. (1963 edition) p. 171
83. Lady Flora, quoted in Martin (1962) p. 58
84. RA VIC/MAIN/L/17/56 (30 October 1897)
85. Ponsonby (1942) p. 81
86. Benson and Esher, eds. (1907, 1908 edition) vol. 1, p. 184 (26 August 1839)
87. RA QVJ/1839: 29 May
88. RA QVJ/1839: 17 April
89. RA QVJ/1839: 15–18 April

10. *The Proposal: Windsor Castle, 10–15 October 1839*

1. Anon., *The Annual Register For the Year 1839*, London (1839) pp. 199, 246, 262
2. *The Satirist*, quoted in Plunkett (2003) p. 31
3. Benson and Esher, eds. (1907 1908 edition) vol. 1, p. 188 (12 October 1839)
4. *The Morning Chronicle* (11 October 1839) pp. 2, 4
5. Stoney and Weltzien, eds. (1994) pp. 40, 39
6. Grey (1867) p. 201
7. Jonathan Marsden, ed. *Victoria & Albert, Art & Love*, London (2010) p. 17
8. Ibid.
9. Quoted in Roger Fulford, *The Prince Consort*, London (1949) p. 31
10. Albert to Prince Lowenstein, June 1838, quoted in Marsden, ed. (2010) p. 17
11. Quoted in James (1984) p. 35
12. Royal College of Physicians, MS 4973, p. 8
13. Quoted in James (1984) p. 41
14. Royal College of Physicians, MS 4973, p. 7
15. *Private Life* (1897; 1901 edition) p. 39; for beefeaters on the stairs, see RA QVJ/1863: 10 March
16. RA QVJ/1839: 6 August
17. Benson and Esher, eds. (1907, 1908 edition) vol. 1, p. 186
18. Quoted in Ziegler (1976) p. 254
19. RA QVJ/1839: 10 October
20. *The Morning Chronicle* (11 October 1839) p. 2

21. Benson and Esher, eds. (1907, 1908 edition) vol. 1, p. 188
22. RA QVJ/1839: 10 October
23. RA VIC/MAIN/Z/294, fo. 7v
24. RA VIC/ADDV/2, translation of RA VIC/ADDA/14/84 (12 October 1839)
25. Benson and Esher, eds. (1907, 1908 edition) vol. 1, p. 188
26. RA QVJ/1838: 11 October
27. Grey (1867) p. 183
28. Benson and Esher, eds. (1907, 1908 edition) vol. 1, p. 188
29. RA QVJ/1839: 13 October
30. Quoted in Woodham-Smith (1972) p. 184
31. Benson and Esher, eds. (1907, 1908 edition) vol. 1, p. 186
32. RA QVJ/1839: 11 October
33. RA QVJ/1839: 14 October
34. RA VIC/ADDV/2, translation of ADDA/14/85 (15 October 1839)
35. Mr Arbuthnot to Robert Peel (12 December 1839) in Charles Stuart Parker, ed., *Sir Robert Peel: From His Private Papers*, London (1899 edition) vol. 2, p. 424
36. Grey (1867) p. 144
37. Ibid., p. 187
38. RA QVJ/1830: 14 October
39. Benson and Esher, eds. (1907, 1908 edition) vol. 1, p. 189
40. Gill (2010) p. 151
41. Margaret Homans, *Royal Representations, Queen Victoria and British Culture, 1837–1876*, Chicago, IL (1998) p. 17
42. RA QVJ/1839: 15 October
43. Ibid.
44. Quoted in Charlot (1991) p. 165
45. RA VIC/ADDV/2, translation of RA VIC/ADDA/14/85 (15 October 1839)
46. Martin (1879 edition) vol. 4, p. 169; Kurt Jagow, ed., *Letters of the Prince Consort, 1831–1861*, London (1938) p. 23
47. Jagow, ed. (1938) p. 25
48. Royal College of Physicians, MS 4973, p. 7
49. RA MRH/MRHF/MENUS/MAIN/WC/1840 (15 October 1839)
50. Healey (1997) p. 134
51. Quoted in Daphne Bennet, *King Without a Crown*, Philadelphia, PA (1977) p. 89
52. RA VIC/ADDV/2, translation of RA VIC/ADDA/14/66 (6 March 1838)
53. Magdalen Ponsonby, ed., *Mary Ponsonby: A Memoir, Some Letters and a Journal*, London (1927) pp. 4–5
54. Warner (1979) p. 89
55. RA VIC/ADDV/2, translation of RA VIC/ADDA/14/84 (12 October 1839)
56. Boykin, ed. (1957) p. 104; Sully (22 March 1383)
57. TNA PRO 30/29/424 (30 June 1837)
58. RA QVJ/1840: 2 February
59. Martin (1875; 1879 edition) vol. 1, p. 5
60. Prince William of Lowenstein, quoted in James (1984) p. 51
61. RA QVJ/1839: 1–4 November
62. Leslie (1860) vol. 2, p. 249
63. Scott (1819; 1858 edition) p. 157
64. Gill (2010) p. 149

65. Müller, ed. (1873) vol. 2, p. 3
66. London street ballad (1841), quoted in Homans (1998) p. 1
67. Sarah Ellis, *The Wives of England*, London (1843) p. 263
68. Quoted in Plunkett (2003) p. 102
69. Benson and Esher, eds. (1907, 1908 edition) vol. 1, p. 191
70. Roger Fulford, ed., *Dearest Child*, London (1964; 1981 edition) p. 209
71. Benson and Esher, eds. (1907, 1908 edition) vol. 1, p. 189
72. Marsden, ed. (2010) p. 335
73. RA VIC/MAIN/Z/296/19 (15 October 1839)

11. Wedding Day: three palaces, 10 February 1840

1. RA QVJ/1840: 10 February
2. Kay Staniland and Santina M. Levey, 'Queen Victoria's Wedding Dress and Lace', *Costume*, vol. 17 (1983) pp. 1–32
3. Jennings, ed. (1884) vol. 2, p. 154, Croker to Lady Hardwicke (24 November 1839)
4. RA QVJ/1840: 10 February
5. RA VIC/MAIN/z/490/24, translated in Benson and Esher, eds. (1907, 1908 edition) vol. 1, p. 217. Interestingly, Benson and Esher make no mention of the language of the original: part of a project to make Albert seem less German and more acceptable
6. Jagow, ed. (1938) p. 61
7. Benson and Esher, eds. (1907, 1908 edition) vol. 1, p. 215
8. Plunkett (2003) p. 29
9. *Penny Satirist*, quoted in Plunkett (2003) p. 36
10. RA QVJ/1839: 5 December
11. Philip Whitwell Wilson, ed., *The Greville Diary*, London (1927 edition) p. 130
12. Ibid., p. 129
13. Quoted in Cecil Woodham-Smith, *Florence Nightingale*, London (1951) p. 16
14. RA QVJ/1838: 20 September
15. RA QVJ/1839: 18 August
16. Wilson, ed. (1927 edition) p. 130
17. RA QVJ/1840: 10 February
18. RA VIC/MAIN/Z/294, fos. 8r–v
19. RA QVJ/1840: 10 February
20. Woodham-Smith, (1951) p. 26
21. RA QVJ/1840: 10 February
22. Staniland (1997) p. 118
23. Ibid., p. 120
24. Ponsonby, ed. (1927) p. 6
25. Fulford, ed., (1964, 1981 edition) p. 44
26. Quoted in Weintraub (1987; 1996 edition) p. 123
27. TNA LC 13/2, fo. 112r, an account of the expenses of the Mistress of the Robes (1839); fo. 46v, Duchess of Sutherland to the Treasury (21 December 1837)
28. Mundy, ed. (1885) p. 413

29. RA QVJ/1840: 10 February
30. Tooley (1897) p. 118
31. Reeve, ed. (1902 edition) vol. 4, p. 276
32. Mundy, ed. (1885) p. 413
33. *The Times* (11 February 1840)
34. Plunkett (2003) p. 102
35. Lady Wilhelmina Stanhope, quoted in Lorne (1901) p. 112
36. RA QVJ/1840: 10 February
37. Wyndham, ed. (1912) p. 297
38. Lady Wilhelmina Stanhope, quoted in Lorne (1901) p. 112
39. Anon., *The Annual Register, 1840*, London (1840) p. 16
40. *The Times* (11 February 1840)
41. Boykin, ed. (1957) p. 243
42. *The Times* (11 February 1840)
43. Lady Wilhelmina Stanhope, quoted in Lorne (1901) p. 112
44. Anon., *The Annual Register, 1840*, London (1840) p. 17
45. Tooley (1897) p. 118
46. Woodham-Smith (1972) p. 204
47. Boykin, ed. (1957) p. 243
48. Jagow, ed. (1938) p. 59
49. RA QVJ/1840: 10 February
50. Lady Wilhelmina Stanhope, quoted in Lorne (1901) p. 112
51. Boykin, ed. (1957) p. 243
52. Mundy, ed. (1885) p. 412
53. RA QVJ/1840: 10 February
54. Mundy, ed. (1885) pp. 401–11, Miss Charlotte Neave (11 February 1840) p. 411
55. Boykin, ed. (1957) p. 243
56. Anon., *The Annual Register, 1840*, London (1840) p. 20
57. Mundy, ed. (1885) pp. 410–11, Miss Charlotte Neave (11 February 1840); Anon., *The Annual Register, 1840*, London (1840) p. 20
58. George Barnett Smith, *Life of Her Majesty Queen Victoria*, London (1887) p. 128
59. Lady Wilhelmina Stanhope, quoted in Lorne (1901) p. 114
60. RA QVJ/1840: 10 February
61. Boykin, ed. (1957) p. 243
62. RA VIC/MAIN/Z/491, fo. 2v (January 1862)
63. RA QVJ/1840: 10 February
64. Ibid.
65. Reeve, ed. (1902 edition) vol. 4, p. 277
66. RA QVJ/1840: 10 February
67. *The Times* (11 February 1840)
68. Boykin, ed. (1957) p. 243
69. Bartley (2016) p. 74
70. RA QVJ/1840: 10 February; MRH/MRHF/MENUS/MAIN/WC/1840 (10 February 1840)
71. RA VIC/MAIN/Z/491, fo. 2v (January 1862)
72. RA QVJ/1840: 10 February
73. RA VIC/MAIN/Z/491, fo. 2v (January 1862); RA QVJ/1840: 11 February
74. RA QVJ/1840: 11 February

75. Anon., *The Annual Register, 1840*, London (1840) p. 28
76. Benson and Esher, eds. (1907, 1908 edition) vol. 1, p. 213
77. Jagow, ed. (1938) p. 69
78. Ellis (1843) p. 76
79. Wilson, ed. (1927 edition) vol. 2, p. 131
80. Plunkett (2003) p. 105

12. 'Oh Madam it is a princess': Buckingham Palace, 21 November 1840

1. William Munk, *The Roll of the Royal College of Physicians of London*, London (1878) vol. 3, p. 297; *The Medical Times*, London (1846) p. 17
2. Thomas Ryan, *Queen Charlotte's Lying-In Hospital*, London (1885) p. 13
3. Quoted in Hannah Pakula, *An Uncommon Woman*, New York, NY (1995; 1997 edition) p. 104
4. John Darton, *Famous Girls Who Have Become Illustrious Women*, New York, NY (1864), quoted in Vallone (2001) p. xvi
5. RA QVJ/1840: 24 April
6. RA VIC/MAIN/QVLB/10 November 1840
7. Royal Pharmaceutical Society, account book for 'The Queen' (1837–1844), p. 64
8. Thomas Bull, *Hints to Mothers*, London (1837) p. 23
9. Ibid., pp. 25–6
10. RA QVJ/1840: 20 November
11. RA MRH/MRHF/MENUS/MAIN/BP/1840 (20 November 1840)
12. Anon., *The Annual Register, 1840*, London (1840) p. 109
13. Royal College of Physicians, MS 4973, p. 10
14. RA QVJ/1840: description of 21 November written up on 1 December
15. Bull (1937) p. 135
16. Munk (1878) vol. 3, p. 271
17. Stratfield Saye MS, quoted in Longford (1966) p. 76
18. Matthew Dennison, *The Last Princess, The Devoted Life of Queen Victoria's Youngest Daughter*, London (2007) p. 3
19. Stratfield Saye MS, quoted in Longford, (1966) p. 76
20. Fulford, ed., (1964; 1981 edition) p. 265
21. Stratfield Saye MS, quoted in Longford (1966) p. 76
22. RA VIC/MAIN/QVLB/10 November 1840
23. In the Royal Ceremonial Dress Collection, Historic Royal Palaces.
24. Staniland (1997) p. 126
25. Quoted in Frances Dimond and Roger Taylor, *Crown and Camera*, Harmondsworth (1987) p. 69
26. Tooley (1897) pp. 42–3
27. Self-portrait dated 19 May 1845, Royal Collection Inventory Number 980025.ag
28. Stratfield Saye MS, quoted in Longford, (1966) p. 76
29. Ibid.
30. Royal College of Physicians, MS 4973, pp. 21–3
31. RA VIC/MAIN/Z/294, fo.12r
32. Ridley (2012; 2013 edition) p. 3
33. Roger Fulford, *Dearest Mama*, London (1968) p. 192

34. Royal College of Physicians, MS 4973, pp. 21–3
35. Fulford, ed. (1964; 1981 edition) p. 151
36. Bull (1837) pp. 130–2
37. Dennison (2007) p. 2
38. Roger Fulford, ed., *Beloved Mama*, London (1981) p. 172
39. Royal College of Physicians, MS 4973, pp. 21–3
40. Ibid., p. 22
41. Fulford, ed. (1964; 1981 edition) pp. 150–1
42. RA QVJ/1840: description of 21 November written up on 1 December
43. Quoted in Charlot (1991) p. 195
44. Quoted in Woodham-Smith (1972) pp. 216–17
45. Royal College of Physicians, MS 4973, pp. 21–3
46. RA QVJ/1840: description of 21 November written up on 1 December
47. *Private Life* (1897; 1901 edition) p. 23
48. Quoted in Woodham-Smith (1972) pp. 216–17
49. RA QVJ/1840: description of 21 November written up on 1 December
50. Royal College of Physicians, MS 4973, pp. 21–3
51. RA QVJ/1840: description of 21 November written up on 1 December
52. Quoted in Woodham-Smith (1972) pp. 216–17
53. Boykin, ed. (1957) p. 276
54. Anon., *The Annual Register, 1840,* London (1840) p. 108; Boykin, ed. (1957) p. 276
55. RA VIC/MAIN/QVLB/14 November 1840; RA VIC/MAIN/Y/36/28 (19 March 1841)
56. Boykin, ed. (1957) p. 276
57. Pakula (1995; 1997 edition) p. 28
58. Quoted in Woodham-Smith (1972) pp. 216–17; RA QVJ/1840: description of 22 November written up on 1 December
59. Fulford, ed., (1964; 1981 edition) p. 115
60. RA QVJ/1840: 1 December; Bartley (2016) p. 77
61. Boykin, ed. (1957) pp. 281–2. Weintraub (1987) p. 149 corrects Boykin's misreading of 'Locock' as 'South'
62. RA QVJ/1840: 1 December; Bartley (2016) p. 77
63. RA QVJ/1843: 19 May; Bartley (2016) p. 82
64. RA QVJ/1840: 28 December; Pakula (1995; 1997 edition) p. 6
65. Wyndham, ed. (1912) p. 332
66. Quoted in Pakula (1995; 1997 edition) p. 105
67. Yvonne M. Ward, *Censoring Queen Victoria*, London (2013; 2015) p. 128
68. Julia Baird, *Victoria: The Queen*, London (2016) p. 166
69. RA QVJ/1840: 25 December
70. RA QVJ/1841: 24 July
71. Staniland (1997) p. 127
72. F.M.L. Thompson, ed., *The Cambridge Social History of Britain, 1750–1950,* Cambridge (1990) vol. 2, p. 38
73. Gill (2010) p. 169
74. Quoted in Longford, (1966) p. 86
75. RA VIC/MAIN/Z/484/43 (5 March 1854)
76. RA QVJ/1840: description of 21 November written up on 1 December

77. Hector Bolitho, ed., *The Prince Consort and His Brother: Two Hundred New Letters*, London (1933) p. 21
78. Pakula (1995; 1997 edition) p. 9
79. Helen Rappaport, *Magnificent Obsession: Victoria, Albert and the Death that Changed the Monarchy*, London (2011) p. 21
80. Ellis (1843) pp. 24–5
81. Martin (1901) p. 70
82. Grey (1867) pp. 288–9
83. RA QVJ/1845: 18 February
84. H. C. G. Matthew and K. D. Reynolds, 'Victoria (1819–1901)', *Oxford Dictionary of National Biography*, Oxford University Press (2004)
85. RA VIC/MAIN/Y/54/11 (20 December 1840)
86. Bolitho, ed. (1933) p. 31
87. Vernon Bogdanor, *Gresham College History Lecture* (20 September 2016)
88. Quoted in Woodham-Smith (1972) p. 299
89. Vernon Bogdanor, *Gresham College History Lecture* (20 September 2016)
90. Longford (1964; 1987 edition) p. 155

13. Christmas at Windsor: 25 December 1850

1. Royal Collection Inventory Number 919812
2. RA QVJ/1850: 25 December
3. Jagow, ed. (1938) p. 134
4. Edward Holt, *The Public and Domestic Life of His Late, Most Gracious Majesty, George III*, London (1820) vol. 1, p. 417
5. Arthur Dasent, *John Thadeus Delane, His Life and Correspondence*, London (1908) vol. 2, p. 14
6. *Private Life* (1897; 1901 edition) p. 84
7. Grey (1867) p. 276
8. RA VIC/MAIN/Z/491, fo. 4 (January 1862)
9. Benson and Esher, eds. (1907, 1908 edition) vol. 1, p. 463
10. Fulford, ed. (1968) p. 23
11. Martin (1875) vol. 1, p. 276
12. Fulford, ed. (1968) p. 23
13. Charles C. F. Greville, *The Greville Memoirs*, second series, London (1885) vol. 2, p. 323
14. Albert to Vicky (1 September 1858) quoted in Weintraub (1987) p. 269
15. Reeve, ed. (1911 edition) vol. 8 p. 128
16. Quoted in Lorne (1901) p. 125
17. Ridley (2015) p. 49
18. Quoted in Rappaport (2011) p. 24
19. Dennison (2007) p. 14
20. RA VIC/MAIN/Z/491, fos. 6r–v (January 1862)
21. Müller, ed. (1873) vol. 2, p. 481
22. RA QVJ/1848: 6 April
23. Wyndham, ed. (1912) p. 340
24. RA VIC/MAIN/Z/491, fo. 32v

25. Benson and Esher, eds. (1907, 1908 edition) vol. 3, p. 240
26. Warner (1979) p. 134
27. Quoted in Ponsonby (1942) p. 85
28. Royal College of Physicians MS 30/1, Sir James Clark's diary p. 60 (24 June 1849)
29. *Private Life* (1897; 1901 edition) pp. 93, 26
30. Quoted in Ridley (2012; 2013 edition) p. 27
31. Stoney and Weltzien, eds. (1994) p. 41
32. Erskine (1916) p. 202
33. Dasent (1908) vol. 2, p. 15
34. Quoted in Lorne (1901) p. 119
35. Marsden, ed. (2010) p. 339
36. RA VIC/MAIN/Z/22/16 (2 February 1868)
37. Fulford, ed. (1981) p. 172
38. Wilson, ed. (1927 edition) vol. 2, p. 584
39. Quoted in Woodham-Smith (1972) pp. 266, 232
40. Royal Pharmaceutical Society, account book for 'The Queen' (1837–1844) pp. 100–2
41. Benson and Esher, eds. (1907; 1911 edition) vol. 2, p. 255
42. Royal College of Physicians, MS 4973, pp. 3–5
43. Fulford, ed. (1964; 1981 edition) p. 162
44. Ibid., pp. 165–6
45. RA MAIN/Y/206, copy of diary of James Clark (5 February 1856)
46. Royal College of Physicians, MS 4973, p. 4
47. Ibid., p. 11
48. RA MAIN/Y/206, copy of diary of James Clark (5 15 February 1856)
49. RA VIC/MAIN/Z/140/60-3 (n.d.)
50. Fulford, ed. (1964; 1981 edition) pp. 143–4
51. Quoted in Weintraub (1987) p. 224
52. Victoria to Vicky (2 May 1859) quoted in Pakula (1995; 1997 edition) p. 121
53. Warner (1979) p. 107
54. RA VIC/ADD/U2/4 (18 January 1842) (translation)
55. RA VIC/ADD/U2/7 (19 January 1842) (translation)
56. Fulford, ed. (1964; 1981) p. 112
57. Maxwell, ed. (1904) vol. 1, p. 667
58. Fulford, ed. (1964; 1981) p. 112
59. RA QVJ/1842: 24 September
60. *The Journal of Education,* vol. 33 (1901) p. 208
61. Erskine (1916) p. 155
62. Stoney and Weltzien, eds. (1994) colour plate section following p. 80
63. Tooley (1897) pp. 137–6
64. Quoted in Lorne (1901) pp. 132–3
65. Lorne (1901) p. 348
66. Quoted in Lorne (1901) pp. 132–3
67. Tisdall (1961) p. 27
68. Bartley (2016) p. 44
69. Fulford, ed. (1964; 1981) p. 44
70. Wyndham, ed. (1912) pp. 407–8
71. Ibid., p. 399

72. *Private Life* (1897; 1901 edition) p. 148
73. RA MRH/MRHF/MENUS/MAIN/WC/1850 (25 December 1850), description of lunch quoted in Gray (2017) p. 61
74. RA QVJ/1850: 25 December
75. RA QVJ/1851: 25 December; RA MRH/MRHF/MENUS/MAIN/WC/1850 (25 December 1850)
76. RA QVJ/1850: 25 December
77. *Private Life* (1897; 1901 edition) pp. 177–8
78. Stoney and Weltzien, eds. (1994) p. 42
79. Dasent (1908) vol. 2, p. 16
80. *Private Life* (1897; 1901 edition) pp. 33, 356
81. Gray (2017) p. 70
82. Ibid., pp. 86, 205
83. Quoted in Woodham-Smith (1972) pp. 329–30
84. Dasent (1908) vol. 2, p. 15
85. RA VIC/MAIN/Y/92/4 (29 October 1844)
86. W. L. Alden, 'Christmas at Windsor' in *Shooting Stars as observed from the 'Sixth Column' of The Times*, New York, NY (1878) p. 26
87. John Ruskin, a lecture 'Of Queens' Gardens,' published in *Sesame and Lilies*, London (1865) pp. 147–9
88. Leconfield, ed. (1912) p. 423
89. Margaret Homans, '"To the Queen's Private Apartments": Royal Family Portraiture and the Construction of Victoria's Sovereign Obedience', *Victorian Studies* vol. 37, no.1 (1993) pp. 1–41; Homans (1998).
90. Ponsonby (1942) p. 70

14. A Maharaja on the Isle of Wight: 21–24 August 1854

1. Stoney and Weltzien, eds. (1994) pp. 29, 35
2. Ibid., p. 31
3. RA VIC/ADDX/2/211, p. 14
4. James O. Hoge, ed., *The Letters of Emily Lady Tennyson*, University Park and London (1974) p. 172
5. Dimond and Taylor (1987) p. 78
6. Staniland (1997) p. 13
7. Quoted in Tisdall (1961) pp. 34–5
8. RA QVJ/1843: 19 October
9. RA VIC/MAIN/Y/91/35 (16 January 1844)
10. Benson and Esher, eds. (1907, 1908 edition) vol. 2, p. 36
11. RA QVJ/1854: 21 August
12. Benson and Esher, eds. (1907, 1908 edition) vol. 3, pp. 47–8, 38–9
13. Lady Login quoted in Christy Campbell, *The Maharajah's Box*, London (2000; 2001 edition) p. 44
14. Peter Bance, *The Duleep Singhs: The Photograph Album of Queen Victoria's Maharajah*, Stroud (2004) p. 29
15. *The Times* (14 August 1854)
16. RA QVJ/1854: 21 August

17. Lena Campbell Login, *Lady Login's Recollections, 1820–1904*, London (1916) pp. 125–6
18. Campbell (2000; 2001 edition) p. 41
19. RA QVJ/1854: 20 May
20. Bance (2004) p. 30
21. Ibid.
22. RA QVJ/1854: 21 August
23. Benson and Esher, eds. (1907; 1908 edition) vol. 3, pp. 47–8
24. Sir Frederick Ponsonby, *Side Lights on Queen Victoria*, New York, NY (1930) p. 190
25. Martin (1875) vol. 1, pp. 322–3
26. Quoted in Marsden, ed. (2012) p. 12
27. Grey (1867) p. 200
28. Leconfield, ed. (1912) pp. 364–5
29. Mark Girouard, *The Victorian Country House*, London and New Haven, CT (1979; 1990 edition) p. 149; The Duchess of York with Benita Stoney, *Victoria and Albert, Life at Osborne House*, London (1991) p. 40
30. Ponsonby (1927) p. 59
31. Stoney and Weltzien, eds. (1994) pp. 33, 34
32. RA QVJ/1854: 22 August
33. Quoted in Michael Alexander and Sushila Anand, *Queen Victoria's Maharajah*, London (1980) p. 51
34. RA QVJ/1854: 23 August
35. Dennison (2007) p. 17
36. Ridley (2012; 2013 edition) pp. 28, 32
37. Weintraub (1987) p. 262
38. Dasent (1908) vol. 2, p. 15
39. Weintraub (1987) p. 262
40. RA QVJ/1854: 23 August
41. RA QVJ/1847: 30 July
42. *Private Life* (1897; 1901 edition) p. 29
43. RA QVJ/1854: 23 August
44. Wyndham, ed. (1912) p. 391
45. RA QVJ/1854: 23 August
46. Dimond and Taylor (1987) p. 113
47. RA QVJ/1854: 24 August
48. Quoted in Campbell (2000; 2001 edition) p. 41
49. RA QVJ/1854: 24 August
50. RA VIC/MAIN/RA/491 (January 1861)
51. Quoted in Ridley (2015) p. 53
52. Quoted in Munich (1998) p. 191
53. Ibid., p. 172
54. RA VIC/MAIN/Z/491 (January 1862)
55. Benson and Esher, eds. (1907, 1908 edition) vol. 3, p. 252
56. S. Ganda Singh, 'Some Correspondence of Maharaja Duleep Singh', *Journal of Indian History*, vol. 108 (April, 1949) pp.1–23, p. 5; Sarah Carter and Maria Nugent, eds., *Mistress of Everything, Queen Victoria in Indigenous Worlds*, Manchester (2016) p. 132
57. Singh (1949) pp.1–23, p. 5; Carter and Nugent, eds. (2016) p. 132

15. Miss Nightingale at Balmoral: 21 September 1856

1. Royal College of Physicians MS 30/2, Sir James Clark's diary p. 153 (Autumn in Scotland 1856)
2. Erskine, ed. (1916) pp. 287–8
3. RA QVJ/1856: 21 September
4. Mark Bostridge, *Florence Nightingale: The Woman and Her Legend*, London (2008; 2009 edition) p. 177
5. Quoted in Bostridge (2008; 2009 edition) p. 177
6. Ibid., p. 177
7. J. B. Conacher, *Britain and the Crimea, 1855–56*, London (1987) p. 6
8. Bartley (2016) pp. 158–9
9. Hibbert (2000; 2001 edition) p. 223
10. Quoted in Hibbert (2000; 2001 edition) p. 223
11. James (1984) p. 39
12. Benson and Esher, eds. (1907 edition) vol. 1, p. 28
13. RA QVJ/1854: 21 April
14. RA QVJ/1854: 18 October
15. Quoted in Dimond and Taylor (1987) p. 38
16. RA QVJ/1855: 20, 22 February
17. RA QVJ/1854: 8 December
18. RA QVJ/1855: 6 January
19. Bostridge (2008; 2009 edition) pp. 265–6
20. Tyler Whittle, *Victoria and Albert at Home*, St Lucia, QLD, Australia (1980) p. 85
21. Queen Victoria, *Leaves from the Journal of Our Life in the Highlands, from 1848 to 1861*, London (1868) p. 13
22. Jagow, ed. (1938) p. 82
23. Ibid., p. 81
24. Queen Victoria, (1868) p. 24
25. Royal College of Physicians MS 30/1, Sir James Clark's diary, pp. 56–7; 24 (September 1848; September 1847)
26. Royal College of Physicians MS 30/2, Sir James Clark's diary p. 159 (1856)
27. Count Helmuth von Moltke quoted in Ronald Clark, *Balmoral: Queen Victoria's Highland Home*, London (1981) p. 61
28. Strachey and Fulford, eds. (1938) vol. 6, p. 185
29. Alison Adburgham, *Shops and Shopping, 1800–1914*, London (1964) pp. 73–4; Staniland (1997) p. 156
30. Stoney and Weltzien, eds. (1994) p. 136
31. Quoted in Hibbert (2000; 2001 edition.) p. 180
32. *Private Life* (1897; 1901 edition) p. 210
33. Ethel Smyth, *Streaks of Life*, London (1921) p. 104
34. Marie, Queen of Romania, *The Story of My Life*, New York, NY (1934) vol. 1, p. 69
35. Stoney and Weltzien, eds. (1994) p. 127
36. Quoted in Clark (1981) p. 56
37. Wyndham (1912) p. 386
38. Elizabeth Longford, ed., *Darling Loosy*, London (1991) p. 147

39. Victor Mallet, ed., *Life with Queen Victoria: Marie Mallet's Letters from Court*, London (1968) p. 37

40. Quoted in King (2007) p. 162

41. *Private Life* (1897; 1901 edition) p. 46

42. Erskine, ed. (1916) pp. 287–8

43. Bostridge (2008, 2009 edition) p. 66

44. *Private Life* (1897; 1901 edition) p. 146

45. Madeleine Ginsburg, 'The Young Queen and Her Clothes', *Costume*, vol. 3 (Sprint) (1969) p. 42

46. Royal College of Physicians MS 30/2, Sir James Clark's diary p. 153 ('Autumn in Scotland 1856')

47. Whittle (1980) p. 88

48. RA QVJ/1856: 21 September

49. Quoted in Bostridge (2008, 2009 edition) p. 308

50. RA MAIN/Y/206, copy of diary of James Clark (5 February 1856)

51. RA QVJ/1856: 21 September

52. Quoted in Roy Jenkins, *Gladstone*, London (1995; 2002 edition) p. 616

53. RA QVJ/1856: 21 September

54. Ibid.

55. Ibid.

56. Quoted in Rappaport (2011) p. 267

57. RA QVJ/1856: 21 September

58. The Dean of Windsor and Hector Bolitho, eds., *Letters of Lady Augusta Stanley*, London (1927) p. 105

59. Ibid., p. 106

60. Quoted in Clark (1981) p. 12

61. Windsor and Bolitho, eds. (1927) p. 37

62. RA QVJ/1856: 21 September; Queen Victoria, *Leaves from the Journal of Our Life in the Highlands, from 1848 to 1861*, London (1868) p. 131

63. Quoted in Bostridge (2008; 2009 edition) p. 307

64. Jagow, ed. (1938) p. 234

65. Albert's diary (21 September 1856) quoted in Martin (1877) vol. 3, p. 503

66. Notes on conversation with Florence Nightingale quoted in Bostridge (2008; 2009 edition) p. 307

67. cwrs.russianwar.co.uk/cwrs-crimtexts-panmure-cont20.html, Queen Victoria to Lord Panmure (9 August 1856)

68. Albert quoted in Clark (1981) p. 69; cwrs.russianwar.co.uk/cwrs-crimtexts-pan-mure-cont22.html, Queen Victoria to Lord Panmure (4 October 1856)

69. Quoted in Bostridge (2008; 2009 edition) p. 307

70. Clark (1981) p. 70

71. Bostridge (2008; 2009 edition) p. 309

72. Quoted in Woodham-Smith (1972) p. 274

73. Bostridge (2008; 2009 edition) p. 308

74. Ibid., pp. 309, 303

75. Ibid., p. 309

16. A Night with Nellie: 6 September 1861

1. Dan Harvey, *Soldiers of the Short Grass: A History of the Curragh Camp*, Newbridge, Co. Kildare (2016) p. ix
2. RA QVJ/1861: 24 August
3. Bartley (2016) p. 95
4. Clark (1981) p. 40
5. Bartley (2016) p. 210
6. Maurice Kingsley, ed., *Charles Kingsley, His Letters and Memories*, New York, NY (1899) vol. 2, p. 125; Munich (1998) p. 141
7. Benson and Esher, eds., (1907, 1908 edition) vol. 2, p. 226
8. Buckle, ed., second series (1928) vol. 3 p. 162
9. Bartley (2016) p. 96
10. *Dundalk Democrat* (6 July 1861) p. 2
11. RA QVJ/1861: 24 August
12. *Dundalk Democrat* (31 August 1861)
13. Charles Dickens, 'Curragh Camp', *All the Year Round* (23 May 1867) vol. xvii, p. 522
14. Harvey (2016) p. 29
15. Con Costello, *A Most Delightful Station*, Wilton, Co. Cork (1996; 1999 edition) p. 36
16. RA QVJ/1861: 24 August
17. Benson and Esher, eds. (1907; 1908 edition) vol. 3, p. 452
18. Charles Dickens, 'Curragh Camp', *All the Year Round* (23 May 1867) vol. xvii, p. 522
19. *Punch, Or the London Charivari* (8 August 1863) p. 59
20. Adburgham (1964) p. 93
21. RA VIC/ADDU/32, p. 178 (21 July 1858)
22. RA VIC/MAIN/Y/107/12 (26 August 1861)
23. Fulford, ed. (1964, 1981 edition) p. 147
24. RA QVJ/1861: 24 August
25. *Irish Times* (14 July 1861) courtesy of Matt McNamara; *Freemans Journal* (25 June 1861) p. 3
26. *Freemans Journal* (28 August 1861) p. 3
27. RA VIC/MAIN/Z/140/29–31 (1 October 1865)
28. Lord Clarendon quoted in Theo Aronson, *The Kaisers*, London (1971) p. 38
29. Rappaport (2011) p. 14
30. Quoted in Lorne (1901) p. 126
31. RA QVJ/1852: 12 February; Bartley (2016) p. 130
32. Fulford, ed. (1964; 1981 edition) p. 73
33. Giles St Aubyn, *Edward VII, Prince and King*, London (1979) p. 33
34. Fulford, ed., (1964; 1981 edition) p. 174
35. Quoted in Ridley (2012; 2013 edition) p. 45
36. Bertie's essay quoted in Sidney Lee, *Edward VII*, n.p. (1925) vol. 1, p. 115
37. Roger Fulford, ed., *Your Dear Letter: Private Correspondence of Queen Victoria and the Crown Princess of Prussia, 1865–1871*, London (1971) p. 165
38. RA VIC/ADD/A3/40 (16 April 1861)
39. Harvey (2016) p. 12
40. RA VIC/MAIN/Z/446/13 (10 March 1861)
41. *Irish Times* (14 July 1861) courtesy of Matt McNamara
42. RA VIC/MAIN/Z/446/13/7 (10 March 1861)

43. *Freemans Journal* (23 July 1861) p. 3
44. RA VIC/MAIN/Z/446/14 (13 March 1861)
45. *Illustrated London News* (13 July 1861); *Belfast Newsletter* (16 July 1861)
46. RA VIC/MAIN/Z/446/38/3 (15 August 1861)
47. RA QVJ/1861: 24 August
48. Lee (1925) vol. 1, p. 119
49. Quoted in Longford, (1966) p. 79
50. Ridley (2012; 2013 edition) p. 41
51. Philip Magnus, *King Edward the Seventh*, London (1964; 1975 edition) p. 39
52. Fulford, ed. (1964; 1981 edition) p. 223
53. RA VIC/MAIN/Z/13/49 (6 September 1862)
54. Ridley (2012; 2013 edition) p. 54
55. RA VIC/MAIN/Z/141/94, Albert to Bertie (16 November 1861). Albert spells her name 'Nelly Clifden'
56. Charles Carrington quoted in Ridley (2012; 2013 edition) p. 57
57. Edmund Yates, *His Recollections and Experiences*, London (1884) pp. 138–9 (with thanks to Lee Jackson's victorianlondon.org); Virginia Cowles, *Edward VII and His Circle*, London (1956) p. 75
58. Anon., 'One of the Old Brigade' [Donald Shaw] *London in the Sixties*, London (1908) p. 35
59. *Daily Telegraph* (4 July 1862) quoted in Cowles (1956) p. 77
60. Anon., 'One of the Old Brigade' [Donald Shaw] (1908) pp. 38–9
61. RA VIC/EVIID/1861 (6–11 September)
62. Horace G. Hutchinson, *Portraits of the Eighties*, London (1920) pp. 239–40
63. James Greenwood, *The Wren of the Curragh*, pamphlet reprinted from the *Pall Mall Gazette*, London (1867) p. 7
64. Costello (1996; 1999 edition) p. 52
65. Greenwood (1867) pp. 13–14
66. Charles Dickens, 'Stoning the Desolate', *All the Year Round* (26 November 1864) vol. 12, p. 370
67. Greenwood (1867) p. 25
68. Seth Koven, *Slumming: Sexual and Social Politics in Victorian London*, Princeton, NJ (2004) p. 27
69. Maria Luddy, 'An outcast community: the "wrens" of the Curragh', *Women's History Review*, vol. 1.3 (1992), pp. 341–55
70. Greenwood (1867) p. 17
71. www.turtlebunbury.com/history/history_heroes/hist_hero_nellie_clifden.html
72. *Freemans Journal* (11 September 1861) p. 3
73. *Irish Examiner* (11 September 1861) p. 312
74. St Aubyn (1979) p. 67
75. RA VIC/MAIN/Z/141/94, Albert to Bertie (16 November 1861)
76. Ridley (2012; 2013 edition) p. 58
77. *The New York Clipper* (April 1862) p. 7
78. RA VIC/MAIN/Z/141/94, Albert to Bertie (16 November 1861)
79. Fulford, ed. (1968) pp. 83, 132, 40
80. Quoted in Weintraub (1987) p. 306
81. Bolitho (1933) p. 17
82. Pauline Panam, *Memoirs of a Young Greek Lady*, London (1823) p. 27

17. The Blue Room: Windsor Castle, 14 December 1861

1. Quoted in Woodham-Smith (1972) p. 428
2. RA VIC/MAIN/Z/142 'Account of my beloved Albert's last fatal illness from Nov: 9 to Dec: 14 1861' (taken from Victoria's journal, with additions 1862 and 1872) n.p.
3. Windsor and Bolitho, eds. (1927) p. 242
4. Ibid., p. 244
5. RA VIC/MAIN/Z/142
6. Quoted in Ridley (2012; 2013 edition) p. 66
7. Quoted in Woodham-Smith (1972) p. 417
8. Albert's diary (24 November 1861) quoted in Martin (1880) vol. 5, p. 346
9. RA VIC/MAIN/Z/142
10. Rowland Ernle, ed., *Life and Letters of Dean Stanley*, London (1909) p. 342
11. RA VIC/MAIN/Z/142
12. A letter by 'Lina' Hocédé, royal governess, printed as 'The Last Hours of Prince Albert' in many British newspapers and in George Barnett Smith, *Queen Victoria*, London (1887) p. 351; Rappaport (2011) p. 268
13. RA VIC/MAIN/Z/142
14. Quoted in Rappaport (2011) p. 60
15. Staatschiv Darmstadt, Alice to Louis in Hesse (3 December 1861) quoted in Rappaport (2011) p. 60
16. RA VIC/MAIN/Z/142
17. Weintraub (1987) p. 371
18. Marsden, ed. (2012) p. 51
19. Martin (1875) vol. 1, p. 487
20. Fulford, ed. (1964; 1981 edition) p. 213
21. Vera Watson, *A Queen at Home*, London (1952) p. 97
22. St Aubyn (1979) p. 213
23. David Duff, *Queen Mary*, London (1985) p. 38
24. William Budd, 'On Intestinal Fever', *The London Lancet*, vol. 1, New York, NY (1860) p. 391
25. Chadwick quoted in Bartley (2016) p. 91
26. Weintraub (1987) p. 148
27. Robert Wilson, *Life and Times of Queen Victoria*, London (1891–2) vol. 2, p. 100
28. William Jenner, *On the Identity or Non-Identity of Typhoid and Typhus Fevers*, London (1850); Rappaport (2011) p. 33
29. Martin (1880) vol. 5, p. 431
30. RA QVJ/1861: 7 December
31. Royal College of Physicians, MS 30/2, Sir James Clark's Journal p. 105 (1865)
32. Martin (1876) vol. 2, p. 359
33. RA VIC/MAIN/Z/171/5 (12 March 1844)
34. Fulford, ed. (1964, 1981) pp. 308, 354
35. RA VIC/MAIN/Y/189/26 (29 September 1855) translated in Woodham-Smith (1972) p. 372
36. Rappaport (2011) p. 259
37. Andreae, trans. (1890) p. 55
38. Royal College of Physicians, MS 30/2, Sir James Clark's Journal, p. 105 (1868)

39. RA QVJ/1861: 15 March
40. RA VIC/MAIN/Y/106/14 (9 April 1861)
41. RA VIC/ADD/U2/7 (19 January 1842) (translation)
42. RA VIC/MAIN/Z/140/46–51 (12 March 1857)
43. Albert to Victoria (22 October 1861) quoted in Rappaport (2011) p. 45
44. RA VIC/MAIN/Z/140/12–13 (9 May 1853)
45. Munich (1996) p. 62
46. RA VIC/MAIN/Z/491, fo. 5v (January 1862)
47. Jagow, ed. (1938) p. 305
48. Sale catalogue, Prince Albert's medicine chest, in the files of Kay Staniland, Museum of London (consulted August 2017)
49. Royal Pharmaceutical Society, account book for 'The Queen' (1861–1869) (14, 17 October 1861)
50. Rappaport (2011) p. 48; Royal Pharmaceutical Society, account book for 'The Queen' (1861–1869)
51. Notes on Sir James Clark's Journal, Royal College of Physicians, AIM25 website
52. Martin (1879 edition) vol. 4, p. 501
53. Benson and Esher, eds. (1907, 1908 edition) vol. 3, p. 469
54. Ibid., p. 470
55. Quoted in Rappaport (2011) p. 268
56. Quoted in Woodham-Smith (1972) p. 417
57. Benson and Esher, eds. (1907, 1908 edition) vol. 3, pp. 464–5
58. Quoted in Rappaport (2011) p. 69
59. RA VIC/MAIN/Z/142
60. Ibid.
61. Edward Walford, *Life of the Prince Consort*, London (1862) p. 96 ('Windsor Castle, December 14th, 4.30pm')
62. RA VIC/MAIN/Z/142
63. RA VIC/ADDU/416 (26 December 1861)
64. RA VIC/MAIN/Z/142
65. Ibid.
66. St Aubyn (1979) p. 55
67. RA VIC/MAIN/Z/142
68. Ibid.
69. Windsor and Bolitho, eds. (1927) p. 245
70. RA VIC/ADDU/416 (26 December 1861)
71. RA VIC/MAIN/Z/142
72. Windsor and Bolitho, eds. (1927) p. 245
73. Ibid., p. 245
74. Erskine, ed. (1916) pp. 388–9
75. RA VIC/ADDU/416 (26 December 1861)
76. Royal Pharmaceutical Society, account book of 'The Queen' (1861–1869) (14 December 1861)
77. Windsor and Bolitho, eds. (1927) p. 245
78. William M. Kuhn, *Henry and Mary Ponsonby*, London (2002) p. 82
79. Tisdall (1961) p. 50
80. Erskine, ed. (1916) pp. 388–9
81. Windsor and Bolitho, eds. (1927) p. 246

82. RA VIC/MAIN/Z/142
83. Erskine, ed. (1916) pp. 388–9
84. Quoted in Pakula (1995; 1997 edition) p. 160
85. Wyndham, ed. (1912) p. 422
86. A. L. Kennedy, ed., *'My Dear Duchess': Social and Political Letters to the Duchess of Manchester, 1858–1869*, London (1956) p. 183

18. 'Sewer-poison': Sandringham, 13 December 1871

1. RA QVJ/1871: 13 December
2. RA VIC/ADDC/18/71 (30 November 1871)
3. RA QVJ/1871: 13 December
4. RA QVJ/1871: 11 December
5. Ibid.
6. Wellcome Library MS 5873 A/53 (1 a.m., 13 December 1871)
7. Wellcome Library MS 5873 B/30 (13 December 1871)
8. RA QVJ/1871: 11 December
9. RA QVJ/1871: 29 November
10. Bartley (2016) p. 204
11. Benson and Esher, eds. (1907, 1908 edition) vol. 3, p. 474
12. Sir H. Maxwell, ed. *The Life and Letters of the Fourth Earl of Clarendon*, London (1913) vol. 2, pp. 250–1
13. Bostridge (2008; 2009 edition) p. 388
14. Hibbert (2000; 2001 edition) p. 308
15. Edward John Tilt, *The Change of Life*, London (1857) p. 6; W. Tyler Smith, 'The Climacteric Disease in Women', *London Journal of Medicine*, vol. 7 (July 1849) pp. 604–5; Munich (1996) p. 105
16. Michaela Reid, *Ask Sir James*, London (1987) p. 107
17. Hector Bolitho, ed., *Letters of Queen Victoria From the Archives of the House of Brandenburg-Prussia*, New Haven, CT (1938) p. 143
18. Royal Collection Inventory Number 55254
19. Quoted in Gray (2017) p. 217
20. David Duff, *Alexandra, Princess and Queen*, London (1980) p. 106
21. Wellcome Library MS 5873 J/3 (29 April 1889)
22. The Dean of Windsor and Hector Bolitho, eds., *Later Letters of Augusta Stanley*, London (1929) p. 148
23. Brewer (2005 edition) pp. 248–8
24. Quoted in Weintraub (1987) p. 365
25. Fulford, ed. (1971) p. 21
26. Staniland (1997) p. 157
27. Plunkett (2003) p. 156
28. Dimond and Taylor (1987) p. 20
29. *The Photographic News* (28 February 1862) quoted in Dimond and Taylor (1987) p. 22
30. RA QVJ/1871: 13 December
31. Philip Guedalla, *The Queen and Mr Gladstone*, London (1933) vol. 2, p. 357
32. RA VIC/ADDC/18/72 (1 December 1871)

33. 'The Illness of H.R.H. The Prince of Wales,' *British Medical Journal* (9 December 1871) p. 671
34. Wellcome Library MS 5873 C/1 (26 November 1871)
35. RA VIC/ADDC/18/80 (7 December 1871)
36. Quoted in Georgina Battiscombe, *Queen Alexandra,* London (1969) p. 116
37. Ponsonby (1942) p. 98
38. Helen Walch, *Sandringham: A Royal Estate for 150 Years*, Norwich (2012) p. 35
39. *The Strand* magazine quoted in Walch (2012) p. 45
40. C. Rachel Jones, *Sandringham, Past and Present*, London (1888) p. 12
41. RA VIC/Add A36/395 (29 November 1871)
42. Ridley (2012; 2013 edition) p. 91
43. Walch (2012) p. 30
44. Duff (1980) p. 108
45. RA VIC/ADDC/18/68 (27 November 1871)
46. Walch (2012) p. 43; Roger Fulford, ed., *Darling Child: Private Correspondence of Queen Victoria and the Crown Princess of Prussia, 1871–78*, London (1976) p. 20
47. Ponsonby (1942) p. 99
48. *The Strand* magazine quoted in Walch (2012) p. 45
49. RA QVJ/1871: 13 December
50. Quoted in Weintraub (1987; 1988 edition) p. 321
51. RA VIC/ADDC/18/72 (1 December 1871)
52. Quoted in Ridley (2012; 2013 edition) p. 78
53. RA QVJ/1871: 11 December
54. RA QVJ/1871: 13 December; Wellcome Library MS 5873 B/33 (14 December 1871)
55. Quoted in Martyn Downer, *The Queen's Knight*, London (2007) p. 266
56. RA VIC/ADDC/18/70 (29 November 1871)
57. Wellcome Library MS 5873 B/33
58. Wellcome Library MS 5873 C/22
59. Windsor and Bolitho, eds. (1929) pp. 149–50
60. RA VIC/ADDC/18/84 (10 December 1871)
61. Quoted in Battiscombe (1969) p. 115, most likely in RA VIC/ADDC/18 but her footnote is not traceable
62. RA VIC/ADDA36/395 (29 November 1871)
63. Wellcome Library MS 5873 B/31
64. RA QVJ/1871: 13 December
65. RA VIC/ADDA/36/401 (13 December 1871)
66. RA QVJ/1871: 13 December
67. *The Times* (12 December 1871) issue 27244, p. 9
68. St Aubyn (1979) p. 215
69. Duff (1980) p. 107
70. *Pall Mall Gazette* quoted in Weintraub (1987) p. 370
71. RA QVJ/1871: 13 December
72. Wellcome Library MS 5873 B/32
73. RA VIC/ADDC/18/88 (13 December 1871)
74. RA QVJ/1871: 13 December
75. Ibid.
76. Richard R. Holmes, *Edward VII*, London (1910) vol. 1, p. 246

77. Windsor and Bolitho, eds. (1929) p. 150
78. Wellcome Library MS 5873 A/53 (8 am, 14 December 1871)
79. Wellcome Library MS 5873 B/33 (14 December 1871)
80. Windsor and Bolitho, eds. (1929) p. 150
81. RA QVJ/1871: 14 December
82. Wellcome Library MS 5873 B/34
83. Holmes (1910) vol. 1, p. 247
84. RA QVJ/1871: 11 December
85. RA QVJ/1868: 13 December; Bartley (2016) p. 215
86. Bartley (2016) p. 15
87. Ponsonby (1942) p. 75
88. Quoted in Philip Guedalla, *Idylls of the Queen*, London (1937) p. 66
89. Wellcome Library MS 5873 E/21 (25 January 1872)
90. Lorne (1901) pp. 278–9
91. RA QVJ/1872: 27 February
92. Vernon Bogdanor, *Gresham College History Lecture* (20 September 2016)
93. Lord Halifax (28 August 1871) quoted in Ponsonby (1942) p. 72
94. Homans (1998) p. xix
95. *Private Life* (1897, 1901 edition) p. 215
96. Homan (1998) pp. 113, 101
97. Benson and Esher, eds. (1907, 1908 edition) vol. 3, p. 476 (24 December 1861)
98. Kennedy, ed. (1956) p. 183
99. Holmes (1910) vol. 1, p. 249
100. Fulford, ed., (1976) p. 28
101. Windsor and Bolitho, eds. (1929) p. 149

19. Lunch with Disraeli: Hughenden Manor, 15 December 1877

1. *Private Life* (1897; 1901 edition) p. 14
2. RA QVJ/1871: 13 December
3. Quoted in in R. W. Seton-Watson, *Disraeli, Gladstone and the Eastern Question*, London (1935) p. 243
4. Quoted in Weintraub (1987) p. 427
5. *Private Life* (1897; 1901 edition) p. 112
6. *The Times*, London (17 December 1877) p. 9
7. Quoted in Wilfred Meynell, *Benjamin Disraeli: An Unconventional Biography*, London (1903) p. 488
8. Christopher Hibbert, *Disraeli: A Personal History*, London (2004; 2005 edition) pp. 331, 333
9. Ibid., p. 184
10. Monypenny and Buckle (1910; 1929 edition) vol. 2, p. 273
11. Zetland, ed. (1929) vol. 2, p. 148, Disraeli to Lady Chesterfield (13 December 1877)
12. RA QVJ/1852: 1 April
13. Fulford, ed. (1971) p. 176
14. Buckle, ed. 2nd series, vol. 1 (1926) p. 505
15. Ibid., p. 385

16. Ponsonby (1942) pp. 244–5
17. Buckle, ed., 2nd series, vol. 3 (1928) p. 38
18. G. E. Buckle, ed., *The Life of Benjamin Disraeli*, London (1920) vol. 6, p. 203
19. Served in 1875. Gray (2017) p. 177
20. *Private Life* (1897; 1901 edition) p. 137
21. RA QVJ/1871: 13 December
22. Tooley (1897) pp. 126-7
23. RA QVJ/1837: 8 February
24. Anon., 'Queen Victoria and the Medical Profession', *The British Medical Journal* (26 January 1901) p. 235
25. Clark (1981) p. 84
26. Gray (2017) p. 229
27. John Parker, *The Early History and Antiquities of Wycombe*, Wycombe (1878) p. 175
28. Ibid., p. 175
29. L. J. Ashford, *The History of the Borough of High Wycombe*, London (1960) p. 327
30. RA QVJ/1871: 13 December
31. Parker (1878) p. 175; *The Times*, London (17 December 1877) p. 9
32. L. J. Mayes, *Chair making in High Wycombe*, Local History Essays, High Wycombe Library Local Studies Collection, (n.d.) p. 1
33. William Judson, *A Local Guide and Directory for the Town of High Wycombe*, High Wycombe (1875) p. 16
34. *The Cabinet Maker & Complete House Furnisher* (6 November 1915) quoted at www.wycombe.gov.uk/pages/Sports-leisure-and-tourism/Wycombe-Museum/Chair-arches.aspx
35. Zetland, ed. (1929) vol. 2, p. 148, Disraeli to Lady Bradford (17 December 1877)
36. *The Times*, London (17 December 1877) p. 9
37. Sally Stafford, *Disraeli and Hughenden: Buckinghamshire: a Souvenir Guide*, The National Trust (2010) p. 17, 24
38. For Mary Anne in particular, see Daisy Hay, *Mr and Mrs Disraeli: A Strange Romance*, London (2015)
39. RA QVJ/1871: 13 December
40. Victoria to Disraeli (27 June 1877) quoted in Seton-Watson (1935) p. 216
41. Quoted in Seton-Watson (1935) p. 236
42. RA QVJ/1871: 13 December
43. Buckle, ed. (1929) vol. 6, p. 217
44. RA QVJ/1871: 13 December
45. Sarah Bradford, *Disraeli*, London (1982; 1996 edition) p. 347
46. Pamela Horn, 'Lord and Lady of the Manor: The Disraelis at Hughenden', *Records of Buckinghamshire*, vol. 51 (2011) pp. 205–213, p. 208
47. RA QVJ/1871: 13 December
48. Zetland, ed. (1929) vol. 2, p. 148, Disraeli to Lady Bradford (17 December 1877)
49. RA QVJ/1871: 13 December
50. Zetland, ed. (1929) vol. 2, p. 148, Disraeli to Lady Bradford (17 December 1877)
51. *The Times*, London (17 December 1877) p. 9
52. Weintraub (1987) p. 429
53. Zetland, ed. (1929) vol. 2, p. 149, Disraeli to Lady Bradford (19 December 1877)
54. Bartley (2016) p. 224
55. Plunkett (2003) p. 16

20. John Brown's Legs: 6 March 1884

1. RA VIC/ADDA/12/899 (23 February 1884)
2. Tisdall (1961) p. 57
3. Quoted in Jenkins (1995; 2002 edition) p. 468
4. Kuhn (2002) p. 4
5. *Private Life* (1897; 1901 edition) p. 175
6. Ibid., p. 227
7. Crook and Port (1973) p. 392
8. Royal Pharmaceutical Society, account book of 'The Queen' (1861–1869) (April–May 1868)
9. RA QVJ/1884: 6 March
10. Mallet (1968) p. 213
11. Tooley (1897) pp. 205–6
12. Dimond and Taylor (1987) p. 23
13. *Private Life* (1897; 1901 edition) pp. 204, 19.
14. Benson (1930) p. 8
15. Ward (2014) p. 60
16. Ibid.; Marsden, ed. (2010) p. 436
17. Randall Davidson in Bell (1935) vol. 1, p. 85
18. Mallet (1968) p. 213
19. Benson and Esher, eds. (1907, 1908 edition) vol. 3, pp. 461–2
20. Quoted in Clark (1981) p. 93
21. *Private Life* (1897; 1901 edition) p. 64
22. Ponsonby (1942) p. 126
23. Quoted in Jenkins (1995; 2002 edition) p. 243
24. *Private Life* (1897; 1901 edition) p. 147
25. Ponsonby (1942) p. 128
26. *Private Life* (1897; 1901 edition) p. 99
27. *Lausanne Gazette* (September 1866)
28. *Punch* (7 July 1866)
29. W. Tyler Smith, 'The Climacteric Disease in Women,' *London Journal of Medicine* (July 1849) vol. 7, p. 606; Munich (1996) p. 108
30. *Harper's New Monthly Magazine,* vol. 36 (December 1867) p. 99
31. Fulford, ed. (1968; 1981 edition) p.106
32. Ridley (2015) p. 77
33. Stoney and Weltzien, eds. (1994) p. 25
34. Quoted in Wilson (2014) pp. 311–27
35. Ridley (2015) p. 80
36. Weintraub (1987) p. 385
37. Royal College of Physicians MS 30/2, Sir James Clark's diary p. 131 (1868)
38. Hibbert (2000; 2001 edition) p. 330
39. Quoted in Charlotte Zeepvat, *Prince Leopold*, London (1998) pp. 51, 60
40. Ponsonby (1942; 1943 edition) p. 129
41. Brewer (2005) p. 251
42. *Private Life* (1897; 1901 edition) p. 8
43. Weintraub (1987) p. 399
44. Queen Victoria (1885) p. 27

45. Ibid., pp. 264, 258, 203, 73
46. Ibid., p. 248
47. Ibid., p. 219
48. Dorothy Thompson, *Queen Victoria, A Woman on the Throne*, London (1990; 2001 edition) p. 62
49. Queen Victoria (1885) p. 226
50. Lambeth Palace Library, Randall Davidson Papers, Private Papers, vol. 4, following f. 79
51. Ponsonby (1942) p. 146
52. Kuhn (2002) p. 220
53. *Private Life* (1897; 1901 edition) p. 10
54. Ibid., p. 166
55. Mallet (1968) p. xxi
56. A. C. Benson, *Memories and Friends*, New York, NY (1927) p. p. 55
57. Ethel Smyth, *As Time Went On*, London (1936) p. 104
58. Quoted in Kuhn (2002) p. 17
59. Randall Davidson in Bell (1935) vol. 1, p. 79
60. Smyth (1936) pp. 90; 93
61. Ponsonby (1901) vol. 193, p. 327
62. Kuhn (2002) pp. 124–6
63. Ibid., p. 194
64. Ponsonby, ed. (1927) p. 18
65. RA VIC/ADDA/36/1566 (30 October 1878)
66. Kuhn (2002) p. 203
67. Mallet (1968) p. 45
68. Ponsonby (1942) p. 62
69. Quoted in Reid (1987) p. 58
70. Randall Davidson on Queen Victoria in Bell (1935) vol. 1, p. 77
71. Ibid., pp. 79–80
72. Lambeth Palace Library, Randall Davidson Papers, Private Papers, vol. 4 (1883–1902) f. 34 (6 December 1884)
73. Tisdall (1961) pp. 106–7
74. Randall Davidson in Bell (1935) vol. 1, p. 80
75. Mallet (1968) p. 159
76. Ponsonby (1942) p. 64
77. Hallam Tennyson, ed., *Alfred Lord Tennyson: A Memoir*, London (1899) p. 406
78. Lily Langtry quoted in Tisdall (1961) p. 132
79. Kuhn (2002) p. 206
80. Quoted in Jenkins, (1995; 2002 edition) p. 336
81. Bell (1935) vol. 1, pp. 82, 81
82. Lambeth Palace Library, Davidson Papers, Private Papers, vol. 4, f. 72
83. Bell (1935) vol. 1, p. 94
84. Lambeth Palace Library, Davidson Papers, Private Papers, vol. 4, following f. 79; Wilson (2014) pp. 426–7
85. Jenkins (1995; 2002 edition) p. 469
86. Marie Louise, Her Highness Princess, *My Memories of Six Reigns*, London (1956; 1979 edition) p. 143
87. Miss Harriet Phipps quoted in Mallet (1968) p. xxiii

88. Tisdall (1961) p. 77
89. Lambeth Palace Library, Davidson Papers, Private Papers, vol. 4, fo. 73 (8 March 1884)
90. Randall Davidson quoted in Bell (1935) vol. 1, p. 95
91. Reid (1987) pp. 227–7; Ridley (2012; 2013 edition) p. 483
92. Kuhn (2002) p. 237

21. Baby Gets Married: Osborne House, 23 July 1885

1. RA QVJ/1885: 23 July
2. Marie, Queen of Romania, (1934), vol. 1, p. 20
3. Quoted in Christopher Hibbert, The Court of St James, London (1979) p. 48
4. RA QVJ/1885: 23 July
5. Quoted in Dennison (2007) p. 11
6. RA QVJ/1858: 14 April; Bartley (2016) p. 126
7. Nina Consuelo Epton, Queen Victoria and Her Daughters, New York, NY (1971) p. 81
8. Erskine, ed. (1916) p. 371
9. Windsor and Bolitho, eds. (1927) p. 207
10. Ridley (2015) p. 85
11. Quoted in Dennison (2007) p. 33
12. Quoted in Epton (1971) p. 109
13. Ibid., pp. 150–2
14. Dennison (2007) p. 124
15. Ibid., p. 120
16. RA VIC/MAIN/Z/140/60–3 (n.d.)
17. Norman Rich, ed., The Holstein Papers, Cambridge (1959) vol. 2, p. 139
18. Fulford, ed. (1981) p. 187
19. Helen Rappaport, Queen Victoria: A Biographical Companion, London (2003) p. 57
20. RA QVJ/1885: 23 July
21. David Duff, The Shy Princess, London (1958) p. 113; Dennison (2007) p. 130
22. RA QVJ/1884: 8 July
23. Fulford, ed. (1981) pp. 176–7
24. Longford, ed. (1991) p. 139
25. Quoted in Ridley (2015) p. 72
26. Quoted in G. B. Tennyson, ed., A Carlyle Reader, Cambridge (1969) p. 495
27. Rich, ed. (1957) vol. 2, p. 139
28. Quoted in Hibbert (1979) p. 47
29. Fulford, ed. (1981) p. 185
30. Buckle, ed., second series (1928) vol. 3, p. 593
31. RA QVJ/1884: 29 December
32. Fulford, ed. (1981) p. 177
33. Walter Bagehot, The English Constitution, London (1867) pp. 85–6, quoted in Homans (1998) p. 107
34. Loewe, ed. (1890) vol. 2, p. 339
35. Watson (1952) p. 255
36. Ibid., p. 252

37. Bartley (2016) p. 231
38. RA QVJ/1885: 23 July
39. Tooley (1897) p. 242; Tennyson (1899) vol. 4, p. 238
40. RA QVJ/1885: 23 July
41. Hesketh Pearson, *Labby*, London (1936) p. 255
42. RA QVJ/1885: 23 July
43. Watson (1952) p. 251
44. John Matson, *Dear Osborne*, London (1978) p. 97
45. Ibid., p. 97
46. RA QVJ/1885: 23 July
47. Anon. *Private Life* (1897; 1901 edition) p. 69
48. RA QVJ/1843: 19 May; Bartley (2016) p. 82
49. RA QVJ/1885: 23 July
50. Pearson (1936) p. 255
51. Dennison (2007) p. 151
52. *Illustrated London News* quoted in Dennison (2007) p. 154
53. Maurice V. Brett, ed., *Journals and Letters of Reginald Viscount Esher*, London (1934) vol. 1, p. 208
54. Recollections of Osborne by Somerset North Gough Colthorpe, MS in possession of English Heritage, kindly shown to me by Osborne curator Michael Hunter
55. Quoted at lukemckernan.com/wp-content/uploads/queen_victoria_diamond_jubilee.pdf
56. RA QVJ/1885: 23 July
57. Quoted in Hibbert (1980) p. 48
58. RA QVJ/1885: 23 July
59. Quoted in Matson (1978) p. 99
60. RA QVJ/1885: 23 July
61. *Private Life* (1897; 1901 edition) p. 122
62. Dennison (2007) p. 155
63. RA QVJ/1885: 23 July
64. RA VIC/ADDA/30/1357 (24 July 1885); Dennison (2007) p. 133
65. Quoted in Dennison (2007) p. 159
66. RA QVJ/1886: 26 April
67. Mallet (1968) p. 71
68. Bruce Vandervort, *Wars of Imperial Conquest in Africa, 1830–1914*, London (1998) pp. 113–14
69. Weintraub (1987) p. 565
70. Mary Lutyens, ed., *Lady Lytton's Court Diary*, London (1961) p. 157

22. *Munshi-Mania: Excelsior Hotel Regina, French Riviera, 4 April 1897*

1. RA QVJ/1896: 28 April
2. Quoted in Nelson (2007) p. 120
3. Advert in *Bradshaw's Watering Places*, London (1904)
4. *L'Eclaireur de Nice*, quoted in Nelson (2007) p. 119
5. Mountstuart Elphinstone Grant Duff, *Notes from a Diary*, London (1905) p. 174

6. Quoted in Michael Nelson, *Queen Victoria and the Discovery of the Riviera*, London (2007) p. 120

7. David Duff, *Victoria Travels*, London (1970) p. 323

8. RA QVJ/1837: 18 April

9. Nelson (2007) p. 9

10. Mallet (1968) p. 153

11. Nelson (2007) p. 7

12. Stoney and Weltzien, eds. (1994) pp. 11–12

13. Royal Pharmaceutical Society, account book for 'The Queen' (1861–1869)

14. Staniland (1997) p. 186

15. Quoted in King (2007) p. 100

16. Princess Marie Louise (1956) p. 141

17. Quoted in King (2007) p. 101

18. Xavier Paoli, *My Royal Clients*, London (1910) p. 340

19. Stoney and Weltzien, eds. (1994) p. 13

20. Tisdall (1961) p. 54

21. Stoney and Weltzien, eds. (1994) p. 13

22. Queen Victoria's 'Rules for Scotland' (20 August 1887) quoted in Reid (1987) p. 129

23. *Private Life* (1897; 1901 edition) p. 14

24. King (2007) p. 102

25. RA QVJ/1892: 18 August

26. Ponsonby (1942; 1943 edition) p. 45

27. King (2007) p. 103

28. Paoli (1910) p. 348

29. Ibid., p. 351

30. Richard Hough, ed., *Advice to a Grand-daughter: Letters from Queen Victoria to Princess Victoria of Hesse*, New York, NY (1975) p. 36

31. Duff (1970) pp. 338–9

32. Lady Paget quoted in Weintraub (1987) p. 539

33. *Galignani Messenger* quoted in Nelson (2007) p. 108

34. Quoted in Shrabani Basu, *Victoria and Abdul,* Stroud (2010, 2011 edition) p. 176

35. Queen Marie of Romania (1934) vol. 1, p. 230

36. Paoli (1910) p. 338

37. Martin (1879 edition) vol. 4, p. 148

38. RA QVJ/1887: 3 August

39. Reid (1987) p. 131

40. Basu (2010, 2011 edition) p. 167

41. Abdul Karim's *Journals* are quoted in Basu (2010, 2011 edition) p. 30

42. Reid (1987) p. 132

43. Ponsonby (1942; 1943 edition) p. 131

44. Kuhn (2002) p. 223

45. Reid (1987) p. 24

46. Frederick Ponsonby quoted in Reid (1987) p. 255

47. Robert C. Abrams, 'Sir James Reid and the Death of Queen Victoria', *The Gerontologist*, vol. 55, issue 6 (December 2015) pp. 943–50, p. 944

48. Reid (1987) p. 139

49. Ibid., pp. 133, 142

50. Duff (1970) p. 333
51. Ibid.
52. Paoli (1910) pp. 339–40
53. Mallet (1968) pp. 152, 76
54. Paoli (1910) p. 334
55. *Court Circular* quoted in Nelson (2007) p. 107
56. RA QVJ/1897: 4 April
57. Reid (1987) p. 145
58. Ponsonby (1942; 1943 edition) p. 131
59. Quoted in Hubbard (2012) p. 318
60. Munich (1998) p. 151
61. Basu (2010, 2011 edition) p. 192
62. Buckle, ed., third series, London (1931) vol. 2, p. 68
63. Reid (1987) p. 144
64. James Reid's diary quoted in Hubbard (2012) p. 325
65. Reid (1987) p. 144
66. Ibid., p. 146
67. Ibid., p. 57
68. Andrew Roberts, *Salisbury: Victorian Titan*, London (1999) p. 680
69. Ridley (2012; 2013 edition) p. 351
70. RA VIC/ADDC/07/2/P (17 August 1909)
71. James Reid's diary quoted in Hubbard (2012) p. 326
72. Roberts (1999) p. 681
73. Eustace A. Reynolds-Ball, *Mediterranean Resorts*, London (1908) p. 74
74. RA QVJ/1899: 1 May
75. Paoli (1910) p. 332

23. Apotheosis: London, 22 June 1897

1. *Private Life* (1897; 1901 edition) p. 12
2. Anon, 'The Queen's Bedroom', *Woman's Life* (23 May 1896) p. 431
3. RA QVJ/1897: 22 June
4. Queen Victoria's granddaughter quoted in Tisdall (1961) p. 145
5. Mary Hannah Krout, *A Looker on in London*, New York, NY (1899) p. 307
6. RA QVJ/1897: 22 June
7. Weintraub (1987) p. 581
8. RA QVJ/1897: 22 June
9. Ponsonby (1942) p. 79
10. Smyth (1921) p. 99
11. RA QVJ/1897: 22 June
12. Gray (2017) p. 243; RA QVJ/1897: 22 June
13. Quoted in Ridley (2012; 2013 edition) p. 168
14. Quoted in King (2007) pp. 220–1
15. Quoted in Weintraub, (1987, 1988 edition) p. 507
16. Quoted in King (2007) p. 43
17. Buckle, ed., second series (1932) vol. 3, p. 124
18. King (2007) p. 21

19. Jeffrey L. Lant, *Insubstantial Pageant: Ceremony and Confusion at Queen Victoria's Court*, London (1979) p. 216

20. Ibid., p. 217

21. RA QVJ/1897: 22 June

22. Lutyens, ed. (1961) p. 25

23. *Private Life* (1897; 1901 edition) p. 59

24. RA QVJ/1897: 22 June

25. Lincoln, President of USA (1865), Prim, Prime Minster of Spain (1870), Alexander II, Tsar of Russia (1881), Carnot, President of France (1894)

26. Ginsburg (1969) p. 43

27. Caroline Chapman and Paul Raben, eds., *Debrett's Queen Victoria's Jubilees*, London (1977) unpaginated

28. Mark Twain, *The Writings of Mark Twain*, New York, NY (1922) pp. 206–7

29. Krout (1899) pp. 313–4; 310

30. Twain (1922) pp. 206–7

31. G. W. Steevens in the *Daily Mail*, quoted at lukemckernan.com/wpcontent/uploads/queen_victoria_diamond_jubilee.pdf

32. See David Cannadine, 'The British Monarchy, c.1820–1977', in Eric Hobsbawm and Terence Ranger, eds., *The Invention of Tradition*, Cambridge (1983), pp. 101–164; p. 121

33. E.C.F. Collier (ed.), *A Victorian Diarist: Later Extracts from the Journals of Mary, Lady Monkswell, 1895–1909* (1946) quoted at lukemckernan.com/wp-content/uploads/queen_victoria_diamond_jubilee.pdf

34. Hobsbawn, ed. (1983; 1999 edition) p. 124

35. Mary King Waddington, *Letters of a Diplomat's Wife, 1883–1900,* New York, NY (1903) p. 177

36. Nicholas II, Tsar of Russia, in his diary (1893) quoted in Miranda Blunt, *The Three Emperors*, London (2009; 2010 edition) p. 133

37. Lord Frederic Hamilton, *The Days Before Yesterday*, London (1920) p. 27

38. Bell (1935) vol. 1, p. 78

39. Homans (1998) p. 5

40. W. T. Stead, *Her Majesty the Queen*, London (1887) pp. 24, 153

41. RA QVJ/1897: 22 June

42. King (2007) p. 138

43. Wilfred Blunt papers quoted in Ridley (2012; 2013 edition) p. 328

44. Ponsonby (1942) p. 109

45. Quoted in Ridley (2012; 2013 edition) p. 320

46. Lant (1979) p. 221

47. RA QVJ/1897: 22 June

48. Grant Duff (1905) p. 245

49. RA QVJ/1897: 22 June

50. G.W. Steevens in the *Daily Mail,* quoted at lukemckernan.com/wp-content/uploads/queen_victoria_diamond_jubilee.pdf

51. Bartley (2016) p. 277

52. RA QVJ/1897: 22 June

53. *Northern Star* (1843) quoted in Plunkett (2003) p. 57

54. Quoted in Weintraub (1987) p. 551

55. Frank Prochaska, *Royal Bounty: The Making of Welfare Monarchy*, New Haven and London (1995)

56. Chapman and Raben, eds. (1977) unpaginated

57. Ridley (2012; 2013 edition) p. 321

58. lukemckernan.com/wp-content/uploads/queen_victoria_diamond_jubilee.pdf

59. RA QVJ/1897: 23 November; http://lukemckernan.com/wp-content/uploads/queen_victoria_diamond_jubilee.pdf

60. Plunkett (2003) p. 240

61. lukemckernan.com/wp-content/uploads/queen_victoria_diamond_jubilee.pdf

62. RA QVJ/1897: 22 June

63. Gray (2017) p. 243

64. *Private Life* (1897; 1901 edition) p. 143

65. RA QVJ/1897: 22 June

66. Gray (2017) p. 245; *Private Life* (1897; 1901 edition) p. 185

67. RA MRHF/MENUS/WC/1850 (22 June 1897)

68. Bartley (2016) p. 294

69. Quoted in Ridley (2012; 2013 edition) p. 325

70. RA QVJ/1897: 22 June

71. RA QVJ/1885: 27 July

72. *The Times*, London (9 April 1863) p. 7, quoted in Plunkett (2003) p. 189

73. RA VIC/ADDX/2/211, p. 29

74. *Private Life* (1897; 1901 edition) p. 69

75. Plunkett (2003) p. 192

76. Munich (1996) p. 8

77. Weintraub (1987) p. 582; Benson (1930) p. 122

78. RA QVJ/1897: 22 June

79. George Warrington Steevens, *Things Seen*, London (1900) p. 195

80. Jenkins (1995; 2002 edition) p. 406

24. Deathbed: Osborne, 22 January 1901

1. *Private Life* (1897; 1901 edition) pp. 204, 19.

2. Mallet (1968) p. 212

3. Quoted in Rennell (2000) p. 46

4. *Private Life* (1897; 1901 edition) p. 139

5. Staniland (1997) pp. 171–2

6. Fulford, ed. (1976) p. 40

7. Queen Marie of Romania (1934) vol. 1, p. 18

8. RA QVJ/1901: 13 January

9. Lady Frances Balfour, quoted in Rennell (2000) p. 74

10. Reid (1987) p. 201

11. *Private Life* (1897; 1901 edition) pp. 203, 7

12. Quoted in Rennell (2000) p. 77

13. Ibid., p. 80

14. Reid (1987) p. 211

15. Rennell (2000) p. 110

16. Lambeth Palace Library, Davidson Papers, Private Papers, vol. 19 (21 January 1901)

17. Ibid. (memorandum as to details connected with the death of the Queen)

18. Lambeth Palace Library, Davidson Papers, Private Papers, vol. 19 (21 January 1901)
19. Ibid.
20. Anon., *The Annual Register For the Year 1901*, London (1902) p. 7
21. Quoted in Rennell (2000) p. 117
22. Ibid., p. 118
23. Lambeth Palace Library, Davidson Papers, Private Papers, vol. 19 (memorandum as to details connected with the death of the Queen)
24. Ibid.
25. Quoted in Rennell (2000) p. 130
26. Brett, ed. (1934) vol. 1, p. 282
27. Lambeth Palace Library, Davidson Papers, Private Papers, vol. 19 (memorandum as to details connected with the death of the Queen)
28. Sir James Reid's diary quoted in Reid (1987) p. 211
29. *Private Life* (1897; 1901 edition) p. 9
30. Lambeth Palace Library, Davidson Papers, Private Papers, vol. 19 (memorandum as to details connected with the death of the Queen)
31. Carter (2009; 2010 edition) p. 268
32. Rennell (2000) p. 137
33. Wilfred Scawen Blunt, *My Diaries: Being a Personal Narrative of Events, 1888–1914*, New York, NY (1921) vol. 2, p. 2
34. Quoted in Ridley (2012; 2013 edition) p. 343
35. Rennell (2000) p. 138
36. Lambeth Palace Library, Davidson Papers, Private Papers, vol. 19 (22 January 1901)
37. Rennell (2000) p. 139
38. James Vincent, correspondent for *The Times,* quoted in Rennell (2000) p. 139
39. Lambeth Palace Library Davidson Papers, Victoria Visitations, vol. 506, f. 20
40. Quoted in Reid (1989) p. 215
41. Reid (1987) p. 216
42. Ibid.
43. RA VIC/MAIN/Y/203/81 (2 December 1867)
44. RA VIC/MAIN/M/5/80 (2 August 1835)

Index

Picture Acknowledgements

Bridgeman Images: 1 above left/engraving by Charles Hullmandel/Yale Center for British Art Paul Mellon Collection USA, 1 above right/portrait by Jeremiah Meyer/Ashmolean Museum University of Oxford UK, 2 above left/engraving by William Westall/private collection, 2 below right/portrait by Henry William Pickersgill/private collection, 3 below/engraving by William Dummond/British Library London UK ©British Library Board All Rights Reserved, 4 above left/portrait by Thomas Sully/Wallace Collection London UK, 6 above right/private collection, 7 centre right/aquatint by William Henry Payne/private collection, 7 below left/music cover/Victoria & Albert Museum London UK, 13 centre left/Florence Nightingale Museum London UK, 15 above right/photo Alexander Bassano Studio/Alinari Archives Florence, text page 7/engraving by George Hayter/private collection, text page 241. Mary Evans Picture Library: 6 below, 16 above/©The Boswell Collection Bexley Heritage Trust, text page 121/©Charlotte Zeepvat/ILN. ©Historic Royal Palaces: 8 below right. ©National Portrait Gallery London: 15 above left/retouched negative Bassano Studio. Royal Archives/ © Her Majesty Queen Elizabeth II 2018: 3 centre right/self-portrait by Queen Victoria. Royal Collection Trust ©Her Majesty Queen Elizabeth II 2018: 10 below/photo Dr Ernst Becker, 11 above left and above right/photos after Bryan Edward Duppa, 11 below left and below right/photos Dr Ernst Becker, 12 above left/photo Hills & Saunders, 12 centre left/sculpture attributed to Mary Thornycroft, 12 below right/photo William Bambridge, 13 above right/photographer unknown, 13 below right/photographer unknown, 14 above right/photographer unknown, 14 below right/photo Byrne & Co, 15 below/photo Gustav Mullins, 16 below/photographer unknown. Royal Collection Trust ©Her Majesty Queen Elizabeth II 2018/Bridgeman Images: 1 below left/portrait English School, 1 below right/portrait by George Hayter, 2 centre right/English School, 2 below left/portrait by Carl Friedrich Koepke, 3 above left/sketch by Queen Victoria, 4 centre right, 4 below left/sketch by Queen Victoria, 5 above/engraving after George B Campion, 5 below/detail of painting by Charles Robert Leslie, 7 above right/engraving by Carl Mayer, 8 above right/portrait by Franz Xaver Winterhalter, 8 above left/sketch by Queen Victoria, 9 above left/portrait by Franz Xaver Winterhalter, 9 above right/engraving by W Clerk, 10 above/painting by James Roberts, 12 below left/watercolour by Princess Louise. Wellcome Collection: 6 centre left. Lucy Worsley: 9 below left. Wycombe Museum Bucks UK: 14 centre left.

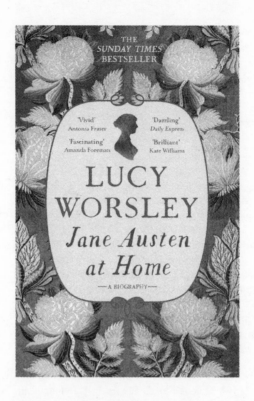

'*Jane Austen at Home* offers a fascinating look at Jane Austen's world through the lens of the homes in which she lived and worked throughout her life. The result is a refreshingly unique perspective on Austen and her work and a beautifully nuanced exploration of gender, creativity, and domesticity.'

Amanda Foreman

This new telling of the story of Jane's life shows us how and why she lived as she did, examining the places and spaces that mattered to her. It wasn't all country houses and ballrooms, but a life that was often a painful struggle. Jane famously lived a 'life without incident', but with new research and insights Lucy Worsley reveals a passionate woman who fought for her freedom. A woman who far from being a lonely spinster in fact had at least five marriage prospects, but who in the end refused to settle for anything less than Mr Darcy.